Small Spaces

Small Spaces
Recasting the Architecture of Empire

Swati Chattopadhyay

BLOOMSBURY VISUAL ARTS
LONDON • NEW YORK • OXFORD • NEW DELHI • SYDNEY

BLOOMSBURY VISUAL ARTS
Bloomsbury Publishing Plc
50 Bedford Square, London, WC1B 3DP, UK
1385 Broadway, New York, NY 10018, USA
29 Earlsfort Terrace, Dublin 2, Ireland

BLOOMSBURY, BLOOMSBURY VISUAL ARTS and the Diana logo are trademarks of
Bloomsbury Publishing Plc

First published in Great Britain 2023

Copyright © Swati Chattopadhyay, 2023

Swati Chattopadhyay has asserted her right under the Copyright, Designs and Patents Act, 1988, to be identified as Author of this work.

For legal purposes the Preface and Acknowledgments on p. xi constitute an extension of this copyright page.

Cover design by Eleanor Rose
Cover image: Staircase in residence, Srirampur, West Bengal, 2020 © Sanjeet Chowdhury

All rights reserved. No part of this publication may be reproduced or transmitted in any form or by any means, electronic or mechanical, including photocopying, recording, or any information storage or retrieval system, without prior permission in writing from the publishers.

Bloomsbury Publishing Plc does not have any control over, or responsibility for, any third-party websites referred to or in this book. All internet addresses given in this book were correct at the time of going to press. The author and publisher regret any inconvenience caused if addresses have changed or sites have ceased to exist, but can accept no responsibility for any such changes.

A catalogue record for this book is available from the British Library.

Library of Congress Cataloging-in-Publication Data
Names: Chattopadhyay, Swati, 1962- author.
Title: Small spaces : recasting the architecture of empire / Swati Chattopadhyay.
Identifiers: LCCN 2022049325 (print) | LCCN 2022049326 (ebook) | ISBN 9781350288225 (hardback) | ISBN 9781350288201 (paperback) | ISBN 9781350288232 (pdf) | ISBN 9781350288249 (epub) | ISBN 9781350288256
Subjects: LCSH: Imperialism and architecture–India–History. | Architecture and society–India–History. | Great Britain–Colonies–India–History.
Classification: LCC NA2543.I47 C49 2023 (print) | LCC NA2543.I47 (ebook) | DDC 720.1/030954--dc23/eng/20221115
LC record available at https://lccn.loc.gov/2022049325
LC ebook record available at https://lccn.loc.gov/2022049326

ISBN: HB: 978-1-3502-8822-5
PB: 978-1-3502-8820-1
ePDF: 978-1-3502-8823-2
eBook: 978-1-3502-8824-9

Typeset by RefineCatch Limited, Bungay, Suffolk
Printed and bound in India

To find out more about our authors and books visit www.bloomsbury.com and sign up for our newsletters.

*To the memory of my mother
Pusparenu Chattopadhyay*

CONTENTS

Preface and Acknowledgments xi

Part One. Small Spaces 1

1 Of Small Spaces 3

Why Small Spaces? 5
In Isolation and Connection 6
Architectural Imagination 8
Axes of Interpretation 11

2 Empire of Small Spaces 13

Long-distance Trade 13
The Aura of Bigness 17
Scalar Alterity 20
Writing Small Spaces 24

Part Two: Trade and Labor 29

3 Dependency 31

Separation 32
Centering 36

4 Locating the Bottlekhana 38

Naming 38
Servants' Spaces 40
Service Spaces at the Apex 46
The Basement Principle 57
Beyond the Compound 59

5 Potable Empire 62

Open Seams 62
The Passage of Liquor 64
Liquor Landscape 68
Storage, Sircars, and Coolies 73
Lines of Control 76
Lumpy Geographies 79

6 Europe Goods 80

Honing Taste 82
Affirming Values 86
"Housekeeping of the Simplest Character" 88
Turab Ali's Artifice 91
Uneven Exchange 95

7 Strange Tongues 97

Command 99
Food Axis 101
Culinary Racism 103
Dirt 106
Recalcitrance 110
Extending the Food Axis 113
Calorie Transfer 117

8 Making Invisible 124

Backstairs 126
Prosthetic Trace 130
Free and Unfree Labor 133
Comfort and Menial Labor 138
Escape 145

Part Three: Land Imagination 147

9 Vantage 149

Abstraction 151
Storytelling 153

10 Connective Spaces 156

Connectors 156
Screen 159
Threshold 162
Roofline 163

11 Anomalous Spaces 168

Edith's Story 171
Verandah as Refuge 172
Verandah as Exposure 178
Anomaly 180
Taxidermic Seams 182

12 An Aesthetic Episode 186

"A Heap of Jasmines" 188
Duration and Materiality 189
Paths that Connect 196
Flood 198
Rani's Story 200

13 Roofscapes 204

Openings 205
Rabindranath's Story 206
Sociopoetics of Circumscription: Terrace Lives 211
Affective Modalities 214
Terrace as Public Space 216

Part Four: A Geography of Small Spaces 221

14 Collections and Containment 223

Grey Zones 225
Containers 228

15 Portable Geographies 231

Boundary-work 234
Portable Gardens, Maps, and Tools 237

Recollection 243
Contraction of Space 245
Jangal 248
Inhabiting a Map 251

16 A Good Shelf 253

Bibliomigrancy 255
Tipu's Library 258
The Material Culture of Reading 262
Vidyasagar's Library 263
An Encounter 265
A New Figure of Space 266

17 A Box of Medicine 268

Vernacularization 269
Therapeutic Kit 271
Death and Survival 272

18 Epilogue 275

Appendix 280
Notes 282
Index 329

PREFACE AND ACKNOWLEDGMENTS

The work for this book was conducted in the margins of other research projects. It has been sustained by small parenthetical notes in the archive and surprising finds on visits to old houses and during fieldwork in the last three decades. The ideas that permeate this book were perhaps first generated over three decades ago when I encountered the work of James Deetz in his classes at Berkeley, where Jim, Dell Upton, and Jamie Horowitz helped me hone my fondness for small things with the fire of intellectual rigor. The writing itself took shape in the last decade and in conversation with friends and family members. Like the contents of this book itself, the sources and sites of research and engagement are scattered. This preface is thus a humble acknowledgment of the many voices in the archives, and the people who helped me think with and about small things and small spaces.

Jeremy White, Arijit Sen, Tania Sengupta, Zeynep Kezer, Sudipta Sen, Nuha Khoury, Dorota Dutsch, Bhaskar Sarkar, Bishnupriya Ghosh, Cristina Venegas, Mark Meadow, William Glover, Abigail van Slyck, Dianne Harris, Zirwat Chowdhury, Romita Ray, Keya Dasgupta, and Subhendu Dasgupta have been intellectual companions in this journey. Sudipta and Will did me the honor of reading the entire manuscript; their intellectual probity and constructive criticism were critical to the finished work. Abby, Arijit, Zirwat, and Zeynep read big chunks of the manuscript and gave detailed suggestions. I can never thank them enough for the care with which they read the work and their generosity and friendship. Shaoni C. White and Jeremy White read the various versions of the work whenever I needed sharp pairs of eyes. Jeremy, as always, helped with the images. Arun Nag, Gautam Bhadra, Sanjeet Chowdhury, Pinaki Das, Aurobindo Dasgupta, Stephen Legg, Alan Macfarlane, Malini Roy, Kalyanakrishnan Sivaramakrishnan, Dell Upton, and Anshuman Dasgupta have been tremendously generous with locating sources and images. My mother Pusparenu Chattopadhyay and my elder brother Dipankar Chattopadhyay entertained questions about their long experience of family practices and spaces with patience and rigor.

I thank the staff of the National Library, Bangiya Sahitya Parishat Library, and the West Bengal State Archives in Kolkata, Rabindra Bhavana Archives at Visvabharati, Santiniketan, and the British Library, London, where I did most of the archival research. Bidisha Chakraborty and Sarmistha De at the West Bengal State Archives entertained odd questions about obscure sources and helped me in myriad ways. Jackie Spafford and Christine Fritsch at the Image Resource Center in the Department of History of Art and Architecture at the University of California, Santa Barbara, were magnanimous with their help and advice with visual sources and documentation.

This work would not have been possible without the image resources of the British Library, Hamburger Kuntshalle, Massachusetts Historical Society, National Galleries of Scotland, Peabody Essex Museum, Royal Institute of British Architects, The Collection of Prince and Princess Sadruddin Aga Khan, Science Museum/Science & Society Picture Library, West Bengal State Archives, Rabindra Bhavana Archives, the US National Park Service, the US Department of Agriculture National Agricultural Library, Victoria and Albert Museum, and Yale Center for British Art. I am particularly grateful to Sanjeet Chowdhury, Swati Ghosh, Alan Macfarlane and Dell Upton for giving me permission to use images from their personal archives, and to Monserrat Pis Marcos of the Holburne Museum, Saswati Karmakar of the Rabindra Bhavana Photo Archives, and to Nicolas Sursock for facilitating image permissions.

I owe thanks to my research assistants—James Bashford in London, Sounita Sengupta and Aaheli Sen in Kolkata, and Thomas Crimmel in Santa Barbara—for their help in completing the research.

Versions of four of the chapters were published in other venues. A different version of Chapter 5 was published in Harald Fischer-Tiné and Maria Framke, eds., *Routledge Handbook of the History of Colonialism in South Asia* (2021).[1] The central argument of Chapter 8 was presented as the Eduard Sekler Talk at the Society of Architectural Historians' Annual Conference in 2021 and subsequently published in the *Journal of the Society of Architectural Historians*.[2] A different iteration of Chapter 13 was published in Anuradha Roy and Melitta Waligora, eds., *Kolkata in Space, Time and Imagination: Rethinking Heritage* (2019).[3] Similarly, a shorter version of Chapter 16 was published in Charlotte Ashby and Mark Crinson, eds., *Building-Object: Shared and Contested Territories of Design and Architecture* (2022). I have benefited from the substantive comments and editorial acumen of Anuradha Roy, Melitta Waligora, Harald Fischer-Tiné, Maria Framke, David Karmon, Judy Selhorst, Charlotte Ashby, and Mark Crinson.

James Thompson, my editor at Bloomsbury, liked the strange idea for an architectural history book and shepherded the project with patience. Anonymous reviewers provided critical feedback. Alex Highfield and Rosamunde O'Cleirigh at Bloomsbury and the production team saw it through the final stages of publication. I am grateful for their assistance with the editorial decisions that went into the book.

I wish I had been able to present this book to my mother who had in small ways and large sustained and inspired my thinking about small spaces. She taught me that all the things that matter in this world reside in small acts and it is vital that we learn to notice the small things forgotten. To her loving memory this book is dedicated.

PART ONE

Small Spaces

1

Of Small Spaces

This book is an invitation to shift our attention to small spaces. These are spaces that have long been considered insignificant because of their size or location or for the minor role they seemingly play in the larger social and political scene. Small spaces are simultaneously evident and elusive. They are lived spaces we don't notice. They span and breach social classes and categories, sensations and materialities, deprivation and delight. As objects of inquiry, they demand that we ask what constitutes smallness.

Small spaces are deemed to lack value, and thus seldom appear in historical narratives, architectural or otherwise. They are service spaces—cook rooms, godowns, and bottlekhanas—spaces with uncertain names and hazy genealogies in the margins of the archive of the British empire. They are peripheral and discontinuous; never front and center. They are work spaces, storage spaces, backspaces. The godown was a fixture of colonial port cities in South and East Asia from Calcutta to Canton: its ubiquitous presence notwithstanding, it has left small footprints in the historiography of empire.[1]

As subterranean spaces, they take the form of root cellars in which rows of bottles are shelved by caring hands. They are often ill-lit and illicit. Lack of illumination obscures, deprives. But it can also enable. They are hidden and hiding spaces: the cellars in which enslaved people were imprisoned, the garrets in which they took shelter, the hidey holes underneath the earthen floor where they stowed away food stolen from their labor.[2] They are forgotten spaces.

Often seen as anomalies because their bounds are ill-defined or because they are fungible—they have *give*—in their shape-shifting characteristics, in their propensity to spill over, they disrupt the decorum of formal spaces that are expected to remain fixed in their propriety. They are spaces appropriated from the dominant infrastructure of grids, roads, and public spaces. These are the hawker stalls and squatting casual workers on sidewalks waiting for customers. We call such spaces informal, unauthorized, and cannot fathom their errant logic.

Smallness may refer to small dimension, though many such spaces by themselves or as collectivities occupy large areas. Even when such spaces are physically substantial, they do not register in the dominant scheme of things. Spaces such as verandahs, courtyards, terraces, fire escapes, stoops are part of a global lexicon of spatial types, and yet are rarely deemed sufficiently important to merit close reading.[3] They are supplementary to the principal spaces in a building. As adjunct spaces they do not press for attention. Small spaces remain peripheral to our vision (**Plate 1**).

As property, small spaces are low in status, even though they are indispensable spaces of production. As utilitarian spaces they constitute the everyday vernacular landscape. They are architecturally undistinguished and rudimentary in terms of construction, and thus are unlikely to be explored in terms of aesthetics. They are not deemed worthy of appreciation for beauty or craft, unless designed by an architect. The marks of labor—the work of those who ensure production, profit, sustenance, and waste removal—are intentionally erased from the kitchen, cellar, and bathroom. They are connected to "master spaces" through distinctive formal devices that ensure the separation of labor from served spaces. Back entrances, service stairs, dumbwaiters create links that are meant to keep labor invisible, while enabling the comfort of the master.[4] Like the dumbwaiter, small spaces are meant to remain mute so they don't presume to interject or share in the glory of formal spaces. Such erasure prevents small spaces from being recognized as spaces of emergence: agentic locales that have the capacity to throw fresh light on power, community, and solidarity.

Size, placement, and nomenclature of buildings are deliberately used to make social distinctions and to marginalize. British residents in India referred to servants' quarters as godowns—storage spaces—since it seemingly made no difference that one was meant to house people and the other was meant to house things. Indeed, storage spaces were often better built than the spaces for servants and the enslaved. Slave owners in colonial America and the United States used scale, size, and location to place the enslaved "literally out, away, apart, down, at the back, to the side, or confined in storage areas within them" to visibly and corporeally render the subordination of labor explicit.[5]

Visibility can be threatening. To be deprived of agency in public is to become invisible in plain sight. The slave auction block and holding pens were fixtures of ports, markets, plantations, courthouses in cities of the Atlantic world, small and large. Their everyday ruthless visibility, their exceptional roles in devastating lives were normalized and stood in contrast to the mostly unnamed multitudes whose presence was erased even as their bodies were enumerated—recorded and marked—for profit. Most such sites remain unmarked; they lack a history to call their own.

In their temporal conjunction, small spaces become singular: the patch of light to which you take a book to read. The steady script on fragile airmail paper charting arrivals, partings, and recipes become openings for conversations, rituals, and remembrances. They are archival photographs of nameless subjects. They record the presence of peoples and spaces, named and unnamed, and provide grounds for speculation of what might have been.⁶

Smallness is a clearing in the woods marked by a modest sculpture of small stones and leaves, a shrine renewed every day. In their impermanence, they constitute geographies that defy description. They can be culturally specific to an extent that does not suffer translation. An accidental step on a wet rice-paste design on a red-oxide floor, they are stowed away in a corner of the mind, a footnote to a marigold morning in early spring. It is Proust's recollection of the smell of madeleines dipped in tea: small spaces as ephemeral sensations carry the promise of return.

To whom are these spaces important? The answers all seem utterly mundane and ordinary; worse, personal—not important to anyone else. Their material impermanence makes them easy to ignore within the long arc of historical narratives. Why bother with small spaces in the age of big data and the hyper object, when we are asked to stretch our extrapolative and conceptual capacities to their limits? Why subject small spaces to historical narration?

To claim history is to claim agency. To claim history is to read singularity in the repetitive and anonymous. To write a history of small spaces is to assert a way of thinking otherwise about space and empire. Small spaces can appear threatening, because they are anything but ordinary. Small spaces, in their very ubiquity, hold unparalleled potential. They have the strength to endure; in repetition they morph and regenerate. Small spaces are resilient spaces. Even when no one is paying attention, they transcend the chasm of time and geography to connect peoples and memories.

Why Small Spaces?

In his book *In Small Things Forgotten*, first published in 1977, James Deetz makes a plea for attending to the small artifacts that comprise our daily lives. Recalling a colonial Anglo-American probate inventory he writes:

> At the end of the listing the appraiser made a final entry, "In small things forgotten, eight shillings sixpence." In this he acknowledged things that he may have overlooked but that nonetheless had value . . . For in the seemingly little and insignificant things that accumulate to create a lifetime, the essence of our existence is captured.⁷

By mapping the "small things forgotten" across different types of artifacts, Deetz suggests, we might be able to discern the logic that undergirds choices made in the production and consumption of objects, be it houses, ceramics, pipe stems, gravestones, or cuts of meat. Paying attention to the small things of everyday life might be the *only* way to access the significance of cultural practices that have not been accorded importance in the traditional narrative of history enamored with battles, great men, and monuments.

I extend Deetz's argument to the small spaces of empire, but in so doing I ask a different set of questions about how smallness is understood and configured, about the relation between size and scale in our imagination of empire, of how scale is given value, and who has the capacity to produce that value. In the next chapter I expand on scalar imagination, but here I want to register that smallness, when it comes to space, exceeds both scale and size. It involves the politics of materials and labor. So, rather than taking smallness as a given, defined by dimension or scale, I ask: how do the small things that comprise our everyday lives become dwelling spaces, enabling imagination, creativity, and habitation? How are small things and spaces related to constitute meaning? How are such spaces and the relation between objects and spaces reappropriated to function as sites of resistance? How do they challenge historical narratives? How do they sit in relation to empire?

Small spaces are fragments, products of division, isolation, excision: a fragmentary landscape created by repeated processes of racial, caste, gender, and class sorting. We habitually ignore such spaces *because* they are productive in more ways than one. And yet they remain as traces in the archive *because* they sustain life and thereby become sites of affect and memory. They are spaces of unanticipated potential, harboring the capacity to spark affect, foster connections in unexpected ways. Servants, the enslaved, children, and women flit in and out of these spaces—once in a while they take charge and become the center of commentary. Small spaces in the hands of the marginalized become tools for hacking the dominant code. Indeed, they are the only way to interrupt the rule of dominance. They cast a challenge to imperial histories and their claims to bigness defined by vast territorial acquisitions, the logic of capital accumulation, and the devotion to large scale and big profit. This book is driven by the desire to hold on to that potentiality in smallness, even as it shifts valence.

In Isolation and Connection

Small spaces as interstitial spaces are connectors. And yet they demand that we not just notice connections, but attend to these spaces' potential for fragmentation and disruption. The modes through which small spaces are connected enable us to imagine other ways of viewing and experiencing the landscape. When we begin with small spaces, we notice subjects and effects that remain invisible at the big scale of analysis. Here we notice connectors as interruptions. It is this potential that helps challenge the understanding of history as a narrative of bigness—great wars and armed conflicts, famous men (and sometimes women, just for a change of pace), big profits, and the voice of authority—unrelentingly telling tales of momentous change, speaking about, over, on behalf of those who are thus made inaudible and invisible.

Small spaces can shock our collective naivete of believing that spaces function as they are intended: that they are what they are named to do, that modernity's gift resides in calling out defined activities for particular spaces at distinct times. In a geography of small spaces, the kitchen in a plantation appears no longer just a place of round-the-clock toil, but a place of sexual assault, of a whipping so brutal that it traumatized a young Frederick Douglass.[8]

Defined by unanticipated expansion and contraction of time, small spaces are experienced in terms of waiting, watching, servicing time. Take Harriet Jacobs's description of the loophole of retreat in the *Incidents in the Life of a Slave Girl* (1861) as an example. As a young enslaved woman, for seven years she hid in a garret to escape the sexual predation of a white enslaver. The garret was connected to the storeroom in her grandmother's house:

> Some boards were laid across the joists at the top, and between these boards and the roof was a very small garret, never occupied by anything but rats and mice. It had a pent roof, covered with nothing but shingles according to the southern custom for such buildings. The garret was only nine feet long and seven feet wide. The highest part was three feet high, and sloped down abruptly to the loose board floor. There was no admission for either light or air.[9]

Her uncle Philip, a carpenter, created a concealed trap door which communicated with the storeroom so that she could enter the garret: "The air was stifling; the darkness total." Jacobs found a gimlet and drilled a hole one inch wide so she could observe the goings-on in the street outside.[10] That inch-wide aperture was her opening to the world.

When there is no space to call one's own, no enclosure that the law would heed, this was a spatial discovery. Jacobs narrated her escape as a movement from one hiding space to another: in a storeroom, under the floorboard, in a garret, as well as the dangerous peripheral space of the swamp. Her sense of self and self-preservation was premised upon utilizing this garret as the "loophole of retreat." The garret was withdrawal and escape.[11] It was also a location that enabled Jacobs to observe without being seen.

We can cite many such examples. Children, women, the outcaste, the marginalized, the enslaved inhabit fragmented worlds. Seen from their circumscribed positions, the world appears not as a panorama, but as fragmented scenes.[12] Correspondingly, there is no easy transition from subjection to subjectivity. Jacobs wrote her narrative when she was much older, having patched together her sense of self as subject by relying on her experience of interstitial spaces between disparate worlds. This understanding of spatial discontinuity, excision, and circumscription resonates with Antonio Gramsci's view that histories of subaltern groups are episodic and fragmentary.[13] The challenge is to write the history of that spatial fragment.[14] How do we restitute the servants and the enslaved—"unseen people," to use artist and writer Abanindranath Tagore's description—to the spaces where they labored?[15] How does one understand the relation between marginalized bodies and interstitial spaces using the tools of architectural history?

Architectural Imagination

For long we have taken recourse to the architectural plan to understand the relation between bodies and space. Robin Evans in his classic "Figures, Doors and Passages" notes: "If anything is described in an architectural plan, it is in the nature of human relationships, since the elements whose trace it records—walls, doors, windows, and stairs—are employed first to divide and then selectively to re-unite inhabited space."[16] Discussing the mid-nineteenth-century work of Robert Kerr in *The Gentleman's House* he observes how domestic space became neatly defined between route and destination, served and service spaces. Kerr, he notes, "made diagrams that reduced house plans to … trajectory (route) and position (destination), proposing that their proper arrangement was the substratum upon which both architecture and domesticity were to be raised"[17] (Figure 1.1).

Keen to read architectural plans as harboring subterfuges and evasions, Evans nevertheless does not question the ontology of the plan as a mode of seeing and knowing. Implicit in his reading of the plan as architectural method is the idea of a fully formed undivided subject who vicariously moves through the building, sees and inhabits the whole. The abstract plan and by proxy the building is wholly available for cognizance, scrutiny, and experimentation. That space is perceived differentially, that space is

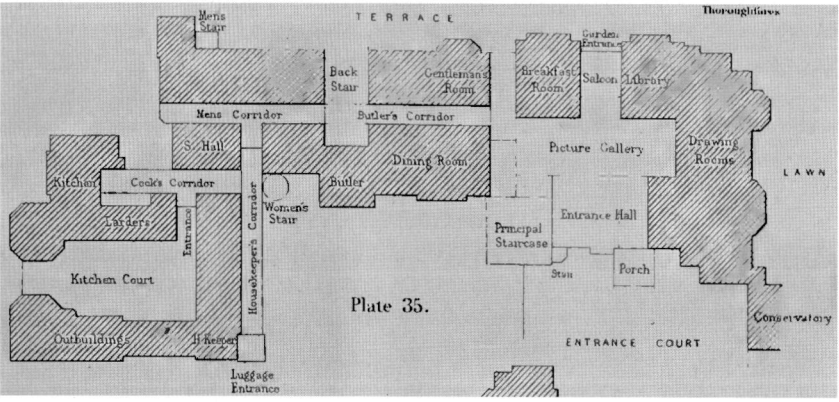

FIGURE 1.1 Robert Kerr, Bearwood, Berkshire, 1865–74, floor plan showing the locations of corridors, staircases, and passages. Source: Robert Kerr, *The Gentleman's House* (London: John Murray, 1864).

fragmented, that the placid plan of domestic space hides just as much as it reveals does not enter the discussion. If it does, it is in the last instance. Because before we get to the everyday terror of that placid domestic space of the main house, we pay homage to authoritative modes of thinking architecture.

This mode of thinking and writing architecture is a product of the imperial enterprise that defined the modern world and continues to shape our imagination of space. As historians of colonialism and empire, as those who analyze buildings and spatial relations, we have not taken stock of the extent to which our analytic methods, our understanding of disciplinary boundaries and the nature of evidence have been shaped by imperial formations. We haven't learned to read the architecture of invisibility, the process through which subjects, names, and histories are excised from the archive. To break that habit would require more than digging for information about one minority architect here, another beautiful artwork crafted by a "native" artisan (where everyone instinctively knows what native means—the colonized/Indigenous), or the proof of a rare text that details the mode of construction in a remote location. We also seem to instinctively recognize what "remote" is: it is at a distance from the metropolitan center of empire. Remoteness in the colonial milieu was constructed through the very technologies that collapsed distance, the forces of colonial extraction that promoted an insatiable desire for resources—minerals, plants, animals, and objects—that could not be procured from proximate spaces.

Writing three decades ago, Edward Said notes: "There is I believe, a quite serious split in our critical consciousness today, which allows us to spend a great deal of time elaborating Carlyle's or Ruskin's aesthetic theories, for example, without giving attention to the authority that their ideas simultaneously bestowed on the subjection of inferior peoples and colonial territories."[18] That problem identified by Said has not disappeared in architectural studies in the intervening decades, despite the labor of three generations of scholars working on colonial architecture and urbanism. The disciplinary segregation of modern Europe from the rest of the world is the norm: colonial histories are left to those who study regions beyond Europe, as if the colonies and imperial thinking never entered the ivory gateways of Britain, France, Germany.[19] Those who study the architecture of American colonies or the antebellum United States scarcely trouble themselves with the abundant literature on colonialism in the rest of the world, or with postcolonial theory shaped through the analysis of European imperialism in the non-Western world, lest stubborn similarities across imperial territories make the United States look less exceptional. Those who take on "empire" as an analytic unit nonchalantly rely on English- and French-language archives to think through empire, as if the vast gamut of languages in the colonies have scant purchase for thoughts about architecture or history.

Said's reference to the split in critical consciousness is meant to explain the need to think of empire in terms of cultural formations that were connected but also had their own life "beyond the laws and political decisions." The importance of novels, he argues, resided in their "worldliness" because of their complex affiliations with their "real setting." Connections would emerge from the references to "explicit places in the various texts, with the enveloping setting—empire—there to make connections with, to develop, elaborate, expand, or criticize."[20] He reads in a selection of novels a geography of spatial relations that constituted empire.

In this work, by *empire* I am referring to such a set of spatial relations—not as the territorial fact that European powers claimed to possess, but in terms of the processes that contributed to the territorial transformations of the world as modern European states sought to control overseas resources for trade, profit, and scientific exploration. This distinction between empire as a self-evident geographical space whose lines can be drawn on a map, and empire as a set of spatial relations produced through construction *and* conjuration, rests on the recognition of the social excess that haunted cherished boundaries between "blacks" and "whites," elites and subalterns, and threatened to undermine lines of control.[21] It is in the terrain of spatial relations created by the trade in commodities, by the forced and unforced migration of vast numbers of people as servants, convicts, the enslaved, merchants, soldiers, state employees, artists, scientists, writers, and tourists, that I locate the small spaces and what these meant or might have meant in terms of creating the infrastructure that was empire.

I look across geographies and cultures to understand the emergence and perpetuation of similar spatial modalities in over two centuries of European colonial dominance between the mid-eighteenth to the mid-twentieth centuries. Thus, while the bulk of my examples are drawn from British India, and specifically from the Bengal Presidency that covered much of the eastern and northern part of the subcontinent, I also signal the parallels and connections with colonial East Asia, Africa, and the transatlantic world, and the experiences of consumption, representation, and collection in the larger colonial world. The effects of empire pop up in unexpected spaces. Despite their historical particularities, in the striking similarity of the representations of spaces, building types, and the location of people within these spaces across the career of the British empire, we can sense the shaping of norms of representation, of the exchange of knowledge, techniques, materials, and expertise that would come to define the modern imperial world and become foundational to modern architectural history. There are also, however, similarities in the modes of resistance to this shaping, and it is in this realm that we might discern myriad approaches to addressing the rule of dominance through small things and small spaces.

The cast of characters in this story is large and varied: from servants and the enslaved, English memsahibs and Bengali homemakers, both European and Indian writers, as well as military and civil servants. They appear sometimes as the protagonist and sometimes as the "chorus"—unnamed, unfelicitated, but as the necessary arrangement that makes the solo performances audible and perceptible.

Axes of Interpretation

The book takes its entrée into small spaces through the things—foodstuff, household goods, furniture, potted plants, and boxes of medicine—with and around which sociospatial relations were constituted, and that became sites for telling stories. In choosing the things and sites I have been partial to those that have received little or no prior historical treatment. And this is not simply because these tell stories that remain untold, but because they dishevel the neatness of imperial understanding of sources, events, and sites.

Three axes of interpretation organize the chapters in this work: trade and labor, land imagination, and objects and collections. As subjects of inquiry, trade, labor, landscape, collections, and collecting have for long been considered central to empire studies. The movement of commodities and labor across regions constituted trade networks and reshaped geographies of production and consumption. Various modes of imagining the land were created through travel and dissemination of aesthetic ideas. Portable objects and collections generated new modes of transmitting knowledge between the eighteenth and nineteenth centuries. I hope we can apprehend in the small spaces a different reading of such enterprise, constituting a geography that not only connected but disconnected.[22]

If space is produced through social relations, I attempt to link the physical (traditionally presumed to be fixed) space of a room, a courtyard, or a field that a person can walk into and inhabit, with the objects around which social relations are construed. Such connections foster possibilities of dwelling. In the stories I have selected, the presumed fixity of a room is disturbed by the movement of bodies and goods, by the passage of time. The boxes and bookshelves are not only movable and thereby help manipulate the space in which these objects are kept, but they constitute spaces within. These become expansive sites of imagination and sociality in a manner that often defy their modest dimensions. The bookshelf becomes more than a container for storing books; it becomes a prop in a social encounter; a small trunk of possessions unpacked, its contents sunned and repacked, becomes susceptible to a mode of caring that instantiates a different kind of spatial relation in its capacity to connect distant imaginaries.

The spaces that constitute this story are, however, meant to be neither exhaustive nor part of an identifiable whole. Their episodic and fragmentary presence is just as important and telling as their connectivity. The reader should be advised that I am not writing an architectural history of the verandah, kitchen, godown, and so on as architectural types. I am invoking their particular presence in the historical archive to rethink what constitutes empire.

In addition to this introductory chapter and the next one on scalar relations, I have devoted a brief chapter at the beginning of Parts Two, Three, and Four to introduce the methodological issues pertinent to the particular set of objects and spaces I am tackling under these headings. The thread that connects them is a refrain of ordinary spaces, even in exceptional buildings. Constellated as a geography of small spaces, the archive I have assembled offers glimpses of *another place* from which a host of actors made room to imagine and reconstruct their worlds. Another place is not a designated or even shared space but emerges out of a sharing, as differentiated openings into the everyday lives of those who lived through the fabrication of empire. In the Epilogue I return to the clusters of meaning that cling to the art and politics of smallness.

2

Empire of Small Spaces

My interest in small spaces was sparked by minor discoveries in the colonial archive: of names such as "bottlekhana" with which I was unfamiliar, from passing comments in the colonial record of the British empire to memoirs in English and Bengali that recalled the time of empire as a geography of small objects, sites, events. To fathom that geography, I had to work against some fundamental assumptions about empire and architectural history.

We are told that empires are big affairs. Building empire is about conquering and accumulating territories, a collective enterprise of enormous proportions. The map of the British empire grew so rapidly and steadily over the span of a century that it defied imagination. In a late-eighteenth-century map of the world the not-yet British empire could be discerned over small strips of land that hugged coastlines of enormous peninsulas in India, Australia, and Africa; by the eve of World War I the empire had appropriated a quarter of the world's landmass. It is thus perhaps not surprising that the expansive logic of empire and its self-fulfilling prophecies of scalar advantage have been endlessly cited as evidence of the fact of empire, leaving scant room for attending to the small spaces that made this big imagination of empire possible.

This story of imperial expansion is told through wars, annexations, and much-prized commercial goods: cotton, indigo, saltpeter, opium, spices, tea. It is a narrative of complex trade networks, vast territorial occupations, large-scale revenue management, and a complicated machinery of knowledge production—surveys, census, official minutes, and reports. These stories are cross-hatched with the massive numbers of forced and voluntary migrations, and the creation of new forms of free and unfree labor. The cacophonous archive assembled to weave these stories is remarkable not always for what it foregrounds, but for the gaps and silences that pockmark its surface, for the spaces that glimmer in the background, seemingly powerless to stand up to the dominant discourse of what makes trade and politics happen.

Long-distance Trade

Take the case of long-distance trade. Trade histories of the British empire have primarily focused on the large scale and on bulk commodities. No doubt this has much to do with the need to grapple with the magnitude of change in the balance of trade between Asia and Europe with the consolidation of the British empire, and with the intertwined histories of colonialism and capitalism that demanded ever bigger scales of production, transportation over vast distances, and generated the territorial sublime of empire. Correspondingly, there is an important literature that examines the movement of commodities along various routes between Europe, Africa, and the Americas, and the vast magnitude of trade in human cargo that was key to the "successful" production and processing of these commodities.

In such histories, smallness is connected to lack of value through the figures of fragmentation and isolation.[1] In his groundbreaking work on the rise of the bazaar in the "age of European domination," Rajat Ray explains that what had been dismissed as small-scale "debased, fragmented and marginal" economies of Asian peddlers were in fact complex processes of banking and shipping with their own spatio-economic hierarchies that defined robust trade networks throughout Asia, Africa, and the Arab peninsula.[2] Ray applies a new optics to the landscape of colonial trade that helps us see how different levels of trade—the market in the abstract sense as well as the urban marketplace of wholesale trade and retail trade—comprised an integrated network through which trade and credit moved "with surprising facility."[3] He makes a case for the practices at the small scale adding up to aggregates with an impact on larger economic and territorial scales:

> To conceive the "modern world system" in terms of "the European world-economy" alone is to miss a dimension in its formation without which its overall shape cannot be grasped. The rise of the bazaar moulded in a vital manner the process by which the capitalist world economy expanded outwards from Europe into Asia and Africa.[4]

Ray demonstrates the interlacing of European networks and the "bazaar economy" in the shaping of modern trade and banking.

Tirthankar Roy cites scale—and specifically the large scale of resources that joint-stock companies could command—as the key to explain the differences in the reach of trade networks and business practices among Indian merchant bankers and the East India Company's (EIC) merchants.[5] It is evident from his discussion of the EIC's practices that there were defined zones of exclusivity within this far-flung global trade that shaped the economic enterprise and politics of empire. If large scale, in terms of the magnitude of capital and the infrastructure that it creates, produces value, one could argue that small-scale entities—often lodged within global networks—have their own complexity and generate value differently than do large-scale entities and transactions. Smallness in terms of scale may signal marginalization, but by that same token may suggest power and exclusion.

The problem with trade histories of empires at first seems twofold: empirically, it has to do with the kinds of commodities that have received the most scholarly attention, and methodologically it is about how these have been studied. The literature on British trade with India, for example, has primarily focused on those commodities that in terms of volume and profit were among the most important exports from India. In the eighteenth and nineteenth centuries these were cotton, saltpeter, indigo, tea, opium, piece goods, and grain. For the same period, we have research on the import to India of woolens, worsted textiles ("stuffs"), cotton manufactures, metals (copper, tin, iron, lead), firearms and munitions, and snapshots of the range of other commodities imported by private traders that constituted the balance of import cargo.[6] B. R. Tomlinson and Huw Bowen have brought attention to the increase in the import of "general merchandise" with growing territorial control from the mid-eighteenth century onwards.[7] In a 2010 essay Bowen makes the important point that a considerable range of such commodities entered the Indian market through private trade before the EIC lost its commercial monopoly (1813), and that these commodities had a considerable impact on Indian patterns of consumption.[8] This latter set of commodities constitutes the realm of what James Deetz would call "small things."

Yet we have only a sketchy idea of the details or the long arc of the impact of these small things. We know little of the spaces through which these goods moved to link sellers and consumers, and what happened at the endpoint of consumption—who bought them, how were these stored, consumed, and managed? We have fine analysis of the volume and price of commodities, the rules and regulations that controlled colonial trade, and the crucial role played by the big agency houses and the merchant bankers—Europeans and Indians—in constructing the paths of trade.[9] Scant attention, however, has been paid to the material culture and spatial correlates of this trade. The exceptions to this trend are few.[10] For the import trade to India, the exception is David Arnold's analysis of the late-nineteenth- and early-twentieth-century everyday technologies of empire: sewing machines, bicycles, typewriters.[11]

Long before the age of "everyday technologies" that is the focus of Arnold's work, "Europe Goods" had entered the markets of Indian port cities and made significant incursions inland, following the tracks of the colonial army and the civil service.[12] The volume of trade in Europe Goods, imported provisions, and alcohol in the late eighteenth and early nineteenth centuries was large enough to show up on import summaries presented by the EIC.[13] Between 1792 and 1811, the percentage of trade in provisions, wine, beer, spirits, glassware, earthenware, and platedware remained modest in relation to the total value of imports, but increased over the course of the nineteenth century. In 1811 the total value of these imports exceeded by a small margin the total value of woolens (Table 1).

TABLE 1 Decadal increase in the import value (in £) of commodities imported by the East India Company from England to India between 1792 and 1811, showing the value of each commodity and percentage of total import value. Source: British Library IOR W5804 (v).

Commodity	1792	1811
Provisions	13,438 1.74%	42,028 2%
Wine, Beer, Spirits	38,125 4.93%	122,340 5.84%
Glass and Earthenware	20,584 2.66%	118,172 5.64%
Plates and Platedware	5,166 0.68%	21,968 1.05%
Woolens	110,524 14.29%	277,196 13.23%

The value of trade in each commodity fluctuated from year to year. In some years such as 1818, the figures for glassware and earthenware imports exceeded that of woolens, and the total import of alcohol and provisions came close to the value of woolen imports.[14] This increase in the value of imports has been typically dismissed because the high price of import goods was beyond the means of most Indians and the demands of these goods "was limited within the circle of Europeans."[15] The size of the market for this class of goods was indeed small, and remained so into the twentieth century. However, it was possible to "secure a wide margin of profit" in such trade.[16]

While each individual commodity within the group was small, as a cluster of related commodities it commanded a significant profile. Everyday commodities such as glassware, tableware, foodstuff, and alcohol defined Anglo-Indian foodways, and even when constituting a modest proportion of the import trade had a remarkable cultural impact. The passage and consumption of Europe Goods gave rise to a variety of spaces, altered spatial nomenclature, and engendered new forms of agency. Enter the bottlekhana and cook room.

An economistic approach to empire fails to take into account the material culture impact of such transactions and spaces. The spatial changes were related not only to the process through which commodities were moved from one location to another, or how ideas about consumption circulated through print and visual media, but the process through which these commodities and media triggered and naturalized scalar identities. Generations of men and women were taught through books on housekeeping, gardening, and home medicine, and imagined from advertisements and news media how to prepare and conduct themselves to extract value as a way of creating and harnessing scalar advantages, including at the small scale. The small spaces of empire as sites for producing and appropriating value had an important role to play in this process.

The Aura of Bigness

My prefatory comments about the movement of trade goods and commodities—from bottled provisions to books—might suggest that I am adopting one of the models of global history that have received some traction in the last two decades. Two significant moves within the discipline of history have addressed the problem of scale and historical narrative. To move past the limitations of the nation-state as a unit of analysis, scholars have turned to "connected histories" as a way of linking economic, cultural, and political processes. Working on histories of the early modern world, Sanjay Subrahmanyam describes it as a project of seeking out the "fragile threads that connected the globe."[17] This has had a significant impact on how empire studies is conducted. More recently, the scalar anxiety of manifold planetary crises, the threat posited by the Anthropocene, and the ecological limits to capitalism have prompted advocates of working-class and subaltern histories, such as Dipesh Chakrabarty, to turn their energy to confront the bigness of historical, geographical, and geological events with a new urgency.[18] The politics of environmental violence that distances the scale of individual perception from "non-visible" scales of the ocean, atmosphere, and distant future relies on scalar disjunction.[19] It is thus critical that we learn to read the entanglements of imperialism with the aura of bigness and see the manner in which the "color line," to use W. E. B. Du Bois's phrase, marks this entanglement.

An enduring legacy of nineteenth-century imperialism is the aesthetics of scale that correlated bigness, power, modernity, and domination with infrastructure. Consider George Parkin's 1892 "Commercial and Strategic Chart of the British Empire" (**Plate 2**). Parkin was an ardent imperialist, author of *Imperial Federation: The Problem of National Unity* (1892), and the second president of the Geographical Association.[20] Parkin's map shows the British empire as a color-coded consolidated entity, distinguishing it from non-empire. Empire's unity is emphasized by delineating trade routes and telegraph lines that span oceans and continents. It celebrates expansion, connectivity, commerce, movement, and construes empire as homogenous. The spatial connections seem to emerge inevitably and surely from the technological and trade infrastructure. The geographical scale of imperial ambition, caricatured in an 1892 depiction of Cecil Rhodes on the map of

Africa after he announced plans for a railroad and telegraph line from Cairo to Cape Town, carries home the point about the grandeur of imperial geopolitics (Figure 2.1). It is not a happenstance that images and plans for infrastructure construction—roads, railways, canals, bridges, hydroelectric projects—were swapped across empires and were eagerly adopted by modern nation-states freshly independent from colonial rule, from Ghana to India, as the very essence of self-determination and modernity—as indicators of moving up in the economic scale.[21]

Such visions glorifying the relation between empire, bigness, and infrastructure as a network may just as well be construed as the stuff of "connected histories." Recognizing the problem of valorizing the history of those with global connections, Subrahmanyam makes the point that the object of connected histories is not to disavow the importance of local, particular events: "not to deny voice to those who were somehow 'fixed' by physical, social and cultural coordinates, who inhabited localities." "But if we ever get to 'them' by means other than archeology," he remarks, "the chances are that is because they are already plugged into some network, some process of circulation."[22] His salutary reminder, however, neglects to foreground the problem of scale and the strategies of reading the archive.

FIGURE 2.1 Edward Linley Sambourne, *The Rhodes Colossus*, Caricature of Cecil John Rhodes, after he announced plans for a telegraph line and railroad from Cape Town to Cairo. *Punch*, December 10, 1892.

Implicit in this statement is a scalar argument that views local, particular events as small in value and "fixed." These particular events gain value—by becoming visible—in being plugged into a larger network of regional and global proportions. A scalar hierarchy kicks into a network model of historical process to assign discrepant values to local and global entities. Scale is conflated with size to support notions of smallness and bigness.

Discussing the aura of "bigness" in global imperial histories, Jonathan Saha has astutely remarked that "connected histories" could just as easily become elite histories with little explanatory power: "a big history of empires written across a huge chronological sweep does not necessarily explain more than micro-studies embedded in particular cultures." It depends on how we construct the connections and how we perceive the "human scale" in it. He puts it plainly: "[I]t is difficult to imagine the important work of explaining and breaking down imperial ideologies of race and gender being achieved through this big history."[23] Within the "connected histories" approach lies the danger of reinforcing colonial ideologies that claim the human subject as a bounded scalar unit, thereby ignoring affective ties and intra-species relations.

Historians who have attempted to bring global histories in conversation with local histories have struggled with the scalar interchanges between the local and global, even as they have done meaningful work by introducing the "small voices" of history into the global sublime of statistics. For Antoinette Burton, the lens of world/global history offers sight lines to various geographical locations that have remained beyond the bailiwick of Western histories.[24] In a 2007 article, arguing along the lines of Charles Picot's work on "village modernity" in West Africa, she calls for global histories to act as "reorientation devices" to register the "off-centre, the ex-centric, the polycentric, the anti-centric and the 'remotely global'."[25] Others have leaned on the potential of microhistory to reduce the "scale of observation" and bring to light those lives and events that global history does not capture.[26] Making an argument for global microhistories, Tonio Andrade in a 2010 article notes that microhistory infuses human drama into global histories of empire and their propensity to narrate flows and processes in the abstract.[27] Global microhistory, he argues, is a form of good storytelling, the value of which is considerable. In contrast, in a 2006 article on associationism and anticolonialism in the Caribbean, Lara Putnam reminds us that microhistories are intended not to put a human face to a process but to challenge the understanding of the process itself. In proposing a method for bringing microhistories in conversation with Atlantic histories, Putnam notes the "purposive manipulation" of scale shared by both microhistory and Atlantic history, and the important distinction between scale and scope. The latter refers to a distinction between the scale of analysis and the scope of interpretation that may exceed the bounds of space and time of the microhistorical instantiation. Here she calls out microhistory's remit in illuminating connections between popular and scholarly knowledge, between victims and accusers, agrarian cults and witchcraft, founded on "close reading of multiple texts." While these forays into microhistories remind us of the migrant, dispossessed, and ordinary subjects who carry the potential for rethinking imperialism,[28] they also point to different modes of engaging space and time.

Scalar Alterity

Both Andrade and Putnam preface their articles with poems. Andrade quotes William Blake: "To see a world in a grain of sand / And a heaven in a wild flower, / Hold Infinity in the palm of your hand / And Eternity in an hour." Putnam's epigram is Edward Kamau Brathwaite's lines: "the unity is submarine / breathing air, our problem is how to study the fragments/ whole."[29] Blake's verse signals a flash of recognition of divine power that illuminates the potential to imagine and comprehend infinity at a corporeal and human temporal scale. The moment of epiphany collapses scales to reveal the universe in a microcosm. In that momentary implosion a whole universe of relations become perceptible. Scalar alterity figures as divine dispensation. Brathwaite's verse moves in an entirely different trajectory to describe scalar alterity as a geographic force. It alludes to connections that once existed but had since been erased or are buried. And yet these connections remain as sensing possibilities, as potential channels for the flow of knowledge, practices, movements, stories, and affects. Putnam notes that both C. L. R. James, the author of *Black Jacobins*, and Eric Williams, the author of *Capitalism and Slavery*, intuited this submarine unity as their lives spanned the British West Indian migratory world across the Black Atlantic.

Brathwaite's submarine unity is prefaced with and grounded in the geologics of continental and oceanic scales. It is the tectonic movement of earth and water—"geological plate being crushed by the pacific's curve"— that generates the landform layers; these scales of transformation predate Atlantic slavery and are thus aboriginal. Analogically, it is from the violent destruction of cultures that new scales of recognition emerge, fragments are reshaped into communities.[30] Brathwaite's call for studying the fragments/whole does not lead to a larger knowable entity, but appears as an insistence to recognize the nature of the fragment, its contours and multi-directionality—"from or *towards* ancestral origins."[31] It calls attention to the resonances in the stories, spaces, and lives that were scattered and now require an empathetical commitment to hear, gather, restructure, and rearrange. Speaking of the plantation as a unit of Caribbean Studies, he remarks, "The plantation model . . . is in itself a product of the plantation and runs the hazard of becoming as much tool as tomb of the systems it seeks to understand and transform."[32] He suggests the insertion of other scales of analysis—inter-structures—to access the "inner plantation." The "unit is submarine."[33] What becomes the inter-structures/infra-structures of empire, if we do not begin with the model of empire as a constituted entity?

Every architectural student, at the outset of their studies, is taught to apply scale to a building or spatial element. Rather, they are taught how to scale down and represent a building with dimensions that would actually fit the space of representation. This follows the cartographic convention of scale which is a relation between two entities: a relational ratio. The entity being mapped is full-scale, while the map as fractional representation conveys dimensions through a proportional logic. Of course, this assumes that the entity precedes the map. When the map or drawing precedes the entity, when a plan is not merely a geometrical projection but also a projection into the future, it is assumed that the same scalar process can be engineered in reverse. Such scaling methods are flagrantly abused. For one, entire analytic methods of scale models, graphs, mapmaking have been devised to make a large entity or problem appear manageable, seeable, and open to analysis and comprehension, even if such mapping/modeling erases things that matter—materials, processes, inhabitants, and even if that comprehension is utterly incorrect, because in scaling down/up we confront multiple problems. One is the discrepant relation between process and size. When Charles Correa criticizes Le Corbusier's "City of 3 Million" by noting that a simple arithmetic of population vis-à-vis floor area does not solve a design problem of mass housing, he is not merely critiquing the logic of aggregates (of filing large numbers of people and objects in space based on principles of efficiency) but suggesting that a larger aggregate of space functions differently than a smaller cluster of space.[34] The social infrastructure changes with scale. This should be commonsensical in design thinking, but it is not. Alternatively, consider how geometry and social process cannot be reconciled. When a political boundary is mapped on paper and then actualized on the ground, it encounters materialities and processes that are simply not recognizable at the scale of representation or are intentionally erased to promote political agendas. As Joya Chatterjee notes in her discussion of the partition line that divided Bengal in 1947, the boundary mark on paper was not a clean line that could simply be geometrically transferred on the ground—such lines could not relate to either geographical features or everyday transactions of agrarian communities in a region where rivers make and remake the land every few years.[35]

Representational scaling down to smaller manageable bits, normalized in our disciplinary thinking, is based on the idea of the small as easily observable and thus comprehensible. The relation between size and spatial affordance is conferred social value. Difference, however, appears not merely between representation and reality, and across scales, but difference, as Zachary Horton has recently argued, inheres in scalar imagination.[36]

Horton usefully summarizes the various disciplinary approaches to scale.[37] While mathematics (when not based on empiricism) assumes scale-invariance—that is, it adopts a "homologous scaling operation" that allows an entity to scale up and down infinitely by keeping its internal relationships invariant—in physics scale is taken as absolute size domain, with each scale being a "conventionally derived slice of reality."[38] Horton uses the term "resolving cut" to describe the action through which such a slice is isolated.[39] A resolving cut isolates and stabilizes a particular scale by allowing individual entities to be resolved at that scale. Size here is absolute, but scale is not. It is thus premised upon a "field of view" that suggests "what sort of entities are resolvable" within a particular field of view. Thus, the same object at various scales may appear different with the use of various techniques of observation (mediations) as comprising different entities—rather than merely being a miniature or a larger version of that same object. A scale thus may be thought of as a "reference frame wherein certain differences can be detected, or resolved, while others fall either above or below the perspectival threshold of differentiation. All differences can be resolved at some scale, but only certain differences can be resolved at any given scale."[40] In biology and engineering, scale is understood in functional terms to describe "the constitutive relationships between size, parts, and whole."[41] In this view, "organisms do not linearly scale: any change in size requires a redistribution of organs and their functions."[42] Entities at different scales will be organized and function differently. Alterity is built into scalar thinking.

In his discussion of scale in Andean art, Andrew Hamilton brings something else to the discussion of scale and size. Scale, Hamilton beautifully demonstrates, is "a perceptual quality of art" which "plays a primary role in the ways viewers engage with and subsequently interpret objects." The comprehension of scale, he points out, is not universal; it is culturally specific.[43] His analysis also suggests that scale is not only related to size in culture- (and discipline-)specific ways, but that scale may be correlated to materiality in complex ways. And this is not about a shift in scale revealing a new elemental structure. A small-scale version of a fan as part of burial practice was not only constructed out of different materials than the larger (usable)-scale artifact, but through the use of materials seemed to have signaled more importance than the larger fan. Scalar alterity in Andean artifacts may appear in a symbolic manner rather than purely as a measure; it might inhere in the Inca notion of objecthood in which *camay* or "generative force" of matter—"neither visible nor tangible"—was assumed to materially infuse substances.[44]

In its territorial imagination, spatial disciplines like architecture and geography assume the relevance of size domains and also in many cases the compositional integrity of entities at each scale that we see in biological sciences and engineering. When we think of scale and empire, we typically think of territorial scale and magnitude of capital and commodities. The three dominant spatial models of empire are nested hierarchies from local to global (e.g., home, city, region, nation, empire), divisions of the world in presumably horizontal zones but which are implicitly hierarchical (core, semi-periphery, periphery), and networks across horizontal and vertical terrains of land, water, and air (infrastructures that enable exchange of commodity, labor, expertise, knowledge, data, etc.). These are not simply three different ways of imagining the structure of empire, but different forms of mediations. They register and occlude processes in distinct ways.

The animated discourse among geographers about the politics of scale in the last three decades stems from an effort to confront these inclusions and occlusions. Scale here ceases to be "geographical heuristics" and comes to correspond with "real material processes, events and spatial formations."[45] As Neil Smith argues, space is produced through scalar construction. From this point of view, scales are social constructions that may be seen as hierarchically nested entities constituted by economic and political forces and which may be circumvented by scale-jumping. Opposed to the many problems of this hierarchical conceptualization of scale, Sallie Marston, John Paul Jones, and Kevin Woodward have proposed a "flat ontology" of scale that can attend to the connections among sites/milieux that are continually being transformed. Adam Moore, Stephen Legg, and others have troubled these models to question the degree to which these scalar designations are discrete or fluid, and have brought into focus multiscalar assemblages and movements across scales that attend to "how scale operates as a category of practice" even if one accepts the epistemological foundations of scalar domains.[46]

The most useful aspect of these debates in relation to the concerns of this book is how scalar assertions were created to retain colonial sovereignty.[47] There are, however, lingering problems with how scalar imaginations privilege certain narratives of empire: that macrostructures are more connected than microstructures, or that inserting microhistories into macrostructures will provide a heterogeneous, dispersed model of social relations that constitute empire. There is little concern with how scale relates to senses other than the visual, particularly smell and touch, which do not obey the optical logics of scale.

In some ways, by focusing on the small things and small spaces I aim for the scale in which the microdynamics of sensorial space and power may become perceptible. The alterity that inheres in the small-scale leads through extension, excess and slippage into a multisensory world where other narrative turns become possible. This project of small spaces addresses both spatial and temporal parameters and begins with artifacts and spaces that are dimensionally small and may or may not add up to large aggregates. It registers evanescent moments that may not concretize as events. Smallness here does not imply miniaturization, but responds to the fullness of the materiality of the artifact or space—in their connectedness and disconnectedness. Small artifacts and spaces, contrary to popular misconception, are not easy to comprehend or analyze.

Writing Small Spaces

Noticing small spaces in the archive and in our everyday lives is difficult. As has been said about infrastructure, we only notice infrastructure when something goes wrong: for example, we become cognizant of water infrastructure only when the faucet runs dry. Only in exceptional moments do small spaces surface in the dominant optical field, appearing as so many problems to be solved, subjects to discipline, punish, and reform. They are expected to remain contained, confined, and working. *It is in working that they become invisible.* In contrast, those who have to fetch water every day from a river or well, who do the working, are hardly unaware of the infrastructure's affordances—the class, race, caste, religious lines that striate the landscape of everyday need. The latter appear in the archive when summoned for their recalcitrance and resistance.

Writing about long-neglected small spaces presents methodological difficulties. How do we recover traces that have been consigned to oblivion? How do we make sense of such traces when they are recovered or that shine through the chaos of the archive? We have a difficult time convincing others that small spaces and minor actors matter. Few believe they are important. Even when we concede their importance, we resist the notion that small spaces are "pivotal." Few consider them paradigm-shifting.[48]

The approach to small spaces I advocate requires us, in a fundamental sense, to unlearn habits of thinking about architecture and history—what matters and what counts as evidence.[49] In my previous book, *Unlearning the City: Infrastructure in a New Optical Field*, I made an argument that to unlearn the city we cannot begin with the dominant discourse as a framing or jumping-off point in a debate about urban infrastructure. We need to begin somewhere else, turning our attention to materialities that dis/connect and constitute communities. There my recourse to urban popular culture was a means to unlearn the term "infrastructure" and put it to a different descriptive task. In so doing, I made a case for looking at horizontal connections that link subaltern and elite practices, rather than assume a so-called bottom-up approach.

The problem with a bottom-up approach is that it risks carrying over, depending upon, and replicating disciplinary prejudices while supposedly reversing the top-down approach. As Upton notes, the tradition of vernacular architectural history was to create a canon of folk buildings, replicating the process of analysis and evaluation used to canonize architect-designed great works of architecture.[50] Those who moved out of canonical frames did little to read the politics of the vernacular. In a more recent article Upton criticizes the implicit or explicit boosterism of much American vernacular studies: "Our tale is relentlessly cheerful. Our farmers and carpenters and shopkeepers couldn't possibly be among those farmers and carpenters and shopkeepers and housewives who committed crimes large and small, participated in anti-Catholic or anti-Chinese riots, or peered out from Ku

Klux Klan hoods."[51] Turning to "vernacular architecture" does nothing by itself to change the racist, masculinist prerogative of architectural history.

While it is possible to locate and "uncover" hidden voices and narratives through ethnographic work to redress the absence of those voices that have been erased from the archive, these voices come no less unmediated than those from the dominant historical archive. Both require a practice of reading and behove us to honor silences as we archive and analyze.[52]

The documents I assemble here from the archive of trade reports, advertisements, probate inventories, records of household expenses and lists of servants, memoirs, housekeeping guides and recipe books, pictorial evidence, photographs and architectural drawings are wide-ranging, but they are also decidedly one-sided, predominantly a product of the British and Indian educated class's effort at documentation, recollection, and reform. My reading of this assembly purports to unarchive—by paying attention to the marginal spaces, that which is left over, refused, unacknowledged, and looking for the openings where the archival line of thought is strained by its banality and becomes too fragile to maintain a countenance of control, where it erupts in anger, frustration, and fear. Unarchiving is thus a form of disassembling: noticing, while unwinding, what might have been erased and left out in the process of archive-making, both intentionally or because some spaces and events thwart representation.

As in the probate inventory that Deetz cites in which the small artifacts were too insignificant to be listed separately, small spaces are ubiquitous in this archive. Yet they resist description. The long list of commodities offered for sale in newspaper advertisements and notices in cities that connected Europe's trade with Asia appear too banal for speculation. The minutiae about dusters and dishwashing that populate housekeeping guides obscure the regimes of labor that were pressed into the service of keeping white homes clean and white bodies comfortable. The descriptions of pickling fruits on terraces appear too minor to be worthy of architectural histories of empire. Servants figure prominently in these records, but their utterances are noticeable in their sparseness. When their voices draw attention, it is because they are ventriloquized by the masters and mistresses as amusing episodes of the insufficient knowledge of the native population, or because they are deemed threatening. Such utterances mark the lines of difference, of an effort to sort relations of class, gender, and race. For the most part, these actors are unnamed. Their *presence*, however, is on record. As they are made into objects of gaze and speculation, they stand as accusations of empire. When I have found the names—the "boy" Turab Ali, already a grandfather, or Bhowany Bose, wine godown sircar, or Syfollah, bottlekhana sircar—I have heeded their names as spatial presence.

In well-regarded memoirs penned by Indians, small spaces are seen as indulgent, ideological excesses of the self, tinged with the illicit. The authors all offer apologies for expending the reader's attention on such indulgence. But they persist with their stories, and along the way speak of spaces in uncommon light: a rice field moving away with flood waters, a verandah that shields a desperately hungry woman from the inquisitive eyes of neighbors. Commonplace objects such as bookshelves and medicine cases become subjects of lengthy reflections, engendering spaces of loss and comfort.

My practice of reading this colonial archive begins with a commitment to question the very idea of smallness as it relates to the geography of empire. This means beginning with ordinary fragments of daily life, lading lists with their numbing routines and patterns, and not the large already always known territory that is empire.

The small spaces, as ordinary fragments, may or may not add up to any larger collective: but I am interested in where they do and with what they do or where the potential for extrapolation and speculation emerge. This means being alert to minor disturbances in routine, the anxious moment when things do not work as usual. It means being prepared for uneasy alliances, accidental overlaps, and not knowing. I have tried to reflect on the clusters of meaning that adhere to small spaces, stretching from the obvious, presumptive, resistant, and criminalized. These constitute a range of invocations in terms of scale, location, power, status, duration, visibility, portability, aberrance, and affect.

I scan these possibilities through a spatial reading approximating what Kathleen Stewart calls "slow looking": paying attention to the ordinary everyday events and watch for their potentiality to emerge.[53] I search for the unintended gaps in spatial articulation, accidental ruptures in the narrative, and brittleness in the material foundations of consumption, noticing the edges of the space, object, argument, where these lead and how they connect to and inscribe, often unwittingly, a larger geography, without being determinant.

There are no heroes or leaders in this story. Given the scattered specks of evidence in the historical archives, there is no unitary story line either. My strategy has been to refuse the attitude toward the archive that determines one moment of Europe's or the British empire's entry into the colonies or a defined exit point, hoping to at least set aside stories of unsullied pasts, glorious victories, and tainted presents. There have been multiple entries and exits, one more violent and rapacious than the other, and each entrée and exit renders a different complex world. And these entries and exits are not limited to the colonizers, just as there is no one way that these small spaces are registered, connected, operate. Their operation is as diverse as their form, use, location, historical specificity. My reading is guided by two features of the way small spaces appear in the archive: their seeming disconnectedness and a somewhat paradoxical similarity across empires and regions.

That is why this is not connected history. Rather, I propose to rethink connections by delinking the spaces of empire from their usual networks and rerouting them through other paths to help us see what the so-called fact of empire obscures. Delinking here borrows the strategic instinct of Samir Amin's and Walter Mignolo's theorizations—a refusal to be preoccupied by imperial formations.[54] By delinking from empire I do *not* mean we ought to (a) ignore the imbalance of power that constituted imperial enterprise; (b) assume that empires lacked decipherable structures or happened in "a fit of absence of mind"; and (c) focus on the ostensibly "local" rather than the translocal to claim some uncontaminated cultural essence. And it does not mean the recentering of empire via small spaces.

On the contrary, the project of delinking is premised upon the idea that global transactions transformed cultural practices at many scales, in the most intimate spaces and the most public arenas, in ways that we are just beginning to comprehend. Social and political boundaries are inherently porous. To understand the peculiar complexity of lifeworlds disrupted and engendered through colonialism, we must keep the edges of our temporal and spatial inquiry open.

I propose *strategic delinking* as an approach to inserting small spaces into the narrative of empire. I aim to not just disrupt the hegemonic accounts of production and consumption, but to refuse the assumption of empire as geographical fact defined by a vastness of scale and a handful of agents. Strategic delinking refutes the idea that imperial spaces are temporally, physically, and categorically congruent. Strategic delinking constitutes seeing the small spaces of empire as sitting askew in relation to the dominant vectors of power, even when lodged within hegemonic contexts. Empire's coherence is splintered by small spaces as fragments residing both within and outside dominant networks. Unarchiving leads us to these fragments, forcing us to rethink the taken-for-granted assumptions about space and architecture which we have unthinkingly, unwittingly adopted in our liberal posture of modernity. The three parts of the book that follow attempt to think smallness through three different approaches to scale, size, location, and materiality.

PART TWO

Trade and Labor

3

Dependency

A small room, no larger than 8-foot square, some shelves against the wall, a table, and perhaps a washbasin. This was the bottlekhana of colonial houses in India. I came across this space with its peculiar name while rummaging through the archives. What was the space used for? Why was it so common in nineteenth-century architectural plans, memoirs, and housekeeping guides, and, most importantly, why is it entirely absent from architectural histories?

"Bottlekhana" literally means a room for bottles. A fixture of Anglo-Indian residences for almost two centuries, it was a storage space for bottled and canned provisions, beverage, wine, and liquor. The suffix *khana*, meaning room or house, connects the space with its precolonial predecessors.[1] Like the gymkhana (athletic club), the advent of new practices and uses with European colonialism introduced a set of nomenclatures to spaces, marking them as distinctly Anglo-Indian.[2]

The bottlekhana is my entrée into the service spaces of the Anglo-Indian house—the extensive range of buildings variously called godowns, cook rooms, or servants' quarters. These, along with the stable, carriage house, and animal pens, comprised the outhouse of the Anglo-Indian compound. Clearly distinguished from the main house in their placement, size, and construction, these outhouses, including the kitchen, were located along the boundary walls of the property or as far from the main house as possible. Their very existence was premised upon a paradox: their physical peripherality was indeed a sign of their central role in keeping the household functioning.

Naming and location confer value. Calling service spaces "support" or "secondary" or "outhouses" or "dependencies" reinforces the centrality of the master's space and sets up a fabricated sense of dependency. Service spaces are made to appear dependent on the master's space. The utter dependence of the master's living spaces on the labor of servants and the enslaved is turned around to convey the latter's dependence on the master. The master's dependency is made *invisible*. It constitutes a classic colonial bio-political relation in which power derives from the right to command, to define social roles through the allowable extent of social interactions. It resides in the ability to exercise physical control over laboring bodies—when and where the servants and enslaved work and reproduce. The value generated through labor is divested from the laborers and this divestment is naturalized through spatial means. That not all modes of separation, naming, and definition worked as intended is the reason to dwell on these techniques of deploying space to constitute social relations.

Separation

Techniques of separation are fundamental to architecture and placemaking. The enclosing wall, whether of a cottage or a palace, is a means of bounding space. Its thickness, materiality, and construction are the features that give it distinctiveness, extending beyond structural necessity. Walls act as means of controlling sensations of light, sound, smell, and the unsightly. The confinement of the indigent, insane, and pauper population in the Edict of Nantes was intended to cordon off "all those incautious, immoral, impolitic beings who insisted on being extravagantly poor or mad."[3] Walls that enclose, partition, and confine space thus cater to the dual motive of producing prescriptions for social intercourse and aesthetics. Robin Evans describes the effort to disarrange, rather than reduce, sound transmission across prison walls in Millbank Penitentiary in 1830 to prevent prisoners from communicating with each other. Inventor Michael Faraday's design for the prison wall was intended to scramble the pattern of sound waves as a means of disabling communication.[4] That a clever arrangement of materials could offer a refracting method, rather than merely damping the passage of sound waves, was also a frank admission of the difficulties in controlling communication and sensations through architectural means. Information destruction as environmental screening, however, originates prior to the 1830s in the modern methods of screening the relation between masters, servants, and the enslaved. Screening, distancing, segregation, and emplacement were all strategic modes of casting the spatial relation of masters and servants in a visible pattern of ordered space.

The eighteenth- and nineteenth-century separation of service spaces from the main house in much of the colonial world was rationalized as a functional need—a matter of differentiating between uses and "natural" or commonsensical grouping of similar kinds of spaces to facilitate workflow.[5] These spaces were seen as emanating such smell and noise that were best distanced from the master's main living space. Cited as fire hazards, susceptible to the dust and dirt of everyday labor, service spaces were potential sites of disorder. In this regard there is little that is different between Anglo-Indian and Anglo-American narratives about service buildings.

The increased separation between master's and servants' accommodations in colonial America has been viewed as a historical process of changing labor relations. The "medieval" pattern of housing both animals and servants under the roof of the main house in the seventeenth century gave way to increased differentiation and separation in the eighteenth century when a more instrumental view of labor led to the construction of outbuildings for both work and living quarters for servant and enslaved populations. This is the case of the Clifts Plantation site in Virginia.[6] Occupied approximately between 1670 and 1730, the site shows evidence of farm laborers being initially accommodated within the main house and later being moved into separate quarters that were enlarged and improved to house the farm hands, while other outbuildings were also constructed.

Such outbuildings or back buildings in plantations and urban locations consisted of a range of spaces, both large and small, their placement and elaboration depending on both the kind of labor undertaken on these sites and their spatial parameters (Figure 3.1). The propensity to build separate structures for each different use, with a dozen such buildings for large plantations, gave the impression of the plantation as a "town" in itself.[7] The outbuildings at Green Hill, Virginia, were located as two distinct sets in the "upper town" and "lower town" (Figure 3.2). The latter, consisting of tenants' houses, grist mill, miller's house, store, chapel, and the main portion of the slave quarters, was located close to the Staunton River. Across from this, a path through woods and fields led to the "upper town," where the service spaces were organized into two groupings. The stables, carriage house, granary, and tobacco barns were located along the lower part of the

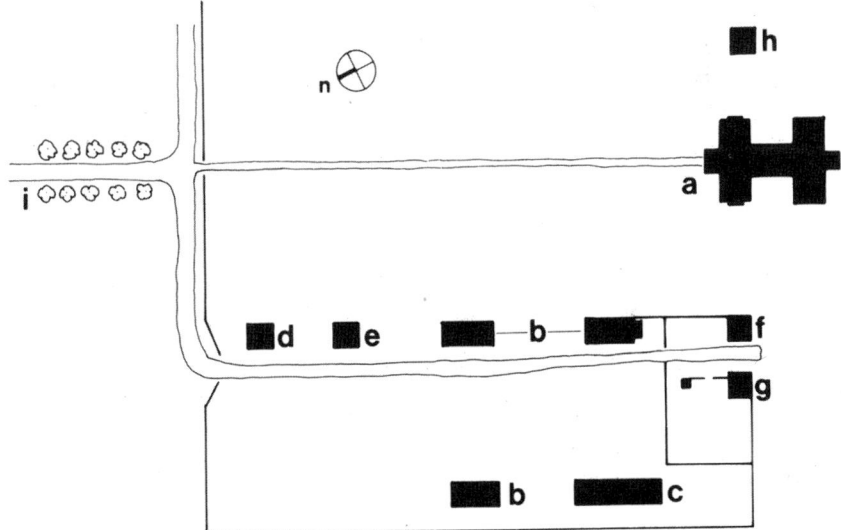

FIGURE 3.1 Site Plan of Tuckahoe Plantation, Goochland County, VA., 18th–19th Century. Main house (a), slave houses (b), stables (c), store house (d), office/dairy (f), kitchen (g), school house (h), cedar lane (i). Drawing by Dell Upton, reproduced with permission.

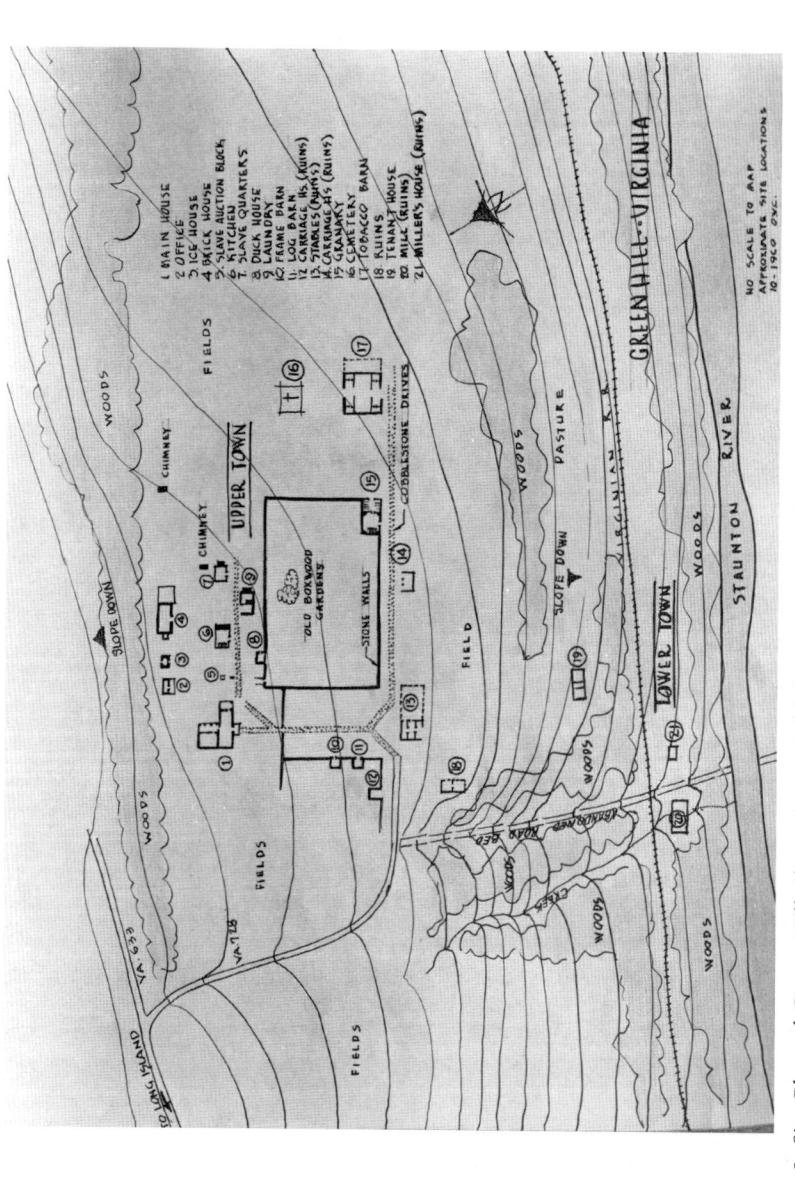

FIGURE 3.2 Site Plan of Green Hill Plantation and Main House, Campbell County, VA. #5 on the plan is the slave auction block. Drawing by Orville W. Carroll, architect, National Park Service, 1960, HABS VA, 16-LONI.V,1–2. Source: Library of Congress.

cobblestone drive to the north, while the office, ice house, kitchen, duck house, laundry, and slave quarters stood in an arc to the west of the main house. Larger plantations such as Mount Vernon and Monticello were outfitted with nailery and blacksmith's shop, carpenter's shop, and other sites of production. The extent of land and the type of plantation crop—rice, tobacco, or cotton—affected the types of service spaces and their scattering.

Green Hill's distinctive feature was the placement of a slave auction block in the center of the yard. Common to town centers in the South, the slave auction block mediated the spatial relation between masters and the enslaved. It stood as a daily invocation of the propertied status of the enslaved. Its conspicuous centrality in the everyday workspace at Green Hill concretized the violence of slavery and the categorical difference between the masters and the property in ways that was not possible through mere distancing, screening, and segregation.

Dimensionally constrained urban sites, predictably, followed a front-back pattern. In mid-eighteenth-century Savannah, Georgia, the kitchen was located behind the main house that fronted the street, while other "conveniences"—"stables and chair houses, servants' quarters, etc. stood further back."[8] The "little back buildings" in Galveston, Texas, included a long list of "secondary" or "support structures" such as the kitchen, storerooms, servants room, wash house, chicken run, hog pen, and "carriage and negro house."[9] Richard Wade notes the screening of information in such town houses where the design of the slave quarters and work yard was intended to seal off the enslaved from the space beyond the master's property. The enclosing walls were thick, and the rooms had no view beyond the property:

> In this arrangement, the walls had an extraordinary significance. Sometimes more than a foot thick, almost always made of brick, generally very high, they transformed a residential complex into a compound. The very smallness of the yards and gardens at the center of the lots seemed to magnify the commanding size of the walls and emphasize the calculated isolation of the slave quarters. The relentless masonry encirclement was broken only by a stark escarpment created by the rear of adjacent buildings—the backs of kitchen, stables or neighboring Negro quarters. Standing in the middle of the plot the bondsman could see only a maze of brick and stone, the forbidding reminders of his servile confinement.[10]

Ward's use of the term "compound" is not a happenstance. Deriving from "kampung," the term was commonly used in colonial Asia and it migrated from there to the Atlantic world. Much was shared across these seemingly different conditions of laboring spaces. The grouping together of storage space, animal pens, and stable with shabbily constructed accommodation for servants and the enslaved was a shared pattern among houses in colonial America and India. Servants' quarters at the back of the lot were a long-standing feature of urban residences in Britain, South Africa, and other locations across the British empire.[11] Functional arguments cannot explain this shared vocabulary. Brought into the service of producing race-based labor relations, the distinctions concretized practices of racial inequity.[12]

Centering

My analysis of service spaces is based on a multipronged approach. First, by treating service spaces as the focus of study, rather than as secondary spaces, I alter the terms of engagement with spatial analysis in architectural history. This means beginning with these spaces in a discussion of spaces of both production and consumption. By centering service spaces in the story of colonial consumption, by examining how they were distanced from the main house—either being placed far away or below the main floor—and how they were clustered, I demonstrate how these spaces were constructed and deployed to facilitate and naturalize iniquitous labor relations. It also enables us to see the links among laboring spaces and their relation to spaces of consumption. This is a story of sorting populations by occupation, gender, and race, and of making servant populations invisible in plain sight, while utilizing their labor for everyday comfort and sustenance.

Second, I attempt to construct the lives of the servants from the scant and scattered sources by attending to their names, descriptions of duties, the modes through which they provided comfort for the colonials, and when they refused to obey orders and instructions. Their refusal and recalcitrance, even small gestures of disobedience or unwillingness to comply with orders, are a rich source of registering the control over space, skills, and technology. One important aspect of this is recognizing the type of labor performed by both highly skilled, literate servants and those who were considered menial labor, and how this menial class of labor was constructed not only by assigning certain tasks and wages but by where they were expected to labor. As Indian servants from previous regimes undertook service in colonial households, there was a distinct loss of prestige as the duties changed even when the appellations survived. For example, the *masalchi* (torch bearer) became a scullery mate, the *khansamah* (head of all domestic assets or chamberlain) became a kitchen servant.[13]

Third, by paying attention to their nomenclature as well as the physical characteristics of the spaces and the kinds of activities that took place in these spaces, beyond their immediate function, I explore the connectivity of these spaces. The bottlekhana, for example, it turns out, was more than a space for storing bottles: the mistress gave out orders and supplies here, servants socialized in this space and entertained children. Beyond the residential compounds, these spaces were connected to the bazaar, to far-flung retail shops, taverns, and stills along networks that linked domestic spaces to port cities in the colonies, East Asia, and Europe. Considering the potentially innumerable sites that can thus be connected, I use the movement of liquor and food to identify the sites of production and consumption and thus the impact of these small spaces on colonial economy, social life, and food distribution itself. Much of this entails analysis of architectural plans and sections, and movement between various territorial scales—house, compound, bazaar, cantonment, city, region, etc.

Finally, I emphasize that some aspects of the social life of small spaces may not be available through plan analysis, no matter how useful these are in demonstrating what kinds of social relations these building and site plans were intended to support and those that were discouraged. Plans become even more useful when we consider *not* what they necessarily show at the building or urban scale, but what they do not reveal. This requires reading stories about everyday life and major political events as cutting through the opacity of the plan.

4

Locating the Bottlekhana

The specific spatial configuration developed in each colonial context—beyond the front–back and central–peripheral relationship—was related to the particularities of laboring practices. And here there were important differences in terms of room nomenclature and its relation to labor. In British colonial India the servant hierarchy was sufficiently complex and different from those in Europe, America, or Africa to invite significant commentary. Housekeeping guides provided lists of servants considered necessary in India and introduced European newcomers to the Anglo-Indian terms for rooms. The variation of terms across two centuries of colonial rule in the Indian subcontinent and across regions suggests changing parameters of social practice and the introduction of new forms of labor and new technologies.

Naming

Naming a space, whether it is main house or outhouse, is a mode of acquiring control over the activities of that space. In this the master's control was not all-pervasive. Consider the bottlekhana. Likely a moniker invented by Indians who worked in Anglo-Indian households, given the sheer novelty of storing so many bottles in one place, the term "bottlekhana" appears to have been more popular in eastern and northern India that constituted the Lower and Upper Provinces of Bengal, where the use of the term lasted into the 1920s. In the Northwestern Province and other presidencies of British India, the usual Anglo-Indian nomenclature for this space was store or godown.[1] Curiously, the term does not appear in *Hobson-Jobson*, the reference book for all terms Anglo-Indian, despite its importance in the everyday life of the colonizers.[2] In at least one instance there is a reference to a "provision room" separate from the "bottle connah, and next to the cook room."[3] It is not unusual to find a house description or house plan with mention of both godown and bottlekhana, or store and bottlekhana, suggesting that these spaces were differentiated in terms of use.[4] In some instances the terms were used interchangeably (Figure 4.1).[5] The term "godown" was more capacious both physically and conceptually, and could refer to a large storage space in both residential and commercial buildings.

The large House No. 13 contains—	The small House No. 12 contains—
An arched Verandah,	A long closed Verandah with venetian,
A Hall,	Windows,
Four Bed-rooms,	A large Hall,
A Cook-room,	Two large Bed-rooms,
A Godown,	A Bottleconnah,
A Bottlecannah,	A Cook-room,
Two Necessaries,	A Godown,
A long Palankeen House,	A Necessary,
A small Godown adjoining it,	A Poultry House,
A Bearer's House, and a Durwan's House;	A Bearer's House,
All standing on 12 cottahs of ground in Dhee Calcutta agreeably to the Pottah.	Durwan's House, and a place for Palankeens—
	All standing on 8 cottahs of ground in Dhee Calcutta agreeably to the Pottah.

FIGURE 4.1 Real estate advertisement in *Calcutta Gazette*, February 4, 1793. Note that the greater number of spaces enumerated in the advertisements are service spaces, with the cook room, bottleconnah and godown forming one unit within these service spaces. Source: W. S. Seton Karr, *Selections from Calcutta Gazettes*, vol. 2 (Calcutta: Military Orphan Press, 1865).

As in other parts of South and East Asia, godowns were a ubiquitous feature of trading centers and port cities (**Plates 3 and 4**).[6]

Memoirs and housekeeping guides from the time convey the importance conferred upon the bottlekhana as a room where imported bottled provisions and liquor were kept, and a struggle to control the use of the space, in particular its use by Indian servants. This had as much to do with what was kept in the bottlekhana as where it was located and how it related to other spaces near and far.

At the more proximate scale, the bottlekhana was a complement to the cook room, and somewhere in between a butler's pantry and a cook's pantry. It is useful to note that the word "butler" derives from bottle, with the butler characterized as a servant in charge of the room in which bottled products are kept.[7] The term "kitchen" was rarely used to refer to the space of food production in the Anglo-Indian compound. The usual term was "cook room," a literal translation of the precolonial *bawarchikhana*, a space where the *bawarchi* (cook) presided over culinary matters. While in precolonial elite houses, the *bawarchikhana* comprised several rooms dedicated to the functions of pantry, storage, and scullery (though not using these terms), the cook room of the typical colonial bungalow was a single room, fitted up with equipment in various degrees of sophistication. Only in the most formal establishments such as Government House, the cook room was distinguished from a bakery, pantry, scullery, and the rest, a pattern that became increasingly anglicized in the late nineteenth century. The division and nomenclature of rooms in the late nineteenth century took on a manner akin to country houses in Britain. Vicereine Lady Dufferin, writing in 1888, remarked: "'Offices' are almost unknown here, and linen, china, plate, and stores are accustomed to take their chance in verandahs or godowns of the roughest description."[8] She was comparing the current state of affairs with the newly built accommodations in the Viceregal Lodge in Simla where stores were differentiated in terms of their use and the cook room was a kitchen with "white tiles six feet high all round the walls, looking so clean and bright."[9] She did not forget to mention that the Viceregal Lodge also had a laundry in which the *dhobi* was now "condemned" to use hot water, soap, and mangles, in deviation from the usual practice of thrashing clothes on a rock next to a stream.[10]

By the time construction of the Viceroy's Palace in New Delhi was started in the second decade of the twentieth century, only two of the early colonial names had survived: godown and *dhobikhana* (laundry). In Viceroy's Palace, New Delhi, the term "godown" was used for most storage spaces: furniture godown, housekeeper's godown, camp equipment godown, tent godown, and so forth.

The nomenclature of these spaces is, however, a small indication of their complex cultural geographies. Multiple factors led to the locational change and spatial organization of these rooms between the late eighteenth and early twentieth centuries. It had to do with the type of goods that were stored in these spaces, and the changing nature of trade in liquor and food provisions, particularly with the change in the frequency of ships arriving from Europe following the construction of the Suez Canal in 1869. The changing political fortunes of the British empire in India and attendant transformations in the administrative and military infrastructures affected the nature of domestic labor as well as who provided the labor. The larger number of European women arriving in India to set up home in the second half of the nineteenth century was decisive, as they became the figures who were primarily responsible for managing the servants in their households. Some of the changes can be attributed to the transformation in culinary habits of British residents in India, and a decided move away from Indian-style food to more European tastes in the second half of the nineteenth century. Normalization of these tastes and expectations were, however, anything but normal. The figure of the Indian servant looms large in this century-long process through which ideas about work and labor were realized.

Servants' Spaces

The figure of the servant is so enmeshed with the description of space and narrative of everyday life in the colonies, it is difficult to carve out these figures from the spatial fabric. The spaces and the figures constitute each other. Listen to Rudyard Kipling's recollection of his Mother Lodge (1894):

I wish that I might see them,
My Brethren black an' brown,
With the trichies smellin' pleasant
An' the hog-darn passin' down;
An' the old khansamah snorin'
On the bottle-khana floor,
Like a Master in good standing
With my Mother-Lodge once more.[11]

The word "lodge" derives from the Anglo-Saxon word "logian" and means "to dwell." Kipling's Mother Lodge as a space of dwelling is grounded in a particular colonial milieu. Here the bottlekhana appears as a fixture of lodge life, its Anglo-Indianness in accordance with the "khansamah" (house steward) and "trichies" (Trichinopoly cigars). Like the lodge, establishments other than residences—clubs, hotel, and restaurants—had bottlekhanas. In Kipling's verse, the body of the lodge defined by its members and their homosocial gathering is dependent on other bodies who reside on the periphery but in such close proximity that the boundaries between the central social space and service periphery are blurred. The image of the old khansamah snoring on the bottlekhana floor in Kipling's imperial nostalgia suggests that the necessity of having servants close by at all hours also meant to a large extent countenancing their unguarded presence and ad hoc use of proximate spaces.

The reliance on a large number of servants for everyday domestic labor, and the paucity of planned spaces for servants within domestic confines, meant that servants were everywhere in these buildings. The scandalous proximity of servants, masters, and mistresses provoked numerous commentaries. Writing in 1835 Emma Roberts noted the "inferior domestics" appearing "in the state apartments, whenever they deem it expedient to do so" and the discomfort in seeing palanquin bearers who "wear very little clothing," "walk into drawing rooms, and employ themselves in dusting books or occupations of the like nature."[12] Apart from signaling that servants undertook a multitude of tasks beyond their presumed job description—in this case palanquin bearers who would normally work and stay outside the main house doing double-duty by dusting household furniture—it also starkly portrays the free access to inner spaces of the household by male servants of all ranks. Rather than a single "neat house-maid," European women found themselves surrounded by male servants—the only two female servant jobs being that of the ayah (either for the lady or the children), and sometimes a female sweeper. Whether inside the house or outside in the compound, the visible extent of household labor, including cooking and washing dishes in the verandah or under the open sky in the compound, appeared to European newcomers as strange and discordant.

Sound, smell, and a babble of tongues flowed across the flimsy distinctions between served and servant spaces. Incongruency—racial, spatial, religious, linguistic—was for Kipling the stuff of Anglo-Indian life. Thus, Kipling's khansamah taking a nap on the bottlekhana floor is a necessary disruptive presence. Housekeeping guides explicitly warned against such disruptive practices, perhaps because it was too commonplace, and insisted on the need to cast an orderly net over servant and served spaces. By the time Kipling was writing, the bottlekhana as a fixture of colonial establishments had migrated from its peripheral location in the compound to the main house under closer supervision of the masters and mistresses. This spatial migration was multifaceted. A long-durée view of this phenomenon helps to understand the nature of the transformation.

The earliest mention of bottlekhana in advertisements are from April 1784:

> A Lower-roomed House, highly raised from the ground, consisting of a hall, two bed rooms, a verandah, bottle-connah, cook-room, and necessary house; standing on five cottahs of ground; at present rented at 100 Sicca Rupees per month; situate to the eastward of the China Bazar.[13]

The one-story house in Calcutta in this advertisement was indeed modest in size, but the specific mention of the verandah, bottlekhana, cook room, and necessary house (a euphemism for toilet) confirms the importance of service spaces even in small houses.

Building plans and real estate advertisements suggest that initially the bottlekhana was part of the other service spaces of the household located on the periphery of the lot (see Figure 4.1). For example, a large house situated on the banks of the Hooghly in the Dutch settlement of Chinsurah, advertised in 1784, contained "out-buildings" consisting of "two large bottle-connahs, in addition to a warehouse, six store rooms, a cook-room."[14] In a 1797 advertisement by Dring & Co., we hear of a "capital upper-roomed House in Chowringhee, containing a large hall and three sitting rooms with a verandah and closet below, and three bedrooms, a spacious hall above," having "two extensive range of Out Houses, one consisting of stabling for five horses, with Coach and Palankeen House, the other a large godown shed, a cook-room, two Bottleconnahs, a Bearer's House, and a necessary apart." The two sets of outbuildings in this property in Calcutta were thus differentiated in terms of use: one for stabling and grooms and coachmen, and the other for servants in charge of provisions and food preparation. The advertisement went on to clarify: "Every part of the house and offices [are] built of the best materials, and finished in the most substantial manner, – and the House is glazed above and below. The whole stands on five biggahs, thirteen cottahs, and a twelve chittaks of ground, which is surrounded by a high pucka built wall."[15] Typically, the larger the house the greater the number of storage spaces. Despite their size, it is not certain that the outhouses in these buildings were "pucka-built," that is were of masonry (fired-brick) construction. Usually, when that was the case, the advertisements clarified this aspect of construction.[16] We know, for example, from an auction advertisement in 1809, that the bottlekhana of Belvedere House in the suburbs of Calcutta (later to become the residence of the Lieutenant Governor of Bengal), at that time a large country house, was "puckah."[17]

This grouping of out-buildings of mud- or fired-brick construction, consisting of warehouse, storeroom, cook room, goes back to the earliest European settlements in Bengal.[18] An economy that thrived on oceangoing as well as upcountry trade necessitated large storage spaces for all kinds of goods. Given the propensity of European servants of the European trading companies to undertake private trade, it is not surprising that both public and private buildings of respectable sizes were built with the provision of large storerooms or godowns. It was convenient to have large storage spaces within one's own compound; otherwise, such spaces had to be rented. An 1814 notice to rent out the godowns in the basement of the Calcutta Town Hall reminds us that large storage spaces were seen as a means of generating revenue in public buildings as well.[19] In offices the record room was sometimes referred to as the records godown and located in the center of the building.[20]

There was another reason for the extensive storage spaces in colonial buildings. Most colonial buildings were built to accommodate a wide range of uses: residences were converted into commercial offices, public buildings, and administrative offices (*kachhari/cutcherry*) and vice versa, with very little change in design, in big cities as well as in provincial towns. The built spaces in these buildings catered to multiple possibilities for use and could be repurposed as the need arose.[21] From an 1823 folio of government buildings in the Bengal Presidency, we have plans that show circuit houses and bungalows of district officers in *muffassil* (provincial) towns. All of these buildings are shown with a large number of small rooms along the boundary walls, ranging in width from 7 to 16 feet and in length from 13 to 35 feet (**Plate 5**).[22]

The physical separation of service spaces from living spaces was premised upon a dual rationale.

First, the separation of servants' quarters from that of the master's living space marked class and racial lines. Servants were ill-provided in terms of housing and their accommodations were rudimentary at best. Eliot James described the servants' quarters as "mud-huts": the kitchen, stables all built in a row on the left side of the bungalow compound.[23] Such descriptions of servants' quarters, godowns, and cook rooms as poorly constructed hovels without windows and proper equipment were the rule. The minimal accommodation for servants—"a smoke-grimed hut in the compound" for each man and his family—was largely justified as the scant needs of Indians.[24] "A native exists on very little," remarked James.[25] Others passed over the poor accommodation of servants without comment. Indeed, there are few detailed descriptions of such accommodations.

Second, in the warm climate of India, the need for storage spaces to be locked, and the living spaces to be kept open to facilitate a cooling breeze was paramount. In addition, the "nuisance" of smoke, smell, and sound from cook rooms, work spaces, and stores in close proximity to the master's living spaces were provided as rationale for the complete separation of service from servant spaces.

Some European residents and visitors were pleased that the servants' quarters were hidden "in some obscure corner where they cannot be seen."[26] For others, the distance between the service spaces and the house continued to be a point of anxious consideration. The very need to keep valuable provisions under lock and key, however, seemed to have enabled the migration of the storeroom or bottlekhana to the main house. As early as the 1825 we see an added-on storeroom in the plan of Lieutenant Colonel Gilbert's bungalow in Hazaribagh (**Plates 6 and 7**).[27] In the late 1850s, Minnie Wood's "own store room" was on her side of the bungalow in Jhelum, Punjab, and like Lieutenant Colonel Gilbert's *abdarkhana* (room for storing beverages under the purview of the *abdar*) it was created by apportioning part of the verandah (Figure 4.2).

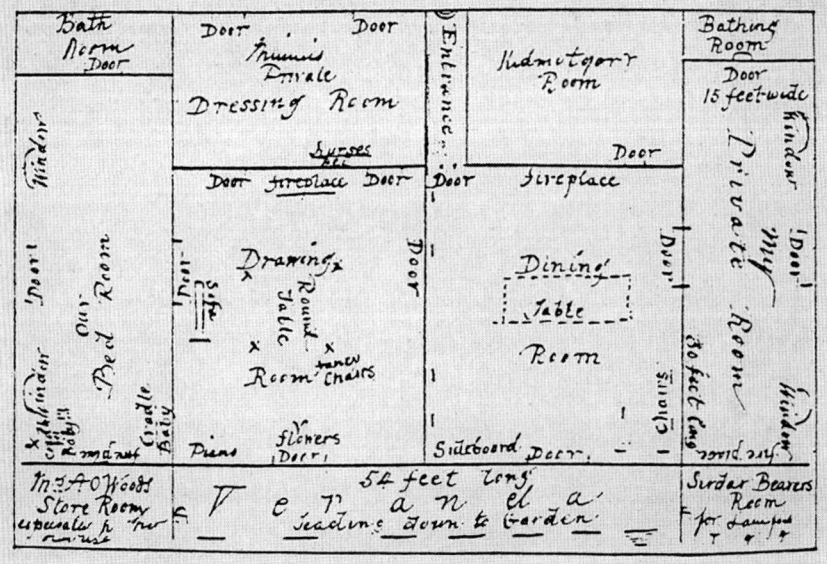

FIGURE 4.2 Plan of Minnie Wood's bungalow, Jhelum, Punjab, late 1850s, with her "Store Room" located in the corner of the verandah. Source: Jane Vansittart, ed., *From Minnie with Love* (London: Peter Davies, 1974).

This space was separate from the "khidmutger's room" which presumably was the space from which food and beverages were served to the dining room. The khidmutger's room or the room of the table attendant functioned as the pantry that mediated the passage of food from the cook room in the servants' quarter to the dining table in the house.[28]

Bottlekhanas inserted within the three-bay plans of residences in Calcutta had become the norm by the late nineteenth century. Consider the relation between the servant spaces and the bottlekhana in two houses on Middleton Street in Calcutta (Figures 4.3 and 4.4). Originally built in the early nineteenth century in the center of their respective lots, the outhouses of these buildings were located along the boundary walls of the compounds. When these houses were given makeovers to render them suitable for multiple occupants in the late nineteenth century, the bottlekhana in 8 Middleton Street was moved inside the house, and in 9 Middleton Street two bottlekhanas and also the cook room were built as adjunct spaces to the main house, with direct connection to the dining room. The latter is also indicative of multiple individuals or families renting the house. The term "bottlekhana" survived into the 1920s. We know from buildings designed in Calcutta in the 1910s

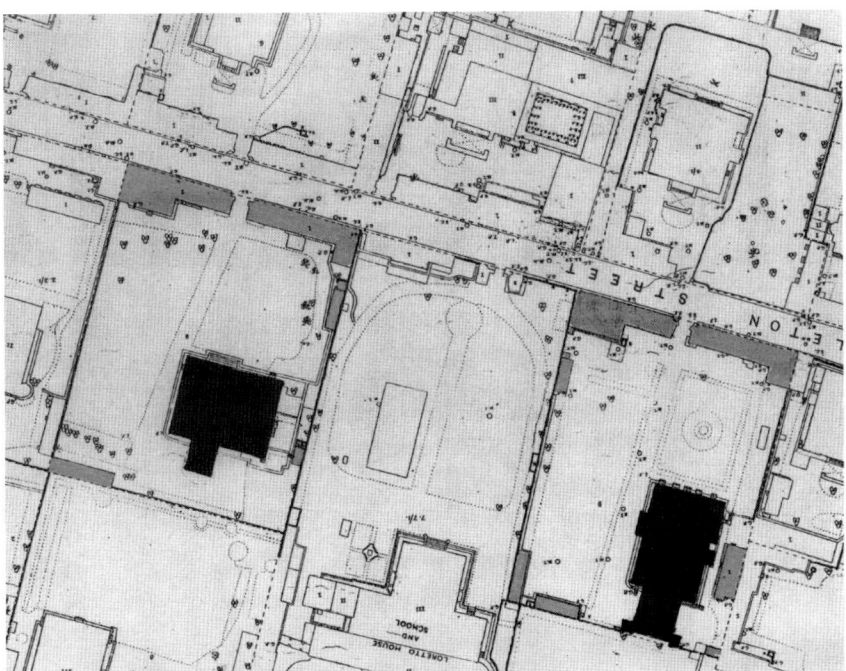

FIGURE 4.3 Site plan of 8 and 9 Middleton Street, Calcutta, 1901. The grey areas indicate outhouses and servants' quarters. Mackintosh Burn Pvt Ltd. © Swati Chattopadhyay.

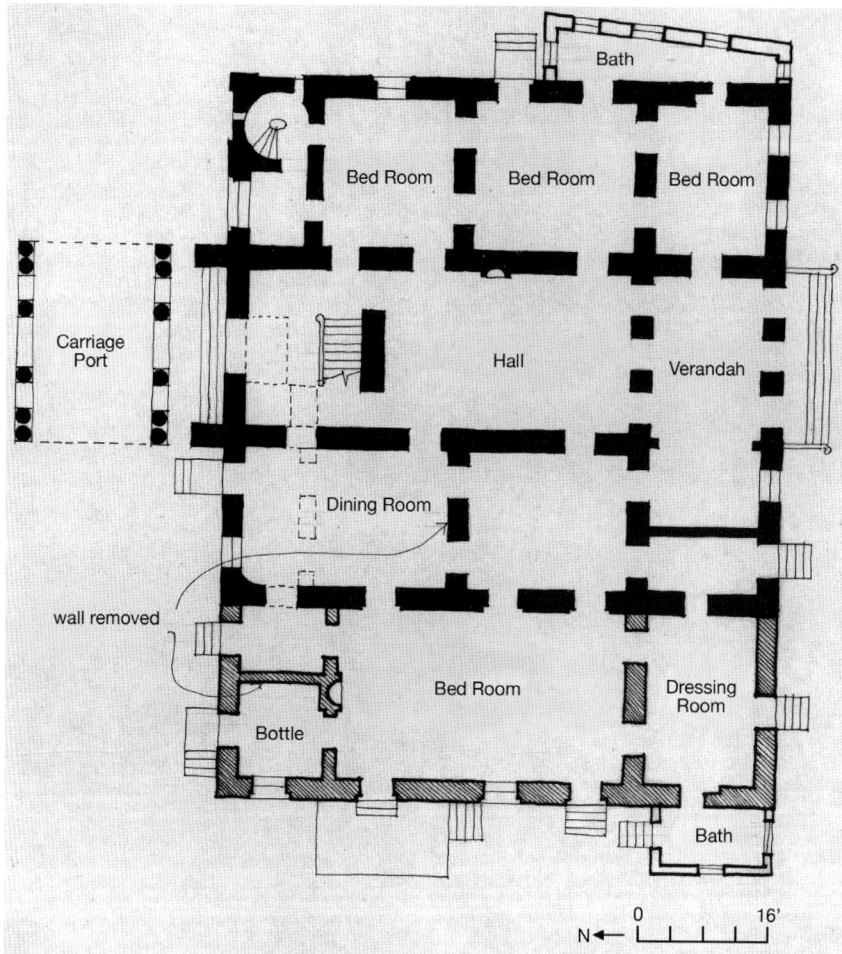

FIGURE 4.4 Plan of 8 Middleton Street, Calcutta, 1901. Mackintosh Burn Pvt Ltd. © Swati Chattopadhyay.

for the Port Commissioners in Alipore Park that the bottlekhana was still considered an integral part of the main house and worked as a pantry that facilitated the passage of food to the dining room (Figure 4.5).

Service Spaces at the Apex

The notion of service spaces as secondary to the main function of a house is so typical and enduring that it is easy to forget the historical specificity of this phenomenon. The spaces that comprised the service wing of colonial houses changed as the expectations and forms of domestic labor changed

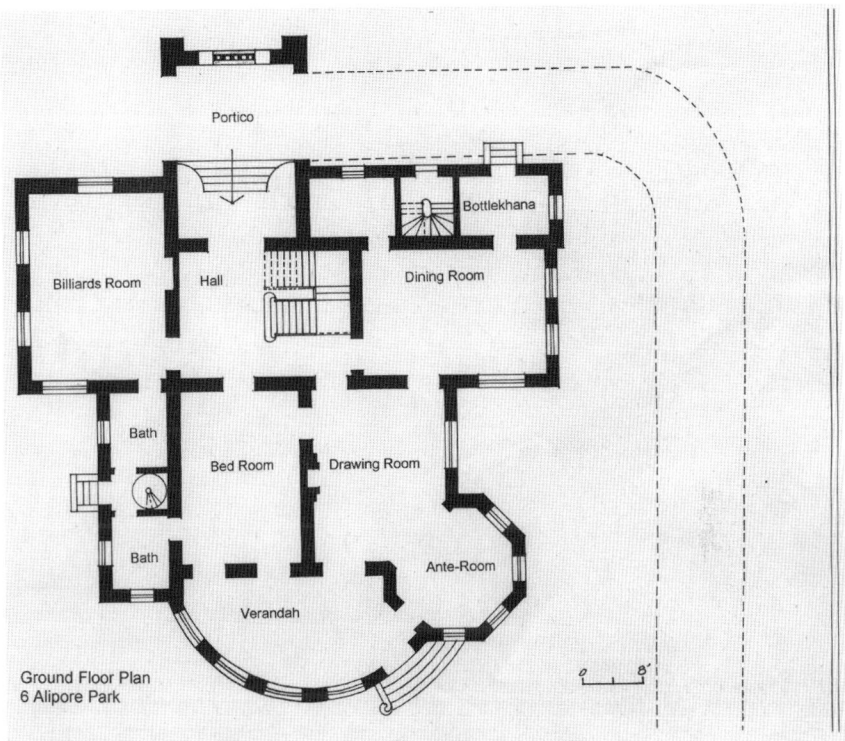

FIGURE 4.5 Plan of residence, Alipore Park, Calcutta. 1910. Mackintosh Burn Pvt Ltd. © Swati Chattopadhyay.

across the span of colonial rule. And here size and rank of the establishment made a difference. We see this in the planning of Government Houses in British colonial India. These buildings served as the residence as well as the office of the Governor-General of the East India Company (later the Viceroy of British India), and in these we can track the elaborate version of this change. In other words, the pattern we find in modest-sized residences was not simply elaborated in large establishments, but a differentiation of spaces accompanied an elaboration of labor categories.

Government House, Calcutta, built in 1803, was intended to convey the imperial ambitions of an emergent colonial state. Based on a Palladian plan, it shared morphological features with other colonial houses in India, in terms of a three-bay central-hall plan supported by ample verandahs, and with service spaces located at a distance from the main house.[29] As befitting a state house hosting large numbers of people, the kitchen, bakery, bottlekhana, store, godown, scullery were separate spaces. This was a practice carried over from the late-eighteenth-century Government Houses in Calcutta and Madras. In addition to those housed in the building's basement, a portion of the service spaces in Government House were located not just away from the main house, but outside the walled enclosure, in a separate set of buildings across the street (Figure 4.6). And yet, the service wing of this grand mansion was not sufficiently large to accommodate the approximately three hundred servants who toiled there. The senior servants would return to their own homes in the city, but a large number of servants, not having a space to retire when not attending to the masters and mistress, crowded the corridors and passageways of the large mansion. This pattern was typical for large houses as well as hotels.[30]

After the capital of British India was moved from Calcutta to New Delhi in 1911 and a new Viceroy's Palace was built as the centerpiece of the city plan, the already large scale of this establishment was magnified. Calcutta's colonial residences had a reputation for spaciousness, and indeed Government House was a magnified version of the elite residences in the city. New Delhi's Viceroy's House exceeded these generous measures by a large margin. With a footprint about twice the size of Calcutta's Government House, and spread over four floors, the building occupied 5 acres and its gardens and golf course another 249 acres (Figure 4.7). Its total floor area was larger than that of the Palace at Versailles. There were 1,779 full-time

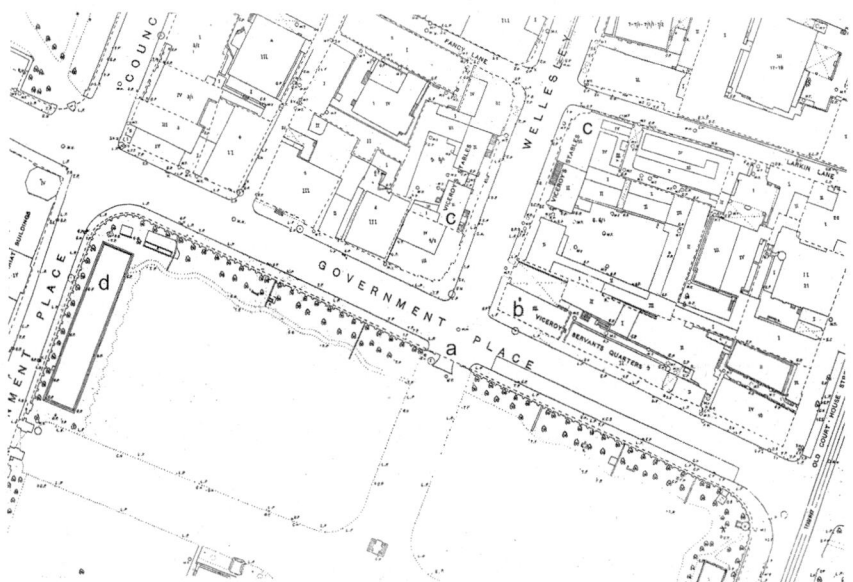

FIGURE 4.6 Location of service wing of Government House, Calcutta, 1911. Detail of Map M8 indicating location of Viceroy's stables and servants' quarters, with the Government House located to the left: rear gate of Government House (a); Viceroy's servants' quarters (b); Viceroy's stables (c); carpenter's shop (d). Map based on survey of 1887–92, revised in 1909 by R. B. Smart.

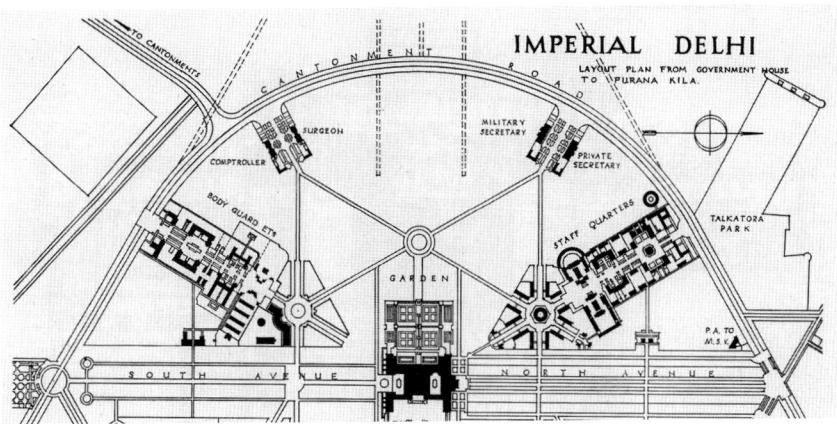

FIGURE 4.7 Plan of Viceroy's estate, New Delhi. Source: A. S. G. Butler, *The Architecture of Sir Edwin Lutyens*, Vol. II (London: Newnes Books, 1950).

staff employed at Viceroy's Palace. This number was considerably augmented by part-time staff.

Apart from the premises in New Delhi, the Viceregal estate included establishments in Calcutta, Simla, as well as a weekend retreat at Mashobra near Simla. Once the Viceroy's primary residence was moved to New Delhi, the erstwhile Lieutenant Governor's residence in Calcutta, Belvedere House, served as the Viceroy's residence when he visited Calcutta (Figure 4.8). Consequently, Belvedere House was operated by a relatively small full-time staff of 68. Plans of Belvedere House, prepared in 1931, show the early-twentieth-century changes that brought the service spaces closer and yet kept the service population at bay.[31] The main house included a kitchen on the ground floor, along with a pantry and other food preparation spaces. This was supplemented with a kitchen and store near the stables, guardrooms, and staff quarters to the east of the building. These quarters were meant for the Indian cook and table staff, whereas the gardener, carpenter, washerman, and Indian clerks were given accommodations on the far south comprising the "back" of the house (Figure 4.9).

In contrast, the entire household service wing of Viceroy's Palace, New Delhi, was accommodated in the building's lower basement floor (Figure 4.10). This did not include accommodation for the staff, which was separate. The service wing was an elaborate affair. All spaces of food preparation and storage, as well as a full range of workshops for carpenters, painters, tinmen, electricians, blacksmith, mason, and stone cutters, utility rooms, and various godowns and cold storage were located in the lower basement.[32] The upper basement level had a few godowns and the top-most level and mezzanine contained storage spaces in addition to rooms for "maids." The relations between master's and servants' spaces, staff and

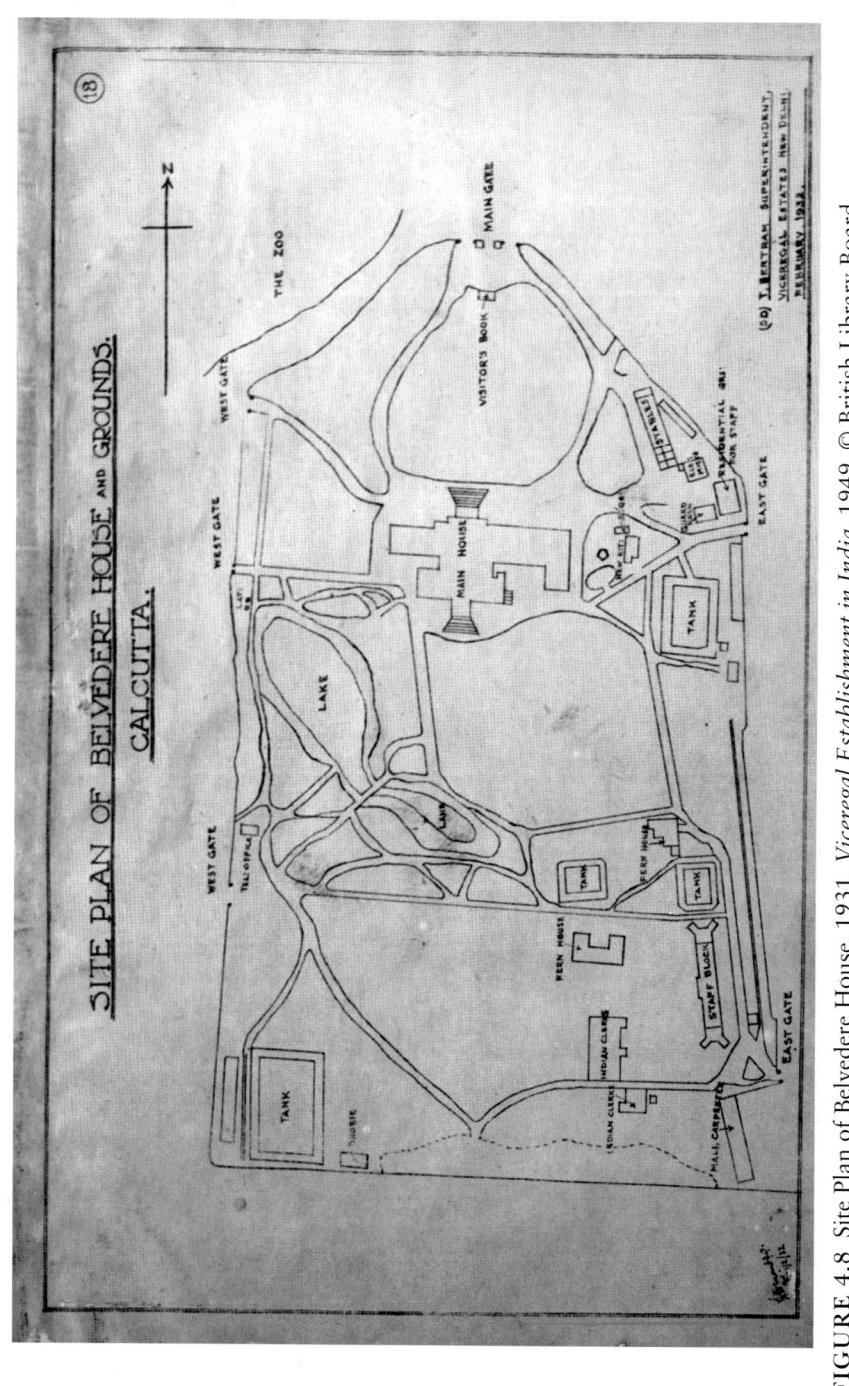

FIGURE 4.8 Site Plan of Belvedere House, 1931. *Viceregal Establishment in India*, 1949. © British Library Board.

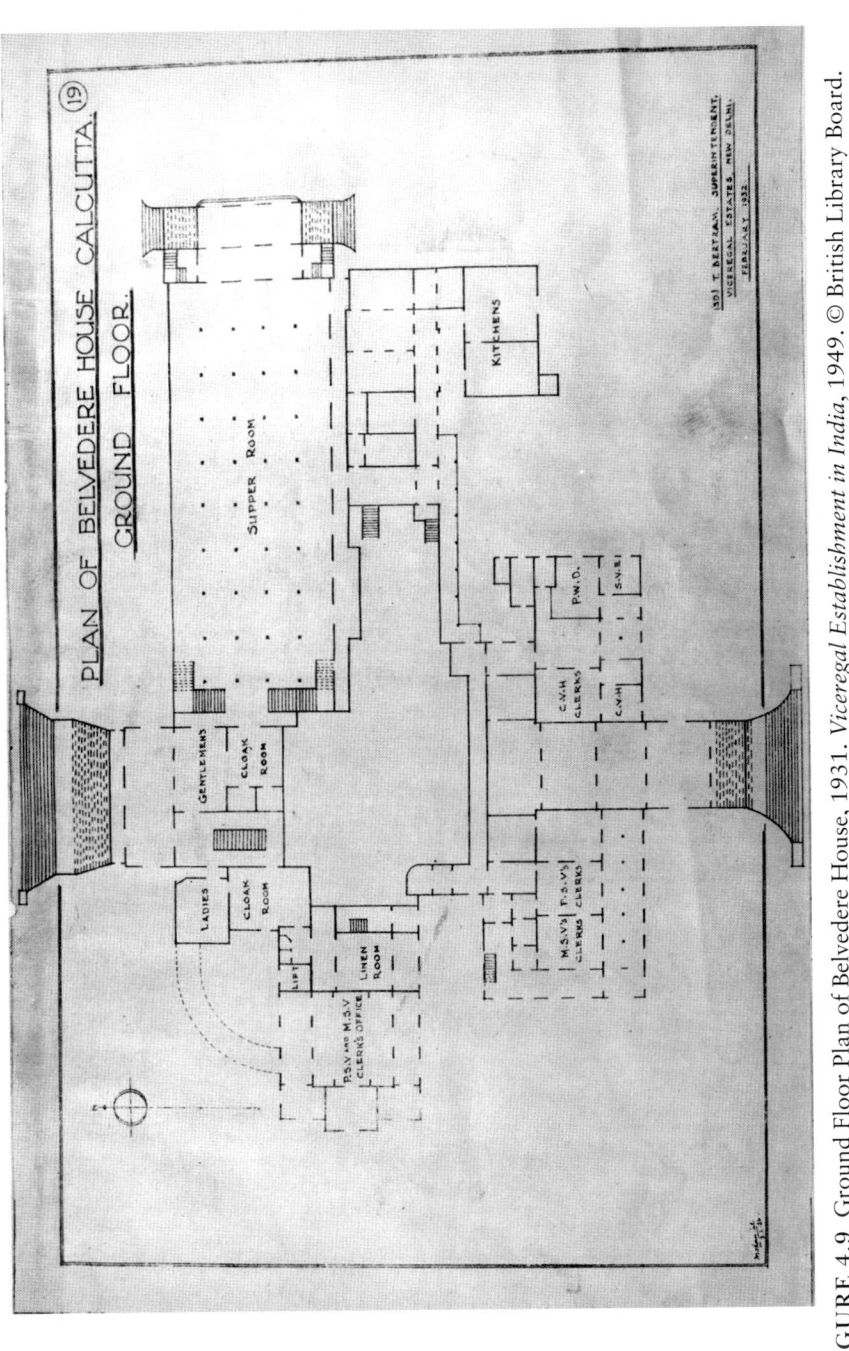

FIGURE 4.9 Ground Floor Plan of Belvedere House, 1931. *Viceregal Establishment in India*, 1949. © British Library Board.

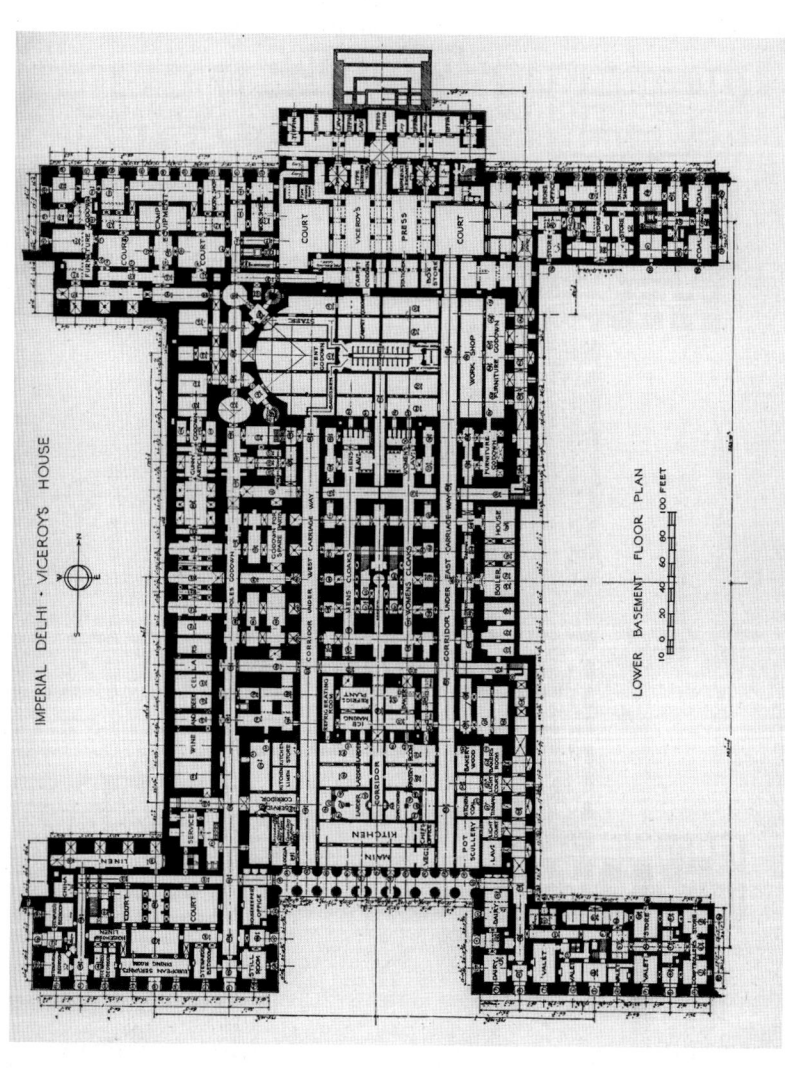

FIGURE 4.10 Lower Basement Plan of Viceroy's House, New Delhi. Source: A. S. G. Butler, *The Architecture of Sir Edwin Lutyens*, Vol. II (London: Newnes Books, 1950).

Coatman's "passing-out parade" in household management in Peshawar took the form of passing out dozens of dusters to a large household of servants. John Coatman, *Portrait of an Englishwoman* (London: Peter Skelton), 40.

11 See, for example, Ann Campbell Wilson's letters of her experience in northern India in the 1880s and 1890s: *Letters from India* (London: William Blackwood and Sons, 1911), 46.

12 An Anglo-Indian, *Indian Outfits and Establishment: A Practical Guide to Persons About to Reside in India* (London: L. Upcott Gill, 1882), 63.

13 Cuthell, *My Garden*, 12.

14 Cuthell, *My Garden*, 69–70.

15 Cuthell, *My Garden*, 121.

16 Cuthell, *My Garden*, 10.

17 For mutiny narratives constructed from site visits, see Manu Goswami, "'Englishness' on the Imperial Circuit: Victorian Englishness, Mutiny Tours in Colonial South Asia," *Journal of Historical Sociology* 9, no. 1 (1996), 54–84, and Ian Baucom, "The Path from War to Friendship: E. M. Forster's Mutiny Pilgrimage," *Out of Place: Englishness, Empire and the Locations of Identity* (Princeton: Princeton University Press, 1999), 101–34.

18 Edith married Captain Cuthell in the early 1870s at his first posting in Lucknow. Captain Cuthell began his military career with the 38th (1st Staffordshire) Regiment of Foot in 1865, and joined the 13th Hussars, Lucknow, in 1870 at the rank of Captain. He subsequently rose to the rank of Lieutenant Colonel.

19 Margaret Macmillan, *Women of the Raj* (London: Thames & Hudon, 1988), 154.

20 Cuthell, *My Garden*, 164.

21 Among her books based in India are a children's storybook, *Little Nellie's Days in India* (1883) and *In the Mutiny Days* (1892); the short story collections *Indian Idylls, by an Idle Exile* (1890) and *In Camp and Cantonment: Stories of Foreign Service* (1897); and two novels, *A Baireuth Pilgrimage* (1894) and *Sweet Irish Eyes* (1897).

22 Martin Heidegger, "The Thing," *Poetry, Language, Thought*, trans. and intro. Albert Hofstadter (New York: HarperCollins, 1971), 163–80.

23 Cuthell, *My Garden*, 74. *Chabutra* refers to a pavilion, in this case set in the garden.

24 Cuthell, *My Garden*, 74.

25 Cuthell, *My Garden*, 89.

26 Cuthell, *My Garden*, 89.

27 Swati Chattopadhyay, "Blurring Boundaries: the Limits of 'White' Town," *Representing Calcutta: Modernity, Nationalism and the Colonial Uncanny* (London: Routledge, 2005).

28 For a representative case of getting a "hold" on household matters, see Steel and Gardiner, *Complete Indian Housekeeper*, 3, 4–5, and A Lady Resident, *The Englishwoman in India*, 2nd ed. (London: Smith Elder and Co., 1865), 5.

29 Cuthell, *My Garden*, 196–7.
30 Cuthell, *My Garden*, 4.
31 Cuthell, *My Garden*, 5.
32 George F. Atkinson, *Curry and Rice on Forty Plates* (London: Day & Sons, 1859), n.p.
33 Cuthell, *My Garden*, 5.
34 Cuthell, *My Garden*, 70.
35 Cuthell, *My Garden*, 14.
36 Cuthell, *My Garden*, 195–6.
37 Cuthell, *My Garden*, 206–7.
38 Cuthell, *My Garden*, 209.
39 Cuthell, *My Garden*, 219.
40 Cuthell, *My Garden*, 277.
41 Cuthell, *My Garden*, 273.
42 Cuthell, *My Garden*, 119.
43 Cuthell, *My Garden*, 25.
44 Atkinson, *Curry and Rice*.
45 For a more detailed account, see Veena Talwar Oldenburg, *The Making of Colonial Lucknow, 1856–1877* (Princeton: Princeton University Press, 1984), Chapter 2.
46 Atkinson, *Curry and Rice on Forty Plates*, n.p.
47 Kenneth L. Ames, *Death in the Dining Room and Other Tales of Victorian Culture* (Philadelphia: Temple University Press, 1992), 196–9.
48 Ames, *Death in the Dining Room*, 202.
49 Ames, *Death in the Dining Room*, 203.
50 Atkinson, *Curry and Rice*, n.p.
51 See Chapter 7 in this volume.
52 I have extended this line of argument in a reading of "nautch" paintings in Chattopadhyay, "Anomalous Spaces: Representations of Dance Performance in Colonial India," in Prarthana Purakayastha and Anurima Banerjee, eds., *The Oxford Handbook of Indian Dance* (Delhi: Oxford University Press, 2023 forthcoming). See reference to one such painting in Chapter 10 in this volume.
53 Thomas Babington Macaulay, "Government of India," Speech Delivered in the House of Commons on the 10th of July 1833.
54 Indeed extraction of even more revenue would be foreseeable in exchange of good governance. The precise language is as follows: "If we have made a good pecuniary bargain for India, but a bad political bargain, if we have saved three or four millions to the finances of that country, and given to it, at the same time, pernicious institutions, we shall indeed have been practising a most ruinous parsimony. If, on the other hand, it shall be found that we have added fifty or a hundred thousand pounds a-year to the expenditure of an empire

Coatman's "passing-out parade" in household management in Peshawar took the form of passing out dozens of dusters to a large household of servants. John Coatman, *Portrait of an Englishwoman* (London: Peter Skelton), 40.

11 See, for example, Ann Campbell Wilson's letters of her experience in northern India in the 1880s and 1890s: *Letters from India* (London: William Blackwood and Sons, 1911), 46.

12 An Anglo-Indian, *Indian Outfits and Establishment: A Practical Guide to Persons About to Reside in India* (London: L. Upcott Gill, 1882), 63.

13 Cuthell, *My Garden*, 12.

14 Cuthell, *My Garden*, 69–70.

15 Cuthell, *My Garden*, 121.

16 Cuthell, *My Garden*, 10.

17 For mutiny narratives constructed from site visits, see Manu Goswami, "'Englishness' on the Imperial Circuit: Victorian Englishness, Mutiny Tours in Colonial South Asia," *Journal of Historical Sociology* 9, no. 1 (1996), 54–84, and Ian Baucom, "The Path from War to Friendship: E. M. Forster's Mutiny Pilgrimage," *Out of Place: Englishness, Empire and the Locations of Identity* (Princeton: Princeton University Press, 1999), 101–34.

18 Edith married Captain Cuthell in the early 1870s at his first posting in Lucknow. Captain Cuthell began his military career with the 38th (1st Staffordshire) Regiment of Foot in 1865, and joined the 13th Hussars, Lucknow, in 1870 at the rank of Captain. He subsequently rose to the rank of Lieutenant Colonel.

19 Margaret Macmillan, *Women of the Raj* (London: Thames & Hudon, 1988), 154.

20 Cuthell, *My Garden*, 164.

21 Among her books based in India are a children's storybook, *Little Nellie's Days in India* (1883) and *In the Mutiny Days* (1892); the short story collections *Indian Idylls, by an Idle Exile* (1890) and *In Camp and Cantonment: Stories of Foreign Service* (1897); and two novels, *A Baireuth Pilgrimage* (1894) and *Sweet Irish Eyes* (1897).

22 Martin Heidegger, "The Thing," *Poetry, Language, Thought*, trans. and intro. Albert Hofstadter (New York: HarperCollins, 1971), 163–80.

23 Cuthell, *My Garden*, 74. *Chabutra* refers to a pavilion, in this case set in the garden.

24 Cuthell, *My Garden*, 74.

25 Cuthell, *My Garden*, 89.

26 Cuthell, *My Garden*, 89.

27 Swati Chattopadhyay, "Blurring Boundaries: the Limits of 'White' Town," *Representing Calcutta: Modernity, Nationalism and the Colonial Uncanny* (London: Routledge, 2005).

28 For a representative case of getting a "hold" on household matters, see Steel and Gardiner, *Complete Indian Housekeeper*, 3, 4–5, and A Lady Resident, *The Englishwoman in India*, 2nd ed. (London: Smith Elder and Co., 1865), 5.

29 Cuthell, *My Garden*, 196–7.
30 Cuthell, *My Garden*, 4.
31 Cuthell, *My Garden*, 5.
32 George F. Atkinson, *Curry and Rice on Forty Plates* (London: Day & Sons, 1859), n.p.
33 Cuthell, *My Garden*, 5.
34 Cuthell, *My Garden*, 70.
35 Cuthell, *My Garden*, 14.
36 Cuthell, *My Garden*, 195–6.
37 Cuthell, *My Garden*, 206–7.
38 Cuthell, *My Garden*, 209.
39 Cuthell, *My Garden*, 219.
40 Cuthell, *My Garden*, 277.
41 Cuthell, *My Garden*, 273.
42 Cuthell, *My Garden*, 119.
43 Cuthell, *My Garden*, 25.
44 Atkinson, *Curry and Rice*.
45 For a more detailed account, see Veena Talwar Oldenburg, *The Making of Colonial Lucknow, 1856–1877* (Princeton: Princeton University Press, 1984), Chapter 2.
46 Atkinson, *Curry and Rice on Forty Plates*, n.p.
47 Kenneth L. Ames, *Death in the Dining Room and Other Tales of Victorian Culture* (Philadelphia: Temple University Press, 1992), 196–9.
48 Ames, *Death in the Dining Room*, 202.
49 Ames, *Death in the Dining Room*, 203.
50 Atkinson, *Curry and Rice*, n.p.
51 See Chapter 7 in this volume.
52 I have extended this line of argument in a reading of "nautch" paintings in Chattopadhyay, "Anomalous Spaces: Representations of Dance Performance in Colonial India," in Prarthana Purakayastha and Anurima Banerjee, eds., *The Oxford Handbook of Indian Dance* (Delhi: Oxford University Press, 2023 forthcoming). See reference to one such painting in Chapter 10 in this volume.
53 Thomas Babington Macaulay, "Government of India," Speech Delivered in the House of Commons on the 10th of July 1833.
54 Indeed extraction of even more revenue would be foreseeable in exchange of good governance. The precise language is as follows: "If we have made a good pecuniary bargain for India, but a bad political bargain, if we have saved three or four millions to the finances of that country, and given to it, at the same time, pernicious institutions, we shall indeed have been practising a most ruinous parsimony. If, on the other hand, it shall be found that we have added fifty or a hundred thousand pounds a-year to the expenditure of an empire

Coatman's "passing-out parade" in household management in Peshawar took the form of passing out dozens of dusters to a large household of servants. John Coatman, *Portrait of an Englishwoman* (London: Peter Skelton), 40.

11 See, for example, Ann Campbell Wilson's letters of her experience in northern India in the 1880s and 1890s: *Letters from India* (London: William Blackwood and Sǿns, 1911), 46.

12 An Anglo-Indian, *Indian Outfits and Establishment: A Practical Guide to Persons About to Reside in India* (London: L. Upcott Gill, 1882), 63.

13 Cuthell, *My Garden*, 12.

14 Cuthell, *My Garden*, 69–70.

15 Cuthell, *My Garden*, 121.

16 Cuthell, *My Garden*, 10.

17 For mutiny narratives constructed from site visits, see Manu Goswami, "'Englishness' on the Imperial Circuit: Victorian Englishness, Mutiny Tours in Colonial South Asia," *Journal of Historical Sociology* 9, no. 1 (1996), 54–84, and Ian Baucom, "The Path from War to Friendship: E. M. Forster's Mutiny Pilgrimage," *Out of Place: Englishness, Empire and the Locations of Identity* (Princeton: Princeton University Press, 1999), 101–34.

18 Edith married Captain Cuthell in the early 1870s at his first posting in Lucknow. Captain Cuthell began his military career with the 38th (1st Staffordshire) Regiment of Foot in 1865, and joined the 13th Hussars, Lucknow, in 1870 at the rank of Captain. He subsequently rose to the rank of Lieutenant Colonel.

19 Margaret Macmillan, *Women of the Raj* (London: Thames & Hudon, 1988), 154.

20 Cuthell, *My Garden*, 164.

21 Among her books based in India are a children's storybook, *Little Nellie's Days in India* (1883) and *In the Mutiny Days* (1892); the short story collections *Indian Idylls, by an Idle Exile* (1890) and *In Camp and Cantonment: Stories of Foreign Service* (1897); and two novels, *A Baireuth Pilgrimage* (1894) and *Sweet Irish Eyes* (1897).

22 Martin Heidegger, "The Thing," *Poetry, Language, Thought*, trans. and intro. Albert Hofstadter (New York: HarperCollins, 1971), 163–80.

23 Cuthell, *My Garden*, 74. *Chabutra* refers to a pavilion, in this case set in the garden.

24 Cuthell, *My Garden*, 74.

25 Cuthell, *My Garden*, 89.

26 Cuthell, *My Garden*, 89.

27 Swati Chattopadhyay, "Blurring Boundaries: the Limits of 'White' Town," *Representing Calcutta: Modernity, Nationalism and the Colonial Uncanny* (London: Routledge, 2005).

28 For a representative case of getting a "hold" on household matters, see Steel and Gardiner, *Complete Indian Housekeeper*, 3, 4–5, and A Lady Resident, *The Englishwoman in India*, 2nd ed. (London: Smith Elder and Co., 1865), 5.

29 Cuthell, *My Garden*, 196–7.
30 Cuthell, *My Garden*, 4.
31 Cuthell, *My Garden*, 5.
32 George F. Atkinson, *Curry and Rice on Forty Plates* (London: Day & Sons, 1859), n.p.
33 Cuthell, *My Garden*, 5.
34 Cuthell, *My Garden*, 70.
35 Cuthell, *My Garden*, 14.
36 Cuthell, *My Garden*, 195–6.
37 Cuthell, *My Garden*, 206–7.
38 Cuthell, *My Garden*, 209.
39 Cuthell, *My Garden*, 219.
40 Cuthell, *My Garden*, 277.
41 Cuthell, *My Garden*, 273.
42 Cuthell, *My Garden*, 119.
43 Cuthell, *My Garden*, 25.
44 Atkinson, *Curry and Rice*.
45 For a more detailed account, see Veena Talwar Oldenburg, *The Making of Colonial Lucknow, 1856–1877* (Princeton: Princeton University Press, 1984), Chapter 2.
46 Atkinson, *Curry and Rice on Forty Plates*, n.p.
47 Kenneth L. Ames, *Death in the Dining Room and Other Tales of Victorian Culture* (Philadelphia: Temple University Press, 1992), 196–9.
48 Ames, *Death in the Dining Room*, 202.
49 Ames, *Death in the Dining Room*, 203.
50 Atkinson, *Curry and Rice*, n.p.
51 See Chapter 7 in this volume.
52 I have extended this line of argument in a reading of "nautch" paintings in Chattopadhyay, "Anomalous Spaces: Representations of Dance Performance in Colonial India," in Prarthana Purakayastha and Anurima Banerjee, eds., *The Oxford Handbook of Indian Dance* (Delhi: Oxford University Press, 2023 forthcoming). See reference to one such painting in Chapter 10 in this volume.
53 Thomas Babington Macaulay, "Government of India," Speech Delivered in the House of Commons on the 10th of July 1833.
54 Indeed extraction of even more revenue would be foreseeable in exchange of good governance. The precise language is as follows: "If we have made a good pecuniary bargain for India, but a bad political bargain, if we have saved three or four millions to the finances of that country, and given to it, at the same time, pernicious institutions, we shall indeed have been practising a most ruinous parsimony. If, on the other hand, it shall be found that we have added fifty or a hundred thousand pounds a-year to the expenditure of an empire

Coatman's "passing-out parade" in household management in Peshawar took the form of passing out dozens of dusters to a large household of servants. John Coatman, *Portrait of an Englishwoman* (London: Peter Skelton), 40.

11 See, for example, Ann Campbell Wilson's letters of her experience in northern India in the 1880s and 1890s: *Letters from India* (London: William Blackwood and Sons, 1911), 46.

12 An Anglo-Indian, *Indian Outfits and Establishment: A Practical Guide to Persons About to Reside in India* (London: L. Upcott Gill, 1882), 63.

13 Cuthell, *My Garden*, 12.

14 Cuthell, *My Garden*, 69–70.

15 Cuthell, *My Garden*, 121.

16 Cuthell, *My Garden*, 10.

17 For mutiny narratives constructed from site visits, see Manu Goswami, "'Englishness' on the Imperial Circuit: Victorian Englishness, Mutiny Tours in Colonial South Asia," *Journal of Historical Sociology* 9, no. 1 (1996), 54–84, and Ian Baucom, "The Path from War to Friendship: E. M. Forster's Mutiny Pilgrimage," *Out of Place: Englishness, Empire and the Locations of Identity* (Princeton: Princeton University Press, 1999), 101–34.

18 Edith married Captain Cuthell in the early 1870s at his first posting in Lucknow. Captain Cuthell began his military career with the 38th (1st Staffordshire) Regiment of Foot in 1865, and joined the 13th Hussars, Lucknow, in 1870 at the rank of Captain. He subsequently rose to the rank of Lieutenant Colonel.

19 Margaret Macmillan, *Women of the Raj* (London: Thames & Hudon, 1988), 154.

20 Cuthell, *My Garden*, 164.

21 Among her books based in India are a children's storybook, *Little Nellie's Days in India* (1883) and *In the Mutiny Days* (1892); the short story collections *Indian Idylls, by an Idle Exile* (1890) and *In Camp and Cantonment: Stories of Foreign Service* (1897); and two novels, *A Baireuth Pilgrimage* (1894) and *Sweet Irish Eyes* (1897).

22 Martin Heidegger, "The Thing," *Poetry, Language, Thought*, trans. and intro. Albert Hofstadter (New York: HarperCollins, 1971), 163–80.

23 Cuthell, *My Garden*, 74. *Chabutra* refers to a pavilion, in this case set in the garden.

24 Cuthell, *My Garden*, 74.

25 Cuthell, *My Garden*, 89.

26 Cuthell, *My Garden*, 89.

27 Swati Chattopadhyay, "Blurring Boundaries: the Limits of 'White' Town," *Representing Calcutta: Modernity, Nationalism and the Colonial Uncanny* (London: Routledge, 2005).

28 For a representative case of getting a "hold" on household matters, see Steel and Gardiner, *Complete Indian Housekeeper*, 3, 4–5, and A Lady Resident, *The Englishwoman in India*, 2nd ed. (London: Smith Elder and Co., 1865), 5.

29 Cuthell, *My Garden*, 196–7.
30 Cuthell, *My Garden*, 4.
31 Cuthell, *My Garden*, 5.
32 George F. Atkinson, *Curry and Rice on Forty Plates* (London: Day & Sons, 1859), n.p.
33 Cuthell, *My Garden*, 5.
34 Cuthell, *My Garden*, 70.
35 Cuthell, *My Garden*, 14.
36 Cuthell, *My Garden*, 195–6.
37 Cuthell, *My Garden*, 206–7.
38 Cuthell, *My Garden*, 209.
39 Cuthell, *My Garden*, 219.
40 Cuthell, *My Garden*, 277.
41 Cuthell, *My Garden*, 273.
42 Cuthell, *My Garden*, 119.
43 Cuthell, *My Garden*, 25.
44 Atkinson, *Curry and Rice*.
45 For a more detailed account, see Veena Talwar Oldenburg, *The Making of Colonial Lucknow, 1856–1877* (Princeton: Princeton University Press, 1984), Chapter 2.
46 Atkinson, *Curry and Rice on Forty Plates*, n.p.
47 Kenneth L. Ames, *Death in the Dining Room and Other Tales of Victorian Culture* (Philadelphia: Temple University Press, 1992), 196–9.
48 Ames, *Death in the Dining Room*, 202.
49 Ames, *Death in the Dining Room*, 203.
50 Atkinson, *Curry and Rice*, n.p.
51 See Chapter 7 in this volume.
52 I have extended this line of argument in a reading of "nautch" paintings in Chattopadhyay, "Anomalous Spaces: Representations of Dance Performance in Colonial India," in Prarthana Purakayastha and Anurima Banerjee, eds., *The Oxford Handbook of Indian Dance* (Delhi: Oxford University Press, 2023 forthcoming). See reference to one such painting in Chapter 10 in this volume.
53 Thomas Babington Macaulay, "Government of India," Speech Delivered in the House of Commons on the 10th of July 1833.
54 Indeed extraction of even more revenue would be foreseeable in exchange of good governance. The precise language is as follows: "If we have made a good pecuniary bargain for India, but a bad political bargain, if we have saved three or four millions to the finances of that country, and given to it, at the same time, pernicious institutions, we shall indeed have been practising a most ruinous parsimony. If, on the other hand, it shall be found that we have added fifty or a hundred thousand pounds a-year to the expenditure of an empire

19 *Calcutta Gazette*, April12, 1810.
20 Public Works Consultations, 5th April 1855. No 80. British Library IOR/P/15/93.
21 For a more detailed treatment of this see Swati Chattopadhyay, "Spaces of Conversation: : The Avant-garde in 1920s Calcutta," in Regina Bittner and Kathrin Rhomberg, eds., *Transcultural Avant-Garde Laboratory: The Bauhaus in Calcutta, 1922* (Berlin: 2013), 161–72.
22 Ruggles, "Making Vision Manifest," 153.
23 Abanindranath Tagore, *Apan Katha, Abanindra Rachanabali*, vol 1. (Kolkata: Prakash Bhavan 1973), 15.
24 For a discussion of the importance of the *otla* in the imagination of princely architecture in the state of Jaipur see Sugata Ray, "Colonial Frames: 'Native' Claims: The Jaipur Economic and Industrial Museum," *The Art Bulletin* XCVI, no 2 (June 2014): 196–212.
25 Chanda, *Amar Ma'r Baper Bari*, 21–22.
26 Chanda, *Amar Ma'r Baper Bari*, 30.
27 Polier's letter to Nawab Shuja-ud-Daula, 26 Rajab, 1187, in Muzaffar Alam and Seema Alavi, *A European Experience of the Mughal Orient the I'jāz-i Arsalānī (Persian letters 1773–1779) of Antoine-Louis Henri Polier* (Delhi: Oxford University Press, 2001), 101; and Polier to Oshra Mistri Gora, 7 Shawwal, in Alam and Alavi, *A European Experience of the Mughal Orient*, 113–114.
28 For more on this see Swati Chattopadhyay, "Anomalous Spaces: Representations of Dance Performance in Colonial India," in Prarthana Purakayastha and Anurima Banerjee, eds., *The Oxford Handbook of Indian Dance* (Delhi: Oxford University Press, 2023 forthcoming).
29 Malini Roy, "Origins of the Late Mughal Painting Tradition in Awadh," in Stephen Markel, and Tushara Bindu Gude, eds., *India's Fabled City: The Art of Courtly Lucknow*, 165–186 (Los Angeles: Los Angeles County Museum of Art and Del Monico Books, Prestel, 2011), 171.
30 Peter Alford Andrews, "The Generous Heart or the Mass of Clouds: the Court Tents of Shahjahan," *Muqarnas* vol. 4 (1987): 148–165.
31 See Chattopadhyay, *Representing Calcutta*.
32 Lady Maria Nugent, *Lady Nugent's East India Journal*, ed. Ashley L. Cohen (1839; London: Oxford University Press, 2014), 55.
33 Nugent, *Lady Nugent's East India Journal*, 59, 63 and passim.
34 Colesworthy Grant, *Anglo-Indian Domestic Sketch* (Calcutta: Thacker and Spink, 1862), 11.
35 W. S. Seton-Kerr, *Selections from Calcutta Gazettes*, vol 3 (Calcutta: Military Orphan Press, 1864), 567.
36 Chattopadhyay, *Representing Calcutta,* Chapter 2.
37 William Clerihew, "View of the Cenotaph and Governor's House seen from across the river, Barrackpore," 1843. Royal Institute of British Architects Collections, RIBA 37341.
38 The only other images of Calcutta drawn by British artists where terraces are clearly indicated are those drawn from the terraces and glacis of Fort William,

which no doubt was meant to be a power vantage. For example, William Hodges, "A view of Calcutta taken from Fort William," 1781. Line Engraving with etching by W. Byrne from Hodges' *Travels in India*, London, 1793; Samuel Davis, "View of Calcutta from Fort William," c 1805, Colored aquatint engraved by C. Duburh, 1807. See Jeremy Losty, *Calcutta City of Palaces* (London: British Library, 1990).

39 Kalyani Dutta notes that in her childhood, in the first half of the twentieth century, the *nyara chhad* was the place, among other found spaces, for school-going girls to hang out. Kalyani Dutta, *Thor Bori Khara* (Kolkata: Thema, 1998), 90.

40 For a good discussion and images of these terraces at #6 Dwarakanath Tagore Lane, see Suranjana Bhattacharya, *Kabi'r Abas*, vol. 1 (Kolkata: Ananda Publishers, 2015).

Chapter 11

1 Edith E. Cuthell, *My Garden in the City of Gardens: A Memory with Illustrations* (London: John Lane, 1905), 37–8.
2 Cuthell, *My Garden*, 3.
3 Cuthell, *My Garden*, 3.
4 Cuthell, *My Garden*, 163.
5 See Part Two of this volume. For earlier works, see Nupur Chaudhuri's discussion of the treatment of servants in "Memsahibs and their Servants in Nineteenth-centiry India," *Women's History Review* 3 (1994).
6 F.A. Steel and G. Gardiner, *The Complete Indian Housekeeper and Cook*, 7th ed. (London: William Heineman, 1909), 7. For a discussion of the empire of home, see Rosemary Marangoly George, "Homes in the empire, empires in the home," *Cultural Critique* (Winter 1993–4), 95–127; Mary Procida, *Married to the Empire: Gender, Politics and Imperialism in India, 1883–1947* (Manchester: Manchester University Press, 2002), Chapter 2; Alison Blunt, "Imperial Geographies of Home: British Domesticity in India, 1886–1925," *Transactions of the Institute of British Geographers*, New Series 24, no. 4 (1999), 421–40.
7 Swati Chattopadhyay, "Goods, Chattels and Sundry Items: Constructing Nineteenth-century Anglo-Indian Domestic Life," *Journal of Material Culture* 7, no. 3 (November 2002), 245–6.
8 Maud Divers, *The Englishwoman in India* (Edinburgh: W. Blackwood, 1909), 62.
9 I am indebted to Sudipta Sen for suggesting the phrase "everyday fussiness that comes with the plenitude of power."
10 Divers, *The Englishwoman in India*, 132–3. Most housekeeping guides for British women in India had something to say about it, and a good many memoirs by Englishwomen in India dwell on that topic. See Divers, *The Englishwoman in India*, 67. Even in the post-World War I years, Theodora

19 *Calcutta Gazette*, April12, 1810.
20 Public Works Consultations, 5th April 1855. No 80. British Library IOR/P/15/93.
21 For a more detailed treatment of this see Swati Chattopadhyay, "Spaces of Conversation: : The Avant-garde in 1920s Calcutta," in Regina Bittner and Kathrin Rhomberg, eds., *Transcultural Avant-Garde Laboratory: The Bauhaus in Calcutta, 1922* (Berlin: 2013), 161–72.
22 Ruggles, "Making Vision Manifest," 153.
23 Abanindranath Tagore, *Apan Katha, Abanindra Rachanabali*, vol 1. (Kolkata: Prakash Bhavan 1973), 15.
24 For a discussion of the importance of the *otla* in the imagination of princely architecture in the state of Jaipur see Sugata Ray, "Colonial Frames: 'Native' Claims: The Jaipur Economic and Industrial Museum," *The Art Bulletin* XCVI, no 2 (June 2014): 196–212.
25 Chanda, *Amar Ma'r Baper Bari*, 21–22.
26 Chanda, *Amar Ma'r Baper Bari*, 30.
27 Polier's letter to Nawab Shuja-ud-Daula, 26 Rajab, 1187, in Muzaffar Alam and Seema Alavi, *A European Experience of the Mughal Orient the I'jāz-i Arsalānī (Persian letters 1773–1779) of Antoine-Louis Henri Polier* (Delhi: Oxford University Press, 2001), 101; and Polier to Oshra Mistri Gora, 7 Shawwal, in Alam and Alavi, *A European Experience of the Mughal Orient*, 113–114.
28 For more on this see Swati Chattopadhyay, "Anomalous Spaces: Representations of Dance Performance in Colonial India," in Prarthana Purakayastha and Anurima Banerjee, eds., *The Oxford Handbook of Indian Dance* (Delhi: Oxford University Press, 2023 forthcoming).
29 Malini Roy, "Origins of the Late Mughal Painting Tradition in Awadh," in Stephen Markel, and Tushara Bindu Gude, eds., *India's Fabled City: The Art of Courtly Lucknow*, 165–186 (Los Angeles: Los Angeles County Museum of Art and Del Monico Books, Prestel, 2011), 171.
30 Peter Alford Andrews, "The Generous Heart or the Mass of Clouds: the Court Tents of Shahjahan," *Muqarnas* vol. 4 (1987): 148–165.
31 See Chattopadhyay, *Representing Calcutta*.
32 Lady Maria Nugent, *Lady Nugent's East India Journal*, ed. Ashley L. Cohen (1839; London: Oxford University Press, 2014), 55.
33 Nugent, *Lady Nugent's East India Journal*, 59, 63 and passim.
34 Colesworthy Grant, *Anglo-Indian Domestic Sketch* (Calcutta: Thacker and Spink, 1862), 11.
35 W. S. Seton-Kerr, *Selections from Calcutta Gazettes*, vol 3 (Calcutta: Military Orphan Press, 1864), 567.
36 Chattopadhyay, *Representing Calcutta*, Chapter 2.
37 William Clerihew, "View of the Cenotaph and Governor's House seen from across the river, Barrackpore," 1843. Royal Institute of British Architects Collections, RIBA 37341.
38 The only other images of Calcutta drawn by British artists where terraces are clearly indicated are those drawn from the terraces and glacis of Fort William,

which no doubt was meant to be a power vantage. For example, William Hodges, "A view of Calcutta taken from Fort William," 1781. Line Engraving with etching by W. Byrne from Hodges' *Travels in India*, London, 1793; Samuel Davis, "View of Calcutta from Fort William," c 1805, Colored aquatint engraved by C. Duburh, 1807. See Jeremy Losty, *Calcutta City of Palaces* (London: British Library, 1990).

39 Kalyani Dutta notes that in her childhood, in the first half of the twentieth century, the *nyara chhad* was the place, among other found spaces, for school-going girls to hang out. Kalyani Dutta, *Thor Bori Khara* (Kolkata: Thema, 1998), 90.

40 For a good discussion and images of these terraces at #6 Dwarakanath Tagore Lane, see Suranjana Bhattacharya, *Kabi'r Abas*, vol. 1 (Kolkata: Ananda Publishers, 2015).

Chapter 11

1 Edith E. Cuthell, *My Garden in the City of Gardens: A Memory with Illustrations* (London: John Lane, 1905), 37–8.
2 Cuthell, *My Garden*, 3.
3 Cuthell, *My Garden*, 3.
4 Cuthell, *My Garden*, 163.
5 See Part Two of this volume. For earlier works, see Nupur Chaudhuri's discussion of the treatment of servants in "Memsahibs and their Servants in Nineteenth-centiry India," *Women's History Review* 3 (1994).
6 F.A. Steel and G. Gardiner, *The Complete Indian Housekeeper and Cook*, 7th ed. (London: William Heineman, 1909), 7. For a discussion of the empire of home, see Rosemary Marangoly George, "Homes in the empire, empires in the home," *Cultural Critique* (Winter 1993–4), 95–127; Mary Procida, *Married to the Empire: Gender, Politics and Imperialism in India, 1883–1947* (Manchester: Manchester University Press, 2002), Chapter 2; Alison Blunt, "Imperial Geographies of Home: British Domesticity in India, 1886–1925," *Transactions of the Institute of British Geographers*, New Series 24, no. 4 (1999), 421–40.
7 Swati Chattopadhyay, "Goods, Chattels and Sundry Items: Constructing Nineteenth-century Anglo-Indian Domestic Life," *Journal of Material Culture* 7, no. 3 (November 2002), 245–6.
8 Maud Divers, *The Englishwoman in India* (Edinburgh: W. Blackwood, 1909), 62.
9 I am indebted to Sudipta Sen for suggesting the phrase "everyday fussiness that comes with the plenitude of power."
10 Divers, *The Englishwoman in India*, 132–3. Most housekeeping guides for British women in India had something to say about it, and a good many memoirs by Englishwomen in India dwell on that topic. See Divers, *The Englishwoman in India*, 67. Even in the post-World War I years, Theodora

19 *Calcutta Gazette*, April 12, 1810.
20 Public Works Consultations, 5th April 1855. No 80. British Library IOR/P/15/93.
21 For a more detailed treatment of this see Swati Chattopadhyay, "Spaces of Conversation: : The Avant-garde in 1920s Calcutta," in Regina Bittner and Kathrin Rhomberg, eds., *Transcultural Avant-Garde Laboratory: The Bauhaus in Calcutta, 1922* (Berlin: 2013), 161–72.
22 Ruggles, "Making Vision Manifest," 153.
23 Abanindranath Tagore, *Apan Katha, Abanindra Rachanabali*, vol 1. (Kolkata: Prakash Bhavan 1973), 15.
24 For a discussion of the importance of the *otla* in the imagination of princely architecture in the state of Jaipur see Sugata Ray, "Colonial Frames: 'Native' Claims: The Jaipur Economic and Industrial Museum," *The Art Bulletin* XCVI, no 2 (June 2014): 196–212.
25 Chanda, *Amar Ma'r Baper Bari*, 21–22.
26 Chanda, *Amar Ma'r Baper Bari*, 30.
27 Polier's letter to Nawab Shuja-ud-Daula, 26 Rajab, 1187, in Muzaffar Alam and Seema Alavi, *A European Experience of the Mughal Orient the I'jāz-i Arsalānī (Persian letters 1773–1779) of Antoine-Louis Henri Polier* (Delhi: Oxford University Press, 2001), 101; and Polier to Oshra Mistri Gora, 7 Shawwal, in Alam and Alavi, *A European Experience of the Mughal Orient*, 113–114.
28 For more on this see Swati Chattopadhyay, "Anomalous Spaces: Representations of Dance Performance in Colonial India," in Prarthana Purakayastha and Anurima Banerjee, eds., *The Oxford Handbook of Indian Dance* (Delhi: Oxford University Press, 2023 forthcoming).
29 Malini Roy, "Origins of the Late Mughal Painting Tradition in Awadh," in Stephen Markel, and Tushara Bindu Gude, eds., *India's Fabled City: The Art of Courtly Lucknow*, 165–186 (Los Angeles: Los Angeles County Museum of Art and Del Monico Books, Prestel, 2011), 171.
30 Peter Alford Andrews, "The Generous Heart or the Mass of Clouds: the Court Tents of Shahjahan," *Muqarnas* vol. 4 (1987): 148–165.
31 See Chattopadhyay, *Representing Calcutta*.
32 Lady Maria Nugent, *Lady Nugent's East India Journal*, ed. Ashley L. Cohen (1839; London: Oxford University Press, 2014), 55.
33 Nugent, *Lady Nugent's East India Journal*, 59, 63 and passim.
34 Colesworthy Grant, *Anglo-Indian Domestic Sketch* (Calcutta: Thacker and Spink, 1862), 11.
35 W. S. Seton-Kerr, *Selections from Calcutta Gazettes*, vol 3 (Calcutta: Military Orphan Press, 1864), 567.
36 Chattopadhyay, *Representing Calcutta*, Chapter 2.
37 William Clerihew, "View of the Cenotaph and Governor's House seen from across the river, Barrackpore," 1843. Royal Institute of British Architects Collections, RIBA 37341.
38 The only other images of Calcutta drawn by British artists where terraces are clearly indicated are those drawn from the terraces and glacis of Fort William,

which no doubt was meant to be a power vantage. For example, William Hodges, "A view of Calcutta taken from Fort William," 1781. Line Engraving with etching by W. Byrne from Hodges' *Travels in India*, London, 1793; Samuel Davis, "View of Calcutta from Fort William," c 1805, Colored aquatint engraved by C. Duburh, 1807. See Jeremy Losty, *Calcutta City of Palaces* (London: British Library, 1990).

39 Kalyani Dutta notes that in her childhood, in the first half of the twentieth century, the *nyara chhad* was the place, among other found spaces, for school-going girls to hang out. Kalyani Dutta, *Thor Bori Khara* (Kolkata: Thema, 1998), 90.

40 For a good discussion and images of these terraces at #6 Dwarakanath Tagore Lane, see Suranjana Bhattacharya, *Kabi'r Abas*, vol. 1 (Kolkata: Ananda Publishers, 2015).

Chapter 11

1 Edith E. Cuthell, *My Garden in the City of Gardens: A Memory with Illustrations* (London: John Lane, 1905), 37–8.
2 Cuthell, *My Garden*, 3.
3 Cuthell, *My Garden*, 3.
4 Cuthell, *My Garden*, 163.
5 See Part Two of this volume. For earlier works, see Nupur Chaudhuri's discussion of the treatment of servants in "Memsahibs and their Servants in Nineteenth-centiry India," *Women's History Review* 3 (1994).
6 F.A. Steel and G. Gardiner, *The Complete Indian Housekeeper and Cook*, 7th ed. (London: William Heineman, 1909), 7. For a discussion of the empire of home, see Rosemary Marangoly George, "Homes in the empire, empires in the home," *Cultural Critique* (Winter 1993–4), 95–127; Mary Procida, *Married to the Empire: Gender, Politics and Imperialism in India, 1883–1947* (Manchester: Manchester University Press, 2002), Chapter 2; Alison Blunt, "Imperial Geographies of Home: British Domesticity in India, 1886–1925," *Transactions of the Institute of British Geographers*, New Series 24, no. 4 (1999), 421–40.
7 Swati Chattopadhyay, "Goods, Chattels and Sundry Items: Constructing Nineteenth-century Anglo-Indian Domestic Life," *Journal of Material Culture* 7, no. 3 (November 2002), 245–6.
8 Maud Divers, *The Englishwoman in India* (Edinburgh: W. Blackwood, 1909), 62.
9 I am indebted to Sudipta Sen for suggesting the phrase "everyday fussiness that comes with the plenitude of power."
10 Divers, *The Englishwoman in India*, 132–3. Most housekeeping guides for British women in India had something to say about it, and a good many memoirs by Englishwomen in India dwell on that topic. See Divers, *The Englishwoman in India*, 67. Even in the post-World War I years, Theodora

19 *Calcutta Gazette*, April12, 1810.
20 Public Works Consultations, 5th April 1855. No 80. British Library IOR/P/15/93.
21 For a more detailed treatment of this see Swati Chattopadhyay, "Spaces of Conversation: : The Avant-garde in 1920s Calcutta," in Regina Bittner and Kathrin Rhomberg, eds., *Transcultural Avant-Garde Laboratory: The Bauhaus in Calcutta, 1922* (Berlin: 2013), 161–72.
22 Ruggles, "Making Vision Manifest," 153.
23 Abanindranath Tagore, *Apan Katha, Abanindra Rachanabali*, vol 1. (Kolkata: Prakash Bhavan 1973), 15.
24 For a discussion of the importance of the *otla* in the imagination of princely architecture in the state of Jaipur see Sugata Ray, "Colonial Frames: 'Native' Claims: The Jaipur Economic and Industrial Museum," *The Art Bulletin* XCVI, no 2 (June 2014): 196–212.
25 Chanda, *Amar Ma'r Baper Bari*, 21–22.
26 Chanda, *Amar Ma'r Baper Bari*, 30.
27 Polier's letter to Nawab Shuja-ud-Daula, 26 Rajab, 1187, in Muzaffar Alam and Seema Alavi, *A European Experience of the Mughal Orient the I'jāz-i Arsalānī (Persian letters 1773–1779) of Antoine-Louis Henri Polier* (Delhi: Oxford University Press, 2001), 101; and Polier to Oshra Mistri Gora, 7 Shawwal, in Alam and Alavi, *A European Experience of the Mughal Orient*, 113–114.
28 For more on this see Swati Chattopadhyay, "Anomalous Spaces: Representations of Dance Performance in Colonial India," in Prarthana Purakayastha and Anurima Banerjee, eds., *The Oxford Handbook of Indian Dance* (Delhi: Oxford University Press, 2023 forthcoming).
29 Malini Roy, "Origins of the Late Mughal Painting Tradition in Awadh," in Stephen Markel, and Tushara Bindu Gude, eds., *India's Fabled City: The Art of Courtly Lucknow*, 165–186 (Los Angeles: Los Angeles County Museum of Art and Del Monico Books, Prestel, 2011), 171.
30 Peter Alford Andrews, "The Generous Heart or the Mass of Clouds: the Court Tents of Shahjahan," *Muqarnas* vol. 4 (1987): 148–165.
31 See Chattopadhyay, *Representing Calcutta*.
32 Lady Maria Nugent, *Lady Nugent's East India Journal*, ed. Ashley L. Cohen (1839; London: Oxford University Press, 2014), 55.
33 Nugent, *Lady Nugent's East India Journal*, 59, 63 and passim.
34 Colesworthy Grant, *Anglo-Indian Domestic Sketch* (Calcutta: Thacker and Spink, 1862), 11.
35 W. S. Seton-Kerr, *Selections from Calcutta Gazettes*, vol 3 (Calcutta: Military Orphan Press, 1864), 567.
36 Chattopadhyay, *Representing Calcutta*, Chapter 2.
37 William Clerihew, "View of the Cenotaph and Governor's House seen from across the river, Barrackpore," 1843. Royal Institute of British Architects Collections, RIBA 37341.
38 The only other images of Calcutta drawn by British artists where terraces are clearly indicated are those drawn from the terraces and glacis of Fort William,

which no doubt was meant to be a power vantage. For example, William Hodges, "A view of Calcutta taken from Fort William," 1781. Line Engraving with etching by W. Byrne from Hodges' *Travels in India*, London, 1793; Samuel Davis, "View of Calcutta from Fort William," c 1805, Colored aquatint engraved by C. Duburh, 1807. See Jeremy Losty, *Calcutta City of Palaces* (London: British Library, 1990).

39 Kalyani Dutta notes that in her childhood, in the first half of the twentieth century, the *nyara chhad* was the place, among other found spaces, for school-going girls to hang out. Kalyani Dutta, *Thor Bori Khara* (Kolkata: Thema, 1998), 90.

40 For a good discussion and images of these terraces at #6 Dwarakanath Tagore Lane, see Suranjana Bhattacharya, *Kabi'r Abas*, vol. 1 (Kolkata: Ananda Publishers, 2015).

Chapter 11

1   Edith E. Cuthell, *My Garden in the City of Gardens: A Memory with Illustrations* (London: John Lane, 1905), 37–8.
2   Cuthell, *My Garden*, 3.
3   Cuthell, *My Garden*, 3.
4   Cuthell, *My Garden*, 163.
5   See Part Two of this volume. For earlier works, see Nupur Chaudhuri's discussion of the treatment of servants in "Memsahibs and their Servants in Nineteenth-centiry India," *Women's History Review* 3 (1994).
6   F.A. Steel and G. Gardiner, *The Complete Indian Housekeeper and Cook*, 7th ed. (London: William Heineman, 1909), 7. For a discussion of the empire of home, see Rosemary Marangoly George, "Homes in the empire, empires in the home," *Cultural Critique* (Winter 1993–4), 95–127; Mary Procida, *Married to the Empire: Gender, Politics and Imperialism in India, 1883–1947* (Manchester: Manchester University Press, 2002), Chapter 2; Alison Blunt, "Imperial Geographies of Home: British Domesticity in India, 1886–1925," *Transactions of the Institute of British Geographers*, New Series 24, no. 4 (1999), 421–40.
7   Swati Chattopadhyay, "Goods, Chattels and Sundry Items: Constructing Nineteenth-century Anglo-Indian Domestic Life," *Journal of Material Culture* 7, no. 3 (November 2002), 245–6.
8   Maud Divers, *The Englishwoman in India* (Edinburgh: W. Blackwood, 1909), 62.
9   I am indebted to Sudipta Sen for suggesting the phrase "everyday fussiness that comes with the plenitude of power."
10 Divers, *The Englishwoman in India*, 132–3. Most housekeeping guides for British women in India had something to say about it, and a good many memoirs by Englishwomen in India dwell on that topic. See Divers, *The Englishwoman in India*, 67. Even in the post-World War I years, Theodora

kitchen gardens could not replicate the desired European dishes, and those who considered all Indian produce—from lamb to mangoes—inferior, were reliant on bottled European provisions, if they could afford them. "Of strawberries, raspberries, cherries, goose berries, pears, and apples we knew nothing, unless we bought them preserved in bottles for pastry purposes," wrote George Clutterbuck from late-nineteenth-century Bombay. He emphasized the difficulty of procuring fresh European fruits because of their prohibitive cost: "Beautiful apples, and strawberries too, grow on the Neilgherries, in the Mysore, but the knowledge had to satiate our longings in Bombay, and indeed throughout the greater part of India."[26] Even those who took the trouble of maintaining a garden could have only grown those "English" vegetables in the cool season, and could hope to reap the benefits of a season's sowing only if they were at that station long enough.[27]

For those in the military and civil services, a peripatetic life—between stations, camps, and on the march—accentuated the need for bottled provisions. Both imported and locally bottled provisions thus extended seasons and produced their own nexus of spaces between the shop, house, road, and camp. When households moved, they could buy a "bottle connah tent" from saddlers and carriage makers.[28] Even a pinnace had a bottlekhana along with the usual ensemble of rooms such as "a hall, bedroom, verandah."[29] In the absence of a bottlekhana tent, a number of boxes of various sizes and descriptions sufficed to carry provisions and beverages. Here is a glimpse of the foodstuff considered necessary for a household on the march in 1865 by "A Lady Resident":

> A square tin box with canisters should be got ready to contain tea, coffee, sugar, and biscuits; other tins should be filled with pepper, salt, gingerbread nuts, sago, arrowroot, &c. Bags with table rice, fine flour and potatoes; jars or bottles with curry powder, jam, pickles, chutney and sauce . . . a few tins of preserved provisions, such as julienne and mock turtle soup, Hogarth's essence of beef, peas and carrots . . . A tin of bacon is a most useful thing; and at first start a piece of salt beef should be taken, some tongues and plenty of bread . . . Coffee for a journey can be boiled and bottled . . . Chocolate and cocoa pastes are useful . . . There are rattan baskets or boxes made with divisions for bottles. Porter is a good thing to take on a march, as a less quantity will suffice.[30]

The long list of goods replicated the contents of the entire bottlekhana. Others in the second half of the nineteenth century would find it sufficient to have tea, coffee, biscuits, bacon, and some preserved vegetables in the "store-box"—"a box fitted with square canisters"—on the march.[31] This was meant to supplement the provisions to be found in markets along the way and a precaution against failure to find fresh produce on the road that was under normal circumstances taken for granted: milk, butter, eggs, chicken, fresh meat, and fish.[32] Steel and Gardiner spoke of the difficulty of procuring a supply of bread, butter, and (English) vegetables unless these are regularly supplied from "headquarters."[33] Prior to the popularization of the railways, when the colonial army or the Governor-General's entourage marched, camp followers ensured a supply of fresh produce. If the march was taking place during a time of political turmoil, however, failure to secure fresh produce from neighboring villages was to be expected.[34] The latter was a sign of refusal on the part of the local populace and served as a political signal.[35] The food provisions taken on a march depended on the route and the proximity of towns with vendors selling European provisions.[36] Indeed these calculations were lodged in the logic of colonial administrative and military infrastructure, and in so doing they constructed a geography of European foodways.

Affirming Values

The list of convenient and necessary food for camp and march enumerated by "A Lady Resident" would certainly have been excessive for most, but speaks of the need to affirm certain Anglo-Indian foodways even on a march. Those such as Steel and Gardiner who advocated taking as little as possible on a march, "especially tinned provisions"—presumably because the reliance on canned food had increased in the late nineteenth century—included the caveat that one ought not to be "uncomfortable for want of things" to which they are "accustomed."[37] This refusal to relax the usual food habits in India, despite the altered circumstances of a march, was meant as a hallmark of one's English identity, and was premised upon the expedient labor of the cook, bearer, and other attendants. Servants were expected to rise before dawn to travel ahead so that a home-style meal could be ready at the next halt.[38]

Not surprisingly perhaps, how much imported provisions was purchased by a household was determined by its socioeconomic status. In giving an account of the kind of expense one ought to expect in running a household in India, Elizabeth Garrett, writing in the 1880s, refused to give a specific sum for "Oilman's store, wine, or beer," as these would vary according to each household's budget and habit. That at least some amount of oilman's stores was necessary for respectable dining was assumed.[39] In 1858, to explain their effort to lessen expenses because of a looming debt, Captain Archie Wood listed Rs. 100 for mess bill including beer, wine, oilman's stores, compared to Rs. 50 for table expenses, Rs. 100 for servants, and Rs. 80 for house rent.[40] A couple of decades later Eliot James considered the following monthly expenses necessary for a middling army officer's household: Rs. 84 for bazaar expenses, Rs. 80 for nine servants, Rs. 20 if a garden is maintained, Rs. 80 for house rent, and Rs. 100 for "incidental expenses and extras, as wine, brandy, soda-water, beer, &c."[41] That the budget for wine and European provisions (even when supplied from the regimental mess) exceeded that of any other single category of expense (except the cost of servants) for families of junior officers suggests the importance accorded to these commodities to maintain a certain lifestyle.

At least some housekeeping guides and recipe books from the late nineteenth century addressed to European women in India suggested minimizing the overreliance on imported canned provisions in the household.[42] Colonel Kenny Herbert's or Wyvern's *Culinary Jottings from Madras*, first published in 1878, is a broadside against the senseless use of canned provisions when fresh alternatives were available. However, he recommended a long list of "*must*" haves in the storeroom that included pickles, sauces, flavoring essences, "the invaluable truffle," tart fruits, olives, capers, dried herbs, Crosse and Blackwell's "grated Parmesan cheese," which he noted "should never be forgotten," and that "no store-room should be without tarragon vinegar, anchovy vinegar, French vinegar, and white wine vinegar."[43] In acknowledging the "necessity" of jams, jellies (particularly redcurrant jelly), dried and candied peels, currants, raisins, and ginger for the store, he made a distinction between these necessities of everyday cooking and those that added a certain continental elan to the table. "*Macedoines, fonds d'artichaut, petits pois, haricots verts* and *asperges* are, of course, excellent, and the dried *Julienne* will be found admirable for soups," he notes.[44]

Despite Wyvern's protests, the *value* accorded to bottled and canned provisions seemed to have increased in the latter half of the nineteenth century. With the easier availability of imported provisions and a more anglicized (and francophile) attitude toward foodways that was seen as a defense against the unavoidable contamination of Indian-ness, the favoring of imported bottled and canned provisions became a mode of projecting and protecting an English imperial identity.[45] Smoked "mangoe fish" and *hilsa*, packaged or not, went out of favor in Anglo-Indian households by the late nineteenth century, as did curries for any but family dinners.[46] Even if one ate Indian-styled meals on a daily basis, formal dinners demanded that everything be English, even if it meant serving canned soup, canned salmon, canned peas, canned ham, and bottled fruit.[47]

The acme of polite cookery, Wyvern, considered the change of eating habits in the late nineteenth century among respectable Anglo-Indian households in India a decided improvement from the days of "our forefathers, who chiefly preyed upon curry and rice, and lived to all intents and purposes *a la mode Indienne.*"[48] This changed attitude toward conspicuous consumption of imported provisions fulfilled a new and different role than it did in the early nineteenth century: imported provisions came to mark the lines of class and racial difference.[49] For Wyvern it meant serving meals along the lines of French haute cuisine, and for others such as Steel and Gardiner it meant affirming the superiority of English foodways.[50] Mildreth Pinkham writing in the third person spoke of the (American) memsahib's desire "now and then indulge in an imported supper of Heinz pork and beans, instead of the seven to eleven course khanas, dinners, which the Boy liked to have the cook serve." The ulterior motive behind the servants' insistence on a multicourse meal, she suggests, resided in their making "comfortable commissions on each course."[51]

The tension we read in Pinkham's story between the oeuvre of Indian servants and the desire of the memsahib was based on a certain discomfort about imported provisions in the hands of Indian servants. Wyvern was categorical about not allowing Indian cooks (in his writings his own cook represented all Indian cooks and were generically referred to as "Ramasámy") to have their own way with bottled condiments and canned food.[52] The discomfort bordering on anxiety was in some ways less about the monetary cost of expensive canned goods and beverages in the wrong hands, and more about the inability to control the precise value given to imported provisions. Control, or the lack of it, was fundamentally related to the spatial location of the bottlekhana and service spaces in the Anglo-Indian compound.

"Housekeeping of the Simplest Character"

From the late-eighteenth-century records of the Marquess of Wellesley's household expenses we know that the bottlekhana was used for storing both wet and dry good, and in bottles, tins, and earthenware pots. A bottlekhana, as in the Governor-General's house, would have a mat on the floor, shelves for storing provisions, and some facility for washing dishes and warming up food.[53]

There is one available depiction of the interior of such a storage space. One of the plates of George F. Atkinson's *Curry and Rice on Forty Plates* shows the "Judge's Wife" giving out her stores, attended by servants (Figure 6.3). She holds a bunch of keys in her hand suggesting that she maintains a locked storeroom/bottlekhana. Of the five servants, a punkah-burdar is fanning her, a servant is cleaning the silverware with a cloth sitting on the floor, a bearer is holding a covered glass of drink, while the khansamah and cook are helping with the selection and weighing of dry ingredients. The Judge's Wife is the only figure sitting on a chair—she orders, inspects, and interrogates—while being fanned for her comfort. Distinctions of rank and labor are clearly marked in having the servants either standing or sitting on the floor. Various sizes of bottles and jars are prominently displayed on shelves. A small round table holds two bottles and another rectangular table in the background has a round cheese or cake dome on it. The narrative sarcastically refers to the Judge's Wife in terms of "her abilities as a household financier and domestic manager." She is "exquisitely unique" as she personally supervises the operation of the kitchen with a "detective's skill." Her "not scorning to assist" in the "manipulation of puddings, pastry and the like" is understood to be both a sign of the economic discipline she

FIGURE 6.3 George F. Atkinson, "Mrs. Turmeric, Our Judge's Wife," 1859. Illustration in Atkinson, *Curry and Rice on Forty Plates* (London: Day & Son, 1859).

imposes on the household by reining in the servants, and the quality control she manages through personal supervision.[54] We are told she is not to be fooled by a bad piece of meat and that she sources her champagne directly from a reputable source in Europe.

If the burra-memsahib's bottlekhana in *Curry and Rice* is a picture of colonial order, its furnishings are entirely in line with contemporaneous sources. For example, Robert Dunlop's 1859 probate inventory noted the following items in the bottlekhana: a teak wood bottlekhana almirah with four shelves, a "defective" breakfast table, a cook room table, a teak wood camp table, a teak wood lamp, and an iron stove.[55] The modest furnishing in this bottlekhana belied the extensive range of tableware, liquor, and furnishing owned by Dunlop who shared the house with another gentleman. The probate suggests that a good deal of the cooking and table equipment were shared among the two, but it is unlikely that their bottlekhana was given the kind of importance bestowed on it by the English women from the mid-nineteenth century onwards.

The bottlekhana as a space and as practice was sufficiently novel for Anglo-Indian housekeeping guides to spend considerable space explaining its arrangement. Garrett, who was Lady Wilson's contemporary, remarked that the "godown" should be "fitted with strong shelves, and situated on the coolest side of the house," as here was to be kept "oilman's stores," "your homemade jams, and also some earthenware jars, called 'mutkhas', full of rice, flour, sugar, dhall, &c. Tea and coffee should be kept in closed canisters." She did not forget to mention the special arrangements during summer when all sweet stuff would need to be kept on tables whose legs "must stand in saucers filled with kerosene oil and water" to prevent the invasion of ants.[56]

Almost four decades later, Theodora Coatman still found the "stores 'godown' a regular general store in miniature: All conceivable kinds of foodstuffs and condiments were there, except of course those which had necessarily to be bought fresh daily."[57] Recalling the bottlekhana of their house in Narayangunj in the 1920s, Jon and Rumer Godden described it "as a scullery-serving room attached to the dining room."[58] They explained that "washing-up is done there, food kept in the dhoolie—a wire-meshed safe—and hot case warmed by a charcoal brazier for dishes carried from the kitchen, and a meeting place for servants."[59] This description of the bottlekhana as pantry as well as a meeting space for servants, suggesting its unlocked character, would not have served the purpose of memsahibs such as Minnie Wood and Flora Annie Steel who had come to see the bottlekhana as their "own" storeroom (see Figure 4.2).

Referring to this storage space as "godown" and using it interchangeably with "store," the author of *The Englishwoman in India* insisted in line with every other housekeeping guide of the time on the absolute necessity of locking up this storage space. "Domestic arrangements in India are of the simplest character," she assured her readers. To ensure the mistress's "comfort" the simple solution was "to have either a locked-up go-down, with a little padlock on it, for stores, or else substantial boxes with locks to contain the articles required for daily use." The latter included sugar, tea, and coffee, lest they disappear mysteriously. The keeping of ground spices in stoppered bottles was also a prevention from the servants pilfering the items. Locking up these provisions was not sufficient, however. "All supplies kept in the house should be registered in a book, as well as everything in the way of liquor; poultry, kitchen utensils, &c, require to be counted frequently, or they are supposed to take to themselves wings in an unpleasantly literal sense," she noted.[60] Fancy plates, kept polished with great care by the servants, would be under lock and key in a "plate chest."[61] The general recommendation from the ordinary officer to the Viceroy was not to bring plates (meaning silver plates) out to India. The rare occasion when they were brought out, they adorned sideboards in dining rooms. This meant the bottlekhana/godown/storeroom in which imported and local food provisions were kept became the only room in the colonial household that was placed under lock and key. The ubiquity of servants in the household and the weather made it impossible to lock living spaces, even if that would have meant more privacy for the master and mistress.

Turab Ali's Artifice

Housekeeping guides devoted considerable space to the proper management of servants, and advised women to take a hold of housekeeping by wresting control from the Indian servants. According to Steel and Gardiner, the first task was to set up an orderly grid of spaces and rationalize household management.[62] As the daily disbursement of supplies occurred here and accounts of expenditure were taken here, the bottlekhana became the staging place for exerting authority. The authors of housekeeping guides believed that the household would be better controlled if the bottlekhana was brought within the main house.

Steel and Gardiner's focus on the bottlekhana as a space of control, and their view that "there is no greater saving of time in housekeeping than a good store room" is somewhat paradoxical. They consider canned provisions "at best the means of evading starvation," and suggest nothing but olives, salad oil, vinegar, and mustard be bought, "if economy is an object."[63] By the time the updated editions of Steel and Gardiner's housekeeping guides were being released in the first decades of the twentieth century, the number of shops supplying European provisions had increased sufficiently to change the geography of foodways. It was no longer necessary in ordinary households in *sadar* towns to keep large stocks of European provisions, wine, and oilman's stores.

What then of value was there in the storcroom of the middling ranks of Anglo-Indian households that these women were to control? Looking at the forms Steel and Gardiner suggested English housewives use for keeping track of domestic accounts—the same forms that were used for keeping accounts by civil administrators—it becomes apparent that it is less the content than the process that was at stake (Figure 6.4). It is in the "*giving out*" of the store punctually, of keeping meticulous accounts of amounts of daily groceries, meat, fish, and beverage that they saw the opportunity to exercise a semblance of control.

Control over the gridded space of the forms simulated a control over material relations that remained elusive. The khansamah, as in Kipling's ditty cited in Chapter 4, would still be found "snoring" on the bottlekhana floor, and, as the Godden sisters remembered, the bottlekhana—a pantry and scullery combined—was the meeting space of servants who entertained the gleeful small children in that space.

The housekeeping guides I have mentioned are not alone in this obsession about the storeroom and the disbursement of stores. In 1857, Minnie Wood wrote to her mother: "I have a very nice storeroom which I have christened the other day by putting three pots of preserve in it, and that is all I can think of, as you cannot as in England go out to shops."[64] Struggling in her role as mistress of the house, the three jars of fruit preserve stood as proof of not just her housewifeliness but also Englishness. Further accomplishments she hoped would "all come in good time."[65]

FORM A.

Date	Daily Memoranda, April 1893.	Dusters. Sent to the wash.	Dusters. Khit.	Dusters. Bearer.	Dusters. Ayah.	Dusters. Saices.	Occurrences among Live Stock.	Grain used. Gram.	Ardawa.	Bajra.	Dalia.	Fowls mixture.	Linseed.	Date.	Eggs.	Loaves.	Milk.	Beer.	Claret.	Soda-water.	Lemonade.	Soup.	Cash Payments. Meat.	Cash Payments. Sundries.	R.	A.	P.
4	Sunday	..	..	..	..	..	..	8	2	2	1	2	..	4	6	2	2	2	1	2	1	2	Beef 2/, fish 8 as.	Apples 2½ as., potatoes 8 as.	3	2	6
5	Dizzie absent	4 glass 6 tea 10 old 10 new	15	8	5	4	Bought 4 ducks	7	2	2	1	2	1	5	6	3	3	1	1	2	1	..	Mutton 1/4	Suji 2½ as., tomatoes 2 as.	1	8	6
6	Carpenter half-day	..	..	..	..	..	Killed 2 chickens	7	2	2	1	2	1	6	5	2	2	2	1	4	1	2	Fish 6 as.	Tinning 1/4, peas 2 as.	1	12	..
7	Gave out tin of oil	..	..	..	..	..	Killed 2 ducks	7	2	2	1	2	1	7	4	2 & 12 rolls	2	1	1	1	1	4	Brains 2 as.	Maida 2 as., rice 3 as.	..	11	..
8	Engaged Kutbdin 10/	..	15	..	..	..	Bought 1 sheep	9	2	2	1	2	1	8	8	3	3	1	1	2	1	..	Beef 1/8, fish 8 as.	Oranges 12 as., Dall 1 a.	2	13	6
9	Gave out saddle soap	..	..	..	..	..	Bought 40 quail	9	2	3	1	2	..	9	3	3	2	1	..	3	1	..	..	Sago 4 as., spices 2½ as.	..	7	6
10	Horses shod	..	..	..	..	..	Killed 6 quail	9	2	3	1	2	..	10	2	2	2	1	..	1	3	..	Kidneys 4 as.	Lemons 5 as.	..	9	..

The Roorkee account book, costing Rs. 2, which can be had at the Thomason College, Roorkee, is recommended as a substitute for these forms.

FIGURE 6.4 One of the forms recommended for housekeeping by F. A. Steel and G. Gardiner in *The Complete Indian Housekeeper and Cook*, 7th ed. (London: William Heinemann, 1909).

Thus, an affective ecology of housekeeping was formed around the bottlekhana/store, one that was shared and sustained because it ultimately revolved around domestic labor, and the ability of Anglo-Indian women *not* to undertake domestic labor "that an ordinary servant could do."[66] An intellectually inclined and adventurous Theodora Coatman took it for granted that the "technicalities of house keeping had to be learnt" from more experienced women at the station. The technicalities involved giving orders and the management of servants. Recounting their arrival in Peshawar in 1917, her husband wrote that Theo received firsthand instructions about domestic duties from senior memsahibs at the station and described giving out stores as a "highly skilled process."[67] It is difficult not to detect a hint of irony in the declarations of arduous housekeeping by the couple and Theo having to inculcate Anglo-Indian prejudices. The *idea* of the bottlekhana teeming with precious imported provisions seem to have lingered longer in the rituals of the memsahib's domestic practice than the space itself.

Interestingly, the fetishization of the bottlekhana and its contents and denizens was often turned around and made a characteristic of Indian servants' fascination and faith in the power of canned provisions and things foreign. Wyvern made a point to remark about the stature of canned provisions in the Indian servants' eyes:

> a butler's ideas about stores are, on the whole, very mixed: he worships "Europe articles" and delights in filling the shelves of the store-room with rows of tins; of which some may perhaps be useful, but many need never be bought at all at Madras, and so remain for months untouched, lumbering the shelves of the cupboard.[68]

When he actually uses the canned article, Ramasámy assumes that "a tin will cover a multitude of sins," Wyvern quipped, and therefore takes little care in preparing that dish.[69] Canned provisions, according to Wyvern, make the Indian cook lazy, and as it is sufficiently foreign to him, he has never mastered its "correct" use.

The impropriety of use, coupled with fetishization, is evident in a remarkable description by Pinkham of the head servant Turab Ali's "godown." The bearer Turab Ali, although a grandfather, is referred to as the "Boy" (Figure 6.5). His living space in the periphery of the residential compound, Pinkham noted, was the most "spacious" of the servants' accommodations: "a perfectly bare, ten-foot square, brick apartment with a straw roof and two wobbling bamboo poles which just managed to support a matting. This arrangement served as a front porch to his domicile." In the corner of this "godown" she was surprised to find "a bewildering array of empty bottles and tin cans which seemed to have been collected from time immemorial."

Turab Ali surely could have kept these to sell later, but he also repurposed them ingeniously. He turned a Heinz tomato and vermicelli can into a jewel

THE BOY WINDS HIS TURBAN

FIGURE 6.5 Turab Ali: "The Boy Winds his Turban." Illustration in Mildreth W. Pinkham, *A Bungalow in India* (New York: Fleming H. Revell Company, 1928).

box for the cook's wife.[70] There was both incredulity and cautious praise in Pinkham's evaluation of Turab Ali's ability to turn cast-off objects into singular affective interventions.

Of course, the reuse of bottles was commonly practiced: Wyvern recommended making a large amount of curry powder and keeping the mix stoppered in "bottles in which tart fruit is imported."[71] Steel and Gardiner pointed out that salad oil should be bought in a large tin and immediately after opening decanted into stoppered bottles.[72] Kerosene tins, because of their large size, were variously repurposed, for carrying water, shaped into sinks and makeshift stoves.[73] But evidently Turab Ali was thwarting expectations by repurposing the cans in a manner that was not about mere utility. He was bestowing meaning on the empty cans by inserting them into a different circuit of value, extraneous to that of Anglo-Indian domesticity and the labor of domestic servants.

Turab Ali and the spaces he inhabited help us reflect on how and why small spaces generate significance in excess of what their monetary worth would suggest. In going through the archival traces of the small spaces that constituted the service wing of Anglo-Indian households three things become increasingly clear: the Anglo-Indian nomenclature betrayed uncertainty; an affective ecology linked long-distance trade with the microdynamics of power in the service wings of the house; and there was concern that the value attributed to Anglo-Indian material possessions in order to shore up a sense of European authenticity was somehow precarious. In Anglo-Indian usage, the term "bottlekhana" slid into a host of adjacent service spaces such as the abdarkhana, godown, and cook room. Referring to the servants' quarter as "godown" insinuates that household stores and servants somehow carry the same valence—they are fixtures of the household. That in the hands of the servants the imported goods (and the containers in which they were transported) and their foreign nomenclature would slide into other uses and significations creating foodways and household objects and affects was seemingly incomprehensible to their Anglo-Indian masters and mistresses. In this they were obeying wider understandings of consumption and cultural change.

Uneven Exchange

Colonial authorities in the late eighteenth and early nineteenth century, looking for deeper penetration of the Indian market for everyday objects of consumption, often despaired about the limited prospect of European imports to India.[74] And this was not only because of the lack of buying power among the majority of the people; it had to do with the "taste" for European goods. A knowledge of the English language, some felt, would inculcate the desire for European material culture. Like present-day trade historians tracking the politics of profit, in some ways they failed to recognize the long-term impact of the full range of everyday European commodities on Indian culture. Even if the short-term prognosis for the import trade in consumables making an impact on mass culture was bleak, certain practices spread beyond the small coterie of Indian princes, merchants, and professionals to larger numbers. By the early twentieth century the Indian urban market had become sufficiently large to create a demand for products such as packaged tea, tinned baby food (Mellins), biscuits (Huntley & Palmer), butter (Brown and Polson's), cigarettes and cocoa (Cadbury). The expansion of the market between the 1920s and 1930s exceeded the import capacity and began to attract multinational companies: Brooke Bond, Britannia, Cadbury.[75]

If tinned butter and baby food, biscuits, tea, and cigarettes altered (Anglo-)Indian foodways, the rearing of children, and sociality, there were other unanticipated effects of buying canned and bottled goods among the middle classes that spread to small towns and rural areas. We get a hint of this in humorist and playwright Amritalal Basu's Bengali short story, *Patit Daktar*. Basu anchored his story in the nineteenth century, when a strange and unequal exchange was set up through colonial relations, by reference to the import-export trade: "At that time the sahibs had opened their business for our benefit—they bought paddy, cotton, and indigo, and Bengalis bought bottles, glasses, glass jars and phials."[76] Basu's sarcasm is directed at the unevenness of transaction in a colonial regime. It was, however, not just about the scale of imports and exports—bulk goods vs. small-scale commodities—but the material culture changes resulting from an altered pattern of consumption that would impact a range of everyday practices: drinking Western-style alcohol, storing food, and buying, storing, and consuming medicine.

Sarcasm aside, Basu's observation was perspicacious. A range of domestic tasks such as the practice of pickling vegetables and fruits in bottles, storing cooking oil in bottles rather than in metal or earthen containers, using cigarette tins as rice measure, slowly but surely changed the practice of storing goods in ordinary Indian kitchens, turning these storerooms into bottlekhanas of a different sort.[77] It is, however, important to point out that the term "bottlekhana" did not rub off on the upper- and middle-class Indian women, although kitchen stores functioned as equally promising spaces for crafting domestic agency.

7

Strange Tongues

Joan paid her cook a monthly salary of thirty rupees—silver coin worth about thirty-three cents at the normal rate of exchange . . . [T]his wage was justified, for he assured his Memsahib that . . . He must serve jellies in quaint forms, and must write CHEKAN POI in baked brown letters on the murghi *pudding.*[1]

The reduction of wages was virtually the great experimental measure as to whether a man could work on one pound of rice per diem, with a small quantity of condiments.[2]

The cook room in the colonial house in British India, located at a distance from the main residence, was a stock figure of shock, ridicule, alarm. A long list of shortcomings was foregrounded in such representations. The rude construction of the cook house, and the scant and primitive kitchen equipment, matched the habits of the cook and his staff, and the trials of communication across languages and tastes.

In his 1859 publication, *Curry and Rice on Forty Plates*, George F. Atkinson invites the reader into this space:

> If your eyes are not instantly blinded with the smoke, and if your sight can penetrate into the darkness, enter that hovel, and witness the preparation of your dinner. The table and the dresser, you observe, are Mother Earth; for niggers—Orientals, I mean—have that peculiar faculty which characterizes the ape and the kangaroo: they can only stand erect on an occasion. Let a nigger alone, and down he drops upon his hams spontaneously, with as much joy as the wretched monkey in our streets when his polka is accomplished.
>
> The preparation for your dinner must therefore be performed in the earth's broad lap, like everything else in this Eastern land.[3]

The pictorial sketch accompanying his narrative shows a "kitchen range" of "mud construction, with apertures for the reception of charcoal," and a paltry set of kitchen utensils (Figure 7.1). Apart from a mortar and pestle and a grindstone on the floor, there is "a spit, two native saucepans, a ladle, and a knife." Here the reader is expected to notice the absence of kitchen architecture. According to Atkinson, the recognizable architectural paucity is not necessarily a problem because the laboring people in eastern lands are used to working and living in minimal shelter. His characterization of the native *chef de cuisine* as ape-like is followed by the counter-assertion that the food delivered to the table could not be bettered by an English cook who is so abundantly provided with equipment. From this follows the inference that sophisticated equipment is not only unnecessary but a positive inconvenience for Indian cooks as they could never fathom or master the intricacies of modern culinary technology.

The crudeness of the cook room appliances was explained away by reference to age-old custom and Indian unfamiliarity with modern technology. Seven decades after Atkinson's publication, Mildreth Pinkham remarked by way of explanation: "For centuries his people had worked over their crude stoves, and if [the mistress] ventured suggestions, their descendant would flounder about in an utterly helpless state."[4] Crudeness suits the Indian kitchen.

Pinkham's narrative of her life in early-twentieth-century colonial India is told through the character of Joan, an American woman who arrives in

FIGURE 7.1 George F. Atkinson, "Our Cook Room," 1859. Illustration in Atkinson, *Curry and Rice on Forty Plates* (London: Day & Son, 1859).

India and steps into a house already outfitted with servants—the previous occupier's retinue. Joan's tour of the bungalow's compound is framed as an official undertaking, as if she is a military or civil administrator on tour, and the kitchen is an administrative "department." She is salaamed into the cook house by the "Boy," Turab Ali:

> She did not find a white enamelled kitchenette! In the little brick building were no fireless cookers, nor modern gas nor electric ranges, but only a crude brick stove built into the wall. Currents of heated air struggled to get out through the door and the loosely tiled roof. The cook-house was shrouded in a blue haze. It nearly suffocated Joan, and she stayed only long enough to see the cook drop lighted coals one by one upon a baking-dish. Joan wondered if she was going to enjoy the food served from her culinary department. That evening a dinner fit for a king was spread before her.[5]

The details and tenor of Pinkham's narrative—the servants as accoutrement of a household, the slovenly kitchen, the rude working habits of Indian cooks, and the limits of training them into reformed ways—were the mainstay of discussion about kitchens in colonial households since the early nineteenth century. The discrepancies between the space of food production and the food that is served, the Indian servants' natural suitedness to such cook rooms in inverse proportion to the white mistress's natural inability to tolerate such environmental conditions, produced heaps of advice that attempted to not so much eliminate such discrepancies as to enlist the differences in expressing the right to command resources and labor. This was the *raison d'être* of culinary racism that shaped civilizational tales of behavioral, moral, and technological improvements necessary to lift the native from his primitive condition into the modern world under European tutelage.

Command

Achille Mbembe argues that *commandement*, the right to command—"issue orders and have them carried out"—is the defining characteristic of colonial rule. Exercising command includes a wide range of claims and prerogatives that attend and exceed resource extraction. "Simultaneously a tone, an accoutrement, and an attitude," through command the distinction between ruling and civilizing is eliminated: power is reduced "to the right to demand, to force, to ban, to compel, to authorize, to punish, to reward, to be obeyed—in short, to enjoin and to direct."[6] Here colonial authority sees no discrepancy between the brutal extraction of labor and "putting an end to scarcity and poverty" by forcing the colonized to undergo a period of tutelage. "The figure of obedience and domination in the colony rests," he notes, "on the assertion that the state is under no social obligation to the colonized and this latter is owed nothing by the state but that which the state, in its infinite goodness, has deigned to grant and reserves the right to revoke at any moment."[7] The violence of *commandement* is made palpable in its "miniaturization." Command replicates itself in smaller scales, showing up in the minutiae of everyday life, "in the form of micro-actions which, becoming smaller, were the source of a host of fears."[8] In the process it coalesces public life with private life.

Thus, in raising the everyday domestic task of visiting a kitchen to a performance of military commandment, Pinkham is not simply using well-worn tropes; she is also signaling through the expected tropes a vision of everyday *commandement* that had become by that time crystallized as ordinary, pleasurable, repeatable. A century-worth of repetition had not worn off its aura. Such language of *commandement*—*because* it is so flippantly and hyperbolically applied—slips back and forth between the formal structures of governance, language, and technology and the utterly small and informal service space of the kitchen. It is in the small interactions surrounding food preparation and consumption that the microdynamics of power is constructed. The servants are made to feel ignorant, child-like, and dependent on the largesse of the master, despite their attempt to cater to the master's tastes and whims and to familiarize themselves with new ingredients and methods. This dynamic of command has larger remit.

When Pinkham narrates the cook's claim to superior expertise deserving a high wage by bringing the reader's attention to the cook's amusing inability to correctly enunciate in the master's tongue, she is effectively noting the simultaneous necessity and impossibility of crossing language and taste worlds. That the cook's desire to show off his language and cooking skills in baking the words Chekan Poi on the "*murghi* [chicken] pudding" falls short of the mark is mitigated by two realizations: that Pinkham's cook is actually cheap labor (so the joke's doubly on the cook), but the pie, regardless of its misspelled appearance (speaking of poor taste), is good to the taste buds. The sensations of the tongue and social distinctions of language do not always correspond. They surprise in ways stranger than *murghi* pie. Between the half-baked English and the well-baked pie, the statement of culinary performance moves between a declaration of the limited utility of Western gadgets in Indian hands and the unlimited potential of cheap labor. The first retains the provision of necessary tutelage, and the second signals the prodigious advantage of a well-laid table in a colonial house.

By locating the colonial kitchen in the collapse of languages of public and private lives I wish to chart a historical understanding of food spaces as critical to the relation between empire and modern metrics of improvement and labor efficiency. One trajectory of this history leads to a demand for reform in several interrelated aspects of food production within the Anglo-Indian household. It involves a recalibration of the degree to which laboring spaces could be separated from the polite spaces of food consumption; the introduction of new English and American gadgets in the kitchen; demanding increasingly Europeanized food to be prepared by Indian servants; and the language of communication in culinary matters. If the ability to command a dinner "fit for a king" is in some fundamental sense the essence of colonial rule, from the 1870s onward this command assumed a particular tenor, mediated by new technologies and ideas about food consumption that powerfully reshaped a broader middle-class attitude toward kitchen as workspace. If the first trajectory is concerned with luxury, comfort, and efficiency, the other trajectory of this history connects efficiency to the withholding of food and leads to the context in which such kitchen reforms and culinary demands were articulated. Of the major events that defined the 1870s in British colonial India were two famines that stretched across much of the subcontinent: the 1873–4 famine in Bihar and the Madras Famine of 1876–8 that went far beyond the Madras and Bombay Presidencies costing the lives of some 8 million people. The command over food became the colonizer's right to determine how much food should the famine worker consume. The debate over dietary needs predated the Madras Famine and fed into the dietary norms that were developed in the 1880s.[9] The Madras Famine, however, was a watershed in quantifying food and how nutritional needs were to be evaluated beyond prisons and military cantonments—the two erstwhile sites of dietary control—and be made applicable to the population at large.

In what follows I bring together these two trajectories to explore how the command of food became a defining feature of colonialism, and how commentaries on the kitchen as work space, as part of an extended "food axis," provide clues to the connection between these trajectories. The calculations that were made to rationalize food consumption through various metrics, and the British colonial determination of wages of famine workers, are important elements of this argument. The extension of the food axis from the colonial house to the military camp ground and to famine kitchens and camps suggests connections that we normally do not recognize in the discussion of foodways of empire. The connective piece is labor—the colonialist view of labor and the laborers' resistance, showing up as demand for better wages, refusal to obey orders, petty thefts, and small acts of recalcitrance.

Food Axis

In discussing the spaces of food preparation, storage, and consumption in the United States, from the first European settlement period to the present, Elizabeth Cromley makes a compelling argument that the food axis defines American residential architecture.[10] The food axis may include spaces of food production and preparation, storage, as well as food serving and consumption.[11] The preference for the term "food axis" over the usual terms such as "kitchen" or "dining room" serves two purposes. It attends to the changing relation between room nomenclature and function: long before the kitchen became the place for cooking, the hall of the Anglo-American house in the seventeenth and eighteenth centuries served as the place of cooking as well as partaking of meals. The food axis changes its character over time and across regions.[12] The "focus on a food axis of activities allows for comparisons across class and region."[13] It helps us see the sociospatial relations between production and consumption of food, inflected by labor dynamics—who actually undertakes the labor and under what conditions—to offer an understanding of residential architecture in which kitchen and storage spaces are not subsidiary but the driving factors of spatial organization.

Attentive to the invisibility of services spaces that are sites of hard physical labor in comparison to the visible and genteel spaces of food consumption in the Victorian era, Cromley discusses the changes in social stratification that attended the changing perception of dirt and distance in organizing food spaces.[14] Her inquiry, however, is confined to the residential premises and what may be called the internal dynamics of food spaces within the house. The house is the spatial unit of analysis.

Cromley's argument may be extended and also applied to other regions of the world, particularly because the primarily Anglo-American world she describes was well-connected to a global regime of food production, consumption, and regulation. Once we expand the food axis to spaces of production and consumption beyond the residential unit, other small spaces and processes emerge into view. Consider the aestheticization of the middle-class kitchen from the mid-nineteenth century onwards. It is generally discussed in terms of the availability and adoption of new technologies, particularly related to new modes of cooking over coal, gas, and electrically powered cooking ranges and improved techniques of refrigeration. The use of coal as fuel indeed required more cleaning than wood-powered ranges and the increasing use of white enameled interiors was meant to allay middle-class anxiety over cleanliness, hygiene, and health.[15] These changes took place alongside large-scale transformation of foodways, enabled by global colonial trade and faster modes of transportation; they were coeval with global colonialism and empire building. Here the modernizing logic of imperialism and nationalism found common cause, if not always a common method.[16] In books on housekeeping and cookery, whether in the United States, England, or British colonial India, we find the emergence of various idioms of domesticity in which technology and its relation to the laboring body are imagined differentially to seek a redefinition of the space of food preparation and consumption.

As the kitchen became a repository of improved gadgets, its aestheticization exceeded its role in staging female identity and good housekeeping. It became tied to ideas about the body, nutritional necessities of peoples in various occupations and ultimately about the body politic. The modern white-enameled American or English kitchen was a "white" kitchen in more ways than just the color of its wall finish. It was premised on dominant white norms of nutrition and hygiene created by scientists, social reformers, and designers in the late nineteenth century who subscribed to a paradigm of white superiority at a time when these norms were being challenged by emancipated African Americans, new immigrants, and anticolonial nationalists harboring other notions of cooking and homecare. Designated as "traditional," "dirty," "primitive," "unhealthy," the culinary practices of non-whites and their food consumption were targeted for control, reform, and regulation. They consisted of a panoply of historically specific practices such as subjecting populations to the principles of home economics, segregating public spaces of eating in North America, and strictly controlling the inclusion of Indian food at the European table.[17] The modern technology of the white kitchen was a hallmark of racial superiority and success.

Culinary Racism

Culinary racism justified the colonizer's command over food and foodways for not just the comfort of the colonizer but for the benefit of the colonized who it was argued could be trained to labor in an efficient manner and thus optimally utilize food resources. Malthusian visions of food scarcity and population growth underwrote many of these arguments about rationalization of food. Culinary racism in the colonies worked in different registers, linking various scales of production and consumption. It was expressed in the aestheticization of European foodways over that of native foods and methods of cooking, in the valorization of the European body and comfort in inverse relation to those of the natives, prioritization of the spaces of food consumption by the colonials over the food production spaces where the colonized labored, and above all, access to native labor while separating the spaces of consumption for Blacks and whites. Racial segregation at no point meant complete removal of Black bodies from white spaces or vice versa. It was about privileging white consumption and access to the labor of the enslaved and colonized. All of these would be construed in aesthetic terms.

It is the method of aestheticization that distinguished clean from dirty, modern Western appliances from primitive hearths, efficient utilization of resources from waste and theft, and refined cuisine from barbaric food. The manner in which the kitchen in the colonial home in India brought together a way to think about language, taste, and labor concretized this aestheticization. Certain foods were expected to be prepared in a particular manner that necessitated certain gadgets and spaces, and the technology was mediated by an economy of language that attributed new values to labor and the laboring spaces. Thus the aestheticization of foodways in the age of high imperialism effectively became a demonstration of the ability to command food. As late as 1958, Iris Macfarlane writing about the opulent life of a managing director in a tea garden in Assam, wrote appreciatively of the well-trained servants: "one simply has to say 'Three for lunch' and leave it at that."[18]

By the late nineteenth century, a dozen housekeeping guides attempted to prepare European would-be residents in India on what to expect when the kitchen was not a kitchen, but a cook room. Like Joan, in Pinkham's narrative, Lady Anne Wilson was shocked with the state of the kitchen in the bungalow compound upon arrival at Shahpur in 1889. "A little dark room, with a board on the mud floor to hold the meat," and "two tumble-down brick ranges in one corner, a stone receptacle in another into which the water is thrown, to run out through its hole in the wall into a sunk tub." There were no plate-racks, scullery, or larder.[19]

The substitution of the quadripartite kitchen, scullery, larder, and pantry with the dual cook room and bottlekhana implicated a whole set of social relations formed around material culture. Unlike the bottlekhana, the cook room was to be located as far from the main house as possible.[20] This separation turned the space of food production into the cook's domain rather than the mistress's, even in modest colonial households. This meant carrying food across the compound in fair and bad weather and relying on the space of the bottlekhana located close to the dining space in the main house to mediate the passage of the food between the cook room and the dining room. That this distance made it difficult for the servants was well recognized, but it was often seen as merely comical, one of those many peculiarities of India and the regime of servants who had to scramble to serve a meal (Figure 7.2). The separation of the cook room from the bottlekhana/storeroom in the second half of the nineteenth century grafted a certain form of invisibility to the cook room. In his representation of the cook room Atkinson is effectively depicting what was better not to *see*, lest it take away from the pleasure of partaking in a multicourse meal "fit for a king" (see Figure 7.1). Lady Wilson's contemporary, Elizabeth Garrett, considered the cook room so "painfully unlike a kitchen at home that a visit to it affords little pleasure to the English matron," and consequently considered a "weekly inspection, to see that it is kept clean and that the chulas (ovens) are in good order," sufficient.[21]

The particularities of the Indian cook room were articulated in reference to the visual and olfactory pleasures of the English kitchen. Atkinson's description of the cook room, for example, is prefaced with an invocation of the fragrant smells emanating from the spotless purity of the English kitchen with its "glittering array of saucepans, the rows of cleanest crockery marshalled on their shelves, the cups and jugs hung pendent from the ledge." The "Oriental kitchen," in contrast, was bereft of purity, precision, and uniformity. The smell of food was too strong, the means of preparation too crude, and modes of food presentation unrefined.

FIGURE 7.2 Madeline Hancock, "Serving dinner under difficulties," 1865–6. British Library shelfmark IOR WD3871, © British Library Board.

Colonel Arthur Kenny-Herbert or "Wyvern," the cookbook author who wrote most vehemently about the need to reform the native cook room, introduced his ideas of new cooking by noting:

> Our dinners of to-day would indeed astonish our Anglo-Indian forefathers. With a taste for light wines, and a far more moderate indulgence in stimulating drinks, has been germinated a desire for delicate and artistic cookery. Quality has superseded quantity, and the molten curries and florid oriental compositions of the olden time—so fearfully and wonderfully made—have been gradually banished from our dinner tables.[22]

Wyvern's menus appeal to the reformed taste of his contemporaries who might be interested in hosting "cosy, little sociable dinners for two to ten people," and with economy in mind.[23] His little home dinners run from seven to nine courses; a dinner for six requires nine to ten courses; and dinners for eight people range from ten to eleven courses. The menus are given in French, with the English names of the dishes provided in "the margins of the details of instruction."[24] Adoption of French cookery as an improvement on English techniques is meant to further distinguish elite European cuisine from the fare that Indian cooks were adept at creating. The refinement demanded of French haute cuisine is recruited to demand more skilled labor from the cooking staff.

Among his instructions are the treatment of the cook and modes of controlling his native inclinations, if the taste and flavor of his prescribed dishes were to be honored. In his view the native cook "possesses admirable materials out of which to form a good cook" because the "work comes to him, as it were, of its own accord."²⁵ However, he was not to be allowed to "grow up at random, clinging affectionately to the ancient barbarisms of his forefathers." Among the Indian cook's "besetting sins" was the use of native herbs, fondness for bottled condiments such as Worcestershire Sauce, and an urge to use spices. Bottled condiments were to be strictly controlled as the Indian cook is wont to overflavor everything, and "spice, if necessary, should be doled out in atoms, the cook ought never to have it under his control."²⁶

Wyvern noted that in engaging the native cook the European master or mistress has to meet the cook halfway in the language of communication. He did not recommend as did some authors of housekeeping guides that a knowledge of the local language is essential to place orders. Indeed, there was no need to learn Indian languages. The cook could be addressed in his pidgin English. He suggested getting proficient in the "patois": "you will soon find yourself interpreting the cherished mysteries of Francatelli or Gouffe in the pigeon English of Madras with marvellous fluency. You will even talk of 'putting that troople,' 'mashing bones all,' 'minching,' 'chimmering,' &c., &c., without a blush."²⁷ This fall from linguistic grace has to be tolerated to elicit the native cook's cooperation. It is important, Wyvern noted, to convey orders directly to the cook, rather than through the butler. The butler in his conceit might feign to understand the nuances of the foreign tongue and practice to the detriment of the meal prepared by the cook: "they pretend to understand rather than confess their ignorance."²⁸ Ignorance of language and process is squarely placed on the servants.

Dirt

Wyvern based his recommendations on the intimate links between culinary reform, the mode and language of instruction directly given to the cook, the appliances that are a requisite for a kitchen in which delicate cookery is to be prepared, and the location of the cook room. Being "part and parcel of a block of godowns," often close to the stables and servants' quarters, kitchens are places for "promiscuous gatherings of outsiders,—the friends, relations, and children (a fruitful source of dirtiness)."²⁹ The argument for plucking the cook room from the domain of the service quarters and placing it closer to the main house is premised upon two essential aspects of reform: improved technology and supervision.

By placing the preparation of food completely in the hands of the khansamah (house steward) and *bawarchi* (cook) "sometimes through sheer ignorance, sometimes on account of idleness, and sometimes because they are not physically equal to the exertion," Wyvern charged his countrymen and women for abetting uncleanliness. Emphasizing the "intense importance of cleanliness in the kitchen, and in all utensils connected therewith," he recommended that if going to the cook room for inspection was impossible (which means disagreeable), the weekly summoning of all cooking utensils to be spread on a mat on the verandah be instituted.[30] And to ensure that soups and sauces do not taste of dirty cloth, washing soda be regularly dispensed.

The better solution to the problem, he argued, is a well-constructed kitchen closer to the main house. The hovel-like kitchen located among the godowns might have sufficed in olden times, when curry was the main fare at the table, but the situation in the late nineteenth century behoves reform: "The delicate cookery which day by day gains popularity in India now demands a clean airy room, properly furnished, with plenty of light, and many accessories borrowed from civilized Europe."[31] Cast as a civilizational reform of gustatory habits, his suggestions are a direct commentary on the habits of Indian servants and how they work.

The colonial conception of dirt as intrinsic to native existence is the cornerstone of environmental racism. Bringing together environmental determinism and racism it justifies differential access to Blacks and whites to spaces and resources. Dirt here is not an "empirical substance," not even "matter out of place," as Mary Douglas explains.[32] Rather, as Stephanie Newell in a study of colonial/postcolonial Nigeria notes, dirt, associated with African bodies, spaces, and food habits, represents systems that are not assimilable within the European colonial economy. As "an interpretive category that facilitates moral, sanitary, economic, and aesthetic evaluations of other cultures under the rubric of cleanliness," dirt links scientific discourse about filth/health to the biopolitics of empire.[33]

Wyvern's recommendation is a purpose-built small building as a standalone kitchen attached to the back verandah of the main house through a covered passage. The building facing either north or south is to consist of three rooms—the work room, the cooking room, and the scullery all opening onto a "good verandah." The work room would be the place for food preparation and pastry making. Well-ventilated, it would have "a good glass window or a sky light," with no direct communication with the cooking room to prevent the passage of smoke. The work room floor was to be surfaced with matting over chunam and should contain the following: "a large dresser, a marble pastry slab, a rack for plates and dishes, shelves for cups, jugs, bowls, &c., a cupboard for culinary stores, and a gauze meat safe to protect meat, &c., from flies." He recommended the cooking room to be well-ventilated, well-lit, fitted with a chimney, and be furnished with an English or American range, and failing that "a country-made range upon English principles." The scullery was to have a water-tight sink and a well-made cistern "covered by a trap door, outside the building." The cistern would be emptied every day and sprinkled with disinfesting powder. He added that a faucet delivering Red Hills water would be ideal in Madras.

Both the cook room and scullery would have floors paved with slabs of stone.[34]

Lady Wilson in contrast, opting for more modest reform, was relieved that her husband promised to put in a brick floor while they were away at camp, and furnish the kitchen with a sink, a range, tables, and "presses." Like Wyvern, she insisted on an English or American kitchen range. She thus demonstrated an emergent set of expectations of improved technology in the kitchen with the availability of reasonably priced imports from England and North America. New technology was deemed cleaner and more efficient.

Wyvern admitted that this model of kitchen would be impractical in all but new constructions in which the owners might be tempted to make the "offices" as complete and home like as possible, but offers other suggestions for remedying the status quo. One suggestion was to repurpose the small building—a former "cooler's godown" (abdarkhana) or a room for hanging meat—if it was still standing near the main house. Both functions—the "cooler" whose task was to cool drinks by various methods and the meat larder had become defunct with the introduction of ice-boxes and zinc-lined meat safes. This newly converted building would be connected to the nearby back verandah with a cheaply constructed covered passageway. The new American or English range would be the centerpiece of this one-room kitchen, with one side contrived up as a washing space. If this was not possible, then a part of the back verandah could be converted into the "working-room" for preparing pastry and all other food before being taken into the cook room: "the making of pastry, the dressing of meat and vegetables, and the mixing of sauces, puddings, &c., should be performed in a cool place, away from the smoke and heat of fires, where wind and dust can be excluded by closing the door, and yet ample light be obtained from a good glass window, and, above all things where the *chef* can be easily supervised."[35]

It is the possibility of dust and dirt carried through the open door (in the absence of a glazed window to permit light) in the old cook room that he considered the chief problem to be solved. A gust of wind blowing fine particles of charcoal from the open fire of the stove would thus not just spoil delicate cookery such as a soufflé, but become an irritant at the dinner table, with both master and mistress failing to understand the real causes of culinary failures. A dust storm, so common in India, might not be a problem to the native cook, and the butler might want to explain away such mishaps with excuses—"little bit yeggshell" or "sugar mistake"—but the master or mistress should not put up with such "accidents." A better appreciation of cleanliness and care on behalf of European masters, he argued, are the only remedies. When seen from the point of view of cleanliness, such a conversion of the back verandah would then appear to be a necessity and not a luxury.

Native cooks, Wyvern argued, were perfectly capable of using Western tools and methods when no other was available to them. The cooks working in houses and clubs that were fitted up with the "Home system" did not complain. Apart from "a dresser of strong wood, a pastry table with marble slab, a cup-board, a rack or plates and dishes, a gauze safe, and a set of shelves," such a working room would contain a mineral oil stove, or failing that, a small charcoal fire upon which all delicate cooking operations could be performed. Then he added, the closeness of the working-room would mean that pilfering would become difficult, long absence of servants would be easily detected, and drinking and gossiping at work would stop.

Dirt and distance go hand in hand. Wyvern sees surveillance as the natural consequence of the native cook's inability to understand that dirt in food is unwelcome at the table, inured as he is to the dust and dirt of his surroundings. Flora Annie Steel and Grace Gardiner, who did not recommend much architectural reform of the kitchen, in the very first page of their housekeeping guide chided housekeepers who "put up with a degree of slovenliness and dirt which would disgrace a den in St. Giles, on the principle that it is no use attempting to teach the natives." They claimed that the Indian servant was amenable to being taught, unlike his counterpart in England, but Indian servants had a propensity to revert back to their slovenly ways with a few days of absence or neglect on the part of the mistress. Native servants were peculiarly susceptible to their "inherited conservatism of dirt." For Steel and Gardiner a regime of cleanliness and regular, scrupulous supervision would remedy the nuisance associated with a dirty kitchen and its defective drainage.

A dirty kitchen and its surroundings, Steel and Gardiner noted, have other implications beyond food. Subscribing to a miasmatic theory of disease they argued that the dirty pools of water around the kitchen might cause typhoid among the white children, if they played near the kitchen, unsupervised. Such views continued to find affirmation even among medical professionals. In 1923, Dr. Kate Platt, former principal of Lady Hardinge Medical College and Hospital for Women in Delhi, wrote that the kitchen in bungalows should be located at a distance of 20 or 30 feet from the house and connected to the "pantry" (located just outside the dining room), with a covered verandah. She rationalized the necessity of the servants' quarters being located at a distance from the bungalow because "Indians have their own ways of living, and in malarious and unhealthy districts especially, their houses may be centers of infection."[36] Here the cook room is seen as a part and parcel of the native servants' quarters. Wyvern's insistence that the cook room-turned-kitchen be located close to the bungalow is premised upon its thorough modernization along European lines; in other words, upon eradication of its perceived Indian characteristics. He, of course, suggested no reform of the servants' quarters that would continue to be located far from the main house and its now-reformed kitchen.

Recalcitrance

Dirt had its place. If four generations of Europeans insisted that the Indian servant was reconciled to dirt, it also meant that there was nothing they could do to improve the living conditions of the servants because they would fall back on their old ways. This came with another advantage. Wyvern and others wrote of the marvelous facility with which Indian servants conjured up dinners at camps: "Given a hole in the ground, and a couple of stones for her range, with a bundle of jungle sticks, a chatty or two, perhaps a degchee, and a fan, wherewithal to prepare a dinner, can you picture to yourself the face of Martha, the 'thorough good cook' of an English household?" (Figure 7.3).[37]

Unlike the English cook who would require proper equipment, Indian cooks would do just fine "left entirely alone." In camps, Wyvern argued this might be allowed and narrated the tale of an army officer who tried to instruct the Indian cook to prepare food using improved military method. After "issuing orders concerning the geometrical lines in which he wished the tents to be pitched," and making sure that the tent pegs are painted white, he turned to the construction of a Wolseley's field kitchen. This consisted of laying out "a series of broad arrow kitchens" (Figure 7.4).[38] The Indian cooking staff ignored the guidelines set by the geometrical layout and

FIGURE 7.3 Cooking at camp, 1882. Illustration in Mrs. Robert Moss King, *The Diary of a Civilian's Wife India, 1877–82* (London: Richard Bentley & Sons, 1884).

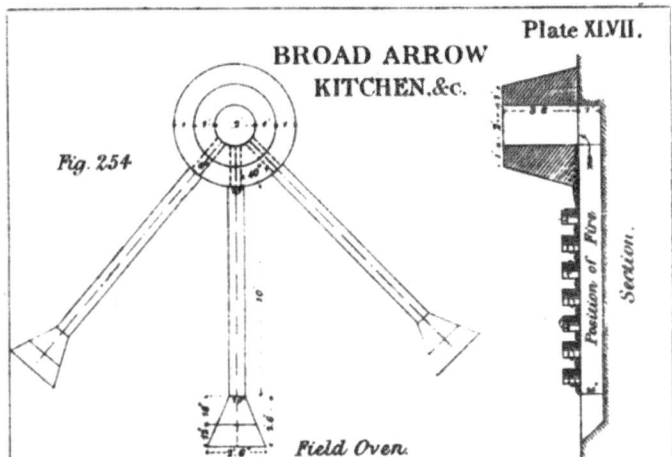

FIGURE 7.4 Wolesley's broad arrow field kitchen, *Manual of Field Fortification, Military Sketching and Reconnaissance* (London: Her Majesty's Stationary Office, 1871).

"efficient" design of the field kitchen, and decided to make their own arrangements in a dry ditch or *nullah*:

> The Colonel furiously demanded why the proper kitchens had not been used, and "all this abominable mess prevented?" Presently a cook of greater daring than his colleagues replied "What sar! that bad sense kitchin, sar, I beg your pardon: too much firewood taking: see sar this proper kitchin only." In the face of such an irresistible argument, the Colonel (albeit irritated beyond measure) was constrained to abandon his cherished project.[39]

The Indian cooks' recalcitrance seen through the lens of resource efficiency made sense, but with a caveat. Wyvern delivers this lesson as a humorous story to present the native cook's distaste for new methods and their preference for technologically uncomplicated solutions. That the cook's experience in this case superseded the colonel's rule-book knowledge is made into an important teaching moment. Wyvern's reason for narrating this story is to get across to his readers the absolute necessity of preventing such blatant acts of refusing modern method: "When presenting Ramasámy with novel utensils, let us guard against his denouncing them as 'bad sense'." The native cook has to be weaned from his habit of thinking by training him to understand the fuel-efficiency of the English- or American-style cooking range and the importance of preventing food wastage:

> The native cook's objection "too much firewood taking" is, let me observe, a downright perversion of fact. If properly understood, and utilized to its

full extent, the English range, with its one fire, must surely consume less fuel than do the numerous open fires in an Indian cook-room. This is self-evident ... A range provided with a hot-plate, an oven, and a boiler, supplies with its one fire all these wants at once. Vessels, the contents of which require rapid boiling, are placed over the fire-hole, while things needing slow treatment, like soups, stews, &c., find a place upon the hotplate, or flat surface of the range. The oven is, of course, always kept hot, and the boiler, if correctly filled, must contain an unceasing supply of hot water.[40]

That this truth was not self-evident to the Indian cook is clear. To make his argument about this constant state of cooking, Wyvern insisted that a correct comparison was not with the barrack room where the soldiers did not have proper multicourse meals and where such kitchen ranges had failed precisely because "too much firewood taking." The comparison should be with hospitals where hot water, soup, and carefully cooked meat is in "constant requisition." Why would a household need such a constant source of hot water or by what metrics is a household kitchen equivalent to a hospital kitchen? Because the house, like the hospital, should be a perfect state of order, discipline, and labor. He pointed out that Indian cooks indeed waste fuel and connected this to their habit of shirking work. An English or American range if it were to be fuel-efficient would require the cook to stay constant watch over the kitchen range and this would mean an elaboration of food courses. An improved cooking range would prevent the rampant waste of food in the Indian kitchen as well: "It is not exaggeration to say that half the quantity of soup-meat and bone required by the ignorant native cook might be saved if he could be prevailed upon to follow the laws of intelligent cookery."[41]

Fifty years later, Pinkham wrote with considerable resignation about the cook's attitude toward new technology being introduced into the kitchen. If the mistress succeeded in getting the cook "to try ideas of which he did not approve, he would outwit her by proving her suggestions utter failures ... It was just as well that Joan did not attempt to introduce too many Western utensils and innovations, for their nomenclature alone would have required special courses of study."[42]

From Pinkham's resignation and Wyvern's insistence we get a palpable sense of tussle over labor time, technology, and wages. The vision of economy, efficiency, and order (including quiet, disciplined service at the dinner table) that Wyvern prescribes is designed to extract labor from the cook in a highly controlled manner so that the table may be served in a "civilized" rather than "barbaric" manner. Elaboration of European foodways becomes efficiency of native labor when properly squared with modern technology. His comparison with the hospital suggests that he hopes to bring the kind of efficiency and improvement that had been obtained at the level of large institutions to the domestic sphere. And here he was in good company. The relation between industry and household was made tighter in the decades that followed, but the argument about waste, efficiency, and progress was part of a larger discourse about food that had emerged in the nineteenth century.

Wyvern's book was published from Madras, where he was stationed, in the middle of the Madras Famine. The plenitude and perfection of European-styled food that he advocated was written when millions of Indians were dying because they did not have enough to eat. As Radhika Mohanram points out, that the famine is not discussed but only alluded to in Wyvern's culinary advice is instructive.[43] In a passage about scarcity of quality meat he wrote: "Owing to the calamity which befell us in 1877, and the two previous seasons of scarcity, our market has, for the past few years, been hardly as well supplied as it formerly was; nevertheless, good meat is to be got."[44] The passive construction in the last sentence, Mohanram notes, delinks European society from the famine and subscribes to the prevailing Anglo-Indian attitude toward the famine as a calamity brought on by Indians upon themselves.[45] Wyvern's culinary racism shared with broader British colonial attitudes toward the famine an understanding of appropriate consumption and means of controlling native labor, and how much a person should eat.[46]

Extending the Food Axis

By the nineteenth century, authorities in Europe and the colonies widely subscribed to the idea that the eating habits of the poor were a consequence of their ignorance. This justified energetic efforts to reform the foodways of recent immigrants in North America, the working class in Europe, and percolated into famine codes formulated in India from the 1870s onward. The various metrics for evaluating healthiness and standards of living that were created between the 1880s and 1920s enabled the social understanding of food habits to become a political tool. These were worked into modern spatial imagination and discernment of the relative status of races, and thus of states and empires.[47] Describing this turn-of-the-twentieth-century phenomenon Nick Cullather writes: "[F]ood lost its subjective cultural character and evolved into a material instrument of statecraft."[48] Cullather's argument is about the history of the calorie as a nutritional measure, and the manner in which it was developed in the 1890s as an instrument—more than a measure—to "render food and eating habits of populations, politically legible."[49] He traces the idea back to Wilbur O. Atwater's experiment with a calorimeter in 1896 on the campus of Wesleyan College (Figure 7.5). The calorimeter was transformed from an instrument for measuring the combustive efficiency of machines and explosives into one that measured energy needs of the human body. The apparatus resembled a meat locker, "a room 'about as large as an ordinary convict's cell' lined with

FIGURE 7.5 Front view of respiration calorimeter, with air pump, water meter, observers table and entrance to the respiration chamber are shown in detail, Judd Hall, Wesleyan University, Middletown, CT. Special Collections, US Department of Agriculture National Agricultural Library.

copper and zinc, its interior visible through a triple-paned glass aperture." An occupant supplied with measured quantities of food performed his daily activities that included physical exercise and reading, while "thermometers, hygrometers, and electrically powered condensers, pumps, and fans precisely measured the movement of heat, air, and matter into and out of the chamber."[50]

An apt illustration of environmental control, the sealed cell provided an exposition of energy consumption and exchange, and directly connected food and labor. The "Wesleyan glass cage" made the body's internal functioning appear transparent—extractable and legible for analysis. This analytic process was intended to differentiate between the subjective sense of food as taste and pleasure in favor of an objective sense of food as fuel. From such calculations could be derived measures that tied nutritional and labor efficiencies, wastefulness in food, and wasted labor, which in turn could be related to idleness, "improvidence," standards of living, and the productivity of citizens.[51]

Calorie confronted culture through racial difference. Once a caloric measure could be attributed to a particular food, irrespective of the individual consuming it, it was a seemingly logical step to compare diets of different social classes, races, and nations. Bodies became fungible through the caloric measure in a more fundamental sense than had occurred under industrial capitalism when the laboring body was construed as a work unit. A man at moderate muscular work became the "man-unit," the standard against which all laboring bodies of men, women, and children were measured as fractions of the full needs of the man.[52] A moderately active woman was deemed to require 0.8 man-units, the equivalent of a 14- to16-year-old boy. A girl of the same age as the boy was deemed to require less: 0.7 man-units. This gendered/age hierarchy could be extended to races within and across nations.

Following German precedents, Atwater and his colleagues, supported by the US Department of Agriculture, had embarked on the caloric measure of food in the 1880s.[53] In 1895, prior to their calorimeter experiment, Atwater and his colleagues conducted research on the nutritional performance of African American farmers in the "Black Belt" of Alabama. The modest foodways of the subjects of the study, primarily sharecroppers, were made the basis for views on racial improvement. Their diet, heavily dependent on corn and deficient in animal protein (by which Atwater meant fresh meat such as beef, mutton, and lamb), was attributed to their "improvidence" and idleness.[54] The researchers recognized that the sharecroppers were debt-bound to their former masters who loaned the farmers equipment and money at ruinous rates. These were the "evils under which the colored people live," and demonstrated "the phases through which they were passing in their upward progress."[55] The researchers documented the housing of the farmers, the extent of their farmed land or landholdings, household animals, clothing, "work, habits and the like," drawing a direct connection between better nutrition, household economy, and improved housing. Reluctant to view the cause rooted in the deep structural inequity of the Jim Crow era that kept the farmers at a subsistence level, the researchers made their findings an argument for education that would teach the farmers the virtues of thrift and wholesome labor.[56] The very tools that were being pushed into European American working-class homes to make them hard-working and thrifty were considered an extravagance for the African American sharecropper:

> When the negro has money he is ready to spend it for almost anything, and the skillful trader may urge goods upon him the purchase of which is most extravagant. After his cotton is sold and the mortgage on the crop is paid, he may spend a large part of the balance for a sewing machine or a modern cooking range, which are ultimately returned to the dealer at a large sacrifice.[57]

Foresight with money, considered a key condition that distinguished primitives from the civilized, was linked to the opportunity for better nutrition.[58] The betterment was visible in those subjects who had closer connection to the civilizing influence of the Tuskegee Institute and "association with people of intelligence and thrift."⁵⁹ The example that illustrated this finding was a carpenter's family who with his "savings and hard work had built a very comfortable one-story frame house with four rooms" (Figure 7.6).⁶⁰ Such improvement, the report noted, was rare, but "illustrated not what the negro is, but what he may become."⁶¹ Race is thus cited as a factor in social, economic, and moral development of the formerly enslaved farmers and at the same time made to disappear by appeal to a scientific analysis of nutritional and bodily needs that viewed bodies as perfectly fungible. The counterpart to the improved caloric balance was the style of the house that reflected a departure from the slave cabin of plantations and suggested upward mobility toward white residential types.

The enthusiasm with which Atwater's experiments and measures were received, Cullather points out, signals the already recognized need for a food index that could put into effect an evolutionary and competitive view of food consumption. With the caloric measure for foods and the caloric needs of a standardized body determined, the management of food in institutions outside the home could be addressed in an efficient manner. Such experiments had precedents in the rationing of food in plantations and early-nineteenth-century prison, barrack, and workhouse reform in both England and India.⁶²

FIGURE 7.6 Houses corresponding with dietary habits. "Fig. 1. Negro carpenter's house (dietary No. 98); Fig. 2. House and barn of negro farmer's family (dietary No. 96)." W. O. Atwater and Chas. D. Woods, *Dietary Studies with Reference to the Food of the Negro in Alabama in 1895 and 1896* (Washington, DC: Government Printing Press, 1897).

The perfect control condition of a prison setting was in particular attractive to those interested in experimentation on human subjects, and food was also used as a deterrence.[63] The caloric understanding conferred on such practices of regulating and withholding of food a modern, universal, and therefore expansive justification: "it could reduce the cost of rations, and test their suitability for the tropics and for varying conditions of work … With a numerical gauge, Americans could begin to imagine the influence to be gained by manipulating the diets of distant peoples."[64] Atwater's contribution was to expand the prevailing idea of "eating cheaply and accepting lower wages" and give it scientific rationale.[65] The calorimeter "translated the vernacular customs of food into the numerical language of empire." And in so doing it inaugurated a new food axis that gave the state direct access to the individual in terms of their caloric needs.[66]

Cullather's argument that the strange tongues and tastes of the "culinary Babel" could be considered neutralized through the invention of the caloric measure of food is important to understand the larger impact of new experiments with food economy and efficiency. In the first place it links the kitchens and dining rooms to a new set of spaces of experimentation, beyond the cannery, department stores, and world fairs of the late nineteenth century. The calorimeter as a scientifically objective, sealed room could now be seen to mediate the food axis to link the home, spaces of food production beyond the house, the nation and its imperial ambitions. In 1898, home-economist advocate Ellen Richards made this connection explicit by noting that while in the past women had been trained to think of the home as separate and protected from the industrial world, it was now important to jettison these protective boundaries and open up the home to industry.[67] This is not simply an extension of the existing food axis that Cromley discusses in her book, but a new articulation of the relation between the state and the individual. The calorimeter emblematized this seemingly transparent relation by divorcing food from affective value and isolating it as body fuel. Rather, all the subjective understanding of food and who should eat what could now be bestowed a scientific, evolutionary rationale tailored to imperial objectives of the modern state.[68] This standardization-impelled politicization of food—that is, food as modern statecraft—worked in tandem with the continuing propensity to speak the rough cultural language of culinary racism that I have cited at the outset of this chapter. Indeed, they support each other.

Calorie Transfer

Famine, Amartya Sen notes, is about the command over food—about the ability to command food through entitlements.[69] It involves some sections of a society gaining from the food loss suffered by another section of a society. In view of this, colonialism may be described as a massive system of calorie transfer from the colonies to the metropole. Britain's rise as a manufacturing power was concomitant with India's loss of industries and increased dependence on agriculture to sustain its economy and meet the financial burden imposed by Britain. In the nineteenth century, Britain's economy depended on food importation from India. Continual impoverishment of the Indian peasantry into the twentieth century was deemed an unfortunate necessity lest the population in Britain starved.[70]

The "causes" of the Madras Famine might have been many-pronged, with the effects of crop failure exacerbated by the policy of wheat importation from India to Britain, the railways that moved grain fast and resulted in delocalizing the food supply, and the colonial state's approach to famine administration.[71] It is useful to note that a recent study of the rainfall pattern in the Deccan shows that the rainfall was not aberrant in the famine years— it stayed well within the norms for that region.[72] That it was not a purely climatic disaster was well-recognized by colonial administrators who denied the existence of food shortage per se. Wheat importation from India to Britain jumped more than fivefold between 1875 and 1877, despite colonial administrators being cognizant of severe shortages in India.[73] Present-day scholars have endeavored to show the inequity and injustice of British colonial policy by comparing the famine wages given out during the Madras Famine with similar regimes of food rationing in prisons and twentieth-century concentration camps. Comparing the famine rations (1,627 calories) with the ration given out at the Nazi camp at Buchenwald (1,750 calories) and the Voit-Atwater standard (4,200 calories for a man engaged in heavy labor), Mike Davis notes the severity of this inequity as a wish to kill.[74] While these comparisons say much about authoritarian forms of the right to command food, reliance on the calorie as a measure to evaluate that inequity also does violence to foodways in terms of understanding the role of food as a cultural form and social modality. As Tom Scott-Smith explains in connection with present-day practices of starvation management by international agencies, such metrical understanding of food disengages the stomach from the full person. In aiming to consider the individual as part of a population, rather than the individual as a person with cultural entitlements, the use of objective bureaucratic metrics acts as a distantiating tool. Such nutritional measures are "based on social distance rather than proximity, managed through the accumulation of statistics, and it always has an eye on speed and efficiency."[75] The calorie, in reducing food to a numerical understanding of nutrients, strengthens the biopolitical assumption on which the necropolitics of famine is hoisted. Colonialism is a method of calorie transfer *and more*. Its racialized geography is essential to understand the process through which seemingly rational measures are deeply implicated in upholding socioeconomic, and consequently political, distinctions.

Richard Temple, Lieutenant Governor of the Bengal Presidency, was deputed to the Madras Famine administration by Viceroy Lytton with an explicit charge of economizing on relief operations and bringing the famine under administrative control. Temple, criticized for overspending on the

Bengal-Bihar famine of 1874 in his capacity as Lieutenant Governor, successfully limited the expenses of the Madras Famine relief by introducing among many directives the notorious "Temple wage."[76] It was, as William Digby noted, essentially an experiment to see how little food intake is required for a laborer to keep working.[77]

The famished person's condition or qualification for relief was determined by spatializing food needs. To determine famine conditions in a region, and among the people in general, certain tests were administered before the Temple wage could be implemented. These consisted of what may be called the four d's: the distance test, distress test, degradation test, and discipline test. The techniques of creating racially striated everyday spaces within colonial domestic confines—separation, distancing, and placement—became the principles on which the spatial organization of famine administration was based. It extended to larger scales and then repeated these techniques at the smaller scale of the poorhouse, relief camp, and kitchen and at the microscale of the bodies of the famished to create a consistent and mutually supportive scalar relation. The impact on a larger scale, however, was not simply greater but of a different order altogether.

To gain access to relief under the colonial administration, the relief seeker had to labor anywhere the state deemed appropriate.[78] Village headmen were responsible for detecting and reporting cases of starvation to the administration. These starving people would then be compelled to undergo methods of relief determined by the colonial state. The distance test formulated during the Madras Famine necessitated those seeking relief to travel to a work site between 7 and 15 miles distant from their home to gain access to relief work.[79] This was considered an effective way to weed out those who were truly starving from those who could fend for themselves. It was understood that no one except those under severe duress would undertake this labor. The very argument for qualification underwrote the death of those who were too famished and could not get to the relief sites or simply refused to do so. Others died near the work sites in the absence of adequate shelter, food, or sanitation facilities.[80] The explicit injunction that food be *not* distributed in each village in close proximity to the famished's place of residence was intended to discourage laziness or dispel any notion that the people are entitled to food without doing labor.[81] The peasantry's willingness to travel a long distance from home for work and food itself was to be a sign of starvation.

For relief work attached to public infrastructural projects such as road, railway, and canal construction, the peasant-turned-construction laborer was expected to stay at relief camps thrown together with minimal care to ensure that the inmates did not wander off or leave the work site.[82] Upon arrival the workers had to build their own huts.[83] Between the distance they were expected to travel and the localization of the famished at construction sites made them a recognizable population category. The distance test created a new geography of labor relations where the peasants were forcibly removed from their home and field. And yet their movement was severely restricted by the spatial logic that determined the location of work and camp sites. To prevent the famished from entering the city of Madras in large numbers, a road works scheme was set up within a 15-miles radius of the city. The works essentially acted as a spatial buffer between the urban residents of Madras and the famished countryside.[84]

The distress test was further evidenced by the physical appearance of the people: unless their clothes were absolutely ragged and dirty, and unless the women had no jewelry on them, they were not considered to have met the distress test and were not admitted for relief work nor for gratuitous relief.[85] It was widely assumed that women were concealing their jewelry and appearing for poor relief when no such need existed. Observable evidence of distress—beyond emaciation—was deemed necessary to confirm a person's state of starvation. Dirt and disease mixed with economic distress to become evidence of bodies needing state intervention.

The wage experiment was "calculated to provide a bare subsistence" for the male participant in relief work, "but not enough to support any non-working member of the family."[86] The goal was to ensure the relief seekers did not get wages from which they could save or live in "comfort." The wage for relief work was 2 annas, a sum well below the normal rate of labor which ran from 4 to 5 annas, depending on the region and type of work. Temple reduced the wages further to 1½ anna per day for a man (and proportionally for women and children) to ensure that only the most appallingly starved submit themselves to such labor.[87] That starving peasants in many locations refused to undertake labor under those wage conditions served as a proof of Temple's estimation that not all who claimed to need relief were actually starving.

The construction works became an opportunity to get access to a labor force that was not otherwise forthcoming. Even though the engineers in charge of construction work protested that emaciated people do not make good laborers, this rationale was not heeded. More than actual construction productivity was at stake. The relief workers were considered not to possess an industrial morale that would make them subject to discipline.[88] What mattered was that the men, women, and children (over 12 years of age) were consigned to hard labor: the value of labor would be taught through its expenditure. It was penal in that the authorities explicitly recognized that no one under normal circumstances would be willing to undertake that kind of back-breaking labor for such wages and under such laboring conditions. Temple expected the famished people would be grateful to the colonial state for teaching them the value of labor so that they could prevent future calamities. Such statements reinforced the idea that the famine was the fault of the unintelligent use of resources, laziness, and improvidence of the peasantry.

Food became a disciplinary tool. Fines were levied on already scant rations for work ill-completed. Meal times were called feeding times, and the workers, each wearing a wooden ticket around their neck like those worn by prisoners, were lined up in rows at "feeding sheds," to be given food under the strictest discipline.[89] The acceptance of cooked food rather than grain at the relief camps was declared to be the "truest and safest test of the need for gratuitous relief."[90] If the people complained about the quality of the food or that this mode of feeding was incompatible with their caste practices, it was argued that since the cooks were high-caste, no such objection could exist.

Temple complained that unlike Bengal which with its compact, tree-studded villages comprised a visually identifiable domain of famine intervention, the geography of the Madras Presidency with its vast rugged territories and scattered villages made observation, survey, and administrative intervention difficult.[91] Aidan Forth explains the method: distressed territories were plotted out "'in groups or sub-circles of villages,' which could be searched by a 'trusty supervisor'." In so doing "famine officials imposed a geometric matrix to convert amorphous landscapes into intelligible units, and illegible, nomadic terrain into an orderly network navigable by the modern state."[92]

Ignoring suggestions that relief operations and famine kitchens should be dispersed and locally managed, Temple insisted on large camps where the inmates could be checked and confined by following penal methods of control.[93] Wanderers, beggars, and charity seekers, seen as a threat to law and order and carriers of dirt and disease, were forced into detention camps which grew in size during the Madras Famine.[94] The relief camp was not to be used as a place for the famished people to get food once or twice a day, but was itself a sorting mechanism: those admitted to a camp had to reside there and work. The "able-bodied" would not be received in such a camp but immediately sent to work sites. "The weakly applicant" would "also be generally sent to a relief work, but may sometimes be detained a few days to be fed up." The camp population then would consist of the aged, infirm, and sick, and everyone except the sick had to work to the degree they were capable. Designed as fenced spaces in which entry and exit were controlled, the camps were laid out on plans that were a cross between nineteenth-century colonial prison and barrack design (Figure 7.7).

If "famine laid bare the coercive apparatus of the colonial state," as Forth notes, there was, however, no contradiction between "life has to be saved at any cost" and the utter importance of minimizing the cost of relief.[95] The first referred to civil and military coercive powers and the second referred to economic measures. In its living condition, process of selection, spatial organization and construction, the camp was made as unattractive as possible.[96] In effect these were detention camps, although terms such as "relief camps" and "poorhouses" were used in official documents. The "degradation of living in relief camps was itself a deterrent," Digby noted. Those who did not want to undergo the degradation, used "passive resistance" and took to "discharging themselves" from relief work.[97]

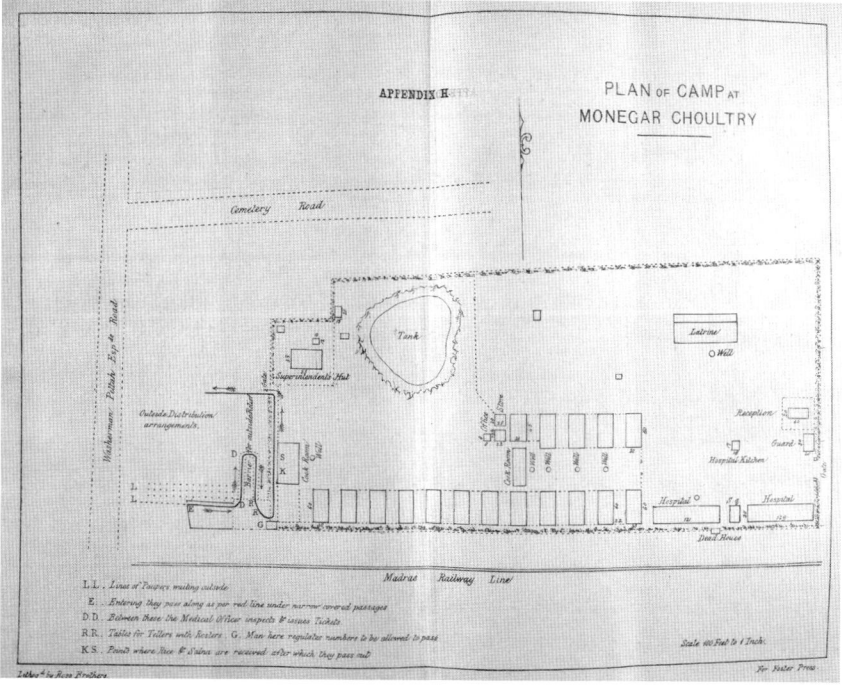

FIGURE 7.7 Monegar Choultry Camp in Madras. The row of rectangles next to the enclosure are 60' × 30' huts holding 60–75 people. The entry and exit are so designed as to make escape difficult. Temple Papers, Mss Eur F86/183, Madras Town Famine Relief 1877. Report by Colonel W. S. Drever, Appendix H. © British Library Board.

The famine did not simply reiterate the gap between the impoverished peasantry and the well-to-do Indians and Europeans but demonstrated in absolute terms the colonial state's right to command: to set policy by fiat, to control the exportation and distribution of grain in the name of free trade, and to determine when, where, and under what circumstances the people affected by scarcity of food should labor, live, and die. A famine fund was created by raising licensing taxes on petty traders and a severe hike in the salt duties in Madras and Bombay from 2 to 45 annas a maund, on the pretext of creating a reserve fund for future famines. These funds were funneled into the Second Anglo-Afghan War to extend British territorial control in the northwest, thereby demonstrating the territorial significance of calorie transfer. Temple argued in defense of this expenditure that "there was no legal contract" between the British government and the Indian people that the funds "must be exclusively devoted to famine purposes."[98]

The colonial food axis thus predated Atwater's experiment and extended far beyond the bungalow compound. It linked the millions of small homesteads of the peasantry with the centralization strategies for labor and food distribution of the government and to reaches that had seemingly no connection to food at all, but which nevertheless had a material impact on the lives of the peasantry. The continuation of figural and spatial representations of culinary racism well into the twentieth century was not separate from the numeric representations of nutritional value that states adopted with enthusiasm. These prior policies and attitudes served an important role in shoring up arguments about caloric content, and indeed places the invention of the calorie as a universal measure in a new historical light. Calorie transfer as an index of colonialism underwrote the methods by which colonial labor was constructed and at the same time made it invisible. In the concluding chapter of Part Two, I turn to the seeming contradiction between the ubiquity of laboring bodies in the colonies and their absence in the archives.

8

Making Invisible

By all accounts, the numerousness of servants in the Anglo-Indian household was its defining feature. Servants often crowd the foregrounds of paintings and photographs of bungalows and camps—working, posing, looking away. The bevy of servants in even middling Anglo-Indian households was a topic of animated conversation, and housekeeping guides provided lists of servants that were necessary to run the household with their job descriptions and salaries. In a diary published in 1884, Elizabeth King, an English civilian's wife provided a list of thirty-two "private servants" for the hot season in India (Figure 8.1). In addition, her husband, a collector in the North-Western

Name of Servant	Best English equivalent	Monthly Wages (Rupees)
Khansáma	Butler	10
Kitmatgár	Footman	8
Bawarchi	Cook	10
Masálchi	Scullion	5
Bearer	Valet, &c.	10
Mate-bearer	Assistant do.	6
Ayah	Lady's-maid	10
Dhaie	Wet-nurse	10
Mehteráni	Low-caste ayah	4
Mehter	Sweeper	5
Dhobi	Washerman	13
Bhisti	Water-carrier	5
Derzie	Tailor	10
Murghiwalla	Fowl-keeper	5
Goála	Cowman	5
Chokidar	Watchman	5
Coachwán	Coachman	8
3 Syces	Grooms	15
3 Grass-cutters		12
6 Punkah-coolies		24
2 Garden-coolies		8
Máli	Gardener	6
Total, 32 servants.	Total monthly wages	Rs. 194

FIGURE 8.1 List of servants and their wages. Mrs. (Elizabeth Augusta) Robert Moss King, *The Diary of a Civilian's Wife in India 1877–1882* (London: Richard Bentley & Son, 1884).

Provinces, had five *chuprassies* or attendants who were "government servants." In the cold weather when tours commenced, they also had "four or five tent-pitchers and a tribe of camel and bullock drivers, elephant drivers, and other miscellaneous camp followers," most of whom were "paid by Government."[1]

Why is it then so difficult in the historical archive to locate the spaces in which these servants worked? The colonial archive reveals endless debates about servants—the large numbers "necessary" in India, the types of servants befitting particular ranks, and their appropriate salaries. We have numbers, types, and ethnographic depictions of these servants. Each servant is rendered typical through the object they carry and which marks their specific role in the master's household. These objects were meant to also represent their caste—and thus they admirably answered the needs of ethnographic documentation. Such representational practice of indexing labor with a tool was transferred from paintings and drawings to photographs without seemingly any representational hitch. In a remarkable conflation, artists and photographers took their own servants and camp followers as model representatives of the labor force and therefore social divisions in Indian society.[2] Domestic servants served as an important lens through which to view native society.

The difficulty of locating servants' spaces in the historical archive is not peculiar to colonial India. Large plantation houses in the antebellum American South had hundreds of servants and enslaved working in the fields and the house. More modest ones had just enough field hands and a few who labored to cook food, wash clothes, clean, and take care of children, alongside the mistress. Plantations by definition were working spaces. So why is it that even in such sites as antebellum Monticello and Mount Vernon, Virginia, where the enslaved numbered in the hundreds, do we find servants and the enslaved rarely depicted—their work spaces parenthetical to the story of the main house?

These questions about the absence of the laboring classes in the archives might appear naive or rather suggestive of a response too obvious: they were not deemed important for representation. In addition, they were not the ones who were undertaking the representation—writing, drawing, photographing. Servants and the laboring population appear in the historical archive as either abstract collectivities—workforce subject to discipline and reform—or when they exceed their role or station by refusing work, by rebelling, by escaping, and as collaborators in exceptional demonstrations of loyalty to their masters.[3] I want to stay with this naivete for a while to ask: how do they disappear?

The fact is they don't disappear, they are *made* invisible, sometimes in plain sight, and at other times through various contrivances. They are present in large numbers but yet are not visible in certain forms of representation—pictorial and photographic representations and architectural plans. In our effort to retrieve their presence from the archive we scour long lists of ship's cargo, census figures, probate inventories—hoping to discover something of their experience. The numbers reinforce the violence of lives erased, of treating people as lives so nominally lived that they do not often deserve a name. Their representation could just be as violent as their erasure. Saidiya Hartman in her discussion of the transatlantic slave trade and Krista Thompson in her study of nineteenth-century photographs of Black laborers in post-emancipation Jamaica argue that it is in exclusion that representations of the enslaved and laboring populations commence.[4] Thompson points out the manner in which colonial capitalism in the shape of American agro-companies continued to use the figures, tropes, and sites of slavery to repackage the Caribbean as a productive and "safe" tropical Eden.[5] The gap between representation and erasure is so perfunctory in the colonial archive that they indeed become interchangeable. As such the spatial tools and techniques that mediate this gap between representation and erasure in the relation between what in architectural parlance is termed "served spaces" and "service spaces" become key.

Backstairs

Consider the backstairs. Whether in the colonial house in India, North America, the Caribbean, or England, backstairs were meant for servants who were not expected to present themselves during their work. In the nineteenth-century English country house, Mark Girouard notes: "[A]s far as possible the servants were kept invisible even when they came into the main house. An intricate system of backstairs and back corridors ensured that housemaids could get up to the bedrooms, dinner to the dining room and the butler or footman to the front door with the least possible chance of meeting the family on the way."[6] There are parallels between such practices and those in colonial India in that the presencing of servants depended on their location in the hierarchy of service. Who could move where described the servant hierarchy. This should not be surprising. It is, however, ill-recognized that in colonial India, caste, class, and racial distinctions were superimposed to determine the access pattern of these houses.

The lowest in the hierarchy of servants in both Indian and Anglo-Indian houses was the *mehtar* or sweeper who cleaned the toilets. The *mehtar* (male) or *mehtarni* (female) was an "untouchable" and no other servant would perform their task. Among the lowest wage earners in such a household, they were responsible for emptying the commodes after each use in covered wicker baskets and depositing the excreta in a shed where the "general receptacle" was kept at a location within the compound farthest from the main house. From there "the contents of the receptacle" were removed by *mehtar*s "at night in a special cart." The term "nightsoil" referring to the removal of wastes from privies at night, whether in Asian, European, or American cities, was a nighttime task designed not to excessively offend the sensory feelings of the citizens. This labor conducted at night, even though absolutely essential to a town's survival, made it invisible. The dilemma, as Tanika Sarkar notes, was how to extract the labor of the nightsoil workers *and* excise the laborer "from one's social horizon."[7] Vijay Prashad, in his discussion of colonial Delhi makes a similar remark: "The task of the sweeper was to remove the accumulated dirt and dispose of it, to remind the residents of their civility and to hide the city's own refuse from itself."[8]

As Dean Ferguson notes in a comparative history of nightsoil removal, the work of those who conducted the various tasks of waste removal—sweepers, scavengers, chimney sweeps, and nightsoil men—"their role is rarely visible in the public record." It is, however, "occasionally possible to catch glimpses of them at work."[9] In the British colonial archive they appear as troublemakers, who because of their caste-community solidarity could partially control this labor process.[10] They defied the municipal commissioners' effort to control the process of refuse removal—when and how houses and streets would be cleaned—and their right to the nightsoil which could be sold to farmers. Dr. Kate Platt, who served as principal of Lady Hardinge College in Delhi, wrote in her guide to home and health that it is absolutely essential that the *mehtar* be available in the house round the clock. She also reminded her readers that the work of nightsoil removal requires "frequent" visits of inspection and at "unexpected times."[11] *Mehtar*s were indispensable and seemingly untrustworthy.

Prashad shows the process through which sweepers in colonial Delhi in the 1880s were slowly wrenched away from their control of *mohalla*s (neighborhoods) in which they had established exclusive rights of waste removal to become municipal employees where the municipality assigned them to a neighborhood. It disrupted the erstwhile relation of clientship and servitude in which they could negotiate with the householder their condition of work. Being disengaged from individual households of the neighborhood "freed the sweepers from the direct bonds of subordination to Hindu and ashraf Muslim families, but it also deprived them of even their limited control over the process of work ... sweepers became merely dalits, rather than Allarakhi or Bunno, as the minimal courtesy of a long-term relationship was now largely unavailable to sweepers."[12] The late-nineteenth-century conflict between the sweepers and the municipality was over keeping the wages to famine rates (increased from Rs. 1 per month to Rs. 4 per month in 1885 and then reduced to Rs. 2 in 1888 sparking a labor strike). They were also subject to Rs. 10 fines for "rebellious behavior."[13]

Colonial sanitation policy was blatantly racist and derived from a convenient environmental determinism that argued that Indians are by nature unhygienic and therefore extending technologies of modern sanitation such as a water-fed sewage system to Indian towns and Indian neighborhoods in large cities was not feasible. Similar arguments were made in colonial towns in other parts of the world. In 1913 a sewerage plan for both Old and New Delhi was shelved, being simply assumed that the new city and the

European civil lines should be connected to a water-fed sewage system "as a matter of policy," while even the "better Indian houses" in the old city would have to wait many years.[14] Such colonial policies of waste removal had important consequences at multiple scales—from the neighborhood to the city and its environments—as these implicated how labor, filth, and social distinctions were pressed into understandings of technology. Technological changes produced newer means of producing social stratification.

It was not until the 1920s that many urban locations in colonial India were regularizing indoor plumbing and flushing toilets by having older houses connected to city-wide sewage systems that made it unnecessary to manually remove the contents of the commodes to a dump. Here too, however, the cleaning of toilets was restricted to members of the *mehtar* community. Drawn from various low castes, varying by region—Bhangis, Khatiks, Sansis, Chamars, Chuhras, Reghars, Lodhas, Doms, Hadis, and others—they were joined "by their menialness."[15] *Mehtars* and their work were considered unclean and therefore their access to the house was controlled. Bathrooms were located on the periphery of the building, and the sweeper's access was typically mediated by a separate entrance exclusively for their use. In houses with multiple stories, a circular wrought-iron staircase gave the sweeper access to the bathrooms from the outside or from a dedicated stair space (Figure 8.2 and see Figure 4.10). Before plumbing, *bhistis* or water carriers also used these back stairs to supply the bathrooms, but their access to other parts of the house was less restricted.

Nikhil Rao in his discussion of apartment buildings in the Dadar-Matunga neighborhoods of Bombay from the 1920s and 1930s shows that there was a lingering preference among middle-class Indians for the toilet to be located outside the house but connected with a verandah. Its gradual incorporation within the enclosed area of the house was made acceptable by its location right upon entry to the house, so the sweeper would not have to traverse through the living spaces to get to the toilet.[16] This was also a plan strategy in contemporaneous houses in Calcutta. Rao makes the important point that the migration of the toilet into the flat "was not simply a matter of increased convenience as it was in the cities of Europe and North America; rather it entailed a conceptual transformation in how the disposal of bodily wastes was perceived by upper-caste middle classes." With efficient plumbing and flushing technologies displacing the nightsoil worker, the disposal of bodily waste was increasingly starting to be seen from a modern "sanitary" point of view rather than from the point of view of caste. This switch to the sanitary point of view, Rao argues, helped upper-caste middle-class families now living in suburban apartments to view themselves *as* middle class.[17]

The acceptance of the sanitary viewpoint did not preclude caste prejudices in terms of the removal and cleaning of bodily waste. The racial-caste prejudices of colonial society were deeply ingrained in the principles of

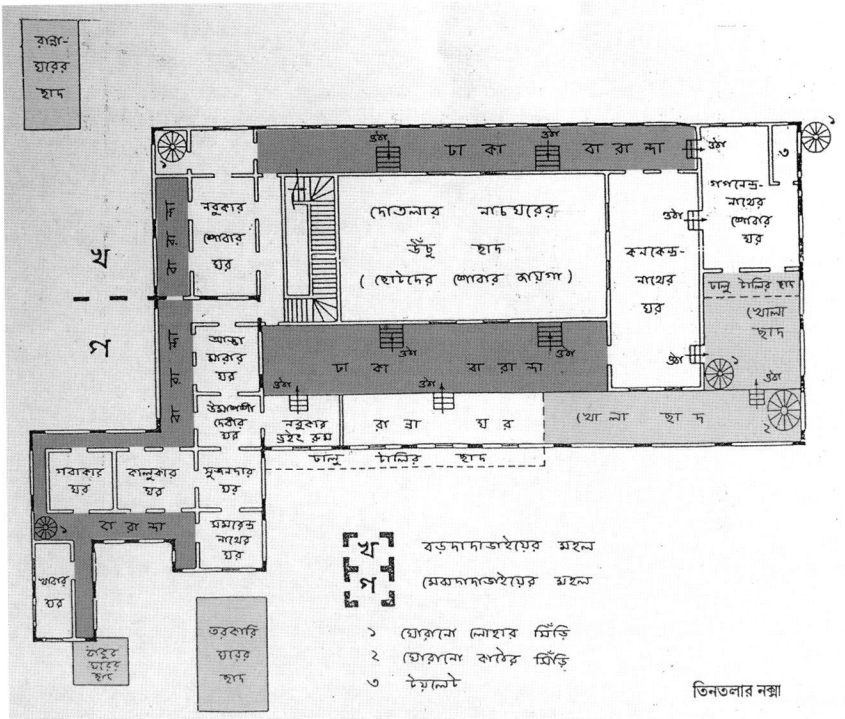

FIGURE 8.2 Third floor plan of Tagore Mansion, 5 Dwarakanath Tagore Lane. Verandahs and terraces are marked in dark and light shades, respectively. The residence had three iron spiral staircases and a larger wooden one in the south verandah. Source: Sumitendranath Tagore, *Thakurbarir Jana Ajana* (Kolkata: Mitra & Ghosh, 2001).

modern sanitation in India. House designs in the first decades of the twentieth century in Bombay, Calcutta, and other locations demonstrate this quite clearly. In a large house constructed in the 1920s in the suburb of Alipore in Calcutta by the colonial government for its senior officers, the bathrooms were located on the opposite side of the "clean" service yard next to the kitchen (Figure 8.3).[18] This distinction between clean and dirty serving spaces in a modern house with running water, electricity, and gas lines, was not so much a function of sanitation as it was a function of caste relations. The two bathrooms on each floor were attached to two bedrooms, but the bathrooms were so planned as to be connected to each other. This created a separate circuit for the sweeper. The sweeper would be let in from the inside and the doors leading to the bedrooms would be closed from the bedroom side. After the sweeper had cleaned both bathrooms, the door to the outside would again be locked. This was a daily practice that completely

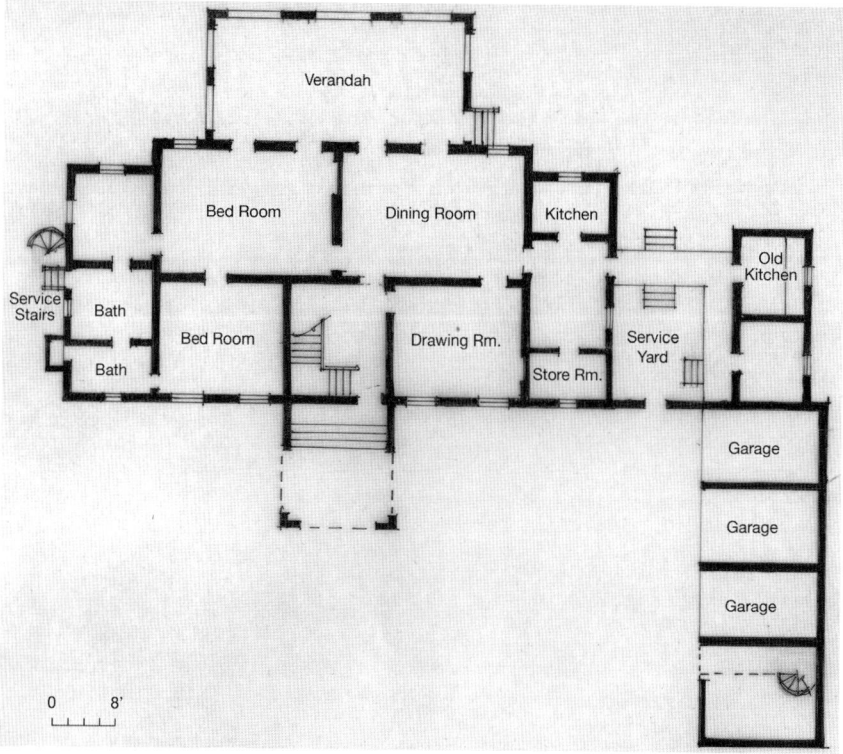

FIGURE 8.3 Ground Floor Plan of 28 Raja Santosh Road, Calcutta, built *c.* 1920s. © Swati Chattopadhyay.

separated the sweeper's movements from that of the residents as well as other servants who had access to other parts of the house.

Prosthetic Trace

Like all representations, architectural plans have their limitations in what they convey about social relations. The information we glean from reading plans—the distinction between servants' spaces and served spaces that we habitually use to differentiate between spaces occupied by servants and those spaces occupied by the master's family—is, however, not as helpful to our understanding of social history as it might appear at first glance. This form of distinction does not pan out when we pay attention to the temporal patterns of social life. Servants and the enslaved were everywhere, at all times. They slept on the floor in the passage in case the mistress needed them at night.[19] Indoors, they pulled fans all day so that residents could dine, relax, and work in comfort. Outdoors, they walked all night to prepare a camp site, waited there for the arrival of the master's family, and then served them a hot breakfast.[20]

In some cases, as at Monticello, we find finely calibrated techniques of separating the enslaved from the master. Design strategies such as placing the service spaces in the basement were intended not so much to remove, as to sublimate enslaved labor—to render it more efficient and acceptable—with the use of ingenious contraptions such as dumbwaiters and revolving service doors that are often, if incorrectly, referred to as labor-saving devices.[21] These are a form of architectural prosthetics: technologies that as extension of limbs and organs compensate for incapacities and thus reorganize the spatial and temporal parameters of labor.

Take the mechanical fan that Thomas Jefferson designed for his dining room at Monticello (Figure 8.4). The design sketch and notes are in the form of instruction. Imagined as a wound-up clock mechanism, this contraption would have relieved the dining room of the presence of an enslaved person fanning the diners using either a whisk fan or a pull-fan known as a punkah, a technology that had traveled to colonial America from colonial India.[22] Making enslaved labor invisible is only one aspect of this contraption. More important for Jefferson was to increase the efficiency of labor by saving labor time, so labor could then be more profitably deployed elsewhere.

His notes are instructive:

> Let a strong axis pass from the W. side of the skylight square through the East wall of the Din^{ing} Rm just below the cornice, presenting it, square end in the passage above stairs at (a) on which a pendulum is to be fixed ... A cord round the barrel of the swing wheel carried to a pulley (e) over the well of the stairs, and having a heavy weight (f) will put the swing wheel into motion.[23]

The task of fanning the diners in person would have cost Jefferson one hour of an enslaved boy's labor. Had this contraption been built, the same labor could have been performed by an adult enslaved man in a fraction of that time. However, to make an 8-foot fan move the air to any degree would require a good deal of exertion in winding up the machine. Jefferson concluded the instruction with the caveat that to make the machine effective "the weight must be proportionally increased & consequently the exertion in winding up."[24]

Machines that could operate without any expendable, or at least observable, power source represented the "holy grail" for engineers and tinkerers in the antebellum United States. Jefferson wrote with contempt about the exhibition of one such supposed device by Charles Redheffer, who charged people a fee to observe a "perpetual motion machine" through a barred window. In this scam, the machine was powered by a hand crank turned by an old man who was shut inside an adjacent windowless room

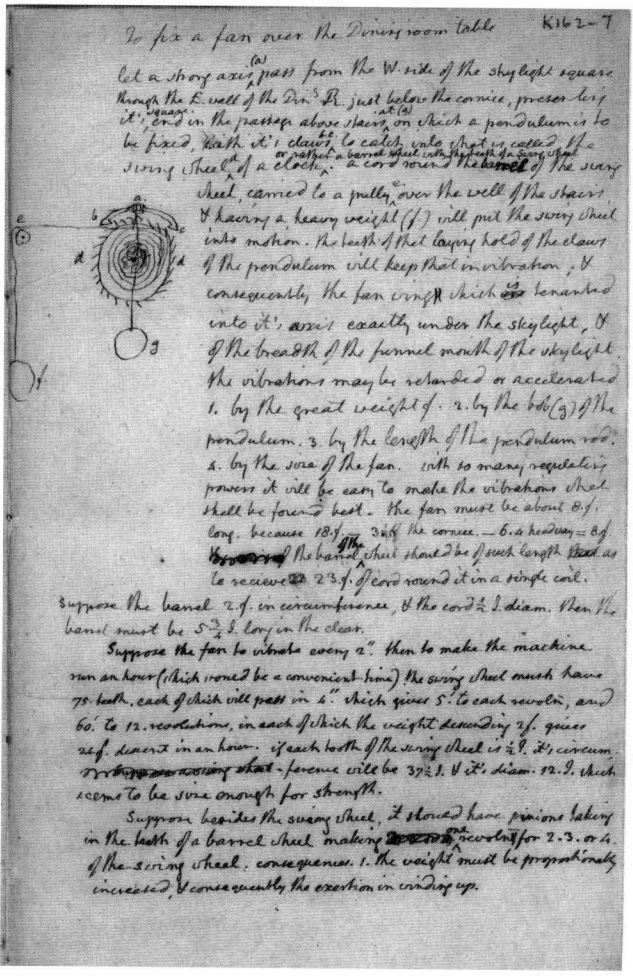

FIGURE 8.4 Thomas Jefferson, "To fix a fan over the Dining room table," Notebook of Improvements, Monticello, Virginia, 1804–7. K 162–7, Coolidge Collection of Thomas Jefferson Manuscripts, Massachusetts Historical Society.

(and fed only bread and water) (Figure 8.5).[25] Jefferson disdained not only the visual trick but also the wasteful labor. His own fan design is haunted by a similar laboring presence, however. The fan-machine intercedes to enhance the aesthetics of comfort and privacy in the dining room and in so doing enables the master to reorganize the field of production—both indoors and outdoors.

The desire for a mechanism that would *extend* rather than "save" labor power remains in Jefferson's architecture as a prosthetic trace, as the adjunct space of the "passage" and the "well of the stairs," as the boundary-work

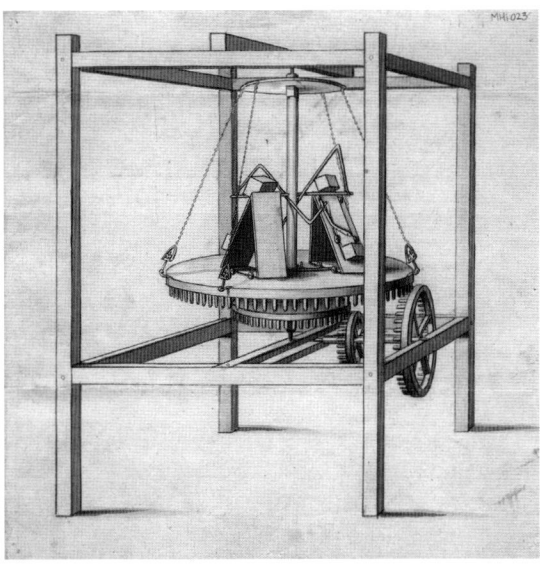

FIGURE 8.5 Charles Redheffer, perpetual motion machine, 1812. Wikimedia Commons.

that sustains the image of consumption as labor-saving creative production. The economy of comfort proceeded along parallel lines in colonial India.

Free and Unfree Labor

Both Indian and European families in colonial India, in addition to wage-earning servants, had enslaved domestic servants well into the nineteenth century. Runaway slaves were advertised in gazettes and newspapers, and they appear in early colonial landscape paintings and portraiture. As Nitin Sinha in his discussion of domestic servants in early colonial India says, "the label 'servant' concealed many other types of relationship."[26] Domestic service resided in a continuum between unfree labor and "free" waged coolie labor.[27] Despite differences in terms of legal definitions between an enslaved person and a wage-earning servant, social conditions permitted "permeability."[28] Hierarchies within the servant rank were based on Mughal practices and caste hierarchies of labor that were reshaped under British colonial rule. Sinha attends to the distinction between two categories, *naukar* and *chakar*. *Naukars* were upper-class servants comprising *munshi* (teacher), *khansamah* (house steward), *sarkar* (manager), while *chakars* were lower-class servants such as *khidmutger* (table servants), bearer, *abdar* (water cooler), *bawarchi* (cook), *mehtar*, all of whom performed "menial labor."[29] As I note in Chapters 4 and 5, depending on the household, some of these servants could not only be well-respected members of their communities, but highly skilled and literate, quite different from menial labor. The cook in Government House was an upper-class servant. This servant hierarchy, already somewhat unstable in the eighteenth century, when the servants also included enslaved boys and girls, would change by the mid-nineteenth century with the emergence of the "coolie" as a particular label for unskilled wage labor.

John Borthwick Gilchrist in his *Dialogues* (1826), a colloquial guide to the language of north India that he termed "Hindoostanee," translated coolie (spelled "qoolee") as "slave." The phrase "bearer is in our tongue a very low word, like slave, or drudge," was to be translated into Hindoostanee as "bearer humaree zuban men buree neech bat hue, juesa qoolee ya muzdoor."[30] Written before the mass transportation of indentured labor from Asia to North American and African plantations commenced, Gilchrist's understanding of coolie as the meanest labor form is likely based on the prevailing use of the term for bonded labor, derived from the Turkic *qul*, meaning slave. Here Gilchrist is specifically pointing out their low status.[31]

Ravi Ahuja in a discussion of labor in the Madras Presidency notes that the fortifications of Fort St. George in the eighteenth century were built by thousands who were recruited from the surrounding villages based on a much older tradition of the government's right to *al-amanji* or corvée service, and such services continued to be extracted into the second half of the nineteenth century "to fulfill transport requirements of travelling government officials."[32] Ahuja also makes the important point that the East India Company (EIC) resorted to military violence when such laborers were not supplied by the upper strata of the peasantry:

> There are frequent references to activities like "pressing coolies" or "catching coolie carpenters" in the Company's records, especially in those of the early 1780s when the most serious crisis of early colonial rule occurred. This was not merely a practice of *al-amanji* or corvée: Tribute in labour was transformed into another variation of involuntary service as a new model state with military despotic features emerged from the almost incessant wars of late-eighteenth-century South India. Armed press gangs recruited labourers not only for short-term tasks but also for longer periods of employment … The labour relations of these construction workers, grass cutters or *kulis* appear to have been created on the model of those of contemporary European soldiers and sailors who had often not chosen their employer (the state) freely though they were compensated with wages.[33]

The description of all menial labor as coolie labor—voluntary and involuntary—likely began in the second quarter of the nineteenth century.

The employment of large numbers of servants was a feature of colonial rule between the late eighteenth and mid-twentieth centuries. Elizabeth

King, the civilian's wife whom I refer to earlier in this chapter, was forthright in noting that the wages were the only cost of the servants since the servants feed themselves, except the "dhai" (wet nurse) who had to be given food in addition to wages. Since the dhai's nourishment had a direct correlation with the production of milk to feed the white baby, the mistress had to ensure this servant was adequately fed. The dhai lost caste by being fed from the house, and had to "pay a fine to be readmitted to caste privileges" on leaving their employment. The only other cost for servants they incurred was a "suit of warm clothes to the coachman and a half a dozen other." These only cost "a few rupees a head, and generally last two cold seasons." She approved the overall economy of this method:

> For this cost you could hardly keep five servants at home, and, however good those five might be, their goodness would not extend to being in thirty-two places at once. So that on the whole you get far more comfort from your Indian than from your English servants.
>
> India would simply be intolerable with only five servants and those five with English ideas and ways.[34]

She hastened to point out that this comparison only works for the "average" servant in each country. And because of their "national characteristics," an Indian servant could not quite match a "thoroughly experienced, devoted, and well-educated English one."[35] Her frequent mention of the trouble her servants took to provide food and comfort for her family under the utmost trying circumstances acknowledged a dependence she deeply felt.

Jefferson's elite European contemporaries in late-eighteenth-century colonial India typically chose to portray themselves with servants: the presence of servants added value, contextualized the European subject's location in the landscape, and conveyed authority. Servants were needed to keep the outside world at bay. Domestic laborers provided a protective envelope for Europeans in India, but the economy of laboring bodies, in their excessive presence, was a constant source of racial anxiety. A painting of the Auriol and Dashwood families in Calcutta by Johann Zoffany is a case in point (**Plate 11**).

Created in the mid-1780s, the painting depicts members of the Auriol, Dashwood, and Prinsep families, which included senior merchants in the EIC as well as officials in the EIC's army and civil service. The families grew wealthy because of these positions as well as through private trade and investment in plantations. In addition to family members, the painting shows five servants, all finely dressed, suggestive of the elevated social rank of the families: a *hookahburdar* standing near a tree prepares John Prinsep's smoking pipe, as Prinsep and two of the Auriol brothers, Charles and John, engage in conversation. On the right edge of the picture, a *hurkarah*, or mail carrier, hands a letter to James Auriol, causing him to look away from his chess game with the seated Thomas Dashwood, while his *sarkar*, or manager, stands nearby with bills in his hand. Two women are seated at Dashwood's right; they are Charlotte and Sophia Auriol, the wives of John Prinsep and Thomas Dashwood, respectively.

At the very center of the composition, just behind and between Charlotte and Sophia Auriol, a servant pours water into a silver teapot held by a darkskinned boy (Figure 8.6). This boy is likely John Auriol's enslaved child servant, euphemistically called Nabob (*nabab* means a royal deputy or prince). We know of this boy because Auriol gifted him to the Calcutta lawyer William Hickey to accompany Hickey on a visit to England.[36] Nabob labored as a personal servant, attending to the immediate comfort of his master and mistress. This would no doubt include the task of fanning them in warm weather, as shown in a contemporary painting of Lady Impey in Calcutta, by Shaikh Zain al-din (**Plate 12**).[37]

Zain al-din's painting shares one feature with Zoffany's painting of the Auriol and Dashwood families: the servants form a spatial envelope of sorts in the representation of the masters and mistresses. The architectural suggestion of Zain al-Din's painting is both specific and capacious. It calls out every object in the room and its architectural details, but in conveying the house as a set of visually connected spaces he registers the spatial organization of elite houses in Calcutta. The diminutive figures of servants and the enslaved in the center of the compositions seem to fit into the crevices of a larger space. They blend with the space—one has to be pay attention to notice them. But they are there for sure. This proximity of bodies, their relation of serving and being served, entertaining and being entertained, comforting and being comforted, creates a spatial link with which to read the architectural space of these settings.

FIGURE 8.6 Detail of Zoffany, *The Auriol and Dashwood Families in Calcutta.*

If writings, paintings, and other visual depictions reveal that servants and the enslaved resided in the very center of the narrative of European families and social life in the eighteenth and nineteenth centuries, architectural drawings do not make this relationship straightforwardly evident, given the putative separation between served and service spaces that we see in plans. The problem is simple. If a modest family of two or three had at least eight to twelve domestic servants, and people in the middling services had about sixteen to twenty servants—the numbers of domestic servants increasing with rank, with the governor-general at the apex with a contingent of 300—where did the servants live? If many of them had homes in the city, that still left a very large number of servants on the premises. Considering they were expected to be at hand all the time, where would they be in these buildings, and how might they have understood their experience of space?

Plans become useful here when we consider not necessarily what they *show* at the building or urban scale, but instead what they do not reveal.[38] Depending on one's point of view, such houses could be seen as protected or besieged. But even that does not show us the ubiquity of laboring bodies. Unless the function is specifically grounded to a space, the plan is blind.

Consider a plan of a bungalow in the town of Jhelum in the Punjab sketched during the years of the Sepoy Rebellion of 1857–9 (see Figure 4.2). The rebellion began as a mutiny of the soldiers or sepoys of the EIC and became a full-scale rebellion against British rule. Arthur or Archie Wood, a captain in the EIC's army, rented this bungalow located just outside the military cantonment of Jhelum, where he lived with his wife Minnie and their infant children. Their house and nearby cantonment were caught in the maelstrom of the rebellion: the regiment stationed at Jhelum mutinied on July 7, 1857.[39]

In this otherwise simple and typical plan of a colonial bungalow, there are two rooms on the left marked with Minnie's name: her private dressing room and the storeroom. The dressing room had two doors opening to the back of the house and was also the location of the nurse's bed. The nurse was the sole European servant—a subaltern's wife hired to care for Minnie during her final weeks of pregnancy and her confinement.[40] The sweeper would have to go through this room to clean the bathroom, and the sweeper was at hand all through the day. The private dressing room was thus not very private. In contrast, Minnie's husband who drafted this plan had a whole room for his private use, and anointed the master bedroom as "Our Bed Room."

The storeroom, on Minnie's side of the bungalow, turned out to be the only room that Minnie felt was her own. The plan's annotation points out that it is "especially for her own use." The storeroom was for the storage of household provisions: Minnie issued daily supplies to the cook from this space.[41] Note that Minnie's storeroom is the size of the room allocated to Captain Wood's personal attendant, the *sardar bearer*. And yet Minnie felt a sense of pride for having her "own store room." The importance of the storeroom was based not upon size or the monetary value of what was stored inside. Rather, it was premised on the fact that servants were not allowed unrestricted access to the room.

Minnie struggled in her role as mistress of the house. She did not know the local language and required her husband's help to translate basic instructions to servants, and her husband was annoyed by her inability to cook jellies and custards—signals of polite status in colonial society. Minnie's house was in constant upheaval: her children cried and she and her husband yelled at the servants.[42] Minnie's failure as a mistress resided in her inability to convey the virtue of idleness—to aspire "by hidden method and management to give a surface impression of large leisure."[43]

Employing between ten and sixteen servants at various times, the Woods fell into debt and had to justify their expenses. One of the two most expensive items on their list was servants. Captain Wood wrote by way of explanation:

> During the hot season, 7 months of the year, we require many more to pull the punkahs and water the tatties, etc. The latter are the reed blinds which are hung in the doorways, etc., and kept sprinkled with water to try to afford a little cool air. Four punkah coolies are *absolutely* necessary to be in attendance *day and night* at our house. *You* cannot imagine what the *heat* is during the *hot months*. These four men each receive four rupees, which makes additional 16 rupees for servants.[44] (emphasis in the original)

In addition to punkahs hung from the ceilings and reed mats over windows, as described by Captain Wood, the Woods' house had a thermantidote—a fan attached to a window that a servant moved manually to generate a breeze.[45]

Comfort and Menial Labor

The punkah, a large fan suspended from the ceiling of a room and manually operated by a servant to create a breeze, was not new to colonial India—it was a precolonial luxury enjoyed by elites, while the vast majority of people in India used handheld fans to cool themselves. By the early nineteenth century, what had been a luxury became a standard feature of the residences of Europeans and public buildings in India such as courtrooms, offices, and churches. As the idea of the debilitating effect of the "tropics" on the European constitution took hold in colonial medical circles, being fanned round the clock came to be regarded as a necessity (**Plate 13**). Initially operated by a servant standing in the same room (see Figure 6.3), the removal of the servant to an adjacent space, still connected by a rope to the fan, erected a visual barrier between masters and servants (Figure 8.7). Punkah design varied from region to region and changed over time. King

FIGURE 8.7 Madeline Hancock, "'Why don't he pull?' or The Sleeping Punkah Wallah," 1865–6. IOR WD3871, © British Library Board.

noted that in Awadh the punkahs in her house consisted of "deep heavy flounce of calico" hung from a stout pole, whereas those in her house in Sardhana had a "flat frame, sixteen inches wide from which the flounce hangs." The frame was simply painted white but King had it decorated with a border "taken from a fifteenth-century missal in two colors." The punkah frills used 15 to 18 yards of calico and some "Turkey red or other bordering to edge the flounces." The flounces cost her 13s each and she had ten of these punkahs in her house.[46] She also had a punkah rigged up for outdoor use when they dined in the garden as the evening temperature outdoors was lower than that inside the house.[47]

Speaking of her experience in the hot dry summers of the military station of Meerut, King made an argument about the peculiarity of the Indian heat to explain why punkahs were not required in Australia where temperatures soared just as high as in India:

> Every one who has been in India, and also in Africa and Australia, knows that, owing to some peculiarity of the atmosphere, heat is felt very much more in India than the same degree of heat in Australia would be. Of this there is sufficient proof in the fact that, although the thermometer

sometimes goes as high in Australia as it does here, yet the country can be colonized by Englishmen, nor are punkahs or tatties required to keep people or dogs alive. Whereas it has always been impossible to colonise the plains of India, as the second generation, or so many as survive childhood, are weak miserable creatures, destroyed in body and mind by the heat.

The heat, therefore, registered by the thermometer does not convey an accurate idea of the heat and suffering felt, and allowance must always be made for this.[48]

By the mid-nineteenth century a new category of menial laborer—the punkah coolie—emerged in India. In Australia no one needed punkahs or punkah coolies because the labor was not available. The job required strength and endurance, and employers recruited low-caste seasonal migrant labor especially for this work. As the residents of a home moved from one room to another, the punkah coolie moved with them the periphery of the building, usually without entering the room. Apart from their cooling function, punkahs hung very low over the bed helped keep away mosquitoes from the masters and mistresses while they slept. Doors and window were left open to facilitate a cross breeze, with light chintz curtains separating the space inside the bedroom from the space outside where the punkah pullers sat and moved the punkah.[49] Europeans regarded these servants as both a necessity and an unseemly presence. An indigenous object of utility and technique of tempering the climate—the punkah—became yoked to a new category of labor—the punkah coolie—to render the laboring body invisible.

The punkah coolie's work space was typically a verandah or hallway adjacent to the room where the punkah was installed; sometimes it was an unsheltered space outside the building (Figure 8.8). Characterized as lazy and recalcitrant, the punkah coolie became the object of a routine form of racialized humor. He was portrayed as negligently asleep at his post, needing to be rudely aroused to continue his task of providing comfort. If throwing a slipper and shoe, and then a chair, at him did not make the fan go faster, the punkah coolie received a good beating:

> The punkah-wind lulled, and the flounce was hushed into repose ... A boot, two boots, — a slipper, — two slippers, did we extend in vain as missiles, projecting with unerring precision at his head. We tried a chair, but no, the vile heathen was impervious to that; until a personal assault, effected to the detriment of our feet in kneading the outcaste's ribs did at last restore him from oblivion to his rope.[50]

The habitual violence was normalized as necessary violence and offered as proof of non-culpability when the coolie died from such assault.[51]

George Atkinson published his caricature of British social life in India, *Curry and Rice on Forty Plates*, in 1859, the year the Sepoy Rebellion ended.

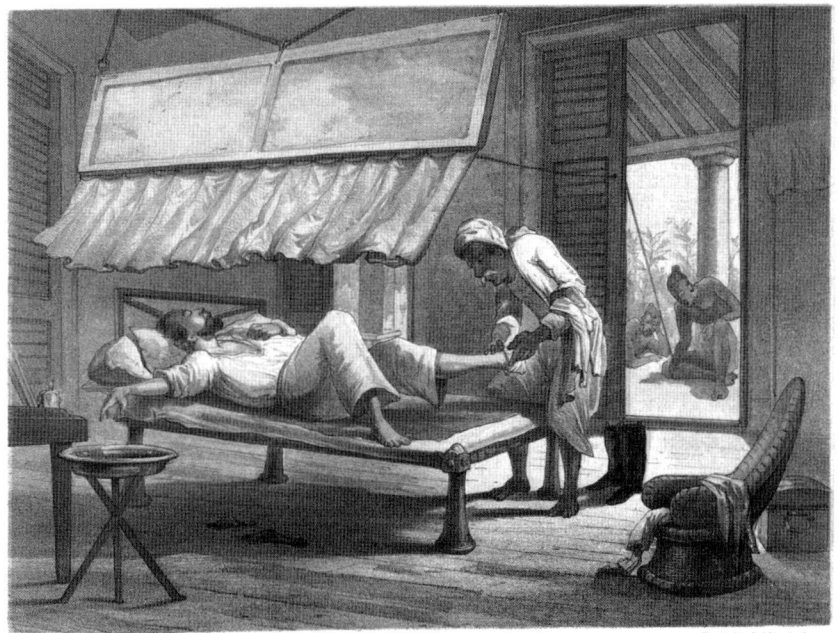

FIGURE 8.8 George F. Atkinson, "Our Bed Room," 1859. Illustration in Atkinson, *Curry and Rice on Forty Plates* (London: Day & Son, 1859).

In that work, he makes no secret of the scandalous proximity of Indians and Europeans in the European bungalow as a residence and work space.

Atkinson pokes fun at the anomalies in British social life, and for him the adjunct spaces such as verandahs offer prime locations for elucidating the odd excesses of colonial living (Figure 8.9). Here the Colonel's wife is surrounded by male tailors busily stitching a dress for her forthcoming ball. She is being touched and measured. The tailors' rude work habits, the closeness of their bodies, and the exposure of the verandah itself all violate the precious privacy and exclusive status to which European women in India were entitled.

The colonel himself is portrayed on his verandah with both a thermantidote and a punkah going round the clock (Figure 8.10). He is devoted to the art and science of keeping cool, reporting that "if you go inside the room, you will practically experience the effects by finding your hat blown off into an adjacent corner, and your hair blown indiscriminately and unpleasantly about your eyes and face."[52]

Atkinson's caricature shows Europeans in various degrees of leisure, even when at work. The Joint Magistrate holds court on his verandah, but his attention is directed toward the sporting page (Figure 8.11). The image militates against every claim of British superiority and authority. The only people who work are Indians. Atkinson transposes the habitual

FIGURE 8.9 George F. Atkinson, "Mrs. Capsicum, Our Colonel's Wife," 1859. Illustration in Atkinson, *Curry and Rice on Forty Plates* (London: Day & Son, 1859).

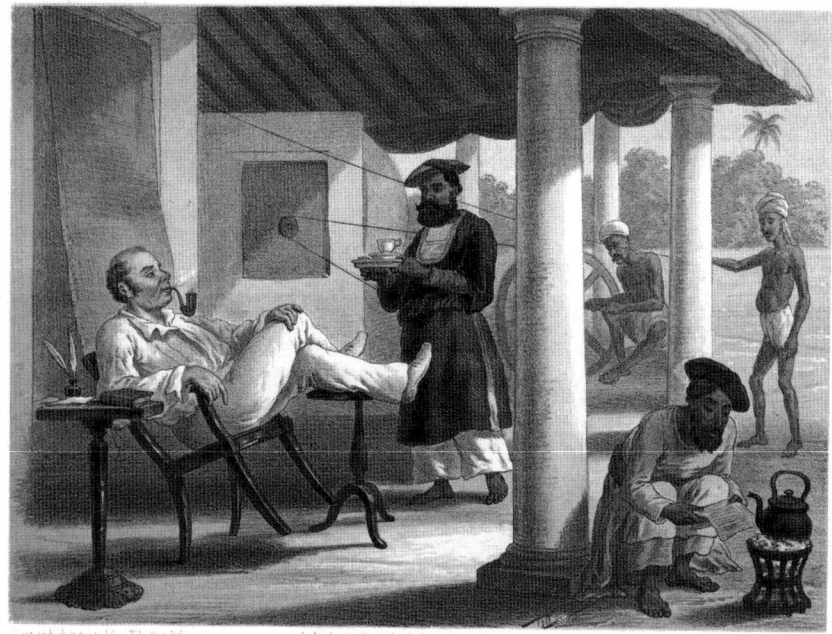

FIGURE 8.10 George F. Atkinson, "Capsicum, Our Colonel," 1859. Illustration in Atkinson, *Curry and Rice on Forty Plates* (London: Day & Son, 1859).

FIGURE 8.11 George F. Atkinson, "Huldey, Our Joint Magistrate and Collector," 1859. Illustration in Atkinson, *Curry and Rice on Forty Plates* (London: Day & Son, 1859). Courtesy of Yale Center for British Art, Paul Mellon Collection.

characterization of the servants as lazy to the Europeans themselves. The blurred lines between authority and laziness, control and excess, Indian and European bodies would have been particularly disturbing in the immediate wake of the Sepoy Rebellion, given the sensational narratives of the deaths of European women and children that came out of that conflict.

As the army was reorganized along racial lines and with the redesign of military cantonments after the Sepoy Rebellion, the methods used to cool army barracks became a prime arena for experimentation. Several attempts involved systems of multiple punkahs in trains of six to eight. The goal of such an assembly was to maximize comfort while economizing on coolie labor. Careful calculations were undertaken to demonstrate how many fans one coolie could pull, and how strong a coolie had to be to accomplish the task: "a train of 6 punkahs in a train is about the average weight that coolies working in three reliefs can be fairly expected to pull." "Occasional cases," demanded a train of eight punkahs which would require "selection of strong coolies and the reliefs should be shorter." The Mortimer frame punkah invented in the 1870s became the model of choice because it allowed the simultaneous operation of several fans in adjacent rooms.[53] In 1878, the army in the Bengal Presidency hired 18,000 punkah coolies.

Colonial military authorities highlighted labor efficiency by providing detailed instructions for the optimal installation of Mortimer punkahs. In a guide to military construction published in 1910 and reprinted in 1921, they recommended precise dimensions for the frames from which punkahs were to be suspended: within a barrack room with a 16-foot ceiling, "the frame should be 10' or more from the point of suspension and about 8' from the floor. This is not always easy to arrange for now that the height of a Barrack room has been reduced to 16 ft. If the points of suspension are made too high the punkah will swing too slowly."[54] Another rod placed above the joist and an elaborate stabilizing contraption of transverse wires provided a solution (Figure 8.12): "Care should be taken that there are not too many punkahs in one train, one Mortimer frame, or two at most, being as much as a man can possibly pull satisfactorily for any length of time. In married quarters a train usually consists of the single punkahs in four or five rooms, and a right-angle pull will be necessary for the central rooms of long blocks."[55]

The diagram accompanying these descriptions fixes on the pulling and stabilizing mechanism of the punkah, as a manual of best practices for military buildings. To think of this as a design detail, however, misses the

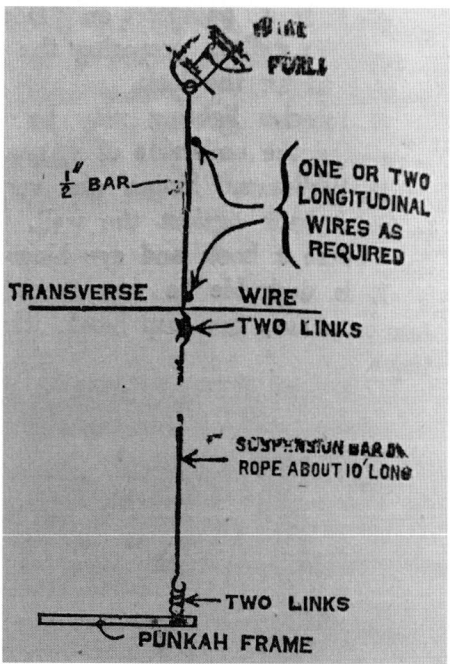

FIGURE 8.12 Diagram for positioning and stabilizing a punkah frame. Illustration in Major E. Stokes-Roberts, *Some Practical Points in the Design and Construction of Military Buildings in India* (1910; repr. Calcutta: Superintendent Government Printing, 1921).

imagination of labor and laboring bodies, the aesthetics of comfort, and the relation between served and service space that this contrivance presumes and prescribes. Represented as a rational design feature—as part of a system—the mechanism erases the coolies and the non-spaces that those bodies inhabited. The abstraction from slave labor to punkah coolie to mechanical device is complete. It is this form of invisibility we take for granted in architectural thinking.

When we read of Robert Kerr strictly separating servants' spaces from masters' spaces for the mutual ease of servants and masters, or Thomas Jefferson's use of elaborate spatial devices to separate servants and the enslaved from himself and his guests, we assign these designs to the category of modern improvement, even while condemning Kerr's and Jefferson's class and race ethics. At the same time, the sheer ingenuity of these kinds of modern improvements invites a glimmer of admiration. Their mechanical cunning helps us to overlook the translation of such methods to the contemporary present we inhabit. We ignore the fact that these strategies and mechanisms achieve their goals by conferring invisibility upon the servants who are still present for cleaning, serving, offering comfort, and providing sexual labor. The abstraction of labor is accomplished when the line between human and mechanical labor becomes a site of prosthetic intervention.

It is this metaphoric transfer that supports the distinction between inhabited spaces and mechanical spaces as served and service spaces in modern architecture.[56] It does so by extending the prejudice of color, caste, and class lines to mute conduits of mechanical servicing of comfort: air ducts, cooling systems, dumbwaiters. We ignore that an entire ecology of labor surrounding dirt, waste, disease, cleanliness, and consumption works as a substratum for such social distinctions. These connections remain invisible unless we begin with the small spaces and laboring bodies, and pay attention to the microdynamics of power that link everyday occurrences, ordinary lives, and epoch-shaping events.

Escape

Returning to the Woods' house plan, one wonders where the punkah coolies sat while they worked. The dining and drawing room could be serviced from the verandah. The fans in the other two rooms were likely linked to the puller through walls facing the garden. Either no provision was made to shelter the pullers occupying the open space outside, or they occupied nominal adjacent spaces simply ignored by the plan. For the Woods the ubiquity of servants in the house was in inverse proportion to their acknowledgment in the plan.

Servants saw this landscape differently. They made broader connections between the domestic spaces in which they worked, the European masters, the cantonment, governance, and labor. The bungalow, as well as nodes of military and civil administration—the cantonment, *kachhari* (office/court), along with railway lines and telegraph and postal connections—were made into expressive targets of insurgency.[57] When the Sepoy Rebellion commenced, one of the *khidmutgers* (table servants) left the Woods' household, saying he would enter the service of "his King," the Mughal Emperor in Delhi, "where he would get much better pay."[58] Minnie could not believe the servant's impertinent and exalted sense of self—that an ordinary servant could draw such connections between employment, labor, and sovereignty. The rebellion was brought "home" to the Woods not only through armed conflict, but also through such everyday open defiance, as servants walked away from their employment, grumbled at not being paid in a timely manner, and dared to speak back to their masters as equals. The servants, Minnie wrote, anticipated a leveling of status distinctions: "They are most insolent, and think nothing of telling you that soon *we shall all be in the service* of the King of Delhi" (emphasis added).[59] That servants could speak back to the masters about a world turned upside down came as a shock to Minnie: in that world the masters, too, would become servants, leaving only one sovereign in Delhi.

The plan of the Woods' bungalow illuminates this conflict. It was prepared when Archie Wood sought payment for damages at the end of the Sepoy Rebellion: the house was "sacked, looted and spoiled by the Mutineers on 7 July," 1857. "We have no compensation," Wood complained.[60]

Four years later, in October 1861, Minnie Wood sailed for England, leaving her husband and her three children in India.[61]

PART THREE

Land Imagination

9

Vantage

The process through which land beyond Europe was transformed into an imperial landscape depended on certain rhetorical conventions: *arrival and first view* at landfall; travel through the interior of a foreign land while the *surroundings are revealed* as landscape; and an *elevated location* from which to survey the land. These modes of seeing the land (and people) as passive and amenable to representation, elicit mastery and control and constitute the vantage of imperial history.

Now consider this description of flood waters in a small village in eastern Bengal (present-day Bangladesh) in the second decade of the twentieth century:

> Before dawn the news reaches that the water has entered Ghosh-bari's *khal*. We run to see—everyone young and old. The water advances in a torrent: the canal is filling up with gurgling water.
>
> The canal fills up. The water from the full canal turns south and enters the *ghat*, the steps of Nandi's Pukur. We run along the water . . .
>
> . . . the fields, the ghats, and all the paths in the village sink under water: the banks overflow, the water approaches the boundaries of the house. And then one day it moves into the *andarmahal*—inside the courtyard of the house . . . the water rises five fingers, ankle deep, knee deep—up to the waist and then the gurgling stops . . .
>
> Grandmother hauls us on to the daowa and make us sit.[1]

Rani Chanda's recollection of running along with the flood waters as a child and her view of the land from the circumscribed space of the "daowa" (raised porch) in this village home invokes a land imagination that cannot be understood through our disciplinary practices of seeing land as landscape, be it in history, art history, geography, or architectural history. The excerpt is from a memoir written as a travel narrative of sorts: a family's seasonal return to their village home. This village, seemingly "not even remotely global," the daowa of which we have no history, and the narrative mode that plays with durational imagination ask us to switch modes of thinking about travel and global connections.[2] The daowa as elevated vantage does not produce mastery, but elicits an ethic of slow looking as the canal, the courtyard, and the land become one with the flood waters.

The vantage creates a narrative frame. Paul Carter notes that the conceit of imperial history resides in a substitution—replacing the contingencies and complexities of a "spatial event" with a stage in which history simply happens. The historian stands outside the frame of events and pulls aside the curtains to show the unfolding drama of history. The goal of imperial history, Carter writes, is "not to understand or to interpret: it is to legitimate." Imperial history's "defensive appeal to the logic of cause and effect" in narrating how a chaotic world is made orderly requires "fixed and detachable facts" such as houses, clearings, and boats at anchor.[3] The peripatetic colonial explorer/administrator finds them as such: "For these, unlike the intentions which brought them there, unlike the material uncertainties of lived time and space, are durable objects which can be treated as typical, as further evidence of a universal historical process." Detached from the historical process of their making, such objects "can be fitted-out with new paternities," enabling their recirculation in historical discourse.[4] The visualization of history as a stage set or as a diorama, available to the gaze of the historian/reader, is so commonplace that we forget to not only question such narrative framing, but to ask who is assumed to be the viewer in this form of history.[5]

In contrast to Carter's insistence on a figure of the traveler "whose gaze is oriented and limited," travel in imperial history is privileged by endowing its subject with uncontained vision. Empire is narrated as a terrain crisscrossed by marching armies and caravans, officials on circuit, and surveyors, scientists, and missionaries traversing the field. It elicits what David Arnold calls the "traveling gaze."[6] The documentary products of this traveling gaze, collated and codified in a few centuries of travelogues, official memos, military reports, scientific musings, paintings, sketches, photographs, maps, and official reports, constitute the bulk of the imperial archive. Arnold's use of the phrase "traveling gaze" is indebted to the Foucauldian idea of the gaze as a disciplining, ordering, and surveilling mechanism that pervades the practice of modern sciences such as botany and zoology. The products of this gaze assert the geographical fact of empire through lines, points, trajectories, grids, and charts. The voluminous archive in its sheer plenitude demands abstraction and generalization. This is where we see an insistence on breaking down phenomena into taxonomies, categories, typologies, disciplines. The viewer remains in control, and manages to be both in the field of action and exploration and distanced from it. It is this dual move that construes land as landscape. It also assumes that only some people would be endowed with the vantage from which to see the totality of landscape and thereby to produce historical narratives.

Carter's and Arnold's critiques notwithstanding, the viewer standing on a high promontory gazing at a land has been so often used in representations of modern landscapes that some historians correlate this disposition with the act and privilege of writing history. The elevated position, John Gaddis contends, shifts perspective from the muddle of everyday life and enlarges experience. His iconic example is Casper David Friedrich's 1811 painting "Wanderer Above the Sea of Fog," an instance of Romantic painting whose rhetorical and compositional structure coincides with that of the imperial gaze and its search for mastery (**Plate 14**). The past for Gaddis is rightly construed as landscape: "[I]t's that act of representation that lifts us above the familiar to let us experience vicariously what we can't experience directly, a wider view."[7] If he recognizes the conscious role of the historian in the staging of history—the capacity to manipulate space and time—it is this ability, he contends, that lends historians their métier. What does the wider view offer? The importance of distance from the object of investigation, distancing, and disinterestedness come together as the value of abstraction, in being liberated from the limitations of time and space. This is an extraordinary claim, suffused with the aura of bigness, lack of constraint, immensity, and totality promoted in imperial history and its mode of imagining the land.

Abstraction

In a pithy article titled "Abstraction is a Privilege," Fernando Lara discusses the pervasive acceptance of abstraction in the language and disciplinary practice of architecture. He begins with Doreen Massey's reading of the encounter between Moctezuma and Cortez in 1519, in which each leader saw a different landscape in Tenochtitlan. Moctezuma, although an authoritarian leader, was "immersed in that space"—he "did not separate himself from all the people, goods, and lands under his government." In contrast, Cortez "developed the ability to remove himself from all that history in order to see only space that could serve his goals of riches and power."[8] Or as Philip Arnold notes, while the Aztec and Spanish occupied the same land, they inhabited "distinct landscapes."[9]

The English word "landscape" has a wide range of meanings and is used as a broad descriptor of land shaped by human intervention. The manner in which social relations are understood to be expressed in the material configuration of land, however, has a specific lineage going back to the early modern world. The terms *landschaft*, *landschap*, *landskip* became transformed into the eighteenth-century idea of landscape as an extensive, cultivated expanse dotted with villages, towns, and cities.[10] A landscape was best seen from a mountaintop and best depicted in a painting or on a map. It opened up a prospect—a vista—that enabled linking the near and far.

The European traditions of privileging sight in representations of land are not unique. In Sanskrit, Persian, and Arabic the idea of landscape has to do with seeing and enjoying a prospect.[11] The Sanskrit word for scenery, *drishya*, derives from the root *drish* (to see). In Persian *chasmaandaz* (outlook) and *tamashagah* (sight or scenery) have to do with sight, and *doornama* (prospect) refers to a distant view (*door* referring to distance). In Arabic, both *manzar* (view/viewing location; from *manzarat*; related to *nazar* or sight) and *mashaad* (view, related to *chahada*, to witness) convey the privilege of seeing.[12] The sense of landscape and atmosphere are brought together in the expression of seeing the land as *jǐngguān* (observe a scene) in Chinese. Like the term *fūkei* that originates in China and means wind and light, *shanshui* (literally mountain+water) is about a way of seeing that lightly touches the land; they refer more to atmosphere than the land itself. In none of these does "seeing," in the nominal sense, exhaust the possibilities of a hermeneutic of land occupation. Neither is the abstraction demanded by representation foreign to any of these pictorial, cartographic, and architectural moves. Abstraction is necessary to representation.[13] But here we might make distinctions about what is entailed by abstraction.

What distinguished the modern European modes of seeing was the "abstraction of human life from its material context."[14] In such a world, everything—the minerals underground, the products of the forests, and the conquered people—could be imagined as commodity. Thus, one could perhaps argue that unlike Cortez, what Moctezuma saw was not landscape in the English sense of the term, but a land ordered by a set of absolute (as opposed to abstract) relations with gods and subjects. This is to say that the social and material relations that constituted the land were quite different for the two imperial leaders. Cortez's sizing up of the land could "never have the locative character of the Aztecs."[15] This is not a distinction between insider and outsider, but the difference in their vantages of observation and enunciation.

Following up on Massey's argument that European colonial modernity reduced space to surface and constructed a geography that disregarded the depth created by a multitude of temporalities, Lara notes that this rise of abstraction as the defining condition of modern epistemes "killed relational processes that we urgently need to bring back to the table."[16] Abstraction, in its threefold incarnation—as geometrical fabrication of land, as flattening of temporality and spatiality, and as a mode of removing the viewer from the field of experience to enable subject formation—made it possible to apprehend conquered territories through the logic of extraction.

If we are not to reduce space to stage and surface, bounded geometrical figures that while admirably suited to a calculus of extraction do little else, we need to do more than look at travel, movement, and flows: we need to notice and shift vantage. By vantage I mean both the locational context of narration as well as the framework for interpreting the land and its occupants, humans and others. Here I question the spatial location and disposition of the subject in imaging and imagining the land. What might happen, I ask, if we abandon the high promontory from which to construct history? What might happen if we begin with a different ground plane and a different idea of staging a land?

Storytelling

In this part of the book, I turn to the verandah, daowa, courtyard, and terrace as launching spaces for telling stories. These spaces are not unmarked by authority. Nor are these always dimensionally small. Quite the contrary. For example, the verandah during the two centuries of British rule in India, spacious and raised from the ground, emerged as a peculiar site of power. But it also came to possess other characteristics that were less directed toward the exercise of dominance. I am interested in their specific articulation amid their repeated appearance in the archive, and their potential as narrative vantages.

In the chapters that follow I look at the manner in which these spaces are strategically mobilized in memoirs to narrate colonial lifeworlds. I deploy the verandah, daowa, courtyard, and terrace to reposition our approach to land and territory. This method acknowledges that different vantages engender different modes of storytelling. Looking from these spaces or making them narrative loci induces a shift in scale: the proximity of people, things, and events that come within purview demand a self-conscious positioning. It encourages "slow looking," dwelling on the materiality of everyday things, the rhythms of daily life, noticing small changes. Slow looking exceeds the practice of close observation conducted in the sciences and art history. In art history close observation focuses on the details of material, color, composition, and assembly, with its primary goal being to elucidate the source, provenance, use, and ultimately to explain the cause: what factors contribute to its creation, form, and circulation, and how it functions as representation. In close observation, the viewer sets the parameters of seeing and analysis. Slow looking, in contrast, is not prompted by the viewer's volition and intent, but from something that occurs without the viewer anticipating: it's a response to a mild tremor in the everyday sequence of events that inflects attention. Slow looking slows down the "quick jump to representational thinking and evaluative critique."[17] It enables picking out connections that are not dominant or bold, those that defy the language of representation and might pass under the radar of authority.

Tying strategies of storytelling to particular vantages does not exhaust narrative possibilities, but acknowledges the sites and conditions of enunciation. The shift allows glimpses of lifeworlds—modes of imagining and inhabiting space—that are not recognizable when the premise of understanding resides in distantiation, in gaining a "wider view" in time and space.

As spaces that draw their meaning from their in-betweenness—as connective pieces between other spaces—the spaces are peculiarly open to multiple uses, significations, and reframing, and as in the services spaces discussed in Part Two challenge the correspondence between form and function insinuated in typologies. In the stories I offer, the spaces erode and exceed their understanding as a type and emerge as spatial events. And once we learn to see the verandah, daowa, courtyard, and terrace not as bounded architectural entities, self-evident in their material articulation, but as spatial events that gather meaning in their immersion in everyday life—changing, transforming, and being transformed—we undertake certain crucial operations.

To begin, we dissolve the unidirectionality that governs the relation between viewer as producer of knowledge and the site that is seen as a source of extraction (of materials, knowledge, people). Here the site is no longer something that the traveler/historian encounters as preparatory to enlarging one's imagination. The site enfolds the viewer in myriad sensory invitations and warps. The assurance of a distantiated contemplation dissolves. In its capacity to generate connections—in its "thingness," as Tim Ingold would put it—the site lays surprising claims on the storyteller/historian.[18] You run with the water as it rushes in. You look fascinated-repelled at the eviscerated body of a bird as it is made into an object. These claims are experienced as affective sparks between humans and the nonhuman world, in the eddies of everyday life in expected and unplanned ways.

The unitary historical narrative and its neat correspondence between evidence and narration, between building and inhabitation, falls apart. We are confronted with the shape-shifting characteristics of space: rather than as fixed objects defined by the obdurate materiality of floors, roofs, and walls, they appear soft, contingent, fungible. If space is perceived differentially based on one's social position, these stories make us aware of how such differentiations are articulated and deployed. Just so I am not misunderstood, this effect is not limited to personalization of space, while that may very well be one part of change in space. And it is not confined to deciphering cultural patterns that invariably assume a group identity.[19] It is about the connections one gathers with that space—the range of images, objects, and associations—that are invoked to tell "spatial stories."

In borrowing the term "spatial stories" from Michel de Certeau, I lean on his insight that stories transform "places into spaces or spaces into places" in innumerable ways. Here space is understood to be "a practiced place," that is a location activated by practice: "Space occurs as the effect produced by the operations that orient it, situate it, temporalize it, and make it function in a polyvalent unity of conflictual programs, contractual proximities."[20] Spatial stories are thus buoyed by ambiguity: "It 'turns' the frontier into a crossing, and the river into a bridge. It recounts inversions and displacements: the door that is closed is precisely what may be opened. The river is what makes passage possible."[21] A range of voices and narrative modes affirm the impossibility of a universal spatial experience or a unified meaning.[22]

In the spatial stories of the verandah, courtyard, terrace we learn to notice modern genealogies of crafting connections among spaces. These are the kinds of conceptual leaps that produce the connective tissues between shooting grounds, woods, garden, territory, and empire. We notice the kinds of turns in a story that short-circuit nationalist narratives. In such stories small spaces shed their character as vantage and transform into something else—a threshold, a fold, a seam—to enable expansion and contraction of narrative parameters.

10

Connective Spaces

Small spaces are thought of as additive to the main spaces of a building. They are seen as inessential to a building's primary function. They perform a certain supplementary role—to enhance, support, and extend the uses of the primary rooms. If that is true for the service spaces I discuss in Part Two, it is perhaps even more so with verandahs, courtyards, and terraces. Rather than seeing them as adjunct spaces, I focus on their role as connective pieces. When Robin Evans writes that corridors and passages as connective devices tell us something important about what kinds of social intercourse are encouraged or discouraged, he offers a critique of the universalizing propensities of architectural thinking about contemporary residential buildings and consequently "the power that the customary arrangement of domestic space exerts over our lives."[1] He urges us to notice that commonplace arrangements have particular histories. Changing modes of linking space suggest changing social relations, and new attempts at connecting across languages and cultural practices.

Connectors

A passage and living space, the term "verandah," of Portuguese origin, had gained popularity by the eighteenth century, and in practice became the standard designation for the semi-enclosed space that mediated between the inside and outside of a building in colonial India. The term became indigenized as *baranda* in Hindi and Bengali, and its use to describe the raised space, typically guarded by a railing in townhouses on the ground as well as upper floors, became the norm by the nineteenth century. The term might have something to do with *ver*, meaning "to see" in Portuguese. And that in Spanish *baranda* refers to "railing" nicely captures the meaning of verandah as a bounded space from which to observe.

The verandah was distinguished from similar porch-like structures prevalent in India, such as otla, daowa, and ro'ak. From India the spatial concept traveled to East Asia, North America, Australia, New Zealand, and Africa along the lines of European colonialism to become a global spatial type. In the process the word was absorbed into the English language. The term was sometimes used interchangeably with porch, and in North America with the term "piazza," where it came to be linked with picturesque landscape design.[2] The widespread use of the verandah in South Asia and port cities of East Asia by the mid-nineteenth century came to be identified as an important feature of "tropical architecture."[3]

The verandah acquired particular connotations of power and pleasure in its association with colonialism and the kind of urban life that emerged during British colonial rule. Seen through the lens of colonialism, the verandah from which European residents of empire viewed the business and pleasure of empire became a spatial trope: the biography of John Pope Hennessey, who served as governor in Labuan, the West African Settlements, Bahamas, Barbados, Hong Kong, and Mauritius, was simply titled *Verandah*.[4] Garth Myers uses the phrase, "verandahs of power," to refer to the sites of administrative power in the British empire, and specifically in colonial Africa.[5] He cites the use of verandahs in a three-story administrative building in British colonial Zanzibar to communicate a racialized hierarchy: the lower-floor verandahs for the governed, the middle-floor verandah for Indian and African bureaucrats, and the top verandah for the British (Figure 10.1).

The verandah, however, slipped off its dominant definition and positioning and came to acquire multiple connotations of refuge, vantage, threshold, and seam. Although it was meant to protect the building from the weather, this function was exceeded by the social uses that it came to support. The open verandah, even when modest in scale, materialized a new set of spatial rules that British visitors and residents in India had to learn and maneuver in everyday life.

FIGURE 10.1 The House of Wonders, Stone Town, Zanzibar. Source: Wikipedia. CC BY-SA 4.0.

The bungalow, that quintessential product of empire, was defined by the verandah that surrounded the rooms, ideally on all four sides, or at least on the north and south sides[6] (**Plate 15**). Multiple doors opened on to the verandah from inner rooms, creating a sensorially porous living space. In cities, the north side was typically the approach road and the north verandah was exposed to the public side of the house. The south verandah in cities was the private leisure space that typically opened on to a garden or lawn. In provincial bungalows, in the absence of a carriage porch, the verandah functioned as a transition zone between the enclosure of the rooms and the openness of the compound. Here the urban front/back relation of the verandah was flipped. It was common for the front verandah to be the south verandah; here officials and guests were welcomed and entertained, the publicity of which was perfectly suited to the official rituals of provincial towns.

As the main unprogrammed space in the bungalow, the verandah hosted a large number of activities. The promise of shade and breeze made it an excellent semi-outdoor living space, for breakfasting in the morning, writing letters in the afternoon, for evening tea and before-dinner drinks, and moonlit summer nights when it was too hot to sleep inside.[7] It also functioned as a day nursery when there were small children in the house.[8] It is here that boxwallahs of olden days would lay out their wares hoping to induce the mistress to buy some lace, chintz, or shawl, to dazzle small children with country-made color toys, and here the *durzee* (tailor) would sit on the floor making new dresses or repairing the linen. Since bungalows functioned as both domestic and office space, the verandah blurred the lines between private and public worlds.[9]

The size and architectural features of the bungalow verandah signaled status, specifically one's rank in officialdom.[10] By the 1870s one could distinguish between verandahs that had been upgraded in terms of construction materials, and those which with their thatched roofs retained a closeness to the rural vernacular. At the turn of the nineteenth century, it was common for bungalows, circuit houses, and *cutcherries* (offices/courthouses) to have thatched roofs, and verandahs in particular often had *chupper* (grass) or thatch covers (see **Plates 5 and 7**), a tradition that continued into the twentieth century.[11] Nevertheless bungalows as government buildings were subject to a number of modifications throughout the nineteenth century. Reports of public works both before and after the establishment of the Public Works Department in 1854 bear evidence of thatched roofs being converted into tiled roofs.[12] A verandah in a *cutcherry* sheltered "the people attending the Court and prevent the rain from beating in."[13] In the *cutcherry* in Bauleah in Lower Bengal, where the "verandah rooms" were used to keep the English records of the court, it was considered necessary to provide adequate roof cover to protect the documents from damage.[14]

Verandahs were seen to improve buildings and premises. In most cases verandahs were not structurally connected to the interior rooms. As add-on elements, they could be extended or removed and rereofed, quite separately from the building proper.[15] In some cases, when treated as a "pucka shed" among service buildings, it could be a freestanding structure. An advertisement in 1794 presents such a verandah—"104 feet long, 20 feet wide and 14-1/2 feet high"—completing the "godowns, coachhouses, cook room, bottleconnah and various other outoffices."[16]

Most verandahs were open on the sides, but often sunshades—venetians—were inserted between pillars to create a cooler space in the verandah.[17] When they were thus "enclosed," either with venetians or rarely with glazing, we notice this detail appearing in eighteenth- and early-nineteenth-century real estate advertisements, indicating the exception to the rule.[18] Advertisements also specified if the verandah was arcaded or pillared, suggesting that their architectural quality mattered to buyers and residents.[19] After the mid-nineteenth century we see more instances of verandahs being glazed, particularly in higher elevations and hill stations.[20]

Screen

In Indian townhouses verandahs were differentiated between work and leisure: service verandahs were used for drying clothes and for housework, while street- and garden-facing verandahs served as gathering spaces for conversation and people-watching. In Bengali, various terms—*ekane baranda* (verandah for one person), *tana baranda* (verandah running a considerable length), *khola baranda* (open-to-sky), *jhul baranda* (cantilevered), *gari baranda* (carriage/car porch)—were coined to describe the myriad forms and uses of verandahs in towns (Figure 10.2).

In at least one instance, the verandah acquired a canonical status. This was the south verandah of the Tagore mansion in Calcutta which the artists Abanindranath Tagore and Gaganendranath Tagore shared with their brother Samarendranath Tagore (Figure 10.3 and see Figure 8.2). It was a salon of sorts: here the brothers painted, read, wrote, and conversed with friends, relatives, and students. The verandah faced the south garden which was designed as a leisure space. From their easy chairs they could see the large mango tree in the garden that shaded the inner compartments of the house. The venetian blinds in between the tall classical columns of the verandah and the decorative wrought-iron railing patterned the red floor with crisp shadows. A wood partition to the right of Abanindranath's seat screened the entry to the inner private compartments. It shielded the private spaces from the prying eyes of a continuous stream of visitors while allowing servants to bring in food and refreshments. In Tagore hagiography this verandah has been described as the birthplace of the Bengal School of Art.[21] The idealism of open-house liberal hospitality that exudes from the recollections of the south verandah of the Tagore mansion is contrasted with the verandahs of the inner compartments of that house. The verandahs of

FIGURE 10.2 Verandah, early-twentieth-century Calcutta. © Swati Chattopadhyay.

FIGURE 10.3 Cover of Mohanlal Gangopadhyay, *Dakshine'r Baranda* (memoir of the Tagore residence at 5 Dwarakanath Tagore Lane, Calcutta), (Kolkata: Indian Associated Publishing Company, 1961).

the inner compartments did not overlook a garden or the street: they faced a courtyard in which domestic labor was undertaken, uncelebrated, and "hidden." Here the view out from the verandah was not designed to be about pleasure, but about observing the work taking place. The verandahs of the inner compartments were linked to rooms of food preparation, storage, and family worship, crisscrossed by servants, women, and children.

When the verandahs of inner compartments faced the street, they were likely to be entirely venetianed to protect the spaces from the gaze of passersby. The use of extensive venetian blinds in verandahs in upper-class city residences introduced a peculiar set of connotations that referred to social and spatial transparency. Meant to "blind"—make sightless, and shade the space—venetian blinds also afforded the resident a screen from behind which they could watch without being seen. To Europeans these were the dark spaces of the Indian city that refused access to the outsider.

The blinds, like the *jali* or *jaffri* of Mughal-Rajput buildings or the *mashrabiya* of buildings in the Arab world, modulate the passage of light, heat, sound, smell. Opaque from the outside, they produce a form of translucency from the inside, casting patterned shade on the floor and walls and on one's body. They work both as a device of separation/connection and framing. The blind constructs a vision as the solid surfaces dematerialize. As D. Fairchild Ruggles puts it nicely: "[S]creens intercept the view, or at least delay it. One can see through the screen to the view beyond, but only by first negotiating the intervening screen, an effort that makes the viewer more conscious of the act of seeing . . . It teases the eye, making the viewer pause and, in that moment of hesitation, become aware of the very act of seeing."[22].

In a society with differential powers of access for women and men, children and grownups, masters and servants, such venetian blinds as screens meant that those who did not have free passage to the street got acquainted with the street through this screen. The world appeared in small pieces: in slices and fragments. This was, however, rarely a one-way seeing: the houses often were so close that such seeing could be reciprocal, contested, too intimate, unavoidable. The fragments with which one could piece together the sights of the city were contingent on a host of other factors not within the viewer's control. The only control, as Abanindranath Tagore recalled of his experience as a child, was that one could choose which slat to open and which slice to see to compose the tableau of daily life; such viewing might or might not correspond with the rest of the sensory surroundings.[23] The venetian blind became a technology and an aperture through which to see and experience the city, albeit darkly. Contrary to most understandings of darkness, the venetian blind as screen signaled possibilities. In transmitting sound and smell the screen complemented and often exceeded the connections made through sight.

Threshold

Like a verandah the terms "otla," "dalan," "ro'ak," and "daowa" refer to strips of space on a raised plinth adjoining living apartments. Though these have distinct origins—*otla* originating in Gujarat, and *daowa* and *dalan* in Bengal, and the spaces these describe are somewhat different in form and use, the terms "dalan," "daowa" and "ro'ak" are sometimes used interchangeably. Daowa and dalan both have rural origins, and daowa, derived from the Sanskrit *darbat,* refers to the raised plinth of a rural vernacular mud house, and dalan, derived from Persian, refers to the raised plinth extensions in a masonry building. Ro'ak, derived from the Arabic *riwaq*, has similar connotations and use. Daowa carries the connotations of earth construction and earthiness, whereas *dalan-bari* refers to a *pucca* or masonry house (**Plate 16**). A key difference is that otla, daowa, dalan, and ro'ak refer to the threshold extensions on the ground floor only, while verandah may refer to lower or upper floor galleries overlooking a courtyard, a garden, or a street.[24]

Calling a daowa a verandah both detracts from and extends the idea of the daowa. The daowa as threshold marked distinctions of wealth, class, caste, gender, and religion in everyday life. Lower castes and those from other religions were not allowed on the daowa in the houses of upper-caste Hindus. The daowa of the outer compartments, often called ro'ak, were a preserve of the men. Describing the neighborhood of her maternal grandparents' house in a small village in eastern Bengal that I have invoked at the beginning of this chapter, writer Rani Chanda recalled small distinctions that marked these spaces. The noise from an impassioned game of dice emanating from Dinanath Kabiraj's daowa signaled Kabiraj's house as a space of male gathering in the neighborhood. His daowa had a railing and against the inner wall stood a series of hookahs set in brass and silver ready for guests.[25] The daowa in the New House on the southwestern part of the village Rani called a verandah, as it had a railing and was of masonry construction.[26] This was a distinction: as one of the only three houses of masonry construction in the village, it was an indicator of wealth.

Daowa and courtyard complement each other as spaces in which a multitude of everyday domestic chores take place. As the social center of a household, a courtyard is also the space of arrival, departure, and festivities. The open-to-sky courtyard as workspace expands the use-capacity of modestly dimensioned interior rooms, even in well-off households. With the sloped roofs draped over the daowa extending into the courtyard, they contributed to a sense of interiority centered on the courtyard, even when multiple entryways give access to this space. In wealthier households, the rooms might touch each other to create a more defined closed geometry, locally called *chak-milano* house, referring to a regular rectangular composition.

Courtyards in Indian townhouses afforded many of the same functions as in a rural household, but different degrees of socialization and seclusion were implied in their arrangement and placement. Elite mansions had multiple courtyards and a clear distinction was made between the public courtyard with its generous spaces and fine detailing and the inner courtyards which were smaller and less refined in their architectural features. These courtyards complemented the open-air terraces of these houses as inner spaces of work and sociability.

Roofline

The practice of building flat roofs was commonplace in precolonial north India. Such flat roofs-turned-terraces made sense in the hot-dry climate of the region with its long extremely hot summer months followed by a short monsoon season. Rooftop terraces were open-air sleeping spaces in hot summer nights. Often an open-sided pavilion on the roof—barsati or baradari—was added to enhance the experience of the roof terrace as a leisure space. The overhead shade protected from the sun and rain while allowing (passage to) the cooling breeze. When the temperature fell sharply in the winter months, the sun-warmed roof terrace provided relief. Scores of Mughal and Rajput miniatures convey the importance of the terrace and the terrace pavilion as a space of pleasure.

The baradari (literally, comprising twelve-doors), or open-on-the sides pavilion, located in a garden setting or on an open terrace, was an architecture of luxury. The open fenestration allowed the passage of breeze and the openings could be screened when necessary for temperature control and privacy. Baradaris were the preferred location for soirées, games of chess, and *pachisi*, dance and music performances, and constituted a spatial tradition that went back to at least the Sultanate period (1206–1526). Often highly ornate garden structures, they were carefully integrated with water channels and chahr-bagh-style parterres. The baradari was also a framing device that created prospects, and controlled the degree of interconnectedness between interior and exterior spaces.

When the French-Swiss adventurer, Antoine-Louis Henri Polier, commissioned portraits of his life in the northern state of Awadh in the late eighteenth century, he chose to have himself depicted under a baradari and on a terrace. Polier had houses in Faizabad and Lucknow (and lived for brief durations in Delhi and Calcutta), and he made sure these houses had baradaris that ensured privacy by virtue of their location and design.[27] The baradari in his house in Faizabad was fitted out with screens, *sayaban* (awning), and *chandni* (floor cover), as was the norm in houses of the Mughal nobility. In the watercolor of Polier watching a "nautch" or dance, the painter Mihr Chand placed Polier under an awning on a terrace. Painted *c*. 1774, we see Polier on a moonlit open terrace overlooking a landscape

(**Plate 17**).[28] He is dressed in the style of an Awadhi noble and sits on a Georgian settee upholstered in Indian fabric, with a decorated hookah pipe in his hand.[29] He is the only sitting figure and the rest of the figures—attendants and dancers—are rendered more diminutive than him, to make sure that the viewer recognizes his authoritative presence. A row of green and red lamps (*diya*) defines the edge of the terrace, and another row of lamps defines the water's edge. The fence and lamps are reflected in the water. The night sky is patterned with fireworks. Conveying refinement and leisure, Mihr Chand's painting brings together eighteenth-century idioms of Mughal painting—the preference for nighttime scenes, entertainment on a terrace or garden setting in open air or under a baradari, and fine clothing and accessories signaling rank. The prominent red *sayaban* is critical in creating the set of associations with Mughal paintings of nobles and sovereigns.[30] In Mughal painting, sovereigns are recognizable among other features by the kind of parasol, awning, or tent cover under which they are seated, and this tradition is carried over to paintings of the Awadh nobles. By rendering Polier through that idiom, Mihr Chand incorporates him into a tradition of representation that had a particular political import. How Polier conducted himself in private—how he was represented in his relation to his household—had direct implications on his public life in the context of late Mughal courtly culture. The latter was critical for his livelihood and business success. The terrace and baradari as spatial practice thus exceeded the realm of private pleasure.

Such flat terraces and baradaris were important enough both in their private and public usages that the flat style of roofing, which should have been an anomaly in the monsoon-drenched Gangetic delta, was adopted with enthusiasm by regional elites in Bengal. Both precolonial and colonial cities borrowed this elite legacy of Mughal north India. Builders in cities such as Murshidabad, Krishnanagar, Dhaka, and Calcutta all adopted flat roofs as a distinct expression of a modern masonry building. And many, such as the Tagore mansion in Calcutta, adopted the style of the baradari for entertainment.[31]

This stylistic preference for flat roofs among Indian elites was reinforced by the Mediterranean-inspired neoclassical architecture brought to India by Europeans. As in the case of transferring a vocabulary from northern India to Bengal, an architectural form that made perfect sense in the temperate climate of the Mediterranean made little climatic sense in England, but stylistic preferences have historically little to do with climatic considerations. When English and French builders and pattern books introduced neoclassicism in the Indian subcontinent as the favored architectural style in the eighteenth century, the overlap of formal preferences ensured that terraces acquired a distinct presence in colonial cities that would continue into the mid-twentieth century.

The roofline was visually important, and dutifully rendered by contemporary artists. As the culminating element of the building's facade, terrace cornices and parapets were conspicuously decorated with urns, garlands, and floral motifs. The Palladian-styled balustrades popularized by pattern books such as James Gibbs's *Rules for Drawing* (1738) were the most common forms of parapet design of eighteenth-century and early-nineteenth-century colonial buildings, both public and private. The form of the Palladian balustrade, amenable to improvisation, became the standard for not only crowning buildings but for verandah railings and boundary walls (Figure 10.4).

While some of these design traits were borrowed from foreign shores and were popular among both Indians and Europeans, in the *use* of terrace space emerged distinct cultural practices. The novelty of the practice of using the rooftop terrace appears in the frequent remarks on the subject made by European visitors to Calcutta in the late eighteenth and nineteenth centuries.

Lady Maria Nugent, visiting Calcutta between 1811 and 1814 with her husband, Commander-in-Chief Sir George Nugent, commented on the style of houses in Garden Reach: "[M]any of the houses look like villas in the neighborhood of London, only they are without chimneys, and the roofs are all terraces, where the inhabitants take air in the morning, or late in the evening."[32] Maria Nugent lived in a house in the neighborhood of Chowringhee, close to the open expanse of the maidan, and maintained a daily journal. From her entries we know that whenever she was unwell, which was frequent, she went to the terrace for her daily perambulation.

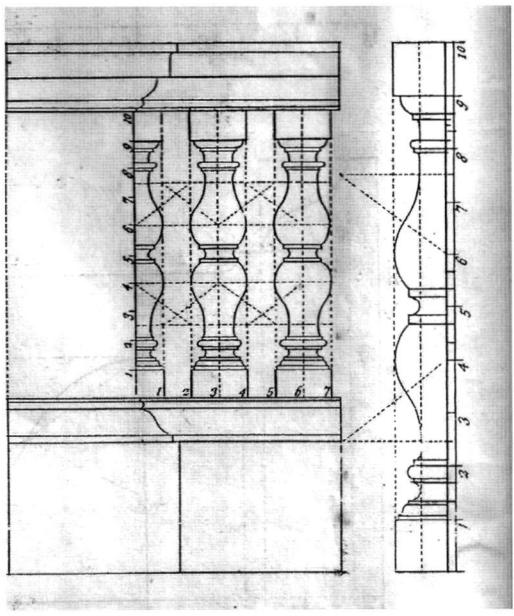

FIGURE 10.4 Drawing of balustrade from James Gibbs, *Rules for Drawing the Several Parts of Architecture*, 1738.

This "walk on the house top," as she put it, was in lieu of the usual ride on the riverside course.[33]

An astute observer of architectural preference and social mores in the mid-nineteenth century, Colesworthy Grant noted that in the Calcutta houses of the early nineteenth century the terrace was "the greatest extent of ground trodden by way of exercise by the European foot."[34] These rooftops would typically have dual access: a service stair, usually on the outside, and an inner staircase for the occupants of the house. The cool southern evening breeze in the oppressive summers of Calcutta was a luxury enjoyed by those who had the privilege of stepping up to a higher vantage.

Such raised terraces came with an added charm: terraces of two- and three-storied houses provided magnificent panoramic views of the city. Sometimes, real estate advertisements would make a virtue of this feature: an 1803 advertisement of an upper-story masonry house to be rented made a point of mentioning the "commanding view of the Salt Lakes" and that miles of country could be seen from the third-floor terrace.[35] Celebratory dinners at Government House located in the administrative heart of the city often ended with fireworks in the maidan fronting Government House and the building's southern terraces (not rooftop terraces) became platforms for enjoying the show. Such viewing from the terrace incorporated the larger space of the maidan into the domain of the Governor-General's palace in a spectacular assertion of power.[36]

It is evident that in depicting the houses in the southern suburbs of the city, still quite close to the city center, the amateur painters of Colesworthy Grant's time portrayed the city from rooftops. Except for two watercolors by William Clerihew who visited India between 1842 and 1845, however, there is scarcely any depiction that actually shows the vantage of the rooftop itself. Most likely painted in 1843, these two paintings by Clerihew not only show the vantage from which they are drawn, but are also exceptional in that they do not depict the city's monuments. One of these is a view of the Hooghly River showing the garden houses on its opposite bank. The slice of the low terrace that is the artist's vantage sets up a reciprocity with the buildings on the opposite bank of the river in Garden Reach.[37] The other painting shows a view of the city from its rooftops (**Plate 18**). In this Clerihew captured the rhythmic volumes as seen from the rooftop of a building located in the densely built center of the city. The roofscape appears as a blurred extension of the vantage: the sepia, pale ocher, and gray tones attempting to portray the massing effect of the masonry buildings rather than accurately define light and shade. What attaches to these paintings is a pleasure of the visual.[38]

The terrace could take on particular regional connotations. The word for terrace in Bengali is *chhad*, and several qualifiers are added to the term to designate various forms and uses of terraces. *Nyara* (bald) *chhad* indicates terraces without balustrades (often a cost-saving measure), and therefore not meant for conventional use.[39] *Chiler chhad* (eagle's perch) and *chile kotha* (eagle's room) refer to the raised attic that leads to the terrace from the floor below. The roof of the attic is typically sloped on one side in keeping with the incline of the stairs. It is possible to climb up the slope to reach the flat rectangular crown that constitutes the horizontal part of the *chiler chhad*. Further distinctions, depending on household practice, were made between the terraces in different locations of a house. We see this kind of nomenclature in Abanindranath Tagore's grandson Sumitendranath Tagore's conjectural plan of the now-demolished house on 5 Dwarakanath Tagore Lane (see Figure 8.2). The different terraces in this house were given different names because they were assigned different functions based on adjacency and location: terrace above the car-porch (*gari-barandar chhad*) accessed by the north-facing verandah, the raised terrace above the *nachghar* (dance room), the large terrace on the fourth floor, terraces on the third floor, terrace in front of the kitchen. The open terrace in front of Abanindranath's eldest brother and artist Gaganendranath's room on the west was partially covered with a tiled roof, providing a shaded space on the terrace. The fourth-floor terrace, the highest in the house, was the space for flying kites, and the annual fireworks on Kalipuja/Diwali were set off from there. Pickles, fruit pulp, and *bori* (dried lentil dumpling) were dried in the square patch of sun on the terrace next to the kitchen, while the *thakurgharer chhad* (terrace above the room for worship) was inaccessible.[40]

Whether it is the verandah, daowa, stoop, or terrace, the significance of these spaces is revealed in their everyday use. It is through the minutiae of everyday life in which working, dwelling, and gathering remain irreducibly heterogeneous that these connective spaces of verandahs and terraces and their regional instantiations gathered their capacity as sites of storytelling. It is to those stories we turn next.

11

Anomalous Spaces

The bird should be placed on its back, and cut open from the top of the breast-bone to within a short distance of the vent. But if the specimen is one remarkable for the beauty of its breast plumage the process should be reversed. The wing-bones should then be broken under the wings, and the bird's skin be removed with the celt handle of the knife, sprinkling the skin as you go with a powder of wood-ash, plaster of Paris, or flour . . . push the gouge well into the back of the eye to separate the ligament which holds to the socket. . . . .

Some people crush the skull to make it come out of the skin more easily, but the Captain Sahib is averse to that proceeding. Remove the brains by taking a piece out of the skull at the back as the neck is cut off. Pull the eyes out of their cavities, and fill up the places with cotton wool soaked in arsenical soap.[1]

Edith Cuthell's step-by-step description of do-it-yourself taxidermy when the catch is brought home reads like a manual of sorts. Its matter-of-factness is very much in accordance with the back verandah in which her husband, Captain Cuthell, undertook this exercise in taxidermy. Prepared well, the catch could continue to adorn the living rooms in the bungalow and be sent abroad to friends as gifts—memorabilia of the couple's time in India. For Edith, it was also part of the everyday life in her bungalow in the Lucknow cantonment that offered a way of seeing the land and create a landscape aesthetic. The seeing, recording, and connecting commenced with her verandah, crowded with plants, servants, small critters, and birds, alive and dead.

Edith's story of her time in Lucknow is presented as a book about gardens, her own and those of others. She begins the book, titled *My Garden in the City of Gardens*, by citing her vantage as a way of introducing her bungalow garden in Lucknow to her readers: "I am writing on my high-raised verandah."² The verandah offers a sheltered position from which to see the goings on in her garden and beyond the bungalow compound. Her observation of life in the verandah and garden—plants, birds, animals—becomes the starting point of a narrative of life, death, and livability in this cantonment town in the plains.

From the perch of her eastern verandah Edith keeps watch, "eagle-eyed" on the *mali* in case he snuck off to eat, snooze, or smoke in the shade of the plantains.³ The "scantily dressed" *mali* or gardener needs constant supervision, Edith reminds her readers. Yet this *mali* was indispensable to an Indian garden because in this climate Englishwomen would not undertake physical labor. Edith wanted to be clear on this account: "Be it well understood that when I speak of doing a thing in the garden myself, it merely means I sit, or stand, and see it done. In this land no one does any gardening personally, but the supervision of the ignorant, untrustworthy, uninterested *mali* is far more trouble."⁴

Edith's casting herself in a supervisory role is not exceptional. Neither is her practically unqualified denigration of Indian servants, seen as slow, dim-witted, and recalcitrant.⁵ By the time Edith was writing, British women were exhorted to take charge of the "empire of home" and treat their bungalow as the unit that held together the functioning and promise of empire. Their task was to make the foreign spatial ensemble of the bungalow into an English home, or at least home like.⁶ At the same time the tropes of "camp," "march," "parade," and "empire" used in describing home life in the colonial context meant that the nurturing role of women espoused by Victorian reformers in England was overwritten by a model of public life directly drawn from the pages of colonial bureaucracy.⁷ Keeping the house in clockwork efficiency was itself the sign of the European wife in India as a woman of "unlimited leisure."⁸

From a gendered perspective, the plenitude of leisure-as-power resulted in an "everyday fussiness," laced with suspicion of subordinates, that came to characterize the vigilant attention to small things in colonial households.⁹ In a location where everything from the architecture to the weather militated against the achievement of Englishness, the women intensely focused on the small things that they felt they could control and rely on for anchoring their sense of self. Nothing else would explain the unrelenting obsession with such mundane details as how many *jharans* (dusters) were handed out to servants and what they used them for.¹⁰

In rare cases and sometimes in hill stations, the architecture of the residences might appear more "English."¹¹ Otherwise, as was the norm, to remedy the architectural dissimilarity of Indian houses from those in England, English residents were encouraged to evoke a sense of "home" by carefully situating a few objects of English manufacture. When the latter was not affordable, they were asked to arrange them as one would in England: "with a few pictures, photographs, brackets for odds and ends of china, japanese scrolls, having books and papers about, and a piano, a room could be made fairly pretty."¹² These small objects were then given extraordinary symbolic value related to the preservation of class and racial privileges, in a context in which proximity to native had to be negotiated on a daily basis.

Edith notes how one cherishes the "common things of everyday 'home' life" in these foreign climes: a patch of watercress planted next to the well;[13] a buttonhole made from English violets grown with the utmost care in the back verandah;[14] English peas—"not the tinned variety"—for Christmas dinner.[15] The effort invested in securing these treasures, redolent of familial affection and distant homes, is considered a reward in itself. It makes her feel she is affirming her Englishness—her nearness to England.

The English home in India in all its privilege and precariousness, constructed around a plethora of small things, was viewed as the nucleus of a larger landscape. In Edith's writing, the verandah is the launching point to construct this landscape that extended her reach far beyond the bungalow gate. And gate she had none; it was an aperture in the bank that defined the compound. The perimeter was marked by pillars and at the entry to their compound was a gatepost carrying Captain Cuthell's name.[16] Often accompanied by her husband, Edith would ride through the cantonment, past the civil lines, to the countryside beyond. Beyond the villages and crop-laden fields beckoned the extensive marshes and open land that were perfect for snipe shooting. Occasionally these excursions took more ambitious forms and involved deer and boar hunts. At other times the outings were more social affairs such as picnics at those sites of Lucknow and its surroundings that were marked by the Sepoy Rebellion (1857–9), creating a series of associations between the domestic realm, official realm, and conquered domains.

The frontispiece of Edith's reminiscence of Lucknow is a view of the city from the garden of the ruined Residency compound. The Residency, where British forces were garrisoned and withstood a long siege, contains the tomb of Brigadier General and Commissioner of Oudh (Awadh) Henry Montgomery Lawrence, who died during the siege. The Residency was left in its ruined state and its grounds transformed into a garden and memorial site. For British residents and visitors, the Lucknow Residency remained the most hallowed mutiny site in the city.

Vignettes of such "mutiny sites," and visits to gardens and the open countryside, holds together Edith's narrative.[17] Written in the present tense even though it was assuredly in the past by the time of publication, she crafts a distinct temporal and spatial arrangement to connect the small elements of her domestic life with larger territorial entities. Edith's story commences with the bungalow verandah and unfolds centrifugally, producing a series of landscape affects that convey the immediacy and authenticity of the moment. Her memoir is presumably untarnished by the passage of time and the vagaries of memory. And it is here that nonhuman animals in her verandah, particularly the practice of taxidermy, comes to occupy an important narrative role.

Edith's Story

Edith E. Cuthell (1853–1929) was married to Thomas George Cuthell, an army officer.[18] She spent several years in India with her husband, and five of her books are based on her Indian experience. The bungalow, camp, cantonment, garden, and hunt are common themes in her stories, as is an autobiographical undertone. As an army officer's wife, she was bound by certain social expectations of hospitality in tune with the official routines of her husband. But unlike the army wife who was only expected to be "a decorative chattel" and accept the masculine order of the day,[19] Edith railed against the infernal custom of midday house calls, "the worship of official rank and precedence," and the interminable badminton games she had to endure to keep society.[20]

Self-aware of her privileged position, in *My Garden*, Edith is keen to assert the need for a space of her own. The garden is her clearing in this convention-bound world, and an entrée to the space of literary ambition.[21] A metaphor for creativity and imagination, and an artifact produced through careful planning and labor, the garden, like the verandah, fulfills a multitude of emotional, physical, and aesthetic needs. But that space is fundamentally shaped by what she understands to be the larger territorial prerogative of empire, one that she consciously evokes. If in Heideggerian terms the garden can be seen not as an object but a thing that gathers and unites, and thus is continuous with the surrounds beyond its boundaries, for Edith the garden as a construct needs to be connected to the larger territory to bring it to significance—to bring it near.[22] It requires a narrative ploy. Thus, Edith's devotion to the garden as a metaphor and an artifact exceeds the prescriptions offered to Englishwomen in India that to raise a garden in India is the duty of empire.

Whereas most Englishwomen in India suffered from a lack of engagement, Edith filled her otherwise ordinary domestic routine with gardening and writing. The sociality of empire she narrates and the methods of gardening, cookery, and taxidermy she prescribes are surely modes of claiming authority over land, far and near. Such authority, however, is at best partial and troubled by the many reminders of the past, specifically, the trauma of the Sepoy Rebellion. The ruins of the older abandoned cantonment on the other side of the river, that had been burnt by the rebels, remains a melancholic reminder of the unexpected turn of events. She constructs the past as an extrapolation of her own sociality:

> They rode, they hunted, they shot, much as we do now, doubtless ... I imagine them sitting in the evening on their *chabutras* in their gardens, the women doing Berlin-wool work or crochet, and talking most microscopic gossip; while the men smoked Indian cheroots, and drank bottled beer from England, or brandy and water ... Then fell the thunderbolt out of the blue ... Their gardens knew them no more.[23]

In this telling the gardens suddenly become alien territory. The bounds of the bungalow that had assured the privilege of leisure and "microscopic gossip" matter no more. As she rides back to her "well-gardened cantonment" at dusk, the present seems less an assurance than a foreboding.[24] The garden in her bungalow, that she oversaw with great interest, becomes unmoored from her authority and turns into a picture of alterity.

Yet, riding out to the countryside brings her great pleasure, having to do with "the overpowering desire ... to be alone." Beyond the line of the cantonment and civil lines of Lucknow, beyond the "European zone of trees and habitations," without another human being around, she imbibes the strange beauty of the land. The loneliness "so delightful, so refreshing" serves as her "mental tonic." She is not looking for authentic India in the space beyond the European zone of habitation; she is seeking a place of solitude. She does not forget to mention that on some of these occasions birds and animals shatter her reverie with unpleasant outcomes.[25]

Edith's rides take her out of the sphere of European sociality, but also from the "ubiquitous native" at home. The "lurking domestic, behind the curtain or screen, squatting somnolently ready for the sahib's shout," tests her patience. It grates against her sense of superiority over everything native: "I have the feeling I am perpetually being watched, as I dare say I am."[26] The gaze of the native turned back is deeply unsettling. Indeed, nothing made the domestic interior more estranged than the presence of servants, most of whom were male.[27] Her own sense of self is thus defined by a spatial architectonic that crucially turns on the ability to choose between inside and outside, an aesthetic fold that links the bungalow verandah with the territorial ambitions of an expansive colonialism.

Her narrative appears as a desire for an interregnum between a traumatic past and an uncertain future. Taking hold of this space and time is, thus, crucial. She does so, not by casting further rules on an already routine-bound life, as was the prescription of many housekeeping guides, but by conferring a set of affective values on everyday practices.[28] The produce of the garden and hunt, and the captive and free creatures that animate her verandah in anticipated diurnal and seasonal rhythms, are essential ingredients with which she constructs this affect. She can speak with equal zeal about producing the most perfect bloom in her garden, and the method of eviscerating a dead bird so it can be made into an aesthetic object. More than that: she intends these home-wrought products to be object lessons in artistic and technical proficiency. Demonstration of this proficiency rests on her capacity to link the domain outside the bungalow with its interior.

Verandah as Refuge

Edith's 1870s bungalow in the Lucknow cantonment sat in over an acre of land, part of which had been planned carefully as a four-square garden. The eastern verandah next to Edith's bedroom was shaded by orange trees and overlooked a small pool she had had built, fringed with ferns. Below the verandah her pet *chital* (spotted deer) was tethered to a tree. She did much of her writing on this eastern verandah. Rather than the southern verandah up front, this eastern location gave her the necessary privacy and also gave the most advantageous position to watch her flower and vegetable gardens.

The private east verandah served another important purpose. It was here that Edith concealed her *durzee* working on a choice design of hers. There he spread a "dirty sheet" on the floor and sat cross-legged, making her dress. It was important that he be out of view, away from the front verandah where she welcomed callers. The tailor's work was perfect, even if the manner of work was rude: "armed with a huge horn thimble, and holding the work in his often grimy toe, he stitches away elaborately." Edith chose to see past the griminess, because it was more important to surprise her compatriots on the day of a *burra khana* with her latest "confection."[29]

The verandah encircled the house, its tiled sloped roof supported on masonry columns. Edith, mindful of the intimate relation between the verandah and the garden, comments on the type of enclosure created to suit the hot dry climate of northern India as well as her personal preferences:

> Between each pillar it is enclosed with bamboo trellis, called *jaffri* work. This answers the twofold purpose of tempering the outside glare to the rooms within, and of supporting the creepers which are now rapidly running up and clothing it from the beds below.[30]

The back wall of this east verandah, which served as the Cuthell's semi-outdoor living space, was lined with potted ferns and palms and the floor was "spread with Chinese matting and littered with armchairs." "India is the land of loll," she remarks in reference to the variety of armchairs that were arranged in the verandah in order to suit "each sex and size": bamboo couch chairs, cretonne-clad small grass chairs, and heavy teak or mahogany armchairs "with wide cane seat and tall curling backs, monsters, with great wide wooden arms splayed out to receive the Sahib's extended legs when he is aweary, and with a hole in them to contain his peg tumbler when he is a-thirst."[31]

The exorbitant potential for leisure, appropriately gendered, was crafted into the furniture design of colonial establishments. George Atkinson, in *Curry and Rice on Forty Plates*, notes with jest that a house with "its round tables, couches, 'whose soft solicitations court repose'; and its marble-topped side-tables, and its easy-chairs" declare "a state of connubial domesticity approximate or anticipated." In this case Atkinson is describing the house of the young bachelor, Dhalbhat. The sahib in this caricature is shown trying to learn Hindustani with the assistance of a native teacher or *munshi*. The setting is an interior space where Dhalbhat sits on the kind of splayed-leg easy chair in which Captain Cuthell spent his leisure hours in the verandah (Figure 11.1). Often referred to as the plantation chair, its dimensions and design were meant to accommodate the adult trouser-wearing male. It invited sitting in an overtly masculinist manner. Even if he is the "student" in this depiction, Dhalbhat appears as the dominant figure who is being catered to by the teacher and an attendant ready to refresh him with "bottles of beer, soda water and brandy."[32] Captain Cuthell's easy chair designed with a placeholder for the brandy peg thus affords a gesture of colonial authority, if not unchallenged control. It is after all placed in the feminine space of the east verandah amid Edith's plants and pet creatures.

Caged ring doves, paddy birds, and parrots completed the verandah ensemble—"green, scarlet and plum, dabs of brilliant colour against the prevailing greenery."[33] Edith evidently takes pleasure in the daytime creatures that visits the verandah: hoopoe birds, and squirrels looking for breakfast crumbs. In the cool weather, pots of petunias and verbenas bring splashes of color. Jasmines, evening glory, passion flower, and ipomea climb the *jaffri* work. The price she pays for the abundant greenery in the verandah is mosquitoes after dark.

The north verandah in the back overlooked the kitchen garden used for domestic chores, including giving out the laundry to the *dhobi* (washerman).

FIGURE 11.1 George F. Atkinson, "Dhalbhat," 1859. Illustration in Atkinson, *Curry and Rice on Forty Plates* (London: Day & Son, 1859).

Here soda and wine bottles in wet baskets were hung from the roof rafters to keep the beverage cool in the summer months. In winter months, it is in this northern verandah that Captain Cuthell would practice his taxidermy after a shooting spree. But it is also in the north verandah's cool shade that Edith grew her violets. The potted plants, "a long unsightly array, with ne'er a glint of the dreaded sunshine flecking them," produced her most treasured blooms.[34]

The verandah changed with the seasons. Edith notes the routines and events that take place in the verandah in sync with the natural rhythms of the seasons. In summer months, one retreats from the verandah during the day, taking shelter in the dark rooms, while in more temperate weather one moves out to more fully utilize the verandah as living space. It is not a coincidence that during these cooler months the bungalow garden is filled with imported "English" species of flowers and vegetables. The verandah and garden become more conducive to moving out of one's shelter, physically, visually, and psychologically.

In October, the verandah becomes Edith's drawing room. From here she gives instructions to her gardener to repot flowering plants and sow winter vegetables. Her geraniums that have been sunned by a friend in the hills had come back to be tended in the favorable autumn weather of the plains.[35] Their pale hue would now join her other flowers whose riotous colors at this season fills her verandah and garden.

The cool season lasts into March, when the "chick" (a screen of green rushes) that separates her bedroom from the verandah makes the nights "delicious." The fragrance of orange blooms mingles with myriad sounds of insects, and frogs, "both continuous recitatives in different keys." The murmurings of the creatures nearby are broken occasionally by the "hellish din" of jackals in the distance.[36] On a full-moon night she stays up in the verandah swept by a cool breeze, "watching in vain for the light flashes from the marigolds and nasturtiums" that Charles Darwin had mentioned. The time, she muses, was perhaps not right. Darwin referred to a phenomenon at dusk during July–August in England, and that would have been the most unpropitious moment in India for witnessing such a remarkable occurrence: as "the atmosphere of the compound is laden with the peculiarly offensive smoke of their cow-dung fuel" being emitted from natives cooking their evening meal.[37]

April brings the hot weather, when except for early mornings and evenings, the verandah provides little respite from the scorching winds of the plains. Then the *punkah*-pullers take over the space to ensure comfort to the family inside.[38] The verandah becomes "sloppy" in summer, she complains. To keep the interior cool, the *bhisti* comes periodically to drench the *khus-khus* screens draping the doors and the thermantidote placed at the dining room door: "From 7 a.m. to 7 p.m. the house is hermetically sealed. It is 80° in the room as I write and 100° degree in the shaded verandah outside."[39]

The tender plants in the verandah, the ferns and palms, have to be secluded in deepest shade and kept constantly watered to counter the effect of the hot winds.[40] As June approaches, the temperature rises further, and she gets up at 4:30 in the morning to have her tea in the verandah, while a servant stands behind waving a large palm fan.[41]

As was the norm for gardening books, Edith's book chapters are arranged by month. She stages the beginning of her book with the month of October. For her the year has just begun at the conclusion of the hot and wet seasons. This marks her full-time return to the verandah. It is also the time of folks returning from "home" in England and from hills stations in India, driven by the cold. She cherishes the idea that social life will be energized by "contact with Western worlds"—life will no longer be bound by "the station."

The Englishness of the cool season is both supported by the labor of Indian servants but also its symbolic import to the European masters mediated by an Indian aesthetic. During Christmas the servants deck the entry gate and the verandah with marigolds and green leaves, as they would on most other Indian festive occasions. The "French" marigold, originally from Africa, was seen as a European flower so indigenized that it was ill-suited for events appropriately "English." But servants seemed to have had their way in this. During Christmas, the servants of the Cuthell household decorated the south verandah with a marigold arch and palm branches. Captain and Mrs. Cuthell sat on the decorated verandah "in-state," giving audience to the servants who brought them *dalis*: "one by one each domestic approached with much salaaming, bearing trays of flowers and cakes, and horrible sticky sweetmeats, receiving in return *baksheesh*."[42]

Whether they were aware of it or not, Edith and her husband were enacting the Indian ritual of *praja*s (subjects) paying homage to *zamindar*s (landlords) in the form of paying rent and gifts on festive occasions. The raised verandah for both the Cuthells and *zamindar*s served as the appropriate platform for performing the rituals of gift-giving in an asymmetrical social order that served to reinforce social and economic hierarchies. On such occasions the verandah becomes a venue, a bounded space of ritual exchange that normalizes the larger social relations within which the bungalow verandah is embedded.

When the Cuthells, for example, were being felicitated by their servants, the honor bestowed upon them was not just the demonstration of loyalty by the servants but a function of their status in the official rank of the colonial order. The image of her bungalow that she includes in the book is a view of the front of the bungalow with the servants populating its foreground (Figure 11.2). Edith reminds her reader that one's residence, the number of servants employed, and above all the size and style of one's garden are the most visible indicators of social status. The garden indexes one's location in the hierarchy of British colonial administration—only the gardens of the upper crust of the administration can afford a green lawn. The rest have to

DENIZENS OF MY GARDEN

FIGURE 11.2 "Denizens of my Garden," Edith Cuthell's bungalow in Lucknow with servants in front. Source: Edith Cuthell, *My Garden in the City of Gardens* (London: John Lane, 1905).

be satisfied with the vast ornamental grass of public botanical gardens, and their own more modest flower and vegetable gardens punctuated with fruit trees, and perhaps an earth-surface tennis court.[43]

While Edith looks forward to the beginning of the season for fresh conversation and company, her enthusiasm wanes as the months progress. The sociality of the cantonment and the callers on her verandah dismay her. She goes into great detail about the gossip and the jealousies of rank she has to endure from two senior women and a younger army wife who happen to "invade" her verandah at the same time. The detailed narrative of this encounter—a conversation about recalcitrant servants—concludes with the sobering reminder that whatever their shortcomings, the elder women at the station, who had lived through the mutiny, had earned their dues, and their advice on servants and cookery were worth every bit of conversational indulgence.

If the verandah as a space of refuge and leisure merge uncomfortably with its official function, the tension between public and private, domestic and official, is not so easily resolved as Edith would have it in this instance. In some ways, verandahs as spatial anomalies—neither inside nor outside, neither wholly public nor entirely private, both essential and nonessential to the building itself—describe the tension between domesticity and officialdom and the peculiar overlap of public and private spheres that characterize colonialism. Verandahs epitomize the anomalies of colonial rule, particularly when viewed less as refuge and vantage, and more in terms of a turn of the fold between inside and outside: as in-between space or threshold and a sutured edge or seam.

Verandah as Exposure

An astute observer of the anomalies of British life in India, George Atkinson, in his pictorial narrative of "the station" in *Curry and Rice on Forty Plates* (1859), portrays his characters through the spaces they inhabit.[44] Atkinson's plates lampoon British social and administrative life in the provinces where the physical environment—a combination of dusty roads, overgrown gardens, primitive technology, and that ubiquitous marker of British presence, the bungalow—defined the limits of social life.

The "station," a permanent site of administration, was a node in the network of British colonial governance that also included smaller "halts." In India these halts were *dak* bungalows, circuit houses, *dak chowkies*, and police stations. Stations implied the presence of the British judge or collector in the case of a civil station, or military personnel in the case of a cantonment. Although such stations as district towns and headquarters would have a significant Indian population, they were marked by the conspicuous presence of Europeans.

In some cases, as in Lucknow, the civil station (or the civil lines) and cantonment were built next to each other. After the Sepoy Rebellion two-fifths of the old Indian city were demolished to create a buffer zone, a wide swath of land between the old city and the line of palatial buildings now converted into military posts and government offices.[45] That open land, the esplanade, created a tangible chasm between the Indian and European populations. Vast garden land in the suburbs of the city were appropriated to build the cantonment, which in area was larger than the native city, while the civil lines were constructed on the demolished southwest portion of the old city. The road that connected the cantonment and civil lines was punctuated by newly planted gardens marking a violent occupation. For someone like Edith, on a day-to-day basis this carves out a clear path of travel from bungalow, cantonment, and civil lines to the countryside beyond the river; there is no need for her to enter the much-reduced Indian city.

However, the palpable presence of Indian servants that so disturbs Edith and makes her feel perpetually exposed is a common theme of British life in India. Atkinson's sharpest critique is perhaps leveled at the exposed life of the verandah. Three of his plates deal with the life of the verandah. In one of these we see the Joint Magistrate and Collector, Huldey, holding his "morning court" in the verandah of his bungalow (see Figure 8.6). A sports enthusiast, Huldey maintains a stud of horses, and during his morning court he reads the racing news in the Gazette while partaking of his *chota hazari* (small breakfast):

> the sable officials, reading away for the very life, utterly regardless of stops, monotonously and nasally race over the documents, swinging their shawled bodies backwards and forwards. Huldey hears all about it, but he does not overlook how that Phizaig with 10 stone has beaten Screwdriver carrying 8 stone 4 1b.; and then he lights his cheroot and sips his tea ... while his favourite dog Forceps, something between a pariah and a buggy-rug, sits by expectantly. Thus public and domestic matters progress congenially.[46]

The drone of legalese emanating from the Indian personnel of the court produces the background noise, so to speak. The monotone is insufficient to attract attention, and enables the Joint Magistrate to read the sports page while holding court. This relaxed, decidedly unofficial, ambience of the morning court mimics Colonel Capsicum's morning routine in the verandah. Both men, holding important ranks in the civil and military administrations, are shown tilting back on their armchairs. With legs raised on the table, they are attended by various servants who oversee their comfort and need, while maintaining a proper distance (see Figures 8.10 and 8.11).

As Kenneth Ames explains in the context of Victorian America, the practice of tilting a chair in the nineteenth century has its own history.[47] Tilting back on one's chair, a decidedly informal, masculine gesture, was a mode of creating a distance from one's surroundings: "Tilting backwards allows one to assess, to order, and to render more abstract a given situation."[48] The masculine posture of tilting is exercised in ordinary, utilitarian chairs, because "these chairs are sturdily constructed, with numerous stretchers to resist the stress of tilting."[49] Genteel parlor chairs would not suffer such abuse.

In Atkinson's depiction, the sahib tilting back on his chair with his feet raised on a side table defies any suggestion of gentility. Here the rigid hierarchy within white colonial officialdom has disappeared to starkly show up as a difference between the sahib who occupies a higher position and the Indians who do not. The Joint Magistrate is not only a figure of relaxed masculinity, comfortable in his verandah—his gesture suggests the ability to take the workings of a court and in extension the empire out of its formal significance and make it into a sport of sorts. Here a formal, official space and activity that ought to be conducted in a courtroom is wrenched from its vestigial official role, and made to appear a matter of whimsical control by the sahib. Seen from a different perspective, the relaxed posture of the sahib signals just the opposite—a lack of control. Wholly dependent on servants, and entirely sure of his superior position, the sahib appears as the lazy figure propped up by laboring natives. The sahib here mirrors the calumny placed on servants and "niggers" ("the Oriental") in general as lazy.[50]

The verandahs in Atkinson's sketches appear interchangeable. The architectural details of the verandahs in the plates are hardly distinguishable, even though they are drawn from different angles. The one with Mrs. Capsicum is the most inward-looking, a cloth hanging from the rafters between the columns serving as a curtain (see Figure 8.9). Atkinson describes Mrs. Capsicum as the colonel's wife who disappears into the darkness of her apartment on returning from her morning ride (rather than keep her husband company on the front verandah). Her drawing room is permanently dark in the colonel's effort to keep the bungalow cool.[51] She rejoices in this "dim obscure." A "dashing dresser," however, Mrs. Capsicum's verandah appears perpetually crowded by a fleet of tailors, and the "tryings on" are infinite. The head tailor checks her measurements, as the others are engaged in various tasks—sewing, twisting thread, ironing. The proximity of the tailors (also considered "servants") to Mrs. Capsicum is much closer than with her male counterparts, her billowing dress in scandalous proximity with the male figures squatting on the floor. The verandah scene, although out in the open, is the counterpart of the dark drawing room of the colonel's wife, and matches the account provided by Edith. The verandah as a space that is neither interior nor exterior is, in both Cuthell's and Atkinson's narratives, flagrantly exposed to the view, and in this case, the touch of natives.

Atkinson's satirical sketch is meant as a humorous take on British life in India, its trials and absurdities. As an exposé, however, it "reveals" the proxemics of colonial life that, despite the desire to draw racial boundaries, were all too compromised by the need to rely on a laboring population. The verandah appears as a liminal threshold, an anomalous space given over to both prescribed and proscribed practices. These everyday workings it would seem could all too easily lapse into a space of excess.

Anomaly

My characterization of the verandah as *anomalous* picks out a strand in the long tradition of ascertaining the appropriate registers in which interactions between Indians and Europeans could be placed within the changing dynamics of imperial power.[52] In 1833, with the future of the East India Company (EIC) and its charter under debate in the British Parliament, Thomas Babington Macaulay proceeded with an argument about governance that was based on asserting the anomalous state of the EIC. In describing the British empire in India as "the strangest of all political anomalies," Macaulay was trying to convince his fellow parliamentarians of the difficulties pertaining to framing laws for the EIC's territorial possessions in India:

> We have to frame a good government for a country into which, by universal acknowledgment, we cannot introduce those institutions which all our habits, which all the reasonings of European philosophers, which

all the history of our own part of the world would lead us to consider as the one great security for good government. We have to engraft on despotism those blessings which are the natural fruits of liberty ... The light of political science and of history are withdrawn—we are walking in darkness.[53]

The argument is lodged in a fundamental difference between Britons and Indians arising from "habits," the traditions of philosophical reasoning and history, as well as the peculiar character of the EIC as a trader and territorial sovereign in one body. The dual character of the EIC was blurred even more as it exercised its territorial prerogative as a vassal of the Mughal emperor until 1858. This composite "undefined" character of the EIC was not merely an historical contingency, Macaulay argued, but had been allowed to survive as policy because it enabled the EIC to treat "the princes in whose names they governed as realities or nonentities, just as might be most convenient." Macaulay did not consider it profitable to adjudicate these contradictions and overlaps, but like his predecessors viewed it necessary for the anomalies to survive, as long as they did not hurt the logics of either pecuniary benefits or the cause of good government.[54] Navigating these contradictions thus needed an anomalous intervention: the grafting of a system of laws conducive to good governance, without the benefit of liberal institutions. Such a move was justifiable because the territorial occupation of the Indian subcontinent by the EIC, "a joint-stock society of traders, the shares of which are daily passed from hand to hand, the component parts of which are perpetually changing," was itself an anomaly. "Where every thing [sic] is anomaly," Macaulay surmised, such a plan of action becomes peculiarly logical. Indeed, there was no point in interrogating the past for general rules "where the whole is one vast exception."

Even if the empire was an anomaly, it still required colonial administrators to sieve out the unnecessary from the necessary anomalies. Here unnecessary anomalies constituted those practices that defied the logic of good governance, now understood as "impartial despotism," a form of authoritarianism based on liberal principles but without representative governance.[55] In everyday life and day-to-day governance the exercise of colonial sovereignty as impartial despotism would appear as a plethora of anomalous interventions each with its spatial correlates.

The verandah as spatial anomaly afforded practices that seemed appropriate nowhere else. In the north verandah of Edith's bungalow, her husband unloads his catch after a hunting expedition. Edith recalls that a morning of snipe shooting in the *jhil* just outside the city yielded "a pretty bag" of thirty-five couple of snipes and twenty jacks. The next day her husband proceeds to demonstrate, "by way of an *amende honorable*," how to skin and stuff the prized painted snipes in the back verandah. The verandah looks like a butcher shop, she notes, but she admires her husband's technique sufficiently to provide a full description.

Taxidermic Seams

Gutting and filling a bird constitutes a precision job. Edith's husband's taxidermic implements were "few, but to the point, in every sense of the word," she comments: "a couple of dissecting-knives with celt handles, a pair of pointed scissors, a large fishhook, and a small gouge for the eyes," as well as "a file for sharpening and a compass for measurements." The goal is to capture the bird whole, disgorge it, and refill it so it can hold its form as an epidermic shell. Time here is of the essence—as the work has to be done against the natural propensities of the dead body.

If the object is to stuff a bird, writes Edith, it must not be killed "with too large a size of charge, or it will be crushed to a jelly, and the skin is not worth using." In case it is merely wounded, it has to be suffocated: "press the breast-bone with finger and thumb till it is dead." Here Edith was directly drawing from her husband's practical taxidermy advice to English boys written in 1887 in the *Boy's Own Paper*.[56] Thomas had assured the boys that this task would not take more than two minutes. Once "life is extinct," it is time to ensure that the bird's feathers are not bloodstained. The small wounds are to be plugged up to prevent the blood staining the feathers, the feathers smoothed down with a handkerchief, and any bloodstained feathers are to be pulled out "as the sacrifice of a feather here and there is immaterial."[57]

A quick transition from death to removing the signs of dying is important in the art of taxidermy. The leaking body of the dead creature needs to be arrested to erase the signs of mortality. The last glimpse of life in the dead creature is, however, important: it helps capture its naturalness in death (Figure 11.3). Notice the color of the eyes when the bird has just been killed, advised Thomas.[58] That color had to be replicated in the choice of the glass eyes that would replace the ones to be gouged. The prescribed method articulated the most effective mode of decontextualization so that a new set of material-spatial relations could be inaugurated.

Unlike Thomas, Edith does not feel she has to elide the fact of actively killing the bird with the intimate press of the thumb. Life in her telling does not just *become* extinct; it has to be made extinct, just as the transmogrification of the bird as animal (endowed with life) to a still life (lively yet lifeless object) needs active disgorgement and attentive curating. After the catch is brought home, and all the flesh, body fluids, and fat have been extracted, and the bird thoroughly "anointed with arsenical soap," she notes, the skin is to be covered with wood ash, the insides filled with paper and wool, and the skin envelope stitched up carefully to avoid a visible seam. Then the reconstructed bird is to be left to dry for a few days before being shipped to be "set up" in a new place.[59]

Taxidermy, popularized in the nineteenth century, was intimately related to the imagination of land as empire. As opposed to big-game taxidermy which was a professional undertaking requiring high precision and ample facilities, domestic taxidermy as the art of stuffing small animals and birds

FIGURE 11.3 "The Snipe," last glimpse of life. Illustration in Lieutenant Colonel Cuthell, "Practical Hints on Taxidermy," *The Boy's Own Book of Indoor Book and Recreations*," ed. G. A. Hutchison (Philadelphia: J. B. Lippincott Company, 1890).

was promoted as a suitably male home-hobby. Domestic taxidermy admirably brought together amateur science, the pleasure of the hunt, colonial collecting, and the "burgeoning culture of hobbycraft," to recenter domestic space not simply as a space of colonial consumption but also one of production and creativity.[60] The death of the nonhuman animal was aestheticized as useful death.

Thomas Cuthell at the outset of his advice to boys impressed upon them not to kill wantonly, but to aim for a good specimen, and to gradually build their skill as they moved up in scale from butterflies to larger animals. The task required cultivating the power of discernment and understanding the logic of a scalar territorial process. The diminished scale of domestic taxidermy is thus not an instance of miniaturization: it is envisioned both as a beginning and an endpoint of large territorial and natural assemblages. Taxidermy as hobby trained boys destined to be future colonial officers how to act in the field. It promoted a distinct *practice* of domestic aesthetic that connected the field with home space, and generated a "special kind of intimacy between producer and object-being."[61]

As the manly labor of the hunt merges into a practical demonstration of taxidermy, the labor of producing an animal-object—part science, part art— becomes a redemptive act. The process of doing and seeing it done confers transcendence in a double move. While each reader can imagine becoming the master of colonial territories, the life captured as death in the stuffed creature serves as a material demonstration of the body transcended: "it is in the *craft* of killing that life is constructed, not in the accident of personal, material birth" (my emphasis), as Donna Haraway notes in a discussion of taxidermy, gender, and natural history.[62] Captain Cuthell's demonstration of the craft of taxidermy in this locale marked by the bloody reminder of the Sepoy Rebellion then becomes a specific articulation of imperial manhood through a conjoined act of transcendence: the animal transcends death in its stilled life and in being crafted grants atonement to the sahib troubled by the failure of English manhood during the rebellion. It becomes a reparative act. Taxidermy's "fatal desire to represent, to be whole" enacts a specific politics of reproduction.[63] It offers the promise of regeneration to a perpetually threatened minority ruling class.

Edith's husband "set up" a valued catch for her: "*Tantalus leucopha*" with its "long yellow beak," "glossy white feathers, tipped with black at the wings, and flecked with rose colour," that he had secured "uninjured."[64] A "triumph of taxidermic art," the "tall and stately" bird adorns her drawing room where it stands supporting a lamp. This zootic furniture located in a bungalow in Lucknow brings the life of the marshland outside the city into the recesses of the colonial home, and in so doing it establishes a new field of meaning. The bungalow is not simply metonymically registered as part of the larger landscape of cantonment, civil lines, and countryside, but the taxidermy bird connects and places it on a par with domestic space in England where such artifacts were eagerly collected and displayed.

The recipe for taxidermy that Edith records carries the same tonality as recipes for cookery and preparation of household medicines and soaps, and falls entirely within a category of domestic avocation. Unlike the short-lived pleasures of roasted snipes, the taxidermy bird serves a more long-term reminder of the triumph of the hunt, and supplies material verity to territorial occupation and wonder. At the same time, the dead bird as still life brought within the circuit of domestic labor helps to refigure the domestic space.

Advice to amateur taxidermists in the United States and Britain emphasized the need to have a home "laboratory": "a good room, if possible 15 × 25 feet, or even larger, with good light, a high ceiling, and an abundant supply of water."[65] This room would have to have a good workbench, a tool case and chest of drawers, a stove, a chopping block, a watertight moveable platform, and a long list of tools. In addition to this work space would be required dry and wet storage space. The semi-open back verandah in the Cuthell's bungalow obviates these elaborate requirements of a home laboratory. Here water is easily fetched through the labor of Indian servants and the cleaning afterwards can also be left to them.

The verandah functioned as an integral part of a larger colonial space, but one in which everyday coloniality—the logic and experience of being in a colonial space and experiencing the power relations it entailed—could be expressed. In Edith Cuthell's writing, as a semi-exposed peripheral space of the bungalow, the verandah is both the beginning and end of the unfolding experience of the colonial landscape. It acts as a seam that could be exposed or folded according to need. The bloody practice of taxidermy, where the Captain Sahib labors, without a shirt on his back, is radically different from the expectations of the non-laboring European body and space, in particular the vision of the European woman in India as a person of unlimited leisure.

The crafting of life in death eradicates the impression of British residents' prolific leisure as a lack of meaningful occupation. In its place it props up a goal-directed avocation that yet holds the scandal of excessive exposure—of body, space, laboring. Containment of this excess is implied by the manner in which the eviscerated body of the bird or animal is put back and carefully cleaned up to be brought inside the house. Edith's narrative of her experience in the colonial terrain is an outcome of her desire to take hold of time and space, one that the verandah's architectural and social placement afforded. Here the verandah is not a "building type" with its assumed correspondence of form and function, but a space that is imbued with the potential of unfolding.

Edith's manner of description—methodical and matter of fact—shuns the appearance of affect that could be suggestive of anomalies. Anomalies have to be acknowledged but written away to evince the effect of authority and control from the verandah to the land outside the bungalow viewed not as "home," but as territorial possession. The exposed and open seam of the verandah reaching into far colonial territory could be folded back into an inhabitable, controllable space: a small space. Therein the small objects, the violets and the bird-turned-lamp, each manifesting a durational aesthetic, could share a role in adorning the interiors of European space and the European body.

12

An Aesthetic Episode

Gangadharpur was earlier called Gangadharkhola; a minor settlement amid better-known villages, unable "to raise its head." Rani Chanda's mother's brothers, when they had moved away from the village to salaried jobs in Dhaka, Asansol, and Calcutta, successfully petitioned to have the suffix in the name of the village changed to "*pur*."[1] The Bengali colloquial term for small settlement, *khola*, was replaced by the Sanskrit suffix *pur*, its classicizing effect intended to make the modest ancestral village sound more respectable, civilized.[2]

Moving away was also coming back. Returning to the ancestral home for festivities, especially in autumn to celebrate the annual festival of Durga Puja, worship of the goddess Durga, was expected by the family. Sons returning home from jobs in distant cities and daughters returning home from their in-laws' house were eagerly anticipated. Rani's story is a narrative of returns: on holiday visits from Dhaka, and later for a permanent stay, until they moved to Calcutta.

Rani's original inspiration to write about this small village came from her mentor, the writer Rabindranath Tagore. A young Rani spoke of her mother's village with such enthusiasm that Rabindranath asked her to write down these remembrances. Express the good in village life like a picture; leave out its unpleasant aspects, he said: "since you won't get back the village life; write, write it down."[3]

But she didn't. "What is there to write about?" she had thought. The stories, sparkling with childhood memories though pleasant in conversation, seemed commonplace, unimportant, ill-suited to a life in ink and print. Only after her mother's death did she realize why Rabindranath might have urged her to commit the memories to paper: writing brought comfort. Rani began with short pieces. Only later did she put together these scattered recollections into a narrative.

An accomplished dancer and painter, Rani Chanda's (1912–97) literary career began when she started writing down the painter-writer Abanindranath Tagore's childhood stories in 1940. In Rani's writing we find the vividness and lucidity that characterizes Abanindranath's stories, as well as the pleasurable tone of reminiscence lined with the pathos of loss.[4]

Taking up the task decades after that first invitation, Rani needed to find an access to that distant time and space of her mother's village. The village home, as ancestral place, was the *permanent* home. Her mother's figure was the point of access and the aesthetic trajectory that she had in mind needed the ordinary practices and events of village life to be articulated *en détail* in all their dynamic exuberance. The journeys that suture that narrative—arrivals and departures of family members and the comings and goings of neighbors, and her own perambulations in that village—might appear to have little to do with empire, too remote from the bustle of burgeoning colonial cities. In terms of physical infrastructure—roads, railways, and river transportation—the village was ill-provided. Its remoteness from the administrative centers in provincial towns and capital cities was not a function of distance as the crow flies, but of the paucity of transportation facilities that moved people and goods.

And yet there were comings and goings from the district headquarter—*sadar* town—where the college or court were located. Clothes, books, fireworks, and jewelry purchased in Calcutta were anticipated. Boxes of dates from Basra—"not like the small local ones but the large variety"—came as a welcome surprise.[5] Bottles of pickles and homemade sweets were sent from this village home to the *temporary* residences in distant locales. News, ideas, goods, and practices from afar tumbled in, creating eddies of excitement, conversation, and exchange amid the calm proceedings of everyday life. They did not fill infrastructural gaps, but sparked affect. The "ordinary affect," both intimate and shared, in Rani's telling illuminates a world of lost connections.

"The ordinary is a circuit that's always tuned in to some little something somewhere," notes Kathleen Stewart in her discussion of everyday life in the contemporary United States.[6] In the world of early-twentieth-century colonial Bengal, the rural ordinary carried the double burden of colonialism and nationalism. Crudely speaking, from the colonialist perspective it was the backwaters whose only recognition was through the logic of extraction—of resources and revenue. And from the nationalist perspective it was the domain of the folk carrying the potential of national regeneration. In such imaginations the village becomes a subject of reform and restructuring. Rani's narrative quietly disavows both these approaches. Her stories delight in the concrete materiality of place, and are alert to the possibility of alighting upon "some little something somewhere." The ordinary in sparking affect brings forth an aesthetic episode. The autographic keeps the ethnographic at bay. Her tunings formed by the memory-desire of her child-self suggest connections—more properly, digressions—without any attempt at resolution. Contrary to Rabindranath's advice, Rani shows no inclination to leave out the unpleasant aspects of this village community. Her understanding of aesthetics is generous—it has no need for jettisoning the unhappy aspects of the village community. It leans toward the word's more capacious Greek derivation from aesthesis—sensation or perception—rather than its more circumscribed meaning of aesthetics as relating to beauty.[7] Finding beauty in the ordinary requires being attuned to this other possibility of aesthetics.

The kind of connections and continuities that emerge in Rani's picture of village life, however, are created not entirely through human volition. The agency as individual will presumed in the modern use of the word "aesthetic" is undercut by a more complex registering of forces and sensory affects. Here ordinary affect sparks connections among land, water, and humans in unexpected ways. The land and the rivers have a pace and story of their own. They disrupt and intervene. And they are accommodated.

"A Heap of Jasmines"

The home was Rani's mother's father's house in Gangadharpur (alternatively Sridharpur) village in the erstwhile Bikrampur pargana in eastern Bengal,[8] now Bangladesh: a small village, "enveloped in shade, filled with water and greens."[9] Rani's story takes shape around the daowa or raised porch.[10] It connects the house with the people in the village, and their everyday lives.

The house comprised four separate buildings, the *bhite*, organized around a large central courtyard or *uthan*. An *angyina*, open front yard, in Hindi *angan* (the terms *uthan* and *angyina* are sometimes used interchangeably), and a row of date palms separated the house from the main path on the south.[11] A *tulsi mandap*—holy basil set in a small platform—in the front yard welcomed visitors to the house.[12] Lit by an evening lamp, it signified the wellbeing of the householder. Each building in the courtyard was designated a different use: the sleeping compartments on the south and east, the dual kitchen for vegetarian and nonvegetarian preparations on the west, and a guestroom that also functioned as a schoolroom to the north. The daowa mediated between the interior rooms of the *bhite* and the open-to-sky courtyard. The entire assembly demarcated by a fence acquired the appearance of an inward-looking space centered on the courtyard.

The spacious courtyard was work space, ritual space, gathering space, and circulation space in one. Busy all day, it was as if "the basket of household work stowed away for the night" got "emptied onto the courtyard every morning."[13] The courtyard was the space of arrival and departure; groceries were unloaded here; pickles and paddy were sunned under the open sky; *muri*, puffed rice, *cheera*, parched rice flakes, and *gur*, jaggery from date nectar, were prepared in makeshift stoves.[14] Neighbors often cut through the courtyard on their way to another destination. Thus, the interiority of the courtyard was always anticipatory to sociality. Meeting with neighbors was a daily occurrence in planned and unplanned ways.

The four apartments of their house were built on high earthen plinths—waist- and chest-high—to ensure the rooms stayed above floodwaters. This was the norm for houses in the village. The walls of their house were of woven bamboo fastened with cane: "fence" Rani called the thin walls. The wood awning windows opened outwards. The tin roof was tethered to a strong wood frame supported on stout *sal* columns. Patterned cane ties completed the construction. The rooms had spacious attic storage—*kaar*—where everything from bedding to foodstuff were stored. Parrot motifs were chiseled into the wooden lintels above the door of the southern apartment. Lotuses were carved on the doors. The *sal* beams of the daowa, shaped like shark heads, celebrated fine craftsmanship.[15]

In the morning, Rani's mother would sit in the daowa of the southern apartment and cut vegetables:

> Aunts arrange the water bowl, wooden platters, knife, plates, vegetable baskets in front of her. Ma cuts vegetables . . .
>
> She has always fancied this task. The manner in which she cuts the vegetables, rinses them in water and arranges them in portions on the wooden platters—it looks as if *naivedya* (ritual offering of food) has been laid out in front of the goddess . . .
>
> Her skill in cutting vegetables is something to learn—something to see. The julienned bottle gourd arranged in a pile looks like a heap of jasmines . . .
>
> Ma cuts vegetables—so many people from the village and the neighborhood drop by. The daowa fills up. They speak and Ma listens . . . So many stories of happiness and sorrow . . . stories of the past and the future.[16]

Her mother's household labor transforms the modest and otherwise undistinguished daowa into a venue and a site for stories; stories of a dynamic landscape patterned by arrivals and departures, droughts and floods, festive times and tastes. Here the white flesh of bottle gourd is rendered light and airy by an expert hand, becoming food fit to be dedicated to gods. The performance of an ordinary chore shines in its skilled brilliance—it becomes an event worth experiencing, and worth recounting.[17]

The present tense in Rani's text conveys immediacy and the expectation of continuity and return. The refrain—"she cuts vegetables"—reiterates the long duration of domestic labor and offers the rhythm of daily routine against which all interactions and events gain significance. Her (re)turn to present tense is an invitation to witness the aesthetic episode, as if it had never ended—it continues into the present.

Duration and Materiality

The characters that populate Rani's narrative gather their authenticity and verve from the spaces they inhabit: as if her story depended crucially on the faithful description of these spaces. Making the characters alive in the present requires paying attention to the materiality and assembly of space.

Duration is essential to materiality. Many of the building materials used in the house—mud and bamboo—require frequent maintenance. The seasonal storms challenge the structural integrity of the thin walls and roofs, and rains erode the earthen plinth. The bamboo walls have to be repaired, the courtyard and daowa have to be resurfaced, and the plinth mended before and after the rainy season. The earthen daowa has to be plastered every day.

The main compartment of Rani's grandparent's house had a tin roof. While a light tin roof requires less maintenance than thatch, and is an improvement of sorts—more modern—it is susceptible to "lift" in stormy weather and can be lethal if carried by a gale. Storms are distinguished in this region by their timing and force. In early summer, before the mango pits had hardened, the nor'wester or *kalbaishakhi* ominously shows up in the late afternoon without warning and the storm—*toofan*—season begins. It is an anxious time. *Kalbaishaki* is an occasional storm; *toofan* is a routine afternoon occurrence in this region.

Daily routines change during the storm season. Dinner is finished early, while there is still some light in the sky. Everyone gets inside the southern sleeping apartment, the strongest structure in the premises. The storm makes the walls shudder, the roof groans under stress; the sound of trees collapsing in the storm adds to the tense atmosphere of early evening. The storm passes and the morning sun shines on the courtyard filled with fallen leaves and branches. By afternoon the courtyard is again made spotlessly clean. Then they wait for the next storm.

During one such storm, while the children huddled under the bed, Rani's uncles stood ready with axes in case they needed to cut the roof ties that bound the roof to the sturdy columns. This was to prevent the entire structure being carried off by the force of the wind. Then came the sound of big rain drops on the roof. And relief. Once the rain starts, the *toofan* calms down.[18]

The summer months bring the gift of mangoes. The anticipation builds in spring as the budding *gopalbhog* mangoes drape the courtyard with fragrance. As the day turns, the colors change. The bright yellow squash blooms on the fence signal the approaching evening. The cooking and washing in the kitchen take place in the dim light of small kerosene lamps. The moon and starry sky brighten the courtyard. Gas lamps are an occasional augmentation during festivities. No one felt the need for additional light, Rani recalls.

Duration is fundamental in another sense. As if in keeping with the riverine landscape, the built spaces ebb and flow with time and with the seasons: "the white-earth courtyard shines all day and night like a brimming tank shimmering with light in the breeze."[19] This aquatic imagery is in keeping with the region's topography—a land crisscrossed by wide rivers and innumerable small streams that braid the land and give sustenance to the humans and nonhuman animals who live in this *jal'er desh*, water-country. The social rituals of the village are intimately tied to the seasons and its riverine geography.

Some spaces are brought close together at certain moments and dispersed at other times. The connectivity revolves around shared religious and domestic rituals in this neighborhood of Hindu households. In the evening the sound of conch shells from every house creates a collective space. Rani's mother's *ashor*, convivial gathering, in the southern daowa is full from morning till evening, and the activities on that daowa and the adjoining courtyard shape the spatial and social links. Rani's aunts flit through the courtyard all day fetching things from one room to another. In the afternoon, the laughter and chatter of the children gathering in the schoolroom fills the courtyard. Rani's eldest aunt was the teacher in this village elementary school. Whether her mother is cutting vegetables, knitting lace, reading, carving stone molds for sweets and mango pulp, or distributing homeopathic medicine among the villagers, the comings and goings create nodes of activity and conversation amid the constancy of domestic chores. These spatial nodes are intersections of multiple temporalities: seasonal and cyclic time of harvesting crops—rice and jute, the homogenous time of print culture, modern medicine and labor in a colonial-capitalist regime, and the ritual time of household gods and community.

The ritual center of the house is the central column of the main southern building. It is the place for the household goddess, Lakshmi. Each year the figure of the goddess is painted on the column by a neighbor, an accomplished painter. She executes her art amid the convivial gathering of women and children after the chores of the midday meal are over. The work takes a few days as layers of paint are added to create the scene: the goddess's figure is set against a blue sky and at her feet is a body of water with lotuses. Every morning her aunts conduct the household worship at this altar, and every evening an oil lamp is lit at the base of the column to signal the arrival of evening. An earthen pot above the flame collects the soot—it is used as *kajal*, kohl for the girls. The mat walls of the rooms are layered with popular prints, torn off from literary journals such as *Prabasi* and *Basumati*: of "Gandhiji, Tajmahal, Rabindranath, Tilak, Kanchenjunga, a turbaned Bankimchandra, and others."[20] Here the mythic time of household gods jostle with the secular time of literary print culture and its pictorial imagination of distant places and noteworthy heroes of the imagined nation.

Rani's family was well-connected to contemporary literary and art worlds in Calcutta, Santiniketan, Tokyo, London, and beyond. Rani's father, Kulachandra Dey, was an officer in the colonial government, a poet, and a close friend of Rabindranath. Rani's experience of this rural world is bracketed by the death of her father in 1917 and the career of his eldest brother, the artist Mukul Dey, whose return from London in 1927 concludes her narrative. By the time Mukul Dey left for London in 1920, his paintings had already been published in *Prabasi*, *Bharati*, and *Modern Review*.[21] His letters bring news from Bombay, Seattle, San Francisco, Chicago, New York, and London. Rani's mother stows away letters, books, and paintings in trunks. Twice a year these works are laid out in the courtyard in the sun to get rid of any dampness.

Rani gets to handle her father's manuscripts, the ink sketches by Abanindranath and Gaganendranath Tagore, and stacks of her elder brother's paintings. Among the letters are those written by Rabindranath to her father, and from Charles Andrews and William Pearson to her mother and brother. Pearson's letters to her mother are in Bengali. The small girl reading these letters is amused at Pearson's misspelling of *mata* (mother) in his address to Rani's mother as *matathakurani* (respected mother). Rani is awed by the illustrations in the books on "Rembrandt, Dürer, da Vinci." It creates a habit of looking at paintings and sparks the imagination. On a quiet afternoon she practices pencil sketches from illustrations in *Prabasi* "in secret."[22]

The interiorized space of daowa and courtyard of each household is turned outwards during festivals such as Lakshmi Puja. Women give alpona with rice-flour paste on the courtyard floor to welcome the goddess. The large intricate patterns are the women's prerogative, while the children are given the task of painting the goddess's footprints in the daowa, the thresholds, and the *tulsi mandap*. On this day the central courtyard is the celebratory focus with the daowa and forecourt relegated to peripheral status.

The elaborate designs in the courtyard are a measure of the skill of the women of each household, and neighbors move from house to house to see the alpona painting in action, eliciting comparisons. The alpona, sometimes as large as the courtyard itself, are both precisely planned—designs of expanding circumference traced on the smooth earthen surface—and also open to improvisation as individual imagination and skill permit. The framework for the alpona is created by tracing circles using a string attached to a central peg, but the rest is the work of skilled fingers. Rani's mother is proficient in this art: her eight-petal, hundred-petal, and thousand-petal lotus designs located at the center of the alpona look crisp. The clusters of thousand petals seem infinite. Her grandmother, however, has the best hand in drawing the bent-lotus design. The central lotus design is surrounded by foliage patterns of various kinds and a snake wrapped around the vine. An urn design completes the painting. Judiciously placed dots—carefully released drops of rice paste—pick out the form of the vines: the alpona "calls out." Now it is time for the goddess to enter and take her place in this patterned habitation. Rice stalks painted on the floor form the paths that the goddess takes to various parts of the house—the *ota* (steps), daowa, thresholds, and the rooms, to the grain storage, the cattle shed, and the grain-husking shed to bestow her blessings of prosperity.[23] The white design of the alpona brims over in the light of the full moon.

The alpona motifs carry mythical connotations but are drawn from the region's land imagination and everyday life: *sanhkalata, chaltelata, kalmilata, khuntilata, chirunilata*—vines patterned after conch shells, the leaves of the banana and the elephant apple tree, water spinach, kitchen spatulas and combs (Figure 12.1). They create a resonance between land, work, and adornment. Since the rituals are performed to celebrate and seek blessing for sustaining life, the region's seasonal crops, fruits, and flowers show up in the pattern as do animals associated with particular rituals: owls, peacocks, butterflies, swans, snakes.

In one register, alpona is a quintessential land art.[24] In another register, calling it land art fails to capture its materiality. Traditionally drawn on the ground without a paintbrush, with fingertips as the guide to drip the thin rice paste, it involves a distinct tactility. You touch the ground. Unlike wall paintings in rural India, alpona and its brethren *rangoli* are not meant to be permanent. They are cleaned up after the ritual is concluded, and thus

FIGURE 12.1 Alpona patterns, from left to right and top to bottom: khuntilata (spatula-shaped vine), *chaltelata* (chalta [elephant apple]-shaped vine), rice stalk and foot print of the goddess Lakshmi, *kalmilata* (*kalmi* [water spinach]-shaped vine), *anshlata* (fish-scale-shaped vine), *kalar chhara lata* (vine shaped like a bunch of bananas), *sankhalata* (conch-shell-shaped vine), *kalalata* (banana-shaped vine). Source: Swati Ghosh, *Design Movements in Tagore's Santiniketan* (New Delhi: Niyogi Books, 2019), 62.

create a soft imprint. Whether indoors or outdoors, alpona is an art of placemaking, where humans, other-than-human creatures, gods, and spirits come into contact. The design superimposes on everyday space a new pattern of inside and outside. Thus demarcated, everyday space is transformed into ritual space. Alpona, Rani recalls, was executed for all rituals. Young girls were initiated in its basics as they were instructed in *brata*s, ritual observances.

As folk art, the regionally specific patterns of alpona were eagerly collected—drawn on paper—by a nationalist elite keen on incorporating these feminine designs into a new nationalist-regional aesthetic.[25] This desire for collecting an ephemeral art meant to last only for a small duration introduced into its planning and execution a longing for permanence that is inimical to the art's *raison d'etre*. It changed its durational parameters. The transference onto paper enabled this art form to be moved from its specific rural milieu to locations far removed from their ritual efficacy. Once drawn into the more rarefied universe of academic training in Santiniketan, it would evolve into an art form in the hands of artists such as Sukumari Debi, Nandalal Bose, Gouri Bhanja, and their contemporaries and successors.[26] The latter version of alpona was detached from its socioreligious moorings and brought closer to the art of mural painting. Artists used paintbrush as well as fingertips to execute the drawings and introduced motifs not found in the rural tradition of alpona in Bengal (Figure 12.2). In its secularization its application was extended to a wider array of events: felicitations of nationalist leaders, university convocations, and such. Gouri Bhanja's alpona art was commissioned for the 1954 Indian National Congress Meeting in Kalyani, West Bengal (Figure 12.3). In such applications alpona was moved from its role in a cyclical time of seasonal rituals to serve the linear homogenized time of the nation. Rani Chanda had experienced this transformation firsthand in Santiniketan, and her "returning" alpona to its womanly rural confines in *Amar Ma'r Baper Bari* signals the possibility of a different set of connections between inside and outside, house, yard, field and waterbodies, and between art and time.

As Rani's narrative moves from the daowa to a larger dispersed landscape of households, flower and fruit trees, canals, ponds, tanks and rivers, her readers are urged to walk with her to the sites that attracted her childhood attention. One such place is the Subachani drawn on one side of the ghat of Nandi's pond. Painted with oil and vermillion, the three female figures, compositely Subachani (literally, delivering auspicious words), are the keeper and conveyer of good news. This is important in a village in which there are so many close relatives who live in far-off places. Letters take time to reach. The women of the village rely on Subachani's providence to receive good news, to know that loved ones in distant places are faring well. When a postcard arrives bearing the good news of Julfi's husband's new job, Subachani is felicitated at the ghat. The sound of ululation runs through the village—a sign for everyone to gather, witness the observance, and so share

AN AESTHETIC EPISODE 195

FIGURE 12.2 Kalabhavan students drawing alpona, Santiniketan. Photographer unknown. Courtesy Rabindra Bhavana Photo Archives, Visvabharati, Santiniketan.

FIGURE 12.3 Kalyani Congress alpona panels. Source: Swati Ghosh, *Design Movements in Tagore's Santiniketan* (New Delhi: Niyogi Books, 2019), 188.

in the good fortune.²⁷ The letter is read aloud at the conclusion of the ritual in consideration of those who can't read.

Sounds of sadness and brutality carry across the village as well: every time Maroni goes to her in-laws' house, she cries. Loudly. This is expected. The in-law's house is in a distant village; it would be heartless not to cry. Her low wail travels across the fields even when the *dooly* (palanquin) carrying her can no longer be seen from the village.²⁸ The wail seems to pick up the rhythm of the palanquin-bearers as they carry her away. When Sasadhar Chowdhury beats his wife, her cries of distress sound different. So do the cries of a wife and a mother mourning their husband/son. Their crying, sudden and at odd hours, is heart-wrenching. It disturbs the composure of the village held together by the everyday materiality of sound.

Paths that Connect

The paths that connect the destinations in this story of a rural community are neither fixed nor available in the same manner throughout the year. In a village with a poor road infrastructure, movement defines paths, rather than paths movement. The clustering of residences based on religious and caste affiliations are overlaid with durational factors to create spatial knots comprising the village. The clusters change as boundaries between land and water shift with the seasons. We see the paths and spatial clusters finding definition through Rani's childhood recollection of the seasons and her access: where she could go, what she could see and hear.

Rani's mother would visit her father's house twice a year, in summer and during the pujas in autumn, when the children were home for the holidays. The rest of the year, she rented a house in the suburbs of Dhaka. This suburban house was very different from the house in Gangadharpur. The masonry building—dalan—sat on a spacious compound filled with flower and fruit trees. It was known for the large sour mango tree that stood just outside its gates.²⁹ Its courtyard was smaller in comparison to the large courtyard of its rural counterpart. This urban courtyard was a necessity, not a space of conviviality, and neighbors would not pass through it on their way to a different destination: the spatial organization precluded that possibility.

The journey to Gangadharpur from Dhaka by boat took an entire day. They embarked from the ghat at Buriganga and proceeded toward the turbulent waters of the Dhaleswari, and then to the placid Ichhamati. In the afternoon they reached the turn in the river that led into a narrow canal or *khal*, lined with the houses of *jola, bhuinmali, shekhs*—lower castes and Muslim families.³⁰ All were on a first-name basis with her mother, and the news of her arrival would reach home long before she reached her father's house.

In the last stretch the boatsmen have to get down into the shallow waters and tug the boat. When they reach the canal that joins the Ichhamati near the roots of the large banyan tree they are close to their destination. Next to the canal is Rani's grandfather's friend Baban Khan's house—Rani's mother calls him Baban-uncle. As the boat nears the Khan household, the eldest son of the family, Ali Hosen Khan, comes out to the water's edge to inquire whose boat it is. Rani's mother pokes her head out. "It's me, Hosen-bhai."

"Oh, it's Puni-boyindi." Her name is Purnashashi, Puni in short. Through familial addresses such as grandpa, sister, and brother, relations with neighbors are constructed as an extended family.[31] Glad to see her, Hosen-bhai sends a stalkful of bananas and a couple of ripe jackfruits to the boat. The boat moves slowly. Everyone, except young housewives, come out of their house to greet the family returning home. Rani portrays the village as an intimate community, despite differences of wealth and status: "A daughter has returned home to the village: everyone shares that joy."[32]

The landscape is fluid, transformed by the rains and *unna*, the dry season. In summer the boat reaches as far as Murali Ghosh's bamboo grove. Then they have to walk to the house. By the puja season in autumn, the monsoon-fed water of the *khals*, tanks, and ponds became connected: then they can land at the ghat of their household pond. Rani's story creates a riverine geography of interspersed spaces—*bhite, uthan, ghat*— connected by canals, *beels* or marshes, and foot tracks that disappear in the rains.

The village had two *paras*—neighborhoods within walking distance—on the east and west side of Ghosh'er Bari'r Khal. The path in front of their house led westwards past the Nandi House to this *khal* and in the other direction it ended at the Eastern House. A *bel* tree in the courtyard of Eastern House, the house of Sushila-aunt, marked the location of the Shiva temple. Further east beyond the fields of mustard and peas was the house of Naran Bhuinmali: standing on the high bank of the pond of the Eastern House, Rani could see the roofs of the houses of this distant *para* sheltered by trees, but she wasn't allowed to go that far.[33] Her daily perambulations took her along the path that led westward. Unlike the houses on the eastern end that were separated by canals and high banks, the houses of the western end were all on one bank, and through this part of the neighborhood stretched the path that connected the large pond of the Nandi's, the resort of the entire neighborhood, to Ghosh'er Bari'r Khal.

The space between the rear of the kitchen of Rani's grandmother's house and the masonry residence of the Nandi's is forest-like, dark, studded with mango trees, and a large *jamrul*, java apple, tree. Ripe, bat-eaten fruits line the path. A little further past the Durga mandap of the Nandi House is a *jhumko joba*, chandelier hibiscus tree. Full of red-and-white-striped flowers, this old tree has a special attraction for Rani—she runs there first thing in the morning to fill her flower basket.[34]

Just south of the *jhumko joba* tree, down the sloped path was Gobinda'r-ma's small house where she lived alone. Gobinda's mother, a widow who had lost her son Gobinda many years ago, still carried the attachment of his name. She scraped a living by foraging greens and doing small chores at the houses of her better-off neighbors in return for a handful of broken rice. To her north lived Dinanath Kabiraj in his substantial residence, his daowa enclosed by a railing. The house adjoining Kabiraj's house was Satya Ghosh's, from which the canal to the west derived its name. In dry weather, Rani splashed across its ankle- or knee-deep water. The canal and the path across it were lined with clusters of bamboos. The leaning bamboo created a dark mysterious stretch that scared Rani: the more she tried to hurry the more she slipped on the smooth bamboo leaves lining the path. Just beyond the bamboo grove was the house of Gopal the washerman. The path led to Subashi-sister's house just beyond the large ancient peepul tree. The peepul tree harbored ghosts.[35]

Rani's recitation of the names of these houses and their inhabitants is not troubled by the concern that none of these people are noteworthy in the historical record. Recognition of their singularity helps her fabricate the spaces of this rural settlement, striated by distinctions of caste, religion, wealth, and position. It is also self-evident that the houses of the upper-caste Hindus—the Ghosh, Bose, and Nandi households—were separated from that of the lower castes and Muslim families by fields and canals. In her narrative, these spaces are not simply connected by an ardor of hospitality, but there are divisions. People, however, move back and forth through these divisions. Most of all they are connected by the movement of water. Floods breach distinctions, highlight others, and connect in powerful ways.

Flood

The arrival of "new water" from the river to the *khal* that borders the villages is vital news and the people react as a community. As the river water rushes into the canals, the village is made alert. The path of the floodwater is predictable as it moves from the canal to the large ponds, sinking the village paths, and then moves into the courtyard of the house: "five fingers, ankle deep, knee deep—up to the waist and then the gurgling stops . . . All around the calm water stands still." Rani's grandmother hauls the kids onto the daowa. Her uncles settle on the bed with their books and papers. Her mother sits down to stitch a *kantha*, while her aunts return to their domestic chores.[36]

Much preparation has already taken place in anticipation of the rainy season. The earthen foundation of the daowa has been strengthened. A temporary bamboo bridge has been suspended across the courtyard to facilitate movement among the apartments. A canoe made from plantain trunk is used to convey goods between the rooms. Moving between households now requires boats.[37] As the "white water" settles just short of the raised daowa, defining a new edge between land and water, the daowa becomes fishing platform and a dock of sorts.[38]

The rains turn the rural landscape into one continuous stretch of water. Houses are built on high ground because the land remain flooded three to four months a year. The water levels increase and recede according to an expected sequence. With the downpour the paths between households—low-lying foot tracks during the dry season—become small canals.[39] The seasonal floods facilitate movement. The region did not have roads to speak of, and therefore travel by boat was easier than travel on foot.

The school inspector visits during the rainy season, as does the matchmaker and the *shankhari*, conch-shell jewelry artisan. The *shankhari* moors his boat on the column of the daowa. The boat's bow extends into the daowa so all can see the boxes full of dazzling white conch jewelry. A variety of patterns are engraved on the conch bangles—crystalline, motifs of leaves, fruits, and flowers like the patterns of alpona. The married women exchange their old bangles for new ones. Young girls get pendants and rings. The appraisal and fitting occupy several hours; Rani's grandmother serves the *shankhari* a plate of *cheera*, flattened rice, and fruits on the daowa before he departs for the next house.

The immersed land opens up fresh vistas and opportunities. Once the muddy waters have stilled, the mud sinks to the bottom—now the children can play in the clarified water. Once in a while Rani accompanies her youngest uncle to the *shapla* woods that defines the edge of the *beel*. They gather a boatload of these edible pink water lilies. The 5–6-foot-long *shapla* stems are plucked one by one and peeled to prepare various dishes: *shapla* bitters and stir fry, and *shapla* fritters shaped like mini canoes. Rani weaves the *shapla* stems into garlands with the flowers hanging as pendants.

One year the central courtyard is raised higher to prevent frequent flooding. The household pond to the east of the house had been deepened and made larger. Now the women would not need to go far to fetch water during the dry season. The earth dug out of the pond is used to raise the level of the courtyard. The new water and new earth complement each other. Fresh earth has been dumped in the banana grove behind the vegetarian kitchen as well; it becomes another courtyard of raised earth. Rani's grandmother plants vegetable seeds in this fresh earth with her hand; no digging, no tools, just a gentle prod into the earth with her fingers—pumpkin and white gourd, snake gourd, and okra. The vine of the white gourd climbs up the bamboo arbor created for it and blooms hundreds of flowers.[40]

The water recedes the same way it arrives. Dramatically. The water in the courtyard is gone in four days. Now the hardships begin. A thick layer of mud everywhere; the stench of foliage rotting in the sun; the proliferation of mosquitoes, snakes, and frogs; and then there is illness.[41] One day their neighbor Satya Ghosh notices the rice fields in the distance moving. He sounds the alarm. Prolonged inundation has loosened the rice saplings from the ground. The receding water is taking away with it this upper layer of rice field. There is no time to consider whose field it is. Bamboo stalks are rapidly cut and hauled onto the boat: the rice fields have to be fenced in because the force of one such rushing field will unmoor adjoining fields. The stalks will end up who knows where in this mobile land. Stabilized, the crop remains in the field. In the days to come the plants will grip the earth, the stalks will stand erect, and the green shoots will smile in the sun.

Mobility, migration, loss, and permanence gather a particular constellation of meanings in this seasonal world-making. Flood here is not an exceptional natural calamity.[42] It is a routine seasonal occurrence that forces a changed pattern of living. It produces a different rhythm of daily life and is accommodated through temporary infrastructure, by raising the levels of courtyards and plinths, and by learning to notice the turns and flows of water. The movement of water moves the land, creates new ones, and destroys existing ones. Building with materials that cannot move with the wind and water, and cannot be easily patched up and renewed, is folly.

Rani's Story

Although the stories constitute several visits, the beginning and end of the book captures the temporal and experiential limits of Rani's acquaintance with the world of this small village. It is the temporal distance and its placement flanked by the two large cities—Dhaka and Calcutta—that makes the ordinary spaces of a rural landowning family appear luminescent with longing. If Rani's story commemorates both Rabindranath and her mother, her narrative is built on loss in more ways than one.

Unlike her mother, Rani did not have a "father's house" to return to. Her father had died when she was a child. The house that he had built on the banks of the Padma in his ancestral village, imagining it to be his retirement home, had long been swallowed by the river. Along with the house the entire village had disappeared. Her mother's natal house, which in the tradition of patrilineal Bengali families would not be considered her mother's "permanent" home, filled that absence. That loss made it possible to create a matrilineal tradition of belonging: "In my connection with the soil of this village," she wrote, "is my link to the soil of all villages."[43]

By the time Rani was penning her memoirs there was a well-established genre of Bengali writing that took the Bengal village as its chief site of exploration. And study of village life from the standpoint of folklore had been advocated and conducted for at least half a century. The Bengal village, as the quintessential site of Bengali nationalist imagination in its opposition to the colonial city, had become both the site of reform—modernizing agriculture, education, and health facilities—and simultaneously a fertile locale of landscape imagination expressed in poetry and paintings. Rani Chanda's story of her mother's father's house cannot be easily assimilated into this genre. It skirts the moralizing tendencies of the bulk of the nationalist writings on the village to carve out a path that can comfortably settle on the prosaic details of rural life. Seen through a joyous aesthetic, the wretched aspects of village life are registered and incorporated in the storytelling. The references to misery in the village community are woven into the bliss so intricately that the negative spaces cannot be pried away from the positive spaces of the village landscape with any resolve.

It is also not possible to isolate the characters from the places described: the characters in the village draw their specificity from the spaces they inhabit. When her grandmother takes Rani along to invite Gobinda'r-ma to fry puffed rice at their house, they sit just outside her open door in the daowa, while Gobinda's mother finishes her scant midday meal of rice gruel. They depart hurriedly when her grandmother recognizes that Gobinda's mother wishes to eat the rice starch salvaged from straining the rice to fill her stomach. But she would have to get up to reach the bowl of rice starch, and as a widow, entitled to only one rice meal a day, she could not bring herself to contravene this high-caste rule in front of Rani's grandmother. Gobinda'r-ma was negotiating two aspects of her marginal standing in the community: as a widow and as someone so poor that she had to consume rice starch. Gobinda's mother needed the seclusion of her small house to do so, out of the prying eyes of her neighbors. The daowa as a barrier between house and village facilitates silence, understanding, looking away.

Rani's recollection is predicated on never returning again. This home was already a distant site of memory; the house might be there, and even some of the people, but that time had passed. The story of this village was already of a village past. When Rani looked back to think of her mother, she saw the village home. As if to express her mother's character she needed the physical settings that comprised her mother's father's home and the extended village community. It was in that village milieu she found her mother fulfilled and appreciated. She belonged there: the only daughter among eight sons, her father's house was Rani's mother's "throne." She was consulted in all matters by her mother and brothers. She was effectively the eldest among the siblings because the only brother older to her had left home never to return. It is clear that this beloved daughter and sister maintained her position in the family by applying herself and assuming the responsibility of the person in charge of the household. She was, however, filling the space of a son who never returned. This position as the head of the family was always temporary. She, too, could never return.

Rani did not remember her mother before she was widowed. This is to say she never saw her mother dressed in colorful clothes, with vermillion in the parting of her hair, wearing jewelry appropriate for a married woman. The possibility of framing her mother within such a convention of beauty was unavailable to her. But there was a small patch of memory that stayed. It was the luminous image of her mother having returned from her *mouni-snan*—silent shower. That day no words were to be uttered before the morning bath. Her mother had just returned from the pond after an early-morning dip. Rani could recall the patch of her exposed right shoulder, and next to it a bit of the wide "biscuit-patterned" necklace:

Her fair complexion and the gold of the necklace mingled, I recall clearly. The color of her skin has faded with the suffering of life, in the sun and rain. But when she comes and stands in the courtyard after her *mounisnan*, the first rays of the sun fall on her body, that image of her shoulder seen in childhood still comes to my eyes.[44]

Where speech stops, sight attains acuity. It produces a singular instance of time-space that stays with her and which her text reaches to recover.

The patches of memory that constitute Rani's narrative forcefully speak to some fundamental issues of home, belonging, and land imagination constructed in the colonial milieu. I have referred to Rani's narrative as a set of digressions that seems to shift their loci and refuse a narrative resolution or the kind of moral efficacy demanded by nationalist narratives. In some ways this has to do with the disappearance of the home of the past, literally and figuratively. It is the absence of her father's house that prompts her to create a diverse set of narrative tracks as acts of placemaking. Thus, her nostalgic return is not geared toward locating a lost site of permanence. Her narrative fabricates space by attending to the ephemeral—to a land that moves, flood water that shapes living space, the light that creates sites of remembrance, alert to small disturbances in the fabric of everyday life—producing an imagination of materiality that subtends the nationalist desire for a pure site of cultural origin. In that way it does not conform to what Susan Stewart calls the "social disease of nostalgia."[45]

Rani's story draws its emotive force from the movement between languages—between "proper" standard Bengali and the local language of her mother's village—an aspect that does not suffer translation. It is impossible to convey in English the affective difference between the local tongue and the standard, urban, reformed Bengali. In the colonial context in which all Indian languages were considered "vernacular," placed in hierarchical opposition to the master's language—English—the local languages (often referred to as dialects) were even more marginalized. Rani's use of the local tongue to convey affective encounters interrupts the hegemony of standard Bengali that had itself been formed in the crucible of colonialism and modern print culture, and carrying with it a strong anticolonial strain. Unlike her uncles who had lobbied to give the village a more respectable name, Rani figured in the colloquialisms of the everyday rural community a geographical specificity that was worth holding on to.

Perhaps behind this linguistic inheritance and insistence resides the messy, drawn-out violence of the 1947 Partition that divided Bengal into Hindu and Muslim territories. In a region in which rivers are "notoriously wayward," Cyril Radcliffe's hastily drawn partition boundary was premised on the assumption of geographical fixity.[46] And as Joya Chatterjee points out, in an instance of "astounding negligence" not only did Radcliffe not bother to understand the geography except on a paper map, neither did the

Hindu and Muslim politicians who clamored for their piece of communal territory as an imagined homeland.[47] To acknowledge the fluidity of home and homeland required a different imagination of space and a different point of view where the impact of such big decisions on small spaces could be registered. That imagination demanded an acknowledgment of the uncertainty that rims the distinction between land and water.

13

Roofscapes

I clearly sense the difference between those days and our present times when I notice that neither humans nor ghosts and spirits frequent the rooftops of today's dwellings.[1]

Rabindranath Tagore (1861–1941) wrote this lament about the vanished charm of rooftops in the last years of life and indexed the lost world of his childhood. The modernity of twentieth-century Calcutta, its crowded streets, and the glare of electric light had banished the enchanted evenings that clung to the nineteenth-century city. Indeed, the loss of rooftop sociality signaled a loss of dwelling space in the city, if by dwelling we mean both a space of habitation and a site of imagination that enable being in the world.

Rabindranath's memoirs and other literary works are replete with references to rooftop terraces. His elaborate recollection of rooftop space in his two memoirs *Jibansmriti* (1912) and *Chelebela* (1940), however, is also a staging. It is his search for an opening—literally and figuratively—to his boyhood days.

As the custom of his family dictated, Rabindranath's early childhood days were spent in the care of servants. Even within the house his access to different parts of their sprawling residence was restricted. He was not allowed in the grown-up world of men or the interior compartments of the women. Confined to the world of servants, he found in the terrace a rare opportunity to overcome the physical limits to his movement. The open space of the rooftop terrace allowed Rabindranath to set up his own relationship with the outside world. This outside never came within his grasp, he recalled later in life, but it cast its enchantment.

That the terrace as an everyday space acquired a special quality is borne out by its repeated appearance in the literary archive of Bengal, in the works of Rabindranath and that of others, in memoirs, poems, short stories, and novels. A space of leisure and intrigue, games and performance, of household labor, and gardens, the terrace was most of all a space for observing and crafting connections. Rabindranath was sufficiently impressed with the promise of the terrace as vantage to have turned the terrace into a trope of liberation in his stories. In the memorable concluding scene of his novel, *Char Adhaya* (Four Episodes, 1934)—a love story set in the context of terrorist nationalism—the rooftop becomes the site for the declaration of romantic love that seeks to oppose the death drive of nationalism.[2] That sense of the terrace as a liberating experience, as a space of deep affect, was rooted in his own experience.

Terraces, like houses in the colonial city, came in all sorts of sizes, and indeed many were not dimensionally small, but they only seem to appear in narrative interstices or as backdrops, rarely emerging as sites important in their own right. We can only catch the narrative moments when they emerge in relief as myriad small references—often only snippets of information. Placing these within a larger historical frame risks violating their character as narrative device that enables the affective spark. At least it requires a recognition that the historical frame is necessarily porous and open-ended.

Openings

The constricted movement to which Rabindranath was subjected as a child opened up a different possibility of seeing the city. The parapet wall of the terrace rose above the child's head, so he would peer through the openings in the parapet:[3]

> I could see the line of coconut palms demarcating the limits of our inner garden; through these could be seen Singir Bagan,[4] a pond in the locality, and next to the pond the cow-shed of Tara, the milk-woman, who supplied us with milk; farther still intermingled with the tree tops the range of Calcutta terraces with their various shapes, sizes and heights, reflecting the brightness of the afternoon sun and disappearing into the pale blue haze of the eastern horizon. The occasional eagle perch, raised attic stairs, stood out on those distant rooftops; it seemed as if with their stilled lifted forefingers and a wink they were trying to signal their inner mysteries to me ... Overhead the searing brilliance of the sky, and from its farthest reach the shrill cry of an eagle would reach my ears and in the lane next to Singir Bagan a peddler passing by the mid-day-siesta-silent houses would give his melodic cry "want bangles? want toys?" turning all my thoughts forlorn.[5]

A play between memory and pictures animates Rabindranath's reminiscence. The past appears as image impressions:

> I do not know who paints the pictures on the canvas of memory. Whoever does so, his task is to paint pictures. He does not sit brush in hand to reproduce whatever that happens in front of him. He deletes much and keeps much else in accordance with his own taste. He reduces big events

to small episodes and enlarges those that are small. He hesitates not a bit to alter the sequence of events . . . Reminiscence of one's life is not history . . . the impressions on the canvas will not suffice to furnish evidence in a court of law.[6]

The sarcasm about evidentiary status aside, his analogy between memory and pictures calls for attention. Rabindranath points out that when he sat down to look back upon his life, the past appeared as image-impressions.[7] These images were not endearing merely because they were the stuff of familial affection. The memories were enchanting because "picture viewing has its own addiction," and when he "found the respite to look back" he became engrossed in "perusing these pictures of the past."

"The variegated colors" of such pictures are "not reflections of outside lights, but belong to the painter himself," he insists.[8] In choosing to dissolve the distinction between the self and the image-impressions, he allows the temporal distance to create a space between the images and the viewer, a process that enables the impressions to be plucked at will and woven into the fabric of a literary narrative.

His declaration—"there is nothing in these memories that deserves to be rendered eternally memorable"—is not mere modesty, but a mode of releasing the picture-memories from the burden of standing as evidence, of revealing more than they possibly could tell.[9] It also frees him from adhering to the norms of male Bengali autobiographical writing. He could indulge in the painfully personal, the affect of prosaic domesticity, and the utterly ordinary details of familial relations, without embarrassment or accusations of emotive excess. As material for an (auto)biography he speaks of these images as trivial—"incomplete and unnecessary."[10] As literary material, he hopes, his recollections would have some merit.

Rabindranath's notion of history was far from naive or reductive. In the heyday of scientific history, he argued for the need to popularize history by injecting it with the magic of good storytelling.[11] Rabindranath's claim that this is not the stuff of history is thus not an academic distinction, but an insistence that imagination (*kalpana*/fancy) be given a free rein in reflecting upon one's experience. His entire reminiscence may be seen as a way of expressing how he came to acquire this habit of imagination.[12]

Rabindranath's Story

The house on 6 Dwarakanath Tagore Lane, begun in 1783, and enlarged in the first two decades of the nineteenth century, consisted of several later additions (Figure 13.1). The most important addition was the construction of a *baithakkhana bari* (literally, meeting house) in 1823 as a separate building on the right of the main entrance to the premises (see Figure 8.2). Built by Rabindranath's grandfather Dwarakanath, this building functioned as Dwarakanath's office/salon/banquet house. He entertained his European acquaintances here, and when his relation with his wife Digambari Debi became strained, he moved into the *baithakkhana bari* for good.[13] After Dwarakanath's death in 1846, his eldest son, Debendranath (Rabindranath's father), inherited the main house, while the middle son, Girindranath (Abanindranath's grandfather), moved into the *baithakkhana bari*.[14] The latter had to be significantly reconfigured with the addition of courtyards and rooms to accommodate the needs and privacy of nineteenth-century Bengali domestic arrangement. The original building inherited by Debendranath received the address 6 Dwarakanath Tagore Lane, while that inherited by Girindranath acquired the address 5 Dwarakanath Tagore Lane.[15] Both houses were modified to suit the changing needs of the extended families, and indeed three new buildings were added in the late nineteenth and early twentieth centuries adjacent to the west and east sides of No. 6 (only two of these later additions are shown in Figure 13.1).[16]

The original house, No. 6, was a sprawling mansion divided into several parts in which the distinctions between the public apartments in front (*bahirmahal*) and the private apartments at the back (*andarmahal*), and that between servants' space and family space were paramount (Figure 13.2). The latter often took the form of a separation between the lower floor for public purposes and services, and upper floors for the family's private apartments. The children of the household were confined to the sphere of

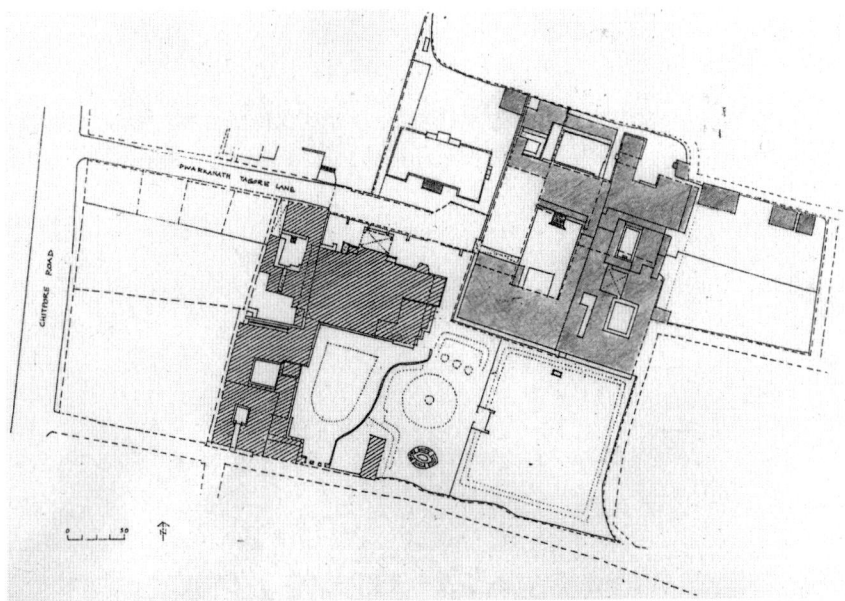

FIGURE 13.1 Site Plan of 5 and 6 Dwarakanath Tagore Lane, based on Plan of Calcutta 1901, © Swati Chattopadhyay.

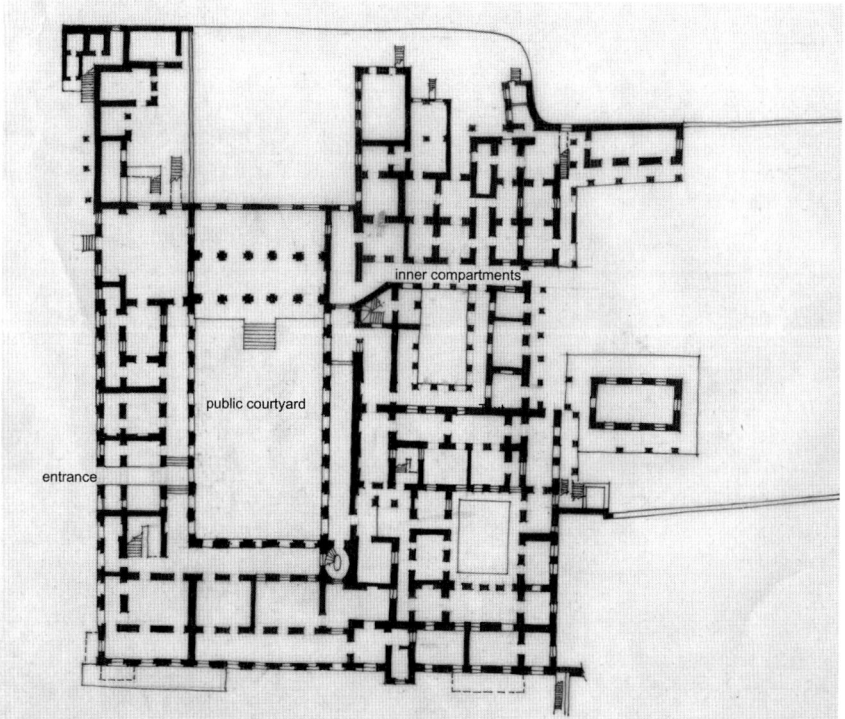

FIGURE 13.2 Ground Floor Plan of 6 Dwarakanath Tagore Lane, based on plan in the collection of Bichitra Bhavan, Kolkata. © Swati Chattopadhyay.

servants, occasionally emerging into the peripheral space of verandahs and terraces. Only when they were a little older could they dwell in either the outer or the inner spaces of the household commanded by grown-up men and women, respectively. The gendered distinction between the inner compartments for the women of the family and the outer compartments for the men began to change only in the 1870s.

Rabindranath's vivid description of the interior spaces of his childhood home and specifically the terrace of the *andarmahal* focus on the many everyday domestic tasks that sustained the large extended family (**Plates 19, 20, 21**):

> This terrace, above the private quarters of the house belonged entirely to women. The place was well in tune with the demands of the pantry. It received direct sunlight which facilitated the pickling of limes. There, the women, their brass vessels full of ground black gram, squeezed out drops of the mixture to form *bori*, lentil dumplings, while they dried their hair in the open. The female attendants would hang out the washing in the sun. Unripe mango was dried to make *amshi*, and mango juice was poured into stacked-up black-stone ornate molds of various sizes, and

left to congeal. Tender jackfruit pickle, steeped in mustard oil, would mature in the sun, *keya-khoyer*, screwpine-scented catechu, was prepared with great care.[17]

In this terrace, work and leisure commingled, with the hard physical labor performed by the multitude of servants that populated the household. The servant population was at least three times the number of family members. A significant amount of labor went into preparing the ingredients for the *bori* and pickles as these needed to meet the demands of a very large household: various kinds of lentils had to be soaked, ground, and mixed with spices to make *bori*. Piles of fruits and vegetables had to be cut and juiced, then seasoned to fill earthenware and stoneware jars. Every evening the *bori* and pickles had to be brought down from the terrace and returned when the sun was up. The pickles and dumplings thus prepared were meant to last the entire year.

Rabindranath saw in the life of this terrace a whiff of village life: the terrace accommodated those activities that would be carried out in the courtyard of a rural household. The lengthy labor-intensive process of food production, from husking grains in a *dhneki* and grinding grains and lentils in a quirn to preparing the daily supply of cooking spices using a grinding stone took place within the household well into the twentieth century. Until the availability of refrigerators in the twentieth century it was imperative to utilize the daily fresh produce and dry or pickle fruits and vegetables for the off-season. Churning milk to produce butter, preparing fresh cheese and yogurt, and evaporating milk to produce sweet confections were routine activities in middle-income and wealthy households.

Life on these terraces ebbed and flowed with the seasons and time of the day. Many of the household tasks were performed in keeping with propitious times of the lunar calendar. Such rituals gave significance to mundane domestic activities and became celebratory occasions for the women of the household. As communal processes, such tasks taught the women skills and familial roles. The purification rites involved in making *kasundi* (prepared mustard) and *bori* were followed dutifully well into the first half of the twentieth century.[18] Young women were taught the art of preparing *bori*; shaping these dumplings such that they retained their erect form was considered an auspicious sign and preparatory for more important ritual tasks at weddings and religious events.[19]

Purnima Debi who grew up in the twin mansion, No. 5 Dwarakanath Tagore Lane, has left us a precise description of the small terrace next to the *thakurghar* (room for worship) on the third floor of the *andarmahal* of this house. This terrace did not have a railing and was specifically intended for drying foodstuff, particularly *bori* and fruits:

> A wire-net-enclosed sliver of terrace; it had a lock and key. After lentil dumplings, mango pulp, tamarind and pickles were put out to sun in this

terrace, the door would be locked. Mango pulp on decorated stone platters would be set out to mature in the sun. When grandma put away the dried mango pulp, *amsattwa*, she would give us the remnants from the plate: "no more now," grandma would say; "once the mango season is over, you'll get the *amsattwa*. Now eat this."[20]

Such autobiographical details convey the importance conferred on these mundane domestic tasks, but also function to document a way of life that by the time Purnima Debi was writing had already become a thing of the past. But she could always return to that moment of postponed desire. Intended to teach the children seasonal variations in food, her grandmother Saudamini's scant gift built anticipation and created a narrative moment that gave depth to her story of the inner spaces of the Tagore mansion. Between the elaborate preparation and the regulated serving the ordinary event became memorable.

Rabindranath's recollection of terrace life of the inner compartments of his childhood, although two generations before Purnima Debi's, echoes that very sense of lost space, a space that wove ordinary household activities with multiple strands of everyday intimacy to produce a realm of deep affect. As if each small insignificant act and gesture, from drying hair to pickling mangoes or reading a book (none of which in and of itself could be explained as the reason for such fond recollection), deposited a kernel of attachment on the space. Each time the act was performed, the attachment was deepened. This is not a form of affect that is anterior to reason or action; indeed, repetition and long duration seemed to have been necessary for the affect to take form and anchor itself to place. The loss that Rabindranath and Purnima Debi seem to convey is perhaps this lost sense of duration belonging to a long-gone world.

Time in the women's world of his childhood moved slowly: it created an interior space untrammeled by the schedule-bound responsibilities of the outside world of the colonial city. Rabindranath's mother Sarada spent her summer evenings on the third-floor terrace at No. 6 with her female companions sprawled on fine mats laid on the terrace floor:

> Their talk required no hard facts. Their only need was to while away their time. Those days, there was no regular supply of diverse pastimes to fill the hours of the day. The day was not a close-knit mesh, but more like a loose net with copious gaps and openings.[21]

Rabindranath had from an early age chafed against the grid of time that dictated the everyday lives of boys and men in the urban world of colonial Calcutta. The child imagined that the inner compartments were a space freed of compulsion—a mysterious space of cherished interiority.[22] Looking back upon his childhood days, Rabindranath remarks that until he realized the "freedom within himself" he failed to learn anything.[23] The realization of this freedom required a time-space to call one's own. He repeatedly writes of the need to fend off the encroachment of business/busyness (*anabasar*) in all domains of life.[24] Time gaps (*phank*) and respite from work (*abasar*), he insists, are necessary for creative pursuits and for shaping one's sense of self.[25]

Terrace leisure had a different connotation in the *andarmahal* at No. 5 where Saudamini, the painter Abanindranath Tagore's mother, presided over evening gatherings. Saudamini, widowed at an early age, ruled her household in a manner quite different from that of No. 6, where Sarada was the mistress of the household and exercised considerable control over everyday domestic matters, but her husband Debendranath as the head of the house set the household norms. The widowed Saudamini was second to none in her household. The terrace next to Saudamini's room was the "center" of activity on summer evenings. There, her servant Mokshada laid out two low divans covered with fine mat, so that a large number of people could be accommodated.[26] Important decisions regarding family events and invitation protocols were made here and Saudamini's three sons along with her brother-in-law participated in the discussions. Access to Saudamini's gatherings was restricted. Children were asked to stay away from such grown-up conversations, and the daughters-in-law did not directly participate in these decisions.[27]

Sociopoetics of Circumscription: Terrace Lives

The recollections of Rabindranath and Purnima Debi about terrace life are as much about their search for creative loci as they are about the servants who sustained everyday lives in these houses through their labor and care work, and the ability of those relatives who managed to craft exceptional spaces from the quotidian fabric of the extended family. The various stories of terrace lives in this household alert us to the sociopoetics of circumscription.

When he was a child, Abanindranath's pictorial sensibility was sparked by one room in his house at No. 5 that stood out as an exception. On the third floor of their house Abanindranath's aunt Kumudini Debi had created a little world of her own, combining her uniquely furnished room with the terrace in front where she kept a variety of fancy pigeons—*lakka, shiraji, mukshi*—in bamboo and wooden coops. Unlike the halls and other bedrooms in the house that were furnished after the European manner, the artwork that brightened Kumudini's room included Indian paintings from Jaipur, Bengal *pat*s that depicted mythical Hindu themes, as well as oil paintings. It brought to mind Suryamukhi's room in Bankim Chandra Chattopadhyay's 1873 novel *Bishabriksha*. Here Kumudini would spend her leisure hours, reading, crocheting, and knitting. This was the only place in the house in which the young Abanindranath could "breathe comfortably." At dusk Kumudini would feed the pigeons on the high-walled terrace. The sight of her aunt sitting on the terrace, swarmed by pigeons, struck Abanindranath's pictorial imagination. The ample sunshine on this terrace and its raised walls also made it suitable for other purposes such as taking family portraits. The novelty of family photographs taken by a European woman on this terrace cast a lasting impression on Abanindranath.[28]

For Rabindranath the terrace became a landscape unto itself. When he was a little older and could escape from servants, he found in the terrace the time-space he yearned for: the key to his "freedom."[29] He recalled walking about aimlessly under a moonlit sky among the shadows cast by the potted palms on the third-floor terrace of the house that his sister-in-law Kadambari Debi had arranged with great care.[30] The terrace was transformed into a sensory field into which he could insert his own desire to rupture the ordinariness of the everyday and his own limits. Rabindranath cited two specific instances of his boyhood days in which the everyday space was catapulted to the realm of exceptional aesthetic experience. Both of these involved the third-floor terrace of the *bahirmahal*.

At No. 6 two sets of third-floor rooms on the terrace were built—one set of rooms in the *andarmahal* and the other in the *bahirmahal*—to accommodate the expanding extended family and to more fully utilize the open environs of the terrace. Though unadorned on the inside, the tiled-roofed verandahs that surrounded these light-filled airy rooms distinguished these spaces from the rest of the house. They helped create private worlds within a house full of relatives and servants.

When Rabindranath's father Debendranath was home, visiting from his usual sojourn in the hills, he would occupy the third-floor room of the *bahirmahal* and make it his private domain. In the early morning he would meditate in the adjacent southeast terrace: "he sat still like a stone sculpture, his hands folded," Rabindranath recalled with awe. When Debendranath was away, the small boy would sneak up to this now vacant closed room and while away his afternoons. He had discovered an "oasis" on this third floor. In 1872 the Tagore household had taken advantage of the introduction of plumbing in the city, and the water had sufficient pressure to reach the third-floor bathroom. The indulgence of an impromptu secret shower thrilled him. The midday hours, when everyone else was asleep, felt like midnight to the child—"time for the child-*sannyasi*, recluse, to renounce the world." In that precious spell of loneliness he would feel the "thrill of high adventure, like crossing the seven seas."[31]

Much later, when Debendranath was at an advanced age, these rooms next to the terrace were refurbished to suit Debendranath's minimalist tastes.[32] When the western balcony suffered damage during the 1905 earthquake, a set of canvas awnings—"like the sails of a ship"—were set up to protect the rooms from the sun. In consideration of his frail health, upturned earthen vessels were installed on the roof of the rooms to enhance

PLATE 1 Staircase, St. Olav's Church, Serampore. Photograph by Sanjeet Chowdhury, 2020. © Sanjeet Chowdhury.

PLATE 2 J. G. Bartholomew, "Commercial and Strategic Chart of the British Empire on Mercator's Projection, Specially Designed for Mr. Parkin's 'Imperial Federation'," 1892.

PLATE 3 Sita Ram, "An opium godown in Patna," from View by Seeta Ram from Patna to Benares Vol. II, watercolor, *c.* 1814. British Library shelfmark: Add.Or.4701 © British Library Board.

PLATE 4 Chow Kwa (active 1850s–90s), *Augustine Heard & Company headquarters, Shanghai*, 1857–62, Oil on canvas, 17 1/2 × 23 1/8 inches (44.5 × 58.7 cm). Museum purchase with funds from the John Robinson Fund, 1943, M5130. Courtesy of the Peabody Essex Museum. Godowns are to the left of the main building.

PLATE 5 Judges of Circuits bungalow in Gageepore (Ghazeepore), 1823. British Library shelfmark: IOR X1004, plate 12. © British Library Board.

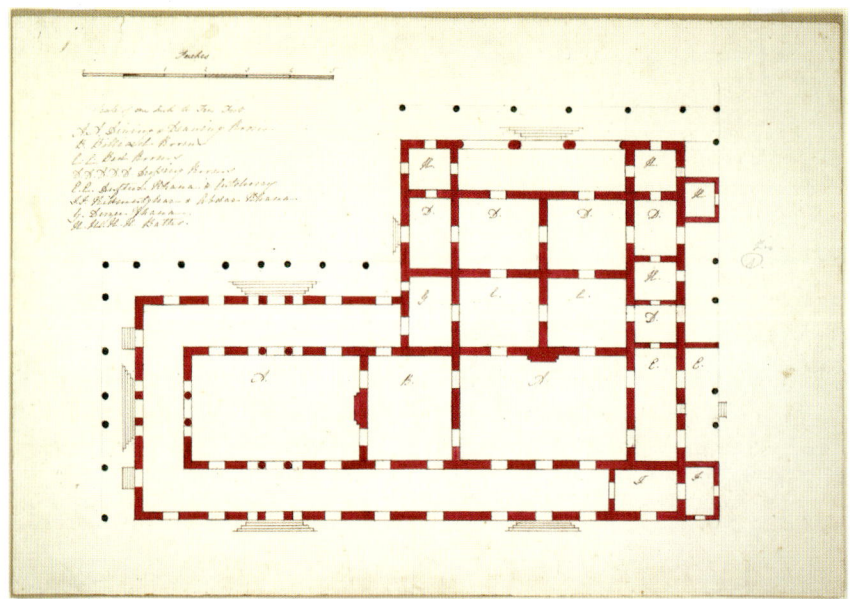

PLATE 6 Plan of Lt. Col. Gilbert's bungalow in Hazaribagh, watercolor, *c.* 1825. British Library shelfmark: Add.Or. 2515. © British Library Board.

PLATE 7 View of Lt. Col. Gilbert's bungalow in Hazaribagh, watercolor, *c.* 1825. British Library shelfmark: Add.Or. 2514. © British Library Board.

PLATE 8 Sita Ram, "The tavern and farm-yard of John Havell outside Dinapore cantonment," from View by Seeta Ram from Patna to Benares Vol. I, watercolor, *c.* 1814. British Library shelf mark: Add.Or.4708. © British Library Board.

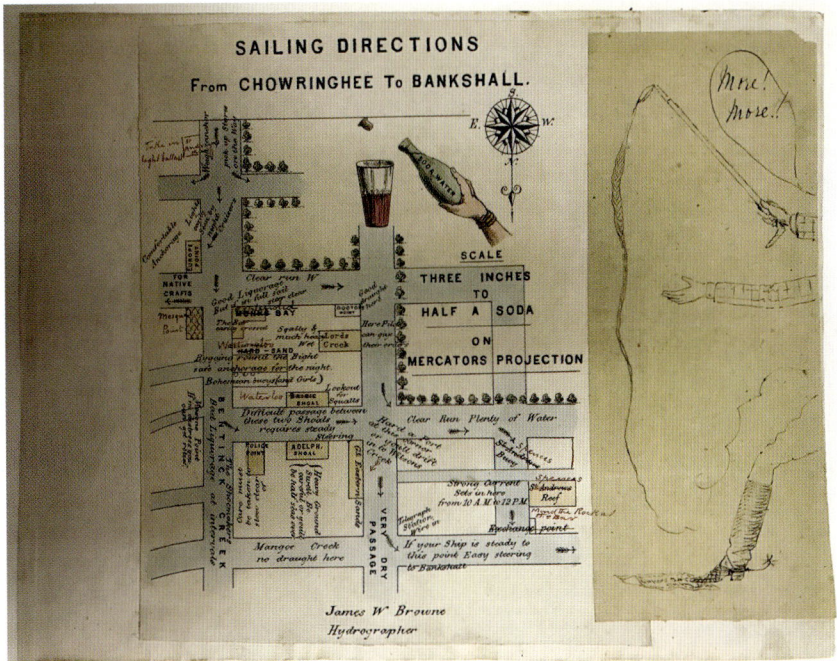

PLATE 9 James W. Browne, "Sailing Directions from Chowringhee to Bankshall," *c.* 1876, British Library WD1346. © British Library Board.

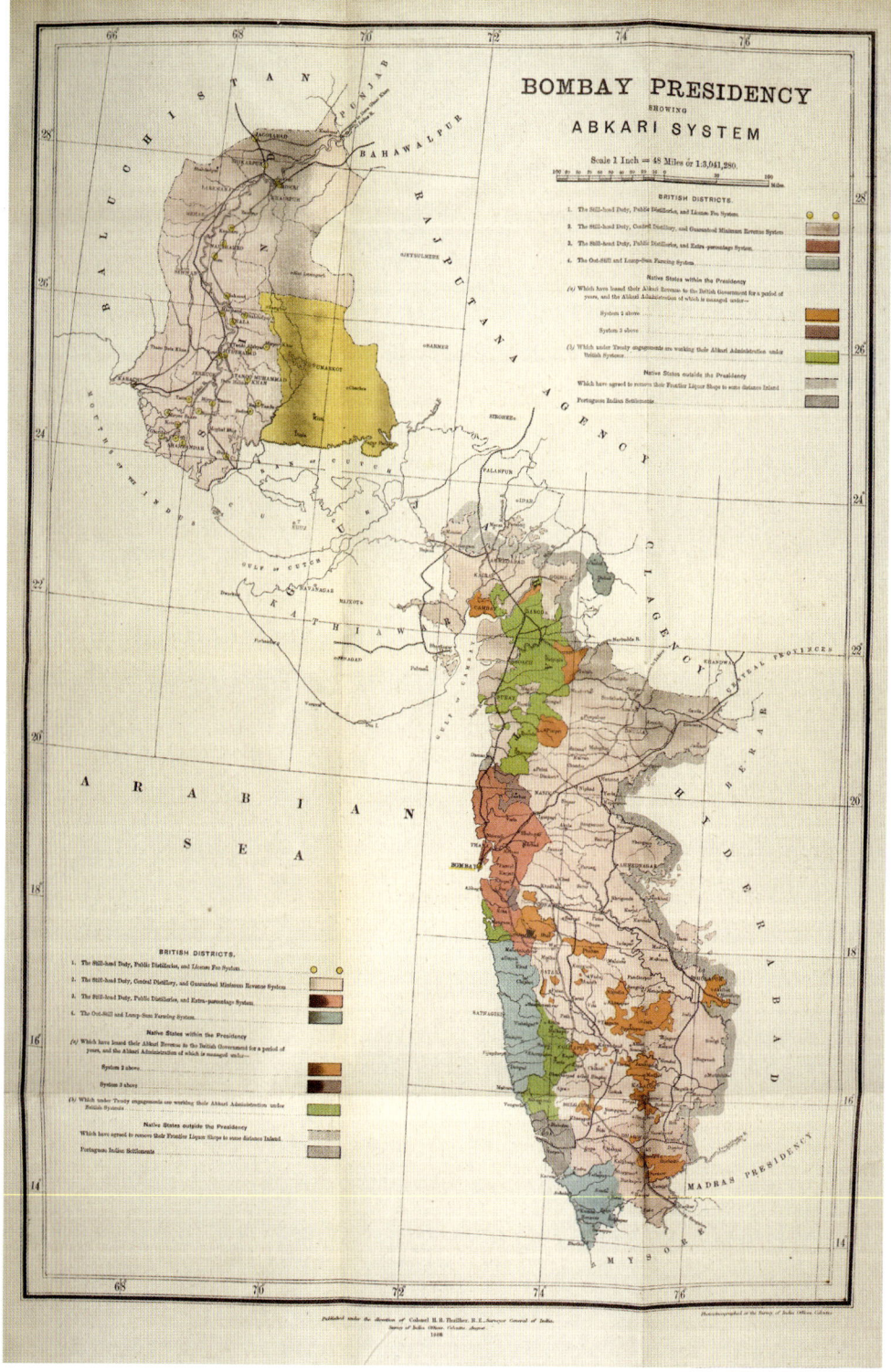

PLATE 10 Bombay Presidency showing abkari system. Source: C. E. Buckland, *A Report on the Systems of Abkari Administration*, 1888. © British Library Board.

PLATE 11 Johann Zoffany, *The Auriol and Dashwood Families in Calcutta*, oil on canvas, *c*. 1783–7. Courtesy of Holburne Museum.

PLATE 12 Shaikh Zain al-Din, *Lady Impey and her servants*, *c*. 1780. Private Collection.

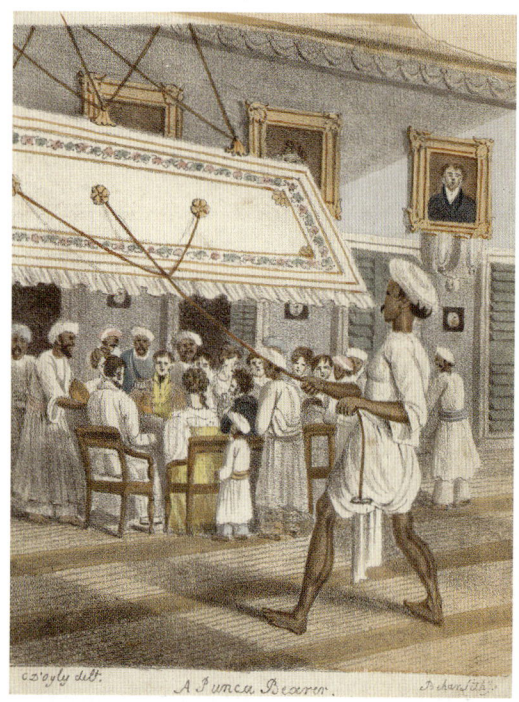

PLATE 13 Charles D'Oyly, *A Punca Bearer*, chromolithograph on paper, *c.* 1813. Courtesy of Yale Center for British Art, Paul Mellon Collection.

PLATE 14 Casper David Friedrich, "Wanderer Above the Sea of Fog," *c.* 1817. Oil on canvas, 94.8 × 74.8 cm. Collection of Hamburger Kuntshalle, on permanent loan from the Foundation for the Promotion of the Hamburg Art Collections. Photo: Elke Walford.

PLATE 15 Anonymous artist, Watercolor of bungalows with extensive verandahs, Maidapur, Bengal, 1795. On the reverse of the painting is inscribed: "South East or back view of Mr. Oldfield's House at Moidapore and Doctor Wilson's Bungalow near it." British Library shelfmark Add.Or.3190, © British Library Board.

PLATE 16 Daowa facing courtyard in rural residence, Daronda, Birbhum. © Swati Chattopadhyay.

PLATE 17 Mihr Chand, Colonel Antoine Polier Watching a Nautch, *c.* 1773–4. From The Collection of Prince and Princess Sadruddin Aga Khan, Accession No. M160.

PLATE 18 Rooftops in Calcutta, William Clerihew, 1843. Watercolor. © Royal Institute of British Architects.

PLATE 19 Inner courtyard of 6 Dwarakanath Tagore Lane, © Swati Chattopadhyay.

PLATE 20 Verandah of Tagore Mansion, 6 Dwarakanath Tagore Lane, © Swati Chattopadhyay.

PLATE 21 Terrace, 6 Dwarakanath Tagore Lane. © Swati Chattopadhyay.

PLATE 22 Garden Bed Design, Illustration in Landolicus, *The Indian Amateur Gardener* (Calcutta: W. Newman & Co, 1881).

PLATE 23 "Front View," Iris Macfarlane's bungalow, Cherideo Tea Plantation, Assam, by Alan Macfarlane, 1959. Illustration in Alan MacFarlane (ed.), *Twenty Years in Tea*, 2019.

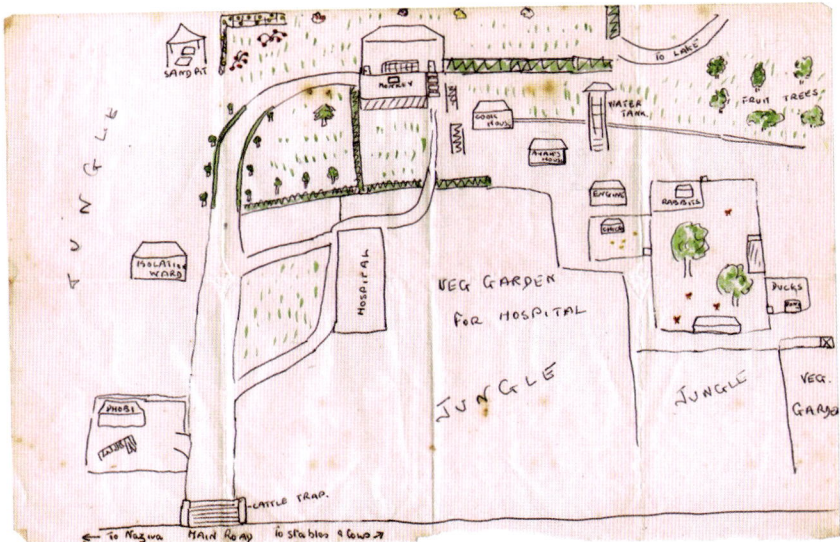

PLATE 24 "Coloured plan of Deopani bungalow and surroundings, with Ayah's house, cook house, rabbits, chicks, ducks, sandpit etc." Illustration in Alan MacFarlane (ed.), *Twenty Years in Tea*, 2019.

PLATE 25 Charles D'Oyly, "English Gentleman and his Munshi," *c.* 1813. Source: Sir Charles D'Oyly, *The Costumes and Customs of Modern India* (London: Edward Orme, 1825).

PLATE 26 Sir David Wilkie, "General Sir David Baird Discovering the Body of Tipoo Sultan after having Captured Seringapatam, on the 4th May 1799," 1839, NG 2430, National Galleries of Scotland, Presented by Irvine Chalmers Watson, received 1985.

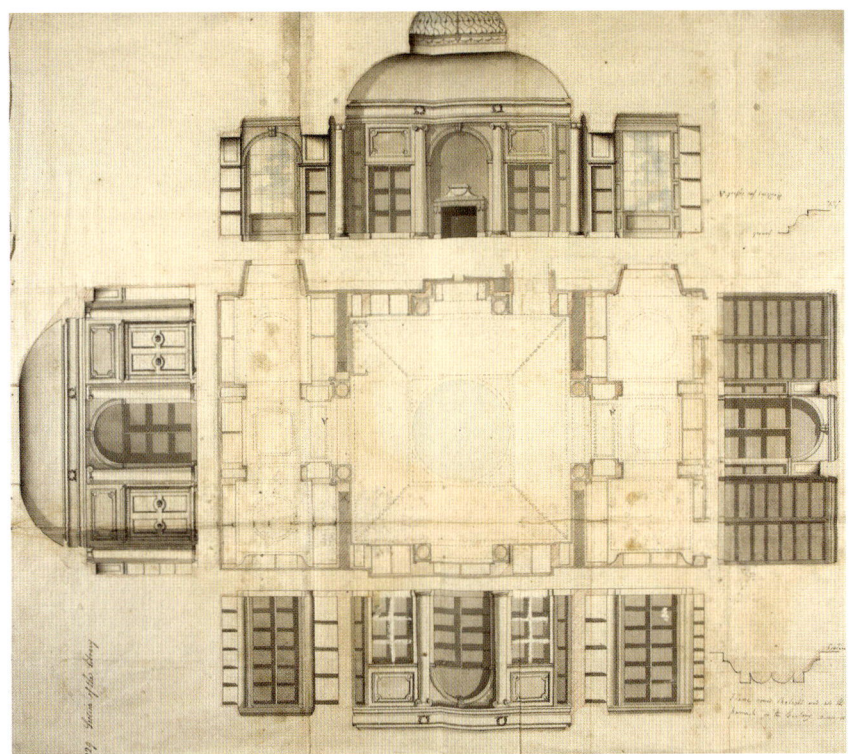

PLATE 27 Richard Jupp, Plan and Elevations of the East India Company's Oriental Repository, c. 1797–8. Accession No. D.1672-1898. © Victoria and Albert Museum, London.

PLATE 28 "The East offering its riches to Britannia," Allegorical ceiling piece commissioned by the East India Company for the Revenue Committee Room in East India House, 1777. British Library Shelf Mark: Foster 245: 1778. © British Library Board.

PLATE 29 Residence of Iswarchandra Vidyasagar, Kolkata. © Swati Chattopadhyay.

PLATE 30 Walnut homeopathic medicine chest, containing 35 bottles and a pullout tray. © Science Museum/Science & Society Picture Library.

passive cooling. At the end of his life, servants would carry him to the terrace in a chair so he could conduct his morning and evening prayers, with Priyanath Shastri reciting the *mantra*s. Rabindranath was summoned to sing on these occasions.[33]

By that time the terraces in the Tagore mansions had become important sites for musical events and plays, but here, too, certain transformations took place in the 1870s when the terrace in No. 6 witnessed some formal and social changes, hastened in part due to the passing of Rabindranath's mother Sarada in 1875. Social relations between brothers-in-law and sisters-in-law, as well as between husbands and wives, became more informal as household members broke gender barriers to participate in plays, edit literary magazines, and collaborate in writing songs and composing music.

In the 1870s Rabindranath's elder brother Jyotinindranath and his wife Kadambari occupied the topmost room in the *andarmahal*. The room had a small added-on kitchen, and a tiled roof attached to the room opened onto the terrace. Such a spatial ensemble provided the couple a private corner; it was not intended to function as a communal space characteristic of Sarada's terrace gatherings on the third floor. Kadambari had "full possession" of her terrace.[34] Some years later the couple moved into two rooms on the third floor of the *bahirmahal* and Jyotinindranath's younger sister Swarnakumari Debi, a writer, took up the rooms next door. This was a novel experiment in modern living within the Tagore household. For Swarnakumari and Kadambari this also meant claiming a time-space to nurture their talents and subjectivity.

Swarnakumari's terrace rooms in the *bahirmahal* enabled her to keep aloof from the day-to-day domestic activities that animated the *andarmahal*. Her children lived in the *andarmahal* in the care of servants, except the youngest who stayed with Kadambari. Swarnakumari's daughter Sarala Debi remembered that they would play on the third-floor terrace with other children of the house, but her mother in the adjacent rooms remained an "unapproachable goddess figure," engrossed in her writing.[35]

For Kadambari, the terrace became an asset for articulating a romanticism that even a decade earlier would have been unthinkable. The new rituals of Kadambari and Jyotinindranath included hosting summer evening musical soirees on the terrace. Kadambari arranged tall potted palms on the terrace and a host of flowering shrubs completed the fragrant ensemble: "jasmine, gardenia, tuberose, oleander, white ginger lily." "There was no concern," Rabindranath writes in hindsight, "that this might hurt the structural integrity of the terrace."[36] Since grown-up women of the household were not yet supposed to use the ground-level gardens in the house, this terrace garden was a refreshing transformation of the old rooftop space. Rabindranath who was admitted to this privileged space recalled the delight of seeing the changes wrought in Kadambari's apartment now furnished in a modern style. Jyotinindranath's morning coffee was served in the shade of the attic, and Rabindranath often accompanied him in finishing the latest literary work until ten o'clock when the sun robbed the terrace of shade and the crows started claiming their food and space.[37] The evening gatherings were more carefully planned and intensely aesthetic:

> At the end of the day, mats and bolsters were arranged on the terrace. There were jasmine garlands wrapped in damp handkerchiefs in a silver dish, a tumbler of iced water, and in a bowl fragrant *paan* of the indigenous variety. Freshly bathed and dressed, her hair coiffed, Bouthakrun (Kadambari) would take her place. Jyotidada would appear, a light wrap cast airily across his shoulders. He would put his bow to the violin, and I would launch into song on a high note ... Across the rooftops my song would carry into the sunset sky. From the far-off sea, the southern breeze would blow, and the sky would fill with stars.[38]

Such soirees at dusk became a family practice of sorts when the three spent time in the garden houses at Chandannagar and Panihati next to the Ganges, and even earlier in Shelidaha on the Padma River. The open expanse of the river here was a welcome substitute to the relentless line of rooftops in Calcutta. What Rabindranath remembered most about these musical evenings was the delightful harmony of the open terrace, the distant views, and the shelter of the open sky in the warm glow of early evening, all of which facilitated the writing and appreciation of music. In his memory, these various terrace experiences were knit together as a finely woven multihued fabric.

Affective Modalities

Kadambari's sudden death in 1884 shattered the poetic haven of the terrace and brought about a deep transformation in the grief-stricken twenty-four-year-old Rabindranath. The terrace in which he had spent evenings strolling about amid potted palms became a different exploratory site, now touched with the agony of loss. Recalling that time in his late years he remarked:

> When *notun-bouthan* died, what heartache I suffered. I remember that time. I would walk in the terrace till late at night, look up at the sky and say, "where are you *notun-bouthan*, appear before me just this once." I would spend entire nights in that manner. At that time I used to sing this song the most, my favorite ... "Who is that went past my heart like the spring breeze, she touched it and bowed the branches, and made a hundred flowers bloom."[39]

For Rabindranath, the gap in life that now appeared was fundamentally different from the time-gaps that he had so cherished. The loss arrived as a gaping hole "in the fabric of life" unsettling the meaning of comfort that he had ascribed to the life of the *andarmahal*:

When death arrived to tear apart in an instant a portion of this closely held world, my mind was perplexed beyond measure . . .

Alone on the roof terrace of our house, in the deep darkness of the night, I longed to see the fluttering banner of the netherworld, at the main entrance of which inscribed on the black stone would be a letter or a sign, and like a blind man, I groped about in search of it the entire night.[40]

Through the multiple metaphors of darkness as loss, the terrace became in his writing an affective space defined by sightlessness and inaccessibility. The haptic, auditory, and visual pleasures that had until then created the timespace of the terrace were radically reversed. He learned to cope with this loss, however, coming to the realization that this dark emptiness, too, could be a creative opening of sorts, preparing "a distance necessary to perceive the world in its completeness and beauty."[41] It alerted him to a different potential of the sociopoetics of circumscription.

Rabindranath's recollection of terrace experience, both his fond memories as well as the agony of loss, highlights, in reverse, the routine temporality of terrace life. His terrace sojourns are remarkable because he is able to slip out of this routine and discover something enchanting, precious. This aesthetic treasure was Kadambari's gift to him. It is therefore not entirely surprising that he professed to have felt a sublime self-realization during one of his strolls on the terrace in Jorasanko at dusk:

The glow of the setting sun commingled with the pale light at the end of day, making the onset of the evening especially captivating. Even the walls of the adjacent buildings appeared beautiful. I wondered whether this lifting of the veil of banality from the everyday world was merely a trick of the descending darkness. But it was definitely not so. I could see plainly that the evening had fallen inside me, I have been shrouded by it.[42]

That this feeling of transcendence did not occur amid the natural surroundings of the country or the hills, the usual favorite retreats of the elite, is noteworthy. As if an environment defined by the patently unromantic stained walls of city buildings was necessary as a banal contrast for the poet's self-revelation.

Here let me make a tentative distinction between two kinds of attachments or engagements that characterize much writing on city terraces. The first is an accumulation of affect around the small things of everyday domesticity. Such affect remains localized and enables the recollection of terrace life as a function of an anchored experience and correspondingly a lost household space. The second is an expansive process, an aesthetic elaboration that tends to subsume the myriad domestic acts to unleash the poetic imagination, traveling outwards.

Kadambari's third-floor terrace garden invokes this latter mode of engagement. In so doing, Kadambari planted the germ for understanding the terrace as an open-air salon, a part of the public sphere of the city. By turning a domestic ritual into a literary event, one that competed with the all-male gatherings in the *baithakkhana* (that continued to be held on the first floors of both No. 5 and No. 6 into the twentieth century), she changed the spatial idiom of the terrace and with it the idiom of cultural events in the late-nineteenth-century city.

A setting for poetry readings, musical gatherings, and plays, though private affairs, the terrace-salon harbored the intersection of the private and public, one in which women could participate relatively freely. This spatial intervention was necessary because women's access to public space was severely circumscribed. "Respectable" women were not expected to visit the public theater, see plays, let alone perform at a public venue in the nineteenth-century city. In elevating the household event into an aesthetic episode, she made the transition from *gharoa* (domestic) space to public sphere, a relation that would be soon mediated by an emergent Indian nationalism, making that passage smoother than it had been for Kadambari.

The tradition of hosting musical events and plays on the rooftop did not end with Kadambari. Numerous plays were held on the third-floor terrace of the outer compartments of No. 6 into the first decade of the twentieth century. Setting up stage on the open terrace sufficed for launching a new play in front of a select gathering of family and friends. Rabindanath's son Rathindranath remarked that the terrace of the outer compartments of No. 6 was so large—"size of two tennis courts"—that the space was suitable for elaborate stage settings, and accommodated large audiences. The center part of the terrace was raised and acted as a "natural" stage. Prompted by the size of the terrace, here we already see the intention to expand the audience. Tugged on one side by the increasing fame of the writers and artists in the Tagore family, and on the other by the "democratization" initiated by the nationalist movement, the line between public and private increasingly began to be blurred. Even though contained within elite space, these events began to shed their private, household character. Whether as sites where the literary magazine *Bharati* was launched or where *Valmiki Pratibha* was staged, there was an incipient claim to these spaces as "public spaces," or in the least as part of the city's public sphere.

Terrace as Public Space

Seeing the city from the rooftop terrace or partaking in activities on the terrace meant very different things for different people, and was highly inflected by gender, class, and age. For example, the practice of young women and housewives gathering or strolling on terraces with low parapets was considered socially unacceptable into the 1870s in both elite and middle-class houses.[43] This was in keeping with nineteenth-century social norms that severely restricted the access of middle- and upper-class women to city streets and public space, unchaperoned. Free movement between terraces even for the boys and men of the household was a privilege of age.[44]

These restrictions were somewhat mitigated by practices that assumed the rooftop terrace in townhouses, large and small, to be part of a larger spatial ensemble. From such perspective, the terraces complemented the verandahs, arcades, and front porches of buildings. The open-air, covered, and semi-covered spaces in such ensembles were to become platforms for watching the city, of seeing the city as a public landscape.

Writer Nirad C. Chaudhuri writes of his first encounter with the skyline of Calcutta when he moved to the metropolis from Kishorganj in the early twentieth century. The cityscape, studded with church spires, seen from the fourth-floor terrace of a house on Serpentine Row, seemed "dream-like." Seeing the city and the neighborhood from the rooftop became his regular preoccupation.[45] Chaudhuri is not alone in this. Abanindranath Tagore's grandson Sumitendranath Tagore recalls the popular seasonal activity of kite flying that stretched the private character of the terrace.[46]

Flying kites, a precolonial tradition and a decidedly male activity, was a mode of getting to know one's neighbors and sharing a competitive spirit. This community camaraderie was a gendered privilege.[47] Sumitendranath in his recollection of No. 5 in the 1930s and early 1940s notes that on *akshay tritia* in spring the kite-flying season would commence and conclude with Viswakarma Puja in autumn. Sumitendranath remembers this seasonal sport lending not just the house but the entire neighborhood a distinct character. The topmost terrace of the two Tagore houses were the chosen sites for unfurling the kites:

> Our fourth-floor terrace was huge. On one side were two tanks that supplied water to all the bathrooms in the house. We stored our kites in the shaded space underneath these tanks ...
>
> You can no longer behold that sky of north Calcutta during kite season. At that time north Calcutta was an elite Indian neighborhood. It had not shifted to south Calcutta yet. The sky was transformed in the late afternoon. The boys from Rajen Mallick's house, Jorasanko Rajbari, and the Daw House, as well as other neighboring houses, would climb on the terrace to fly kites. The variety of color and shapes of these kites is beyond description.[48]

The boys brought down the kites when the light faded and "the flocks of bats" began their journey southward at dusk. Although the passion for kite flying cut across socioeconomic class, the edge between public and private was more easily controlled in large houses such as those of the Tagores, Mullicks, and Daws. These were relatively self-contained buildings, and stood out as large figures in a tightly knit and fine-grain urban fabric in the northern and central parts of the city. Most middle-class townhouses shared party walls or were separated by narrow lanes. So, chasing a kite took on a different meaning for boys from the middle and lower classes; it required a different facility in navigating the roofscape of the city. Middle-class houses would often have small bridges between them at the roof level so that women of the households could move between the houses without stepping onto the street. These connectors came in handy during kite season. The continuity of such a roofscape afforded other uses as well. During the nationalist period and afterward, it was possible to move between houses undetected by the police on the street.

The taboo of respectable women not appearing on the public streetside verandahs and terraces had eased by the first decade of the twentieth century. At the slightest intimation of a procession or demonstration, people, young and old, flocked to these streetside venues. While in the nineteenth century religious festivities, weddings, and funerals were the main occasions for watching street processions, by the twentieth century nationalist processions and political rallies were added to the list of spectacular events. Sisir Kumar Bose recalls visiting his granduncle Satyendranath Dutta's house in Wellington Square to watch nationalist processions from the rooftop terrace.[49] Enterprising homeowners rented out their rooftops on such occasions.

The provisional transformation of the terrace from a private to a public space did not go uncontested. Bose narrates one such incident involving their house in Woodburn Park in south Calcutta. Built by his father, barrister and nationalist leader Sarat Chandra Bose in 1928, this spacious house was designed as a modern detached residence (Figure 13.3). The tradition of using the verandah for work and meals and the rooftop for exercise, prayers, and soirees, however, retained practices from the past. Mahatma Gandhi stayed in this house during his visits to Calcutta in 1937 and 1938. Gandhi took his morning and evening walks on the rooftop terrace of the house, often slept on the terrace, and his prayer meetings were held there. Dance, *bratachari*, and music performances were organized for such gatherings. The house has two large roof terraces, of which the lower one above the second-floor verandah must have been used for Gandhi's prayer meetings. The plan configuration of the house with its curved rear and side walls created a terrace space that could be conveniently divided into two sections, one for the performers and one for the audience.

Mahatma Gandhi's presence in this house prompted the gathering of immense crowds, so large that even the spacious terrace could not accommodate all those who wanted entry. Masses of people crowded nearby streets and occupied the terraces and verandahs of nearby houses in the hopes of catching a glimpse of Gandhi. On one such occasion, the force of the crowd wanting to move past the main entrance to the house damaged the color-glass panels of the front door. When Sisir Bose tried to explain to those gathered in the car porch that this was a residence, not a public space, so it was not possible to accommodate everyone, someone in the crowd

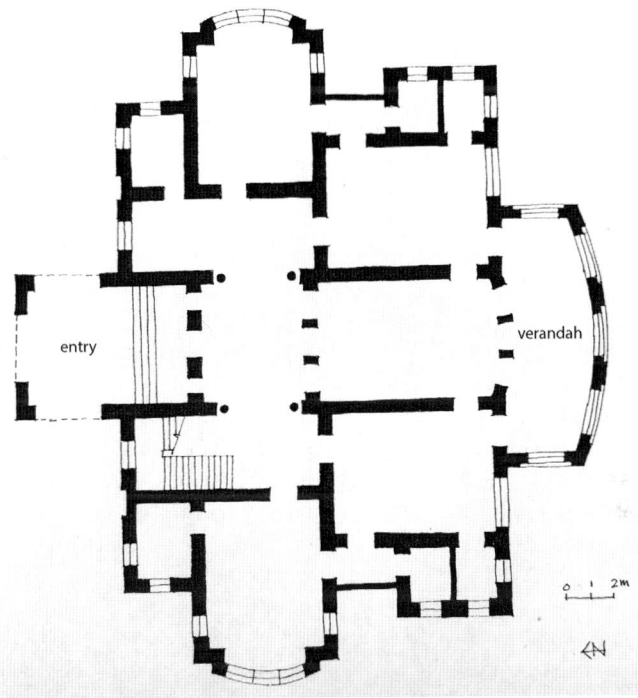

FIGURE 13.3 Plan of the residence of the Bose family, 1 Woodburn Park, Kolkata. Based on drawing in the collection of the Kolkata Municipal Corporation. The curved verandahs at the back and on the sides culminated on the terrace level to produce suitable configurations for performers and audiences. © Swati Chattopadhyay.

remarked: "Mahatma Gandhi is a public man, wherever he stays becomes a public place."[50] That the meeting was held on the terrace and not in one of the interior halls of the house perhaps encouraged such claim to access. Terraces as open-to-sky spaces had become in the imagination of the city's residents a part of the city's public space.

Public space, seen from this angle of political claim, was something unstable, manipulable. What constituted "the public" as well as the appropriate form of public gatherings and felicitations remained largely unsettled at that time.[51] After all, much of the anticolonial nationalist movement in India could be seen as a way of claiming political space from the colonial state. Long before the incident at the Bose residence, the radical wing of the nationalist movement had cast a challenge to the colonial state that if it chose to refuse access to interior public spaces such as town halls for political meetings, then all spaces of the city—outdoors and indoors— would become political space.[52]

While Rabindranath himself had much to say about the idea and construction of public space, his writings on terraces and small spaces are less troubled by the idea of public-private than with the idea of inside-outside. Narrating his experience in many other locations throughout his life, in Karwar at his brother's house, at the garden house in Chandannagar on the Ganga, alone on his boat on the Padma, or in his late years in the many terraces of the houses built to his wishes in Uttarayan, Santiniketan, he repeatedly wrote about the terraces that became his vantage for observing and communing with the outside world. Dealing with the problem of articulating the self in the world, his poems as well as his memoirs struggle with crafting connections between inside and outside. Even with the freedom of his matured age, he lamented that the Distant remained distant, his self-realization hindered by the impossibility of overcoming the barrier between inside and outside. Something beyond the spatial confluence seemed necessary to bridge the gap.

In the concluding portion of the book, I turn to some strategies by which such gaps were negotiated. Here the sociopoetics of circumscription is played out through portable artifacts to defy geographies of containment.

PART FOUR

A Geography of Small Spaces

14

Collections and Containment

In 1970, a young Ghanaian filmmaker, Nii Kwate Owoo, produced a short documentary on the collection of African artifacts in the British Museum in London. Titled *You Hide Me*, the film portrays the museum as a prison house of masks, jewelry, robes, statuettes, baskets, and tools. Stored in the museum's basement, the loots of a "conquering army" are stowed away in boxes, crates, and plastic bags. The Africa collection is remarkable for its indiscriminate diversity: "a statue used for worship, an ancestor's image, a pipe with tobacco still in it, a comb, a vessel to contain food."[1] In contrast to the basement, selected "masterpieces" are exhibited in large glass display cases in "high-ceilinged halls" of the museum's above-ground exhibit space. As in colonial world fairs Western curators set the terms of engagement and discourse. Owoo links this collection directly to colonial conquest and administration—"an all-out attack on African civilization, social structure, religion, language and art." A civilization is destroyed and then selected fragments from that civilization are used to create a historical narrative in which Europeans emerge as the experts in African art and society. The opacity of the storage space and the visibility of the display space share an ontology of colonial dislocation.

In a 2021 interview, Owoo describes this subterranean space as a city within a city, a tightly guarded fortress.[2] While a museum as a tightly guarded premise ought not to surprise current readers—from their own experience of conditions of entry to museums, art heist films, and Banksy-style interventions—the analogy posits an important dimension of collections that is recognized but is seldom the focus of inquiry. Only in a couple of shots do the museum staff momentarily appear in the frame.[3] Owoo notes that he didn't want the museum staff and security personnel in front of the camera. Their parenthetical presence, however, conveys much that is important to understand this instance of annihilation of culture. In the museum's refusal of access, it exceeds the "dislocation of culture" to use Robert Young's phrase.[4] It is a deadening of objects as life forces.

In her recent exposé on the debate about restitution and repatriation of collections from Western museums to the Third World that took place between 1965 and 1985, Bénédicte Savoy remarks that Owoo's polemic is directed against the "uselessness of keeping African cultural goods in the depots of the museums, in Britain or elsewhere. Unseen in the West and inaccessible to Africans—the objects shown in the film appear as an enormous capital hoarded in the basement of the museum."[5] While Owoo is responding to these objects being taken out of their ritual and everyday circulation in African societies, he is also clear that such collections serve a set of very specific economic, political, and cultural *use* as hoarded capital. These are assets that enable Western museums to generate revenue, profit from tourism, and place themselves at the center of the nexus of cultural and educational institutions. The process supports Western powers to reproduce relations of coloniality decades after colonialism has formally ended. It allows them to compete with each other in a game that has shifted from projecting colonialism as political and economic guardianship to cultural guardianship of the formerly colonized. Critically, the space of collection not only hides the objects from view but obscures African knowledge and culture, precisely because such knowledge is a direct challenge to Western intervention and expansion. It is not coincidental that while strenuously refusing repatriation, Western museums were keen to "offer aid" to expand museums, and thus their own expertise, in Africa.[6]

Savoy shows that the many attempts by Third World, specifically African, countries to force the issue of repatriation ended in political "defeat." One could also argue that Third World countries were unsuccessful because they were playing by the same rules as the Western powers: they were abiding by the rules of Western museology that construed a historical narrative through civilizational staging. Here the assertion of Western authorities that museum conditions in the Third World are "appalling" is particularly important. Even if these authorities acknowledged the moral premise—the ontological claim—behind repatriation or restitution, in the end it didn't matter because in that worldview the Third World is "incapable of preserving and presenting its own history." Museum staff in these countries are "hardly sufficiently educated and unfortunately in many cases rather susceptible to corruption."[7] In contrast to the entropy of the Third World, the cosmopolitanism of Western museums, their facilities and expertise legitimize their claim to these cultural objects—only they have a claim to the life and death of these objects.[8]

That Western authorities know more about the colonies than the colonized themselves is the oldest argument in the colonial game book. Savoy quotes Paulin Joachim—poet, journalist, and editor of *Bingo*—caricaturing this Western posturing in a 1965 editorial: "We plundered in order to save the artistic output of the black world from the worms and termites, from the smoke of your huts."[9] The "glorious uselessness" of these captured artifacts was precisely a matter of containment. When Adolf Tullmann, head of the Goethe Institute in Kinshasa, wrote an article titled "Cultural Property Back to the Jungle" in 1982, arguing against restitution, he was pointing out that the status of objects from the Third World as cultural property is only valid in their being safeguarded by Western museums.[10] It is not the object, but the dislocation and spatial containment of the object that by denying Black ontology permits discourse and creates value. The ghostly piles of ordinary and exceptional artifacts that Owoo documented is also a poignant reminder of the unseen corresponding spaces in the colonies—palaces, markets, shrines, ordinary houses, graveyards— that were emptied to create such collections in the metropole. Collections are a scattering—of artifacts, lives, and knowledge systems. In that scattering, however, there remain fugitive possibilities.[11]

Grey Zones

Owoo's film is a meditation on the relation between object and space in multiple ways. As the voiceover narrates the story, we see a young woman and a young man opening these boxes, and removing the plastic covers to look at the objects (Figures 14.1 and 14.2). In one of the shot sequences the young man unlocks a series of glass display cases, as if to free the objects from imprisonment. We sense a fleeting possibility of escape. The stacks, containers, protective covers, and artificial light that comprise this space of hidden dislocated artifacts appear spectral: in the shadows and shimmers is figured a zone of "occult instability" instigated by the violence of colonialism.[12] The shimmer presages eruption of meaning.

The possibility of thinking of the collection otherwise is lodged neither in the artifact collected nor the building that houses a collection, but that which frames the relation between the two. It is in the space of the containers in which the artifacts are stored. The space expands and contracts as objects are taken in and out of the containers and the containers are moved, opened, and put back.

FIGURE 14.1 Film Still from Nii Kwate Owoo, *You Hide Me* (1970).

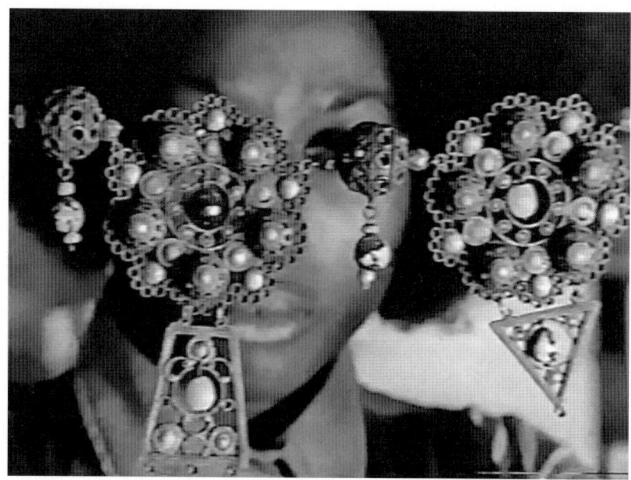

FIGURE 14.2 Film Still from Nii Kwate Owoo, *You Hide Me* (1970).

Danielle Bobker in a recent work on closets show the space of the closet as having developed from a room to a piece of furniture and again back to architecture as paneled walls for collections.[13] This contraction and expansion is not simply a transformation of the closet over time, but can be viewed as synchronous, where the object and architecture become indistinguishable as bodies move in and out of these spaces and frames. In *You Hide Me*'s foregrounding of the apparatus of boxes, containers, and shelves to demonstrate the implications of colonial collecting, we recognize the context-specificity of the role of containers as framing meaning. Containment makes the collection: the apparatus that contains scattered objects frame the meaning of collections. By mediating the relation between object and space they present the forces and constraints that inform collecting.

Collecting in the nineteenth century, however, was not merely an elite avocation nor confined to the expert realm of museum professionals, archivists, and the state. Collection as a practice of consumption, as a mode of affirming one's identity and aspiration, became a part of middle-class cultural vocabulary. And such objects, particularly of foreign and exotic origins, had an aura that exceeded their fetishization.

Writer and consummate collector of books, Nirad C. Chaudhuri, reminiscing of his childhood in early-twentieth-century rural Kishoreganj in eastern Bengal, recalls housewives being "obsessed" with trunks: "No matter how many there were at home, each year they would buy one or two. Big ones, flat ones, in the end these added up to twelve or thirteen trunks in the house. The trunks were chained together so they could not be stolen by breaking through the earthen floor."[14] In addition, each house had a heavy iron chest in which money and jewelry were kept. The trunks were tied to this iron chest as a form of additional security. The steel trunks were foreign imports sold at a local seasonal fair where an entire area (*patti*) was designated for these goods. That local fair was clearly hooked into international circuits of commerce even if in other respects it might appear globally remote.

Chaudhuri's remembrance conveys the respectability of his Bengali home and their status as *zamindar*s (landlords). Attuned to the spirit of collecting as a mode of conspicuous consumption, he relates this womanly passion of collecting trunks not as a connoisseurial act, but as an indicator of a new type of interior space oriented toward new consumption practices. The imported trunks contributed to the proliferation of storage spaces in the house and conveyed wealth:

> In our house there were almirahs and book shelves. There were different kinds of shelves for other things. And despite the earth construction, the interiors were lit with large imported glass hanging lamps from England, Bohemia, and Czechoslovakia. Reflector covers above the lamps directed light downwards . . . And there were framed pictures.[15]

The framed prints included Raphael's *Madonna*, a child with a dove, and two paintings of the Boer War. His mother would point out Raphael's painting: "This is Madonna della Sedia." The framed picture was placed above a pair of deer horns that adorned the space above the door of their sleeping apartment. The books and magazines in his house introduced him to Western art and literature as well as contemporary Bengali works published in journals: his mother subscribed to three Bengali literary journals: *Bamabodhini, Prabasi, Pradip*.[16]

While the selection of paintings and the imported lamps speak of a certain predisposition toward Western-style objects, Chaudhuri makes an astute observation of the role of the containers of the family's collection of artifacts: these artifacts were not merely Western objects in the house, but as collections they served as a framing device. A rural building tradition—mat walls, tin roof, and earthen plinth—and the taste for modern things—imported, alluring—come together in the depiction of an aspiring rural gentry. Imported furnishing in houses of mud and bamboo construction was not uncommon in the houses of the Indian or European elite in India. Bungalows were often of mud construction and thatched roofs remained the norm in many locations in elite houses until the mid-twentieth century.[17] What set apart this well-off upper-caste household from the houses of the common folk in the region was likely not just new objects but how they were stored and where they were kept. The containers describe a zone of space in which the stuff of modern culture—literary magazines, printed paintings, imported lamps—could be enframed and appreciated.

Charlotte Ashby and Mark Crinson refer to this kind of space between object and building as a "grey zone." Neither the "conventional objects of design nor those of architecture," it "reminds us of the knock-on effects that reverberate back and forth between people, things, buildings and their environment, and further to the wider infrastructure, transportation networks, utilities, legal frameworks, new forms of media and political systems within which all these effects take place."[18] Grey zone is an often-nebulous space whose coordinates are uncertain. It is defined only contingently, but also assuredly as a space of scalar mediation.

Containers

Since the eighteenth century, the types of containers used in trade, transportation, and everyday life had proliferated to meet the demands of portable lives and expanding consumption. Colonialism and capitalism had unleashed global movements of goods and people. From specially manufactured crates for tea, fruits, and botanical specimens, the Wardian case that allowed seedlings to be transported and nurtured in inclement weather, to wine casks, bottles, and tins for provisions, packing, and storing, as I have suggested in Part Two of this book, had become highly specialized.[19] Thacker, Spink and Co. of Calcutta, well known for their reputation as publishers and book importers, also imported boxes and cases for specialized uses: jewel cases, writing cases, dispatch boxes, cash boxes, stationary cabinets. Their 10" x 8" x 6½" jewel cases, fitted with "three lifted spring trays, inside lined with best silk velvet and silk fillets," had a cover of brown russia leather and locking facilities. Stationary cabinets of walnut or oak would be fitted with "revolving date range, two ink bottles with screw tops, memo slate, drawer" to fit foolscap-size paper.[20] The variety of such containers clearly indicate their appeal to a growing base of middle-class consumers who saw these appurtenances as signifying professional and social status.

Containers elicited social connotations by serving as the intermediary space between objects and space. They precipitated sociospatial relations by virtue of their materials and design and also through where they were stored, how they were conveyed, and who was in charge and how they were packed, unpacked, and used. Ships and trains designated classes by how much they could carry. From the enslaved who were not allowed to carry any possessions with them to the coolies who were allowed one small box for all their belongings, the containers of goods became extraordinary markers of social worth. In contrast to the laboring migrants, Englishwomen traveling to India in the nineteenth century were given elaborate instructions of how many pieces of luggage to carry and how they should be lined and stored. Eliot James advised her counterparts to carry good trunks because inferior ones would be the "very worst economy." On a sea voyage they would need "at least" the following for one person: "Two air-tight tin cases of large size. Two bullock trunks, one lined with tin. One smaller trunk for cabin, regulation size, to go under berth—that is, if you are an officer's wife, and go by troop-ship. One clothes-bag, with lock and key. One square-mouthed leather-bag. One hand-bag, fitted as a dressing-case." The luggage would be divided into three parts: hold, officers' baggage room, and cabin. The ones in the hold were to be tin boxes or boxes lined in tin, and then soldered down. The "intermediate" trunks in the baggage room would be used for change of clothing as needed, and the cabin baggage for everyday use.[21] She also advised those who intended to set up house for the first time to send separate luggage carrying linen, glass, china, lamps, and other household fittings.[22] Tradesmen in England would pack this last sort of goods and ship them for the owner to their destination. Trunks were often so designed that when opened on a journey or in a tent they worked as shelves and cabinets.

Containers and modes of conveyance feature prominently in Flora Annie Steel and Grace Gardiner's highly detailed advice on moving house during the summer months from the plains to the hills. "In England the smaller amount of luggage you have the greater your peace, but in India it is just the contrary, and happiness consists in carrying all kinds of creature comforts, and being able to get at them easily," they remarked.[23] Luggage for the mistress, three children, and an English nurse would require two dozen trunks, cases, boxes, chest of drawers, and additional furniture such as iron cots and tea tables, which could be distributed among eleven camels.[24] A piano would require a separate cart. "Servants," they wrote "love *guthris*, those indescribable bundles, which, do what you will, they will bring with them, and which often turn out as useful as the lucky-bag in the 'Swiss Family Robinson'."[25] They, however, cautioned about the need for strict limitations as it applied to servants:

> Servants are best left to make their own arrangements for themselves and their goods and chattels; but a stand should be made against mill-stones and bedsteads, and extra special conveyance should as a rule be refused. They will perch on carts, camels, and mules, much as birds of the air do; and they will quarrel among themselves. But it is best to be inexorable when appealed to.[26]

Between the indescribable bundles of Indian servants and the well-defined luggage of English colonizers we read not just social differentiation among classes and between masters and servants, but spatial differentiation of a particular kind: of separating bodies from spaces. The furnishing and ornaments packed for the European family are intended to create the same envelope of space irrespective of the actual configuration of the house—they stand in for their identity which has to be created and affirmed at their summer abode. The bundles of native servants from the colonizer's point of view, however, are a tangle and a puzzle—they can be expanded or contracted without changing the material. The container takes the shape of the objects it contains.

In this concluding part of the book, I focus on the small spaces that emerge between objects and collections as a back and forth between framing and scattering. By focusing on a humble sort of portable artifacts—maps and potted plants, bookshelves, and boxes of medicines—not just for the limits of communication and discourse in a colonial milieu that they convey, but the surprising connections they insinuate, we alter the way we imagine the materiality of these artifacts. My concern is with their potential for enabling transgression—a fugitive crossing over in search of meaning.

The location of an object changes its materiality. To explore the kinds of materiality engendered by location, I focus on the containers themselves as sites and spaces. This means paying attention to the intermediate zone between objects and buildings. But this is not merely a matter of scale. Straying from their treatment as backdrop or appurtenance is to examine how objects are actively deployed to construct social meaning. Even as props, they foreground social relations. Seen as frames they suggest possibilities of reframing. As Bobker writes, this is to resist the idea that the space of the collection or the closet is emptied "of any relevance other than the (collecting) subject."[27] Closets and containers as architecture exceed their function of representing the self and are entangled with the larger social. As spatial entities that are meant to contain and define bounds, they are indeed peculiarly porous to processes and intentions.

Accustomed to think of walls, floors, and roofs as building envelopes, as architectural historians we are attentive to the materials with which these are constructed.[28] Far less attention is given to the materiality of the envelope as in the social relations that are embodied in these materials—the mostly invisible adjacencies and connections that enable them.[29] And here I am thinking of not simply the materials of construction, their haptic, thermal, and sonorous properties, but the degrees to which their social and material connectivity beyond their surface/envelope is recognized and mobilized to transmit values. How and to whom do they transmit value? How do they reverberate, reframe? Once we think in such terms of materiality, the portable artifact, even if a person cannot be physically placed inside the space, sheds its fixed identity as object defined by the bounds of its enclosure, and takes on the attributes of inhabitation—spatial extensions of life that confer meaning on actions. Since they are movable and manipulable—more so than a wall or a roof—they are more susceptible to transformation and reconfiguration of meaning.

The mutually supportive role between containers and collections produces a geography of small spaces that took peculiar turns in the transactions of empire. The next three chapters use maps, bookshelves, and medicine boxes as artifacts and collections to elicit the limitations and possibilities of that geography.

15

Portable Geographies

Theodora Coatman was fond of maps. Her collection of maps, her husband and biographer John Coatman noted, was worthy of a "military map room." The couple had returned to England after John's service in the imperial administration concluded.[1] In a *Portrait of an Englishwoman* (1958) John recalled an evening as Theo stood looking at a map "which she had fastened to the wall." She smiled:

> I knew that she was thinking of something happy in the past. Then, "Come and look at this," she said. "Now tell me what you see." The map was the high moorland region of Northumberland—Durham—Westmorland and I studied it carefully, noting heights, steepness of contours, streams and the rest, and then I smiled too.
>
> "Pah pukhto khke wowayah," she said, also smiling, and speaking in Pushtu. "Akhpul alaquah pa shan de" (Say it in Pushtu. It's like our own old country). So it was. Heights, contours and other physical features were those of the lower Bhogarmang Valley . . .
>
> She made a dot with her pencil on the map and said, half to herself, "I wonder."[2]

A few days later they drove to that dot on the map: "Across the beck was a grassy ledge like the one where we had stayed the night with our guide and sepoys on our journey over Musa-ka-Musalla to the Kaghan Valley. It was strangely like it, so like as to bring tears to the eyes of both of us." Earlier in the narrative John writes about their admiration for the natural beauty of the Kaghan Valley, which they had on their visit compared with that of the Lake District, although the former was at a "greatly magnified scale."[3]

The Coatmans' nostalgic recollection of Northwestern and Afghan territory is so seamlessly woven into the narrative of their retirement experience in England and Scotland that there is no jarring separation between "home" in India and in England, between public and private experience, between the garden Theo planted in India and the one she planted in England. She was delighted by the utter Englishness of their bungalow in Hazara (present-day Pakistan) with its "English" apples, pears, plums, and strawberries.[4] In Bayswater Farm, Oxford, she planted crocuses imported from Hazara. Mailed by John's successor at his former post, each package carried its provenance: "from the bungalow compound Abbotabad," "From the rest-house compound at Shinkiari," "From the head of Loudwater Pass."[5] The specificity of each locale of collection thus could be reconstructed in the home of the gardener in a different part of the world. Aptly mediated by a topographic map, Afghan/Northwestern territory and English territory become translatable in the imagination of empire, the abstract geometry of lines and dots creating a portable geography.

Theo and John display none of the disdain with which Europeans treated colonial peoples and lands. Rather their profound happiness in empire is based on being able to and desiring to move between longitudes. Theo's journal and letters as well as John's (auto)biography evince their interest and confidence in forging connections—physical, intellectual, emotional, aesthetic.

John emphasizes how well Theo managed to reconcile disparate realms during their sojourn in India. Theo managed to be "at home" with her domestic duties as a housewife and mother of a small child and at the same time—rather because of which—she was able to serve as an emissary of the British government. She and her child, John junior, had created such rapport with the locals that people in the far away "border hills and glens, and even far beyond them, deep into independent territory thought of the all-powerful Indian 'Sarker' in terms of Theo and her baby."[6] Here John is at pains to emphasize Theo's intellect as well as her feminine touch.

Theo traveled with him on his inspection tours, living in tents or in government rest houses, and their tours took on the character of "genuine explorations" of "trackless" mountains and forests: "She had opportunities of seeing Indian conditions at first hand, of coming into touch with primitive life in the raw."[7] Capable of studying the "system of Government in India with precisely the same detachment as she studied our Old Colonial System or Roman Provincial Administration," she opened John's eyes to the habitual dominance of Englishmen, detecting "the basic weaknesses, actual and potential" in the British position.[8] Theo studied Urdu with a *munshi* and learned Pushtu from John's orderly—personal attendant—seemingly without any difficulty.[9] She picked up Jatki spoken in the lowlands of Hazara as one would pick up a cold.[10] She was keen on collecting histories and folklores of tribes who were seeing an Englishwoman for the first time.

What makes Theodora and John Coatman's approach toward geography, work, and pleasure imperialistic is not that they served under a colonial government and enjoyed the privileges of race and rank, or that they made "historical" connections between the Roman empire and their contemporary imperial administration, not even that they thought of connecting as collecting. It resides in their sense of having unbounded access to spaces, peoples, and things. This manner of imagining access completely coalesces their private and public roles. Theo's collection of maps and plants sublimate the territorial, historical, and botanical prerogatives of empire as one of personal growth and pleasure. No dissonance or difficulty disturbs this move. We hear nothing of the trials and tribulations of communicating. Gathering of information and construction of knowledge are presented as such transparent acts that there is no recognition of the limits and failures of knowledge accumulation, or of the subterfuges, refusals, or the "sly civility" of the native.[11]

John worked as an official in charge of publicity and must have been acutely aware of the function and impact of the rhetoric of communication. *Portrait of an Englishwoman*, written as a tribute to his beloved wife, is partly intended to demonstrate how an educated Englishwoman could assume responsibilities in the world of politics without sacrificing her family responsibilities. And how the experience in the colonies could prepare a woman for her political or public role in England. The text thus treads on an overwrought arena of debate about women and the public sphere in the nineteenth and twentieth centuries, but by suturing the relation of the colonies and home in a seamless geography. What interests me here is John's characterization of Theo's gardening instincts as an indication of her greater capacities, her fitness for participation in the public world of politics, and how he links her map collection with her practical acumen.[12]

Theo is presented as the consummate gardener. On their first arrival at the bungalow in Hazara, she went into the garden—before entering the house—and picked up a handful of earth and crumbled it. Here she is represented as arriving already equipped with her English knowledge of soils and plants and techniques of gardening. She instinctively understands how to make this bungalow in Hazara a home. Hazara thus appears already known. This small vignette of her in action—her tactile and down-to-earth assessment—communicates her practical and intuitive grasp of not only how to tackle her garden and its future possibilities, but this assessment as suggestive of the productive leaps she could make between the house, garden, woods, and routes. That she could translate her expertise to a larger territorial appreciation as indicated by her map collection is what made Theo's story worth recalling. The maps are not just tools; the potted crocus is not just a favorite flower; rather they are conduits for translating worlds and inhabiting empire.

The effortless connections that Theodora and John Coatman made between travel, home, garden, and empire were unlikely. Rather the imperial rhetoric of the text smooths over the disconnects, and relies on the topographic map to make conceptual leaps. If the territorial prerogative of empire sways between unbounded access to land and the lived spaces of Europeans as enclaves of protection, the colonial domestic garden with its abundance of potted plants epitomizes the tension between these two trajectories of power.

The garden itself is seen as a framing device, as a critical buffer zone in which the rhetoric of imperial control could be expressed as an aesthetic order. It conveys multiple connotations of territory, cultivation, productivity, and consumption and serves as the perfect trope of empire. At the same time, its "living," generative character grants it an unpredictability that could be challenging. The colonial domestic garden turned out to be a fragile entity precisely because of its framing practice. Here is Sara Duncan writing from the hill station of Simla in the latter half of the nineteenth century:

> The jungle triumphs in the rains, it overwhelms the place . . . creeping up, licking and lipping the garden through the paling, but out upon the public khud-sides it is unchecked and insatiable. We hate the jungle, it is so patient and designing and unremitting, so much stronger than we are. Such constant war we have to make upon it merely to prevent it swallowing us alive. It will plant a toadstool in your bedroom and a tree in your roof; it shrinks from nothing.[13]

It didn't help that the English plants did not heed the social boundaries of European occupation. They succumbed to the wantonness of "unregulated living." The dahlia had gone rogue, alighting on everything and "everywhere along the khud-sides that border the public highway," and the nasturtiums, tiger lilies, and convolvulus had followed suit, propagating beyond the garden without permission or invitation.[14] It is in the face of these formidable obstacles when newcomers rhapsodized about the "glorious freedom of the wilderness" that seasoned residents such as Duncan would point "to the crooked squares of our pathetic little estates, painfully redeemed and set smugly with posies, saying, 'Admire *that*!'"[15]

Duncan's text is laced with sarcasm, but in her view of the small victories in a jungle warfare of sorts, she quite astutely figures the ambitions and absurdities of the gardening guides published in the decades after the Sepoy Rebellion (1857–9). These gardening guides, flush with the prospect of territorial occupation made possible by the British victory in the rebellion, found eager audience among an increasing number of British soldiers and civilians in India. Elaborate advice about seasonal planting, soil treatment, and garden design were offered, asserting the basic principles upon which the unit of territorial occupation—the garden and the bungalow—was to be organized. Most of the gardening books that were published went through several editions, testifying to their demand.

Boundary-work

Garden-making in the colonies was boundary-work. For domestic gardens in British colonial India, it meant setting up a series of spaces whose edge conditions secured the imagination of the English home as a protected space. Irrespective of their urban or rural location and for the most part irrespective of their geographical specificities, this ideal propagated through scores of housekeeping and gardening guides gained value through repetition and replication. In a situation where the house—the bungalow—itself did not conform to the design and spatial expectation of an English residence, the garden offered the promise of an envelope of Englishness:

> Gardens around European bungalows where Europeans live should be made to look as "homelike" as possible. Characteristic sweeping drives bordered with shrubs and flower borders, beds of flowers, bowers of roses and verdant lawns should be the predominating ideas. The layout of the garden should be considered the framework of the residence.[16]

I am using the term "boundary-work" in a dual sense to describe the sociospatial relations materialized through garden design. First is the sense in which Thomas Gieryn applies the term to describe the rhetorical methods used by scientists to distinguish the domain of science from nonscientific knowledge.[17] This involves attributing certain values to the institution of science, referring to "its practitioners, methods, stock of knowledge, values and work organization" for purposes of constructing a social boundary between science and nonscience.[18] I am also using the term in its more literal sense to describe the physical boundaries that were constructed to secure the institution. The rhetoric of garden-making in the colonies not only articulated methods, produced a stock of knowledge, and created values about the work, it materially depended upon the practice of gardening on the ground—quite literally—in the construction of walls, hedges, fences, and the distribution of spaces in the garden that created a set of enclosures within the bounds of the property.

The garden fence or hedge can connect and disconnect. Unlike their English counterparts, the fence in the colonial garden was construed as a cultural, social, and physical barrier against the jungle/native spaces outside. The jungle in this view is neither just a social construct nor a form of rank vegetation. Constituting a set of negations—uncultivated, unhealthy, unregulated, dangerous—it is a proxy for native society. What is important is that the jungle's very fecundity is its threat—its capacity to overcome the small clearings of European occupation. The bigger the garden, more is the possibility of conveying the impression of the jungle held at bay. One could well argue that the boundary wall in its delimiting function defined and merged the jungle with native space.

No wonder gardening was projected as a moral imperative—*the* civilizing mission of empire. In his discussion of the US intervention in the Canal Zone in Panama, Stephen Frenkel shows how the Canal Zone was engineered to produce a safe, manicured—and "civilized"—landscape in contrast to the jungle beyond. The aim was to create "a parklike effect" with "open vistas, to the avoidance of the close confusion of the jungle into which native vegetation lapses when left alone or indiscriminately cultivated." Jungle here was not forest land, but land from which its previous inhabitants had been removed. Jungle and native habitation were thus interchangeable. Even though the gardens utilized some of the very same plants found in the so-called jungle, when placed within domestic confines under the supervision of American mistresses, "arranged and trimmed back in a controlled fashion jungle plants were redefined as safe." The garden in the tropics, with the "zeal and taste of the mistresses," could be reframed "as miniature representatives of the jungle."[19] Miniaturization as domestication and control appealed to the idea of territorial imperative as personal comfort. Gardens and the cost of maintaining large gardens was understood to be a compensation for the "hardships" in the tropics.[20]

In the routine advice peddled to British residents in India about gardening as a duty, a pleasure, and wholesome physical exercise, one might sense a pattern similar to managing class expectations in England.[21] To be sure allotment garden advocates considered gardening for the working class as a process of moral upliftment in addition to an economic supplement. Advice given to English soldiers in India adopted a similar tone. Crucially, it endowed the European gardener in India, irrespective of their class status, a position that distinguished them from the Indian gardener, the *mali*, who was deemed deficient in skills and scientific understanding of plants and planting, not to mention garden design. There was no expectation that either European men or women would do the actual labor of gardening—the objective was to see the work getting done. It was assumed that workers—*malis*—would be available for the hard work of tilling, hauling water, pruning, mixing of composts, and other dirty work involved in gardening. The garden came with the *mali*, so to speak. There was a neat correlation between the number of *malis* and rank in colonial society. Iris Macfarlane put it clearly: as a tea-planter's wife, of her twelve full-time servants four were *malis*, and there were others who were temporarily hired to pull weeds and do the seasonal work of clearing unwanted growth. The tea company's managing director's house had exactly double the number of servants with eight *malis*.[22] For the 249 acres of gardens and golf course at the Viceroy's Palace in New Delhi there were sixty-eight full-time garden staff and three hundred and fifty part-time employees.[23] Thus in their supervisory role of maintaining a garden, European "gardeners," both men and women, found territorial occupation exercised quite directly as a privilege they might not have had in England.

In addition to leisure and cheap labor, colonial gardens promised rapid return of time and money. In the tropics plant growth could be hastened and thus there was more room for creativity in planning gardens in the tropical colonies. The scary tropical fecundity parodied by Duncan was made into a boon by pointing out how rapid growth suited gardening plans in a context where short stays at a station were the norm. Gardens, properly planned, could deliver flowering plants for the drawing room, English vegetables for the table, and a space of congenial labor and sociality, all in a short time between planting and harvesting.[24] Agnes H. Harler began her gardening guide for amateurs published in 1901 by noting the many advantages of a garden in the Indian plains:

It is true that borders of mixed flowers often refuse to bloom all together or to give the effect of herbaceous border as planned, and many well-known favourites will not thrive in the plains. On the other hand, trees and shrubs grow quickly enough in most parts of India to give one a chance of playing with the land in a way quite impossible in a colder climate where big plants grow slowly. Indian gardens are often spacious and provide a large canvas to work upon. The flowering trees, shrubs and creepers are so brilliant and varied that it is possible to experiment with broad colour effects and, what is more, to have a reasonable expectation of seeing the results of one's work.[25]

The authors of these guides seem to always assume the bungalow compound as their arena of experimentation. Harler spells out the sequence of works to be undertaken. The first task is to lay out a wide tree-lined drive from the gate to the garage via the bungalow. Second is defining the boundaries. If hedges are going to be useful as protection these should be thorny and impenetrable or else protected by a wire fence. Meant to keep cattle away, it worked equally well to keep away natives from entering the garden at will. She advises growing a further line of defense against the wind with a line of bamboos or tall trees outside the compound, and if control of the land outside the compound is not possible, the solution is to plant a tall hedge within the compound on the windward side.

As in English picturesque gardens, the enclosure is the first move. Then the boundedness had to be made to disappear. A wide expanse of green lawn, unbroken by paths and flower beds in front of the front verandah, was thus the next item on the design agenda.[26] While the effect of spaciousness and the illusion of far boundaries as a desideratum was to be achieved through a lawn—"even in a small garden"—it was important to avoid rectangular lines that might give the impression of containment. Small flower beds were to be avoided in favor of large clumps of trees and massing of coloring shrubs to enable "long perspectives and open views" and to lead the eye away from the house.[27] The rhetoric of picturesque gardens of "borrowing" a distant scenery from well beyond one's property was applied here as well. In more immediate reaches, it was important to plant a lawn with shrubbery to hide unsightly "back-yard activities."[28] All work spaces were to be screened from the pleasure grounds.

Portable Gardens, Maps, and Tools

Garden design in the colonies was described as a distinct, scientific field of knowledge that even amateurs could participate in by subscribing themselves to its principles. Aspiring gardeners were encouraged to obtain membership in horticulture garden societies that proliferated between the early nineteenth and early twentieth centuries.[29] Botanical and horticulture gardens gave away free seeds, hosted lectures, and provided expertise to create a culture of gardening that poached on but sharply differentiated itself from indigenous practices of gardening.[30] The expertise of colonial gardening critically depended on translation—the ability to translate European, often specific English ideas—into a vernacular idiom, without jeopardizing the principles upon which the gardens were to designed.

The ideal plan of the garden was transplanted from Europe and fitted out with trees suitable for the Indian climate. Botanist George Woodrow's gardening guide, originally meant for European soldiers in India, provided garden plans that were copies of those published in *Gardener's Chronicle* for gardeners in England (Figure 15.1). The names of the plants were simply switched to recommend both imported and local varieties as stand-ins for their English counterparts.[31] The geometry of the garden plan was assumed to follow a fixed sequence in terms of spatial demarcations as one approaches the house: "The main characteristic in the designs is a close following of nature in the curving paths and groups of trees and shrubs to hide

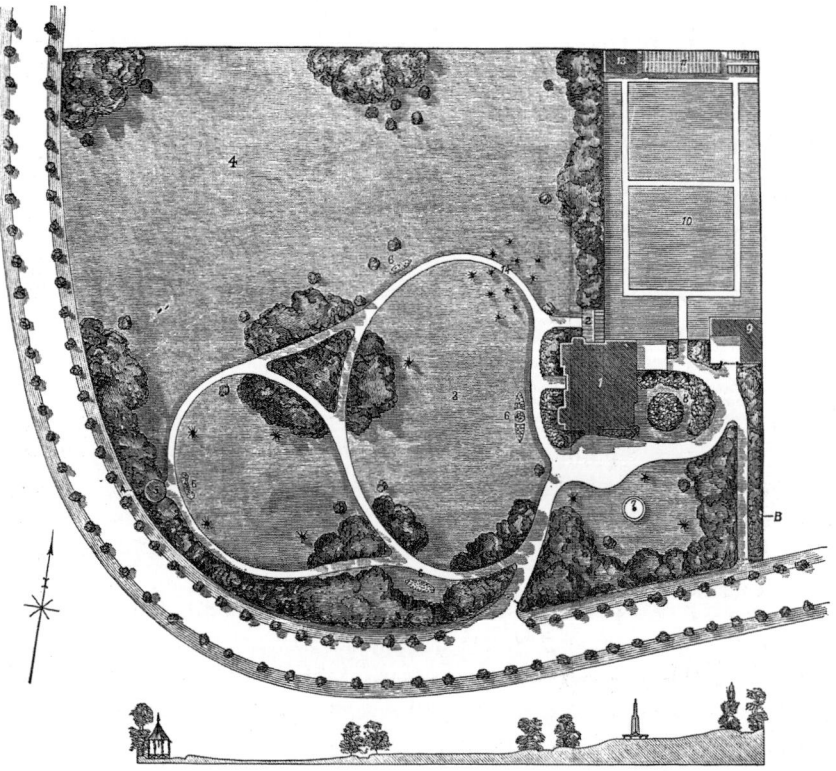

FIGURE 15.1 "Plan of a Villa Garden and Section of the Ground." Illustration in G. Marshall Woodrow, *Gardening in India*, 3rd ed. (Bombay: Education Society Press, 1903).

objectionable and display pleasing features in the landscape. The natural groups become more and more formal as they approach the dwelling house, gradually breaking from the curves of nature to the stiff lines of architecture."[32] Woodrow ignores the fact that these plans do not have the usual spatial arrangement of the Indian compound with servants' quarters at the back. The only service buildings shown in the English plan are a toolshed, green house and vinery, frames and potting shed.[33] Perhaps to compensate for these shortcomings, he inserts a plan of his own design for a 10-acre bungalow compound. Here he does not neglect to include the usual arrangement of the servants' quarters (Figure 15.2). The inclusion of these service spaces changes the tenor of the plan. Trellis-covered passageways now connect the service space and the main house, but their diagonal footprints sit awkwardly, as if an afterthought. This plan also has a profusion of ornamental flower beds, whereas in the plan of the English garden the front lawn and flower edges dominate the composition.

In Europe geometric grid plans for planting go back to the early modern period, when trees in "forests" as well as parterres in enclosed gardens were recommended to be planted in an orderly manner to distinguish cultivated land from waste land. Casting a geometrical order on the land was an achievement of cosmic significance. The varying heights of the trees and tall hedges that created the spaces of the formal gardens, however, were quite different from the low-height flower beds that became popular in the nineteenth century.[34]

The Victorian practice of "bedding out"—starting flowering plants in nurseries and then laying them out in geometrically designed beds resembling a carpet—was dutifully transferred to gardens in India, and enthusiastically approved by Woodrow. These designs, borrowed from English gardening books, came as a set of abstract diagrams. Designs in various shapes and of various degrees of complexity were to be cut into the turf and filled with appropriate groupings of colors and massing of annuals (Figures 15.3 and **Plate 22**).[35] Since the bed designs were denuded of any reference to particular garden contexts, Woodrow helps his readers understand how these patterns are to be applied: "No.14 is a useful figure where watering by hand is necessary, and many opportunities for its use may be found in laying out small gardens," or "No. 21 may be employed in front of a plain building."[36]

The patterning technique and instructional format used to explain the use of garden bed design shares a graphic mode with other do-it-yourself crafts of the nineteenth century such as Berlin wool work.[37] Meant to be easy to follow as long as one could keep count of the spaces, such instructions treat the white paper as the ground and the lines of the shapes provide guides for filling in with color to create the field. A proper counting in Berlin wool work and a precise line on the turf in garden design produce the desired fill-effect.

The garden bed design was a shared vocabulary between the English garden and the colonial garden to the extent that a grouping of colors was the prime objective. At the same time, it was frequently noted that the colors

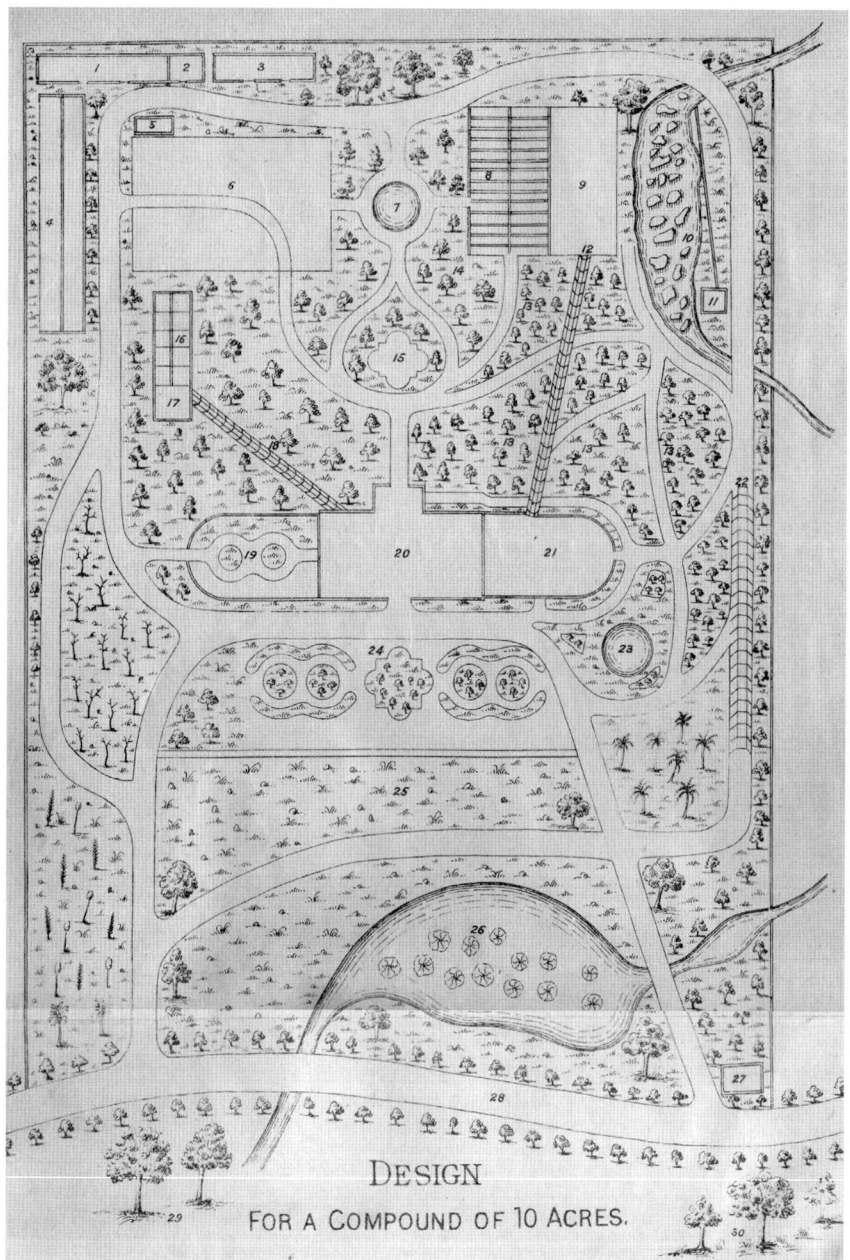

FIGURE 15.2 "Design for a Compound of Ten Acres." Illustration in G. Marshall Woodrow, *Gardening in India*, 3rd ed. (Bombay: Education Society Press, 1903).

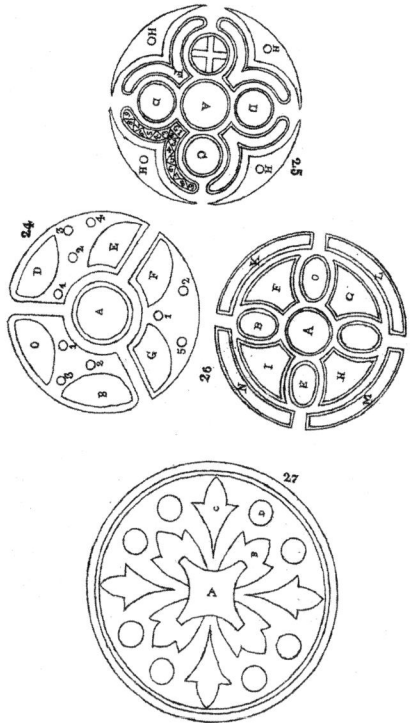

FIGURE 15.3 "Design for Flower Garden Bed." Illustration in G. Marshall Woodrow, *Gardening in India*, 3rd ed. (Bombay: Education Society Press, 1903).

in a colonial garden in India produce a stronger effect. Nevertheless, these designs provided models for replication and constructed a common visual sensibility. Most of all they attempted to lend a certain assurance of success to a process that was resource- and labor-intensive.

The neatness of the edges of borders in the garden was paramount. Woodrow mentions the specialized edging cutters that are necessary to create tidy margins. The edging cutter is one among fifty-four tools in his description of a "tool house" (Figure 15.4). These tools include books, as the gardener should be "a reading and thinking man." The books, the stamps for making labels, and a cabinet for tools indicate that he expects the gardener to be a fellow educated man and not the *mali* who is considered to be the laborer. Such detailed rendering of gardening tools went back to the sixteenth century when the modern notion of the garden was being given shape in the making of elaborate gardens on a scientific basis.[38] The vast majority of colonial houses would not have even a fraction of these tools, or a designated toolshed, but the vision of an orderly toolshed, even though a small space in the house, is telling in terms of conveying the specialized knowledge required for even amateur gardening if the garden is to abide by any semblance of

FIGURE 15.4 "Tool House in an Indian Garden." Illustration in G. Marshall Woodrow, *Gardening in India*, 3rd ed. (Bombay: Education Society Press, 1903).

order expressed in well-trimmed hedges, a uniform lawn, and precise edges of decorative flower beds.[39]

Going against the advice of their male counterparts, women authors of gardening books and those who perused them in India delighted in surrounding their houses and lining the approaches to their bungalows with flower pots. The flower pot as a portable artifact realized the imagination of garden as found in maps. Here they were aligning their goals with their counterparts in England who had found in the potted plant a mode of inhabiting empire.

Though the idea of a potted plant goes back to the ancient world, in the eighteenth and nineteenth centuries amid the rage for botanical expeditions and creation of botanical and horticulture gardens as colonial interventions, the potted plant as a portable artifact found a new relevance. Elizabeth Kent, in her book *Flora Domestica* (1823), advised readers about how to grow a "portable garden" emphasizing the value of potted plants in situations where garden ground was not to be easily found, whether it be in cities like London or Venice.[40] The potted plant in casement windows and porches elicited a touch of the countryside. And even in situations where there was a garden ground or a green house, potted plants could be brought within the domestic space and nursed with a personal touch. While her object in writing the book was to advise those who were inexperienced in nursing potted plants, the list of plants Kent included shows the range of imported plants from the Americas, Asia, and Africa that had become "domesticated" in England by then. Thus, the potted plant, cultivated as a fragment of a larger landscape, represented the logic of colonial transplantation by which objects and spaces could be invested with new values.

Precisely because flower pots were moveable and could be rearranged—moved between inside and outside, from one side of the house to another in keeping with the vexations of the sun and wind—and importantly because its size allowed the mistress to work at a more controllable scale. Flower pots suited smaller gardens, were portable from one station to another (Edith Cuthell's geraniums were sunned in the hills), and were amenable to personalization and creation of intimate spaces.[41] Here potted plants, caged birds, the verandah, and garden created a new geography that took on exceptional significance by allowing women in their circumscribed reach to carve out their own space. An English rose, an African violet, nurtured with great care, became fragments of the portable European home. Just as the garden as boundary-work delivered the promise of visually abstracting space, literally detaching it from the immediate surroundings, so that a set of distanced spaces could be pieced together as one imagined fabric, the flower pot simultaneously concretized both detachment and attachment.

What happens when these guides and assurances of class and race insularity fail? In the balance of this chapter, I want to pursue the idea of boundary-work as a disconnect, emblematized in the colonial garden, by recourse to the story of Iris Macfarlane. Unlike Edith Cuthell, who figured out a strategy for connecting and folding back the larger territory beyond the bungalow into her verandah, Iris felt trapped in the verandah overlooking the garden. Iris's story provokes questions about how we might understand the limits of fostering connections in a colonial milieu through the small spaces I have invoked in earlier chapters.

Recollection

In 1939, Iris Macfarlane (1922–2007), then 16 years old, returned to India from England with the hope of finding a suitable marital prospect. Iris wrote regularly, and her journals, memoirs, and articles convey a sense of her attempt to make a life in India. The verandah and garden as spaces of refuge as well as the potted flowers and pet animals she collected played a large role in her story, but in ways that strain against the narrative grain of empire.

Born in 1922 in Quetta (present-day Pakistan), Iris was the daughter of a military officer in the British army in India, and as was the norm she was sent to be schooled in England only to return in 1939. Before embarking for India, she had finished high school and been to a "finishing school of sorts." There she learnt flower arrangement, how to write cheques, and how to use makeup. "Most of all," the school groomed girls for their expected role in the world: "to be elegant, submissive, feminine, and thus a credit to our sex." It was a waste of money, Iris later reflected, because the next thing on her "agenda" was to travel to India and "having a man to write my cheques for me, and servants to do the flowers." The family's modest situation in England was left behind on arrival in India. Here paths were cleared for white families and their pets. White-only hotels, "superior tents," and bungalows with ample servants provided a life of comfort. In December 1941, she was engaged to a handsome young Scotsman, Donald Macfarlane or "Mac," an engineer in a tea plantation in Assam in northeastern India. She spent much of the next two decades in Assam as a tea planter's wife and gave birth to three children, the couple retiring to England in late 1965.

Looking back decades later, piecing together "the story of four generations of a family and its connections with the east," Iris wondered why that life of comfort, frivolity, routine didn't suit her.[42] As a woman in British colonial elite society, her world consisted of the club and bungalow in the cantonment and plantation, studded with picnics, shooting and fishing parties, and occasional trips to the bazaars "where you could 'beat down' the sellers of the polished stones and brass and exquisite carved ivory." She was expected to stay with her husband in whatever remote locations he was posted and enjoy the circumscribed life of a privileged race:

> For my grandmother and my mother, the pain of separation [from the children who were sent back to England] was alleviated by the pleasure they found in the Eastern scene, or rather their view from the bungalow and club verandahs. I felt myself imprisoned on those verandahs a lot of the time, a matter of temperament I suspect, an influx from my father's side. One lot of his forebears settled near Calcutta as missionaries and became part of the scenery, a subject my mother avoided. Her Jones instincts alerted her to the dangers they must have run into of becoming *desi*. I think their venturing outside the conventions must have been communicated to me in some eccentric gene.[43]

Iris's journal and letters to her children make amply explicit how much she had imbibed the lesson of the dangers of becoming part of the native scene, of being defiled by the "tar brush." Indeed, most of her life in India was spent within the physical confines and therefore the expectations of the social life of the bungalow and club. Her journal contains luminous vignettes of her time with her small children in the bungalow in the tea plantation at Cherideo, Assam:

> Notebook: October 10th 1953. The days drifting past in a flowering of bougainvillea, scarlet flame & purple. Dew on dahlias and cabbage leaves, wood smoke from the stable fire, mixing with manure & cut grass. Brown eggs and radishes. The children eating oranges (always) rubbing rosy faces against their horses' necks, racing the goats across the lawn, making felt needle cases with much-sucked bits of silk, working at a table dappled with sun & butterflies wings, lifting their heads as a golden

oriole swoops & jerks across the lawn or to watch a woodpecker in the Japanese bamboos. ("Mummy do you know where it gets its red crest?" "No tell me later" ...)[44]

Even when the children were sent home to England, she enjoyed her garden and the animals she had collected to populate the bungalow and its surroundings. She also did not hesitate to say that she would gladly give up "the whole of lovely, warm April in Assam, in exchange for one day of soft grey English rain, the glitter and slide of our Lake District streams, the beautiful, restful clouds." She hastened to add that this is an exilic feeling: "this, as Browning knew and every exile before and after has discovered, is the month for home-sickness."[45]

Iris Macfarlane's memoirs have much in common with Edith Cuthell's recollection three quarters of a century earlier: their minute, almost clinical, observations of plant and animal life around their bungalows—seasonal, routine, remarkable: the spider that makes a web every morning between the teapot and the chair, their pet deer, dogs, and kittens.[46] Iris's domesticated animals helped fill her time and make her feel useful.

The difference is that Iris had more opportunities for removing herself from the immediate environment into a cocoon of comfort. Their house had an air-conditioned room to which she could escape to write, "like a fish in an aquarium, cool & quiet as I stare out at the sweating *malis* pushing lawn mowers outside" under a 93-degree temperature. Iris and Mac had a refrigerator and could go to the movies once in a while. When Mac was appointed for a short duration as the managing director at Nazira Plantation, they moved into an even larger bungalow manned by twenty-four servants.

Iris wrote about these days in the tea plantation after India's independence from British rule. Little seemed to have changed as far as white privilege was concerned in the Assam Tea Company's world of tea plantations. Their social life still revolved around the bungalow and club among Europeans. For "official" functions, however, they had to greet Indian ministers, raise the Indian flag on India's Independence Day, tolerate desultory prize-giving ceremonies at the local school, and invite the junior Indian staff and their wives over for tea once in a while.

Contraction of Space

Iris's story dwells upon the formidable structural difficulties she faced breaking the usual model of expectations, but even more how she flailed around in trying to connect with the immediate world outside her verandah so as to construct her own space: "to create what I felt like a useful life suited to my own needs."[47]

Iris started noticing what others chose not to see. She began discovering the small and large corruptions perpetrated by English managers in tea gardens: godowns stashed with the booty collected from the US army—jeeps, fridges, canned food, and whisky. She came to recognize the ease with which the mangers could "cheat" on a tea garden, while at the same time watching their servants like "hawks." She started noticing the difference between Europeans (even junior staff) living in four-bedroom bungalows and the Assamese staff living in "little brick boxes with tin roofs," and the labor force from the states of Bihar and Orissa (Odisha) living in "mud shacks in squalid settlements called 'the lines'," where there was only one water tap between twenty houses and of course no electricity. That her servants could "emerge" from such squalid environments to "become the crisp, efficient bearer of trays round [her] polished rooms" appeared marvelous.[48] She so routinely assumed their "inferiority" that in retrospect she wrote: "It never seemed my business to enquire about their families, nor to wonder what they felt handing round the six course meals at my dinner parties, they who lived on one meal of rice and lentils a day."[49]

After years of valiantly attempting to keep up with her compatriots at the club, she stopped altogether. She drew up a cane chair in the verandah and started a novel. It didn't sell. When she raised her eyes from her typewriter to find something else to do, she was surprised at her own blindness:

> Once a week I had driven to the club through the villages I had never entered, past people whose language I couldn't speak, living lives I knew nothing of, dancing and singing to unknown tunes. I had not, honestly, thought of them as people; they were a brownish blur, like the greenish blur of the rice and the bluish ones of the mountains.

This brownish blur was categorized by the planters as "lazy, effeminate—the men tended to walk hand in hand—and spineless. Many of the women were very beautiful but would not be lured into white men's beds. They had to go to the carefree Khasis for their mistresses." The brownish blur of approximate-humans and the greenish blur of jungles, tea plantations, and rice fields, and the bluish blur of the mountains all were distanced to appear as scenes that one looked at but did not see.[50] The scene acted as a screening device to discourage noticing what resided behind its assured appearance as a picture. As Dell Upton notes in reference to the visual dominance of landscape studies, "the scene demands that we not see."[51]

Iris started learning Assamese, teaching pro bono at the local school, and trying to improve the sanitary conditions of the local hospital. She daydreamed of starting a model school with airy classrooms, new books, and a new crop of enlightened teachers imported from England. Her reforming zeal did not materialize. She found no one who could empathize with her alienation and guilt. She turned to nurturing wild animals rescued from the jungle as pets—an orphaned deer, a little gibbon. The gibbon adopted her: he was clingy, wrapping his arms around her neck as she went about her usual rounds between the house and garden. She worried about the deer wanting to leave the premises and join a mate in the jungle. Poachers would certainly kill her. As a bird in her garden kept saying "you are ill," "you are ill," she tried to dismiss the creeping recognition that she was on the brink of a mental breakdown.

Just before her return to England, knowing she was on her last "tour," she remained determined to make the most of the last warm season in Assam: the blue jays on the grass, the parrots, the moonflowers, the scenery from the verandah, and her pet deer Miranda who she would release into the jungle—"a distant one so that this time she wouldn't return."[52] Iris found herself mirrored in Miranda's captivity and release.

Iris's return back to England was in sharp contrast to her arrival. Sick in mind and body, she had to be carried home "more or less prostrate."[53] One morning during their last warm weather she retreated into her verandah in a terrifying state of mind:

> I found myself jumping aside as I passed an allamanda bush, terrified of touching one of its poisonous golden flowers. In case I had accidentally brushed against one, I hurried back to the bungalow to wash my hands. Who knew what else might poison me? My hands became white and bubbly from constant washing, and my beautiful garden turned into a deadly dangerous area through which I tiptoed, my arms clamped to my sides. Quite soon I didn't dare venture into it, and every day grew too weak to walk further than faltering steps round the verandah, since food was certain to be contaminated and unsafe to eat.[54]

Her sense of feeling trapped in the verandah is registered as being caught between the hope of leaving the life of a tea planter's wife and not wanting to leave Assam. The structure of attitudes which had shaped the formative sense of her self in the empire did not prepare her for this in-betweenness: a deadly ambivalence. The very garden that she had delighted in, and had tended with care and authority, seemingly turned against her in a violent reproach. When she set out to make connections with people and animals beyond her ken, she did not realize that such trespass was unwelcome. Domestication of the wild—clearing a space in the jungle to call home—had gone awry. In the end the boundary between the wildness and unpredictability of the jungle and the order and predictability of the garden no longer held. This sense of feeling unhomed was no sudden irruption of the unfamiliar/unhomely in the familiar/homely that characterizes the uncanny.[55] Iris describes a closing in—a contraction of space—that negates the possibility of her locating a sense of self. The personal space of comfort by virtue of which she could travel between her house and garden and the world beyond had collapsed. Her expansive and well-tended garden and generous verandah had contracted into a small space in a painful and sharp disconnect (Figures 15.5, 15.6, **Plate 23**).

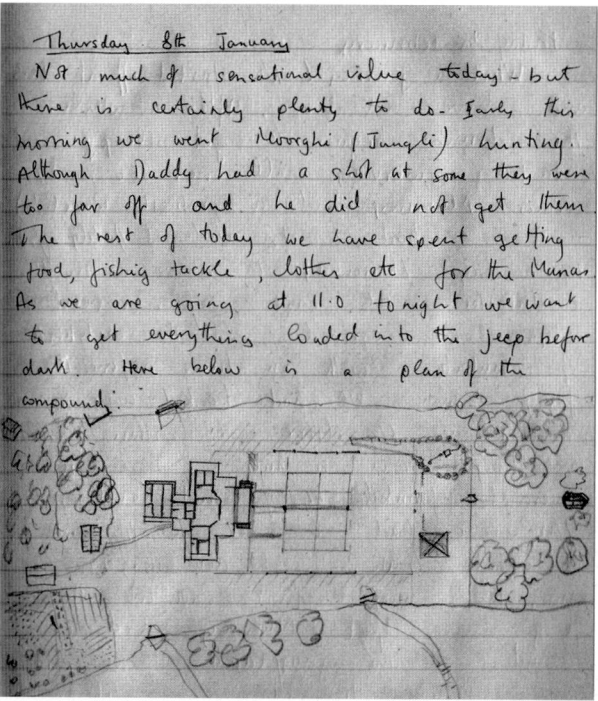

FIGURE 15.5 Page from Alan Macfarlane's journal with site plan of Iris Macfarlane's bungalow, Cherideo Tea Plantation, Assam, 1959. Illustration in Alan MacFarlane (ed.), *Twenty Years in Tea*, 2019.

Jangal

Iris wrote of feeling that her attempts at making home in India were a lot of waste: wasted time, energy, talent. She had led an unproductive life, despite having three children and a caring husband. By virtue of her whiteness in a colonial milieu, she had taken for granted the connections between bungalow, club, hunting, fishing, and leisure only to find these relations unsatisfying. She had assumed a certain coalescing of her private and public selves when as the *burra* (senior) memsahib in the locality she wanted to be useful and expected to find entrée into the social spaces of Indian laborers, the local children, and teachers, only to be reminded that she could not do so with any degree of efficacy. The connections were fragile, unidirectional on her own part, even when language barriers were surmountable.

Years before this turn of events, Iris had drawn a plan of her bungalow in Deopani in a letter sent to her son at school in England (**Plate 24**). The drawing shows a bungalow at the head of the plan with a separate cook house, a water tower and ayah's house to the right within close reach, but distinctly separate. Other servants' quarters and work spaces are further

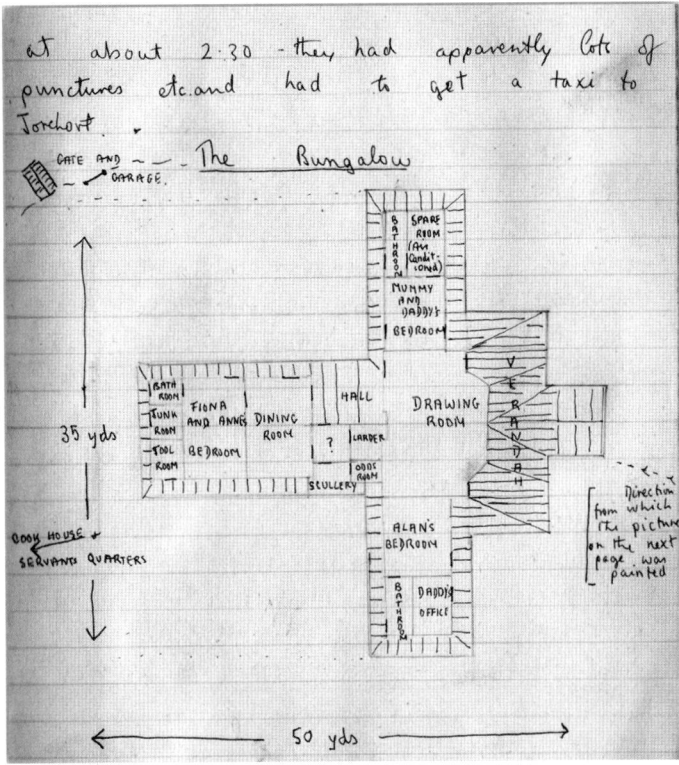

FIGURE 15.6 Floor Plan of Iris Macfarlane's bungalow, Cherideo Tea Plantation, Assam, by Alan Macfarlane, 1959. Illustration in Alan MacFarlane (ed.), *Twenty Years in Tea*, 2019.

away with the ducks and the vegetable garden. The approach road to the bungalow breaks off from the main road and goes past the enclosure of the washerman (*dhobi*) and the tea plantation's hospital wards. She had colored in green the edges where the bungalow premises commenced. Hedges define her front and back gardens. A road past the fruit trees leads to a lake. Scrawled on the blank spaces to both the left and right of the entry road is "Jungle." The jungle is proximate and precariously warded off with hedges. There is seemingly no boundary between the vegetable garden of the hospital (meant for workers in the plantation) and the jungle. The jungle is not rendered through pictorial means, but the words on a blank space suggest itself as the very ground amid which the bungalow, hospital, and the adjoining buildings are designated as living space.

In precolonial India, the word *jangal*, from which the English word "jungle" is derived, had a range of meanings from grass savannah and dry scrubland to land that had been left uncultivated and was therefore unkempt.[56] This was arid land but fit for human habitation and growing crops, and appeared in surveys and legal codes on land tenure. Nathaniel Brassey Halhed, in his *The Code of Gentoo Law* (1776), referred to the extant legal status of jungle as land that has been left uncultivated for five years or more. Halhed translated jungle as "waste." By the late eighteenth century, the idea of clearing and enclosing wasteland in England had been brought within the moral imperative of improvement. Such improvement justified enclosure and appropriation of common land from the peasantry.[57] The translation of an idea of waste from England to India gathered other connotations not evident in the English use of the term. Notably, the idea gained a new importance in its application in the colonies to justify imperial expansion.[58]

In a late-eighteenth-century military report on the Jungle Terry (Jangal Terai) we see the term "jungle" being used for land that remained uncultivated or had been abandoned, and to dense bamboo growth as well as thick grassland. Seen through the lens of warfare the jungle is an obstacle, impeding passage and visibility. Here it is associated with unhealthiness.[59] Lord Cornwallis in his advocacy of the Permanent Settlement of Bengal used the term "jungle" to refer to "land inhabited by wild beasts from which no rent could be extracted."[60] Beyond the failed opportunity to yield revenue he viewed such tracts of unreclaimed land as evidence of native laziness—unwillingness to labor, and moral laxity. Jungles demonstrated the native incapacity to govern themselves.[61]

The visual and physical impenetrability of the jungle was also used to describe a very different land and riverine form, that of the Sunderbans in the lower Gangetic delta. In the 1760s, James Rennell used both jungle and woods to describe the geography of the Sunderbans, whereas W. W. Morrieson in the second decade of the nineteenth century used only jungle. By the late nineteenth century, this same land form would be described by W. W. Hunter as forest.[62]

Thus, by the nineteenth century the term "jungle" was being used in English in government reports as a catchall term for scrubland, dense forests, hunting ground, and often used interchangeably with woods and forests. While in Hindi and Bengali usage, all these meanings were implied in the use of the term *jangal*, there was a wider set of terms used to designate what came to be called "wasteland," encompassing a range of land types. Importantly, the rules of designating wasteland changed over the course of the nineteenth century. With the establishment of the Imperial Forest Department in 1864 and subsequent laws that extended state sovereignty over forest lands, the forest emerged "as a specific category of wooded land or land reserved for the production of woody crops." In contrast, jungle came to stand in for "residual wooded land (which may be largely trees and shrubs considered less valuable)" and "also unkempt, poorly managed, dangerous, weedy and in many other ways devalued or deprecated land."[63] That is, despite the revenue-generating capacity of jungles or the exercise of usufruct rights in them (to gather honey, wood, game, and for swidden cultivation), in both the official language of administrative records and in popular use such as memoirs and gardening guides, the jungle slid into a figure of not simply uncultivated/unkempt land but a threat to the spaces of civilization.[64] As the use of the term was extended from India to other spaces across the empire, jungle came to embody "the outer extremes of colonial expansion," even when such spaces were physically proximate.[65] The jungle resisted enclosure, seemingly defied utility, and harbored disease, and from the colonialist point of view beseeched destruction.[66] The jungle was deemed to lack "utility" from a very specific modern state-centric point of view, and it is in this respect that the jungle came to be seen as interchangeable with the term "waste." We can observe this switch in Hunter's characterization of the "jungle" in Cornwallis's text as "waste." Attribution of the category of waste to land implied its reclaimability by the state, of taking it out of reach of inhabitants who used such land for subsistence or profit.[67]

In light of this century-long deployment of the word, it is useful to reflect upon the implication of the garden-turned-threat in Iris's narrative of her efforts as a litany of wastes. Her desire to be useful beyond her homemaking responsibilities, of partaking in the public sphere, is fueled by the same moral imperative that drove the arguments for land improvement. This extended to her wanting to take care of wildlife, salvaging the ruins of an Ahom temple, writing novels, and teaching (none of which she was trained to do), to improve the conditions she found around her. To her, making a mark in the public sphere in these capacities would have meant leading a useful life.

In figuring her incapacity to maintain the distance and distinction between home and jungle, the terms of engagement between waste and productivity were reversed. In the shock of recognition, the well-tended garden embodied waste—of labor, resources, affective investment. It is after all the calculated disconnect between European enclaves and native spaces that could uphold the fiction of European-style gardening as improvement. For Iris, the figure-ground relation between home and jungle had become reversed, or appeared interchangeable.

Inhabiting a Map

When Alan Macfarlane published his mother's letters and journals in 2019, he included a map used by the Assam Tea Company for representing its tea plantations in Assam (Figure 15.7). There you can see the location of Deopani, Cherideo, Nazira, and the other plantations of the company and the infrastructure of roads, railways, and waterways that connected the plantations. This diagram of the infrastructure as a set of connective pieces is starkly self-referential—even the boundaries of the map are simply blank as if these plantations and infrastructure are not introduced within a geographic context of land and habitation. The map was intended to locate Iris and her family's story within the operations of the Assam Tea Company's domains. But unlike Theo, Iris had not managed to inhabit such a map. Her

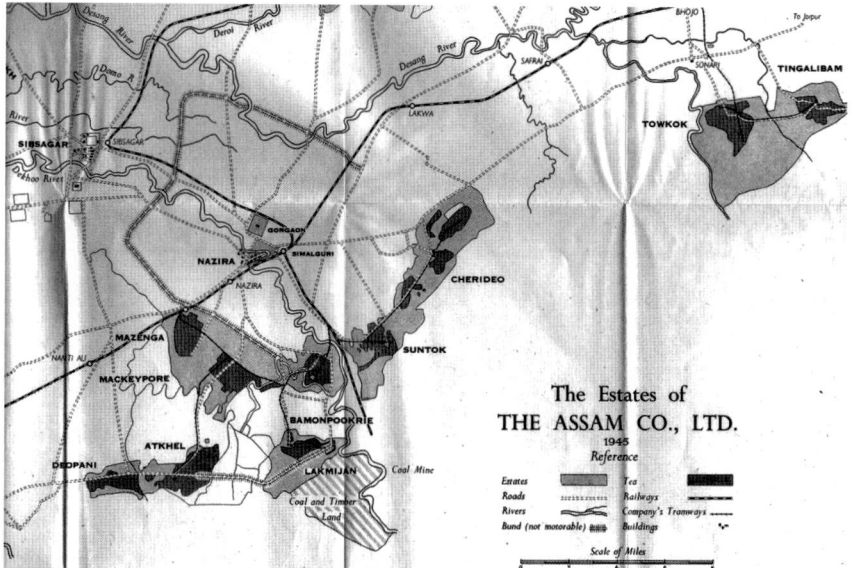

FIGURE 15.7 Map of the Estates of Assam Tea Company. Illustration in Alan MacFarlane (ed.), *Twenty Years in Tea*, 2019.

visceral discomfort with her space of habitation contradicts the abstraction of social and material relations that such a map insinuates and rationalizes.

The map does represent the tea plantation estates in so far as it embodies the social infrastructure of the tea planters. In 1963, in a letter of complaint to the Assam Tea Company's Managing Director, a senior tea planter in Assam, R. Higham wrote of the need for managers to have higher wages, a guaranteed salary "irrespective of any future increases" in income tax, annual salary increments, increased pension, and better perquisites—including paid cooks, improved bungalows fully furnished with crockery, cutlery, and linen, etc., air freight for "an individual's cold storage and 'dry' stores, from Calcutta." He based his argument for these incentives on the hardships the European tea planter had to endure being away from England: "Our main reason for being out here is to earn sufficient to keep our families in reasonable comfort, and to save enough to retire [to England] comfortably."[68] The same crew who regularly sought compensation for roughing it "out here," claimed that the tea plantation coolies, whose living conditions were notoriously wretched, had it "a lot better than they'd get at home." Iris wryly noted that "none of them could have put a finger on the map to show where was home to their fortunate labour force."[69] Such differential expectations of migration and abstraction were built into the imagination of portable geographies.

16

A Good Shelf

The Bangyia Sahitya Parishat Library in Kolkata is home to a collection of books that once belonged to Iswarchandra Vidyasagar (1820–91), a luminary of the nineteenth-century public sphere of Calcutta (Kolkata). The books are housed in twenty-four bookshelves that Vidyasagar had custom-made for his Sanskrit, Hindi, Bengali, and English books as well as his collection of *puthi* (manuscript scrolls).[1]

A renowned Sanskrit scholar, social reformer, educator, author, and publisher, Vidyasagar had intended his book collection to be donated or sold after his death. According to the instruction in his will he wanted the person or institution acquiring his book collection to take the books *with* the bookcases in which he kept them. Those bookshelves ultimately arrived at the Bangiya Sahitya Parishat Library with much of the original collection still intact.[2]

Perhaps Vidyasagar anticipated that his heirs would not understand or heed the integrity of his book collection, and that is why he put in the clause about bookshelves in his will. He did not want his book collection to be dispersed and forgotten. Perhaps they were bequeathed to future generations of literary Calcutta as a mark of his scholarly range and taste. The books, he hoped, would acquire real value in transmission. Perhaps we would get to know him by the company of books he kept. We do not know why he made this decision, but it is evident from contemporary sources that he went to great lengths to accommodate those bookshelves. He had a new residence built to house this large collection.[3]

I stood in front of one of these bookshelves on a dimly lit stair-landing at the Bangiya Sahitya Parishat Library, hoping to find something extraordinary. The dark varnish of the solid wood spoke of age. The stout legs of the bookshelf made room for a few inches of space between the bottom shelf and the floor, making it convenient to clean underneath. The frame itself was unadorned. The clear glass door-leaves of the bookshelf were locked. I peered through the glass to see the titles of the volumes inside. Nothing appeared exceptional about the object, except a solemn presence (Figure 16.1).

The bookshelf, viewed as a window into the material culture of reading, rather than an object of historical significance, helps us contemplate empire

FIGURE 16.1 One of the bookshelves that once belonged to Iswarchandra Vidysagar, presently in the Bangiya Sahitya Parishat Library, Kolkata. © Swati Chattopadhyay.

as a process of assembling small spaces. It helps us unfold the relation between architecture (the building) and the object (bookshelf) as a set of practices—economic, social, political—that shaped the culture of empire. For this we have to abandon the methodological inhibition of thinking of objects in buildings as distinct from the architectural space in which they are located. The bookshelf exceeds its function as a container of books to suggest a larger geography of social relations that it supports and mediates. It connects spaces not simply through a linear set of scalar relations—book, shelf, library, house, city, empire—but throws up surprising revelations in how scalar advantage may be negotiated to generate new figures of space.

The relation between the bookshelf as a spatial container of books and the space in which the bookshelf was located accrued peculiar meanings in the nineteenth-century colonial milieu. The changing practice of storing books—specifically, the gradual obsolescence of the practice of storing books in chests, hampers, and wall niches, and the emergent practice of keeping books in rows of horizontal shelves either set inside a wall or as a freestanding furniture—is key to this story. While the use of wall niches and cupboards for storing books continued, the widespread use of the shelf specifically meant for books was coeval with the rapid growth of the print industry in the late eighteenth and nineteenth centuries that transformed habits of reading, collecting, and keeping books. It was also a consequence of what B. Venkat Mani describes as global "bibliomigrancy"—the movement of books from one language to another and across the world, made possible by modern colonialism.[4]

The social significance of bibliomigrancy exceeded its literary content. An entirely new set of social relations of race, class, and caste—between colonizer and colonized, Indians and Europeans, intellectual elites and the barely literate—was created around the mode of storing books. The bookshelf, first as a tool of display, and second as an emblem of knowledge acquisition and transmission, emerged as a central reference in calibrating power relations.

The location of the collections, whether in a secluded space as opposed to a public space, in the domestic realm, or oriented toward a public sphere, was paramount to the attribution of meaning.[5] As a fragment linked to the public world of letters and of colonial collecting, the bookshelf in the colonial milieu framed the contentious relation between public and private spheres. Viewed in relation to an intended user/audience, it both helped articulate a new public display of colonial power and a new idea of literary space within domestic confines. The bookshelf in this sense emerged as a new *figure of space* that mediated relations of power.

By figure of space, I mean the social constitution of space around a social role—when a space is attached to a social role and thus becomes connotative of an expected performance of power relations, and through this linkage becomes tropic. This is the case of the housewife and the drawing room in nineteenth-century literature on domesticity, the verandah as a site of European authority in the colonies, the salon in the space of bourgeois domesticity that negotiated the line between public and private spheres, and the terrace as a space of literary jouissance, as I have described in this book. Though historically specific, a figure of space exceeds its particular spatial parameters to signal an expanded social imaginary where debates on social ideals and expectations may be launched.

Bibliomigrancy

The bookshelf as a figure of space was particular to the colonial milieu and differed from the comfortable cosmopolitanism that pervaded the practice of book collecting in the nineteenth and early twentieth centuries. Let's take Walter Benjamin's essay, "Unpacking My Library" (1931), for example.[6] Benjamin endowed the contingent act of collecting with a quasi-mystical aura, and noted that collections are dwelling spaces in the maelstrom of capitalism. As his bookscape extended from the personal to the larger world of Europe, Benjamin assumed the universality of the bookshelf as space: his cosmopolitanism would not allow anything short of that.

We see Benjamin sitting amid the crates in which the books had arrived: "The books are not in shelves yet, not yet touched by the mild boredom of order," ready to be paraded in front of an audience. Until then Benjamin could rejoice in the disorder of the crates that had been "wrenched open, the air saturated with the dust of wood, the floor covered with torn paper."[7] The books would see light after two years of crate-life: the tactile pleasure of opening the crates and handling the books is what presumably prompted Benjamin to reflect how this collection was acquired and the legacy of that transmission: through remembrance he could travel to the cities and auction houses where he found his treasured editions. The most valued works had distinctive proprietary lineage or they were treasured family inheritance. No surprise there. A personal history of collecting as a form of self-fashioning is necessarily connected to the larger history of printing and collecting. In contrast, the bookshelf was the place of stasis, waiting to be disturbed by the owner-reader's volitions. In Benjamin's world, the bookshelf as container is rather too obvious, taken for granted. It disappears from view and enables us to contemplate the significance of the act of collecting.

Benjamin had inherited a culture of book collecting in which bibliomigrancy was both assumed and expected. The ability to fill the empty space of the bookshelf with works from all over the world and from all times gave the bookshelf a universal space-time feature not shared by any other space in the house until much later.[8] However, if for a moment we leave Benjamin's twentieth century for the nineteenth-century colonial world, the assumption of universality appears fraught. Not everyone could claim their literary heritage so assuredly without being reminded of the power relations of bibliomigrancy shaped by the "command of languages and languages of command," to borrow Bernard Cohn's phrase.[9]

Advocating the introduction of English education in India in 1835, lawmaker and historian Thomas Babington Macaulay remarked that "a single shelf of a good European library . . . is worth the whole of the native literature of India and Arabia."[10] Macaulay acknowledged that he had no knowledge of these other languages, but he was satisfied with the opinion of Orientalist scholars who advocated the study of Sanskrit, Persian, and Arabic—none of whom would apparently contradict his assessment of the superiority of European languages. He was not discussing specific works; he did not have the language competency to do so. The comparison in which the whole of "native" literature fell short of Macaulay's good shelf was a connoisseurial space: it could be filled in by the reader's imagination and verified by their literary taste and judgment. Macaulay's single shelf of books was a synecdoche of empire—the basis for claiming the superiority of European language, law, justice.

That the authority of the written word would be used to justify European superiority ought not to be a surprise; much has been written about the interface between literate and nonliterate cultures and between different language systems in shaping regimes of conquest.[11] The space in which

Macaulay sought to intercede, however, was a scribal culture of governance with a complex system of rules and hierarchies, and a literate culture in which libraries already functioned as power symbols. Libraries of princes and elites as well as monastic institutions were well known and their valuable collections eagerly sought by European adventurists and Orientalists. By the time Macaulay penned his Minute, classics of Persian, Arabic, and Sanskrit had already made their way into Europe to adorn personal libraries and fatten state and corporate archival holdings. The eighteenth- and early-nineteenth-century Orientalists prized their collection of oriental books and manuscripts.

What was at stake for Macaulay was not just the colonial state's support of schools that taught oriental languages but the expectation that the British administrator in India would have to learn Indian languages.[12] In 1800, Governor-General Richard Wellesley instituted the Fort William College in Calcutta to teach Indian languages—Persian, Arabic, Sanskrit, Urdu, Bengali, and others—to newly arrived British civilians. A firsthand knowledge of Indian languages, it was argued, would not only aid the work of governance, but was a necessary antidote to the untrustworthiness of Indian personnel who manned the expanding bureaucratic apparatus of the colonial state. Here European professors taught alongside Indian scholars who prepared texts, grammars, and dictionaries. Language instruction at Fort William College formalized the informal process through which British administrators and merchants in the eighteenth century acquired familiarity with the principal languages of the subcontinent.[13]

The culture of knowledge accumulation and exchange that characterized these pre-1835 decades are depicted in an 1813 lithograph by Charles D'Oyly (**Plate 25**). Here we see a young European man learning the Arabic alphabet from an elderly *munshi* (language instructor). The *munshi* sits in a dignified manner as a person of authority with a book in hand, while the young man appears exhausted in his attempt to master the first steps of language preparation. In the background is John Gilchrist's *Grammar of the Hindoostanee Language* (1796). A bookcase against the wall provides a literal and metaphorical background of bibliomigrancy. The open bookcase as artifact designates the space as a study/office. Its rows of uniformly bound volumes, conforming to the practice of having books custom-bound for one's library, represents the authority of the world of European texts. That world of ideas, however, has to be mediated through the language practices of the colonized if it is to gain salience. The relation between the European sahib and the Indian *munshi* is presented in a subtle tension, as the hierarchy between the ruler and ruled appears skewed when the colonized teaches the language of command to the ruler. Macaulay's Minute sought to change the terms of exchange portrayed in this image.

The new nexus of language and governance imagined by Macaulay was grounded in powerful currents of bibliomigrancy that had been set in motion in the late eighteenth century. Now I turn to one such event of pivotal significance: the looting of Tipu Sultan's library in Seringapatam (Srirangapatnam), and its subsequent reestablishment in London.

Tipu's Library

When the Battle of Seringapatam (1799) concluded the Fourth Anglo-Mysore War (1798–9) with a decisive British victory, Tipu Sultan was dead and his library of between 3,000 and 4,000 volumes was scattered, a substantial portion destroyed.[14] Of these a collection of about 2,000 manuscripts in Persian (court language), Kannada (language of administration), Marathi, Telegu, Arabic, French, and English was removed to Fort William College Library in Calcutta. Governor-General Wellesley used Tipu's collection to buttress his decision to found Fort William College without the East India Company (EIC) Court of Directors' permission, and to post facto justify waging the Fourth Anglo-Mysore War. After Wellesley's term as Governor-General ended, the EIC asked for the collection at Fort William College to be sent to London where it was placed in the Company's Oriental Repository. Few originals and a large number of copies remained in Calcutta at the Fort William College and the Asiatic Society. The remains of Tipu's library in Calcutta and London would anchor the emergent vision of British imperial sovereignty.

Wellesley's acquisition and distribution of Tipu's library was an old and tried method of appropriating the signs of authority to justify the right of conquest. In this case, he wanted access to the documents in Tipu's library to establish the Mysore ruler's venality and determination to destroy British presence in India in order to justify the Fourth Anglo-Mysore War. The territorial and inquisitorial became linked in an assertion of the library as a representation of sovereignty: the right to rule. In a recent article, Joshua Ehrlich points out that in the eighteenth-century libraries were emblems of power as repositories of *both knowledge and beauty*. In turning the plunder of Tipu's library into greater ideological use, beyond the monetary worth of the books, the EIC's administrators were appropriating the value that Tipu himself placed on his fine book collection as a mark of his sovereignty.[15]

Tipu had acquired this collection from the libraries of vanquished rulers and had manuscripts prepared at his court. He employed calligraphers, bookbinders, and illustrators to reproduce works, which were then distributed. The works in the collection were marked with his imperial seal, individually wrapped, and kept in chests. This method of storage was common in collections attached to monasteries and religious institutions in the subcontinent, and ensured "excellent preservation."[16] Following a much older and widespread practice of marking paintings and books with the owner's seal, in placing his royal stamp next to previous seals Tipu was claiming dynastic legitimacy.[17] This legitimacy exceeded affairs of the state and contained a personal impress of rulership.

The relation between buildings and objects is key to understanding this articulation of sovereignty. Unlike the treasury (*toshakhana*) which was located behind the audience hall facing the public courtyard, the library was located in the inner courtyard of the palace.[18] Besides books and manuscripts, the library also contained state papers, legal digests, and private correspondence.[19] In combining the functions of a *muhafizkhana* (record room) and a *kitabkhana* (library), the collection strode the line between public affairs of the state and the personal/dynastic collection of a king. This collection was carefully ordered and maintained by managers who were obliged to provide daily reports. From this repository of knowledge—literary, historic, scientific, legal—Tipu's sons were instructed in the affairs of the state.[20]

The narratives of British encounter with this collection suggests a reversal of meaning in how the space of the library was received and accorded value by the British. These narratives register both the value of the library as a *treasure house* and its difference from contemporary European libraries. For those who first encountered the library, it looked like a warehouse:

> The library and depôt of manuscripts, was a dark room, in the S.E. angle of the upper virandah of the interior quadrangle of the palace. Instead of being beautifully arranged, as in the Bodleian, the books were heaped together in hampers, covered with leather; to consult which, it was necessary to discharge the whole contents on the floor.[21]

The distinction between Tipu's library and Oxford's Bodleian resides in the use of bookshelves in the latter. Bookshelves here are synonymous with an enlightened institutional order, facilitating an orderly placement and display of books, providing easy access to that repository of knowledge. At the same time bookshelves define the space of the modern library. They enable a collection to be turned into a library: here books may be placed in the light to engender the acquisition and dissemination of knowledge. In the absence of shelves, the vision of a library as a space of knowledge and enlightenment appeared errant. Tipu's library was seen as a dark space in which valuable content was secreted away, and seemingly betrayed Tipu's character: his coveting of beautiful objects, as well as his cunning and cruelty. Pairing the racialized metaphors of darkness and light with (heathen) ignorance and (Christian) knowledge, the distinction between the architecture of a depot and a library is used to signal the move from despotism to enlightened occupation.

The reference to the beauty of the Bodleian library is important in this context. Beauty itself was a matter of adjudication. While a "Hindu goldsmith" was retained to provide a valuation of the treasury jewels, the inspection of the books in Tipu's library was presumably undertaken without the presence of an Indian scholar. British officers in charge selected from the larger collection over 300 manuscripts "of the choicest description" for delivery to the EIC.²² Penmanship and fineness of illustration were considered the chief criteria of value. The status of the books as artwork was prior to their importance as treatise. In this regard the valuation of the works in the library was akin to the valuation of jewels in the treasury.²³ Unlike the jewels, however, the books were not distributed among the officers and soldiers. Their status as art *and* information—something potentially more revealing—demanded a different kind of processing.

Tipu's state papers and the rest of the library were considered invaluable as reflective of his personal character. His peculiar "barbarity," Alexander Beatson wrote, following William Kirkpatrick who translated some of the papers, could be deduced from state correspondence and a journal of dreams "written in his own hand."²⁴ The discovery of Tipu's library in a dark vault-like space was thus an encounter with the figure of Tipu as a ruler. The description corresponds with the much-publicized depiction of General Baird discovering the body of Tipu in a dimly lit dungeon-like space: English victory brings light to the dark spaces of oriental despotism (**Plate 26**).

That collections and characters were seen as mutually constitutive or even interchangeable is not surprising. There is a much longer pre-eighteenth-century history going back to antiquity of thinking of a library as peculiarly reflective of the collector's intellectual and social disposition.²⁵ What is striking in this instance is the intent behind disturbing the extant order of a collection. The actions of the British officers on the scene are a demonstration of the ability to appropriate, invert, and disseminate a new order. Captain Price, one of the officers in charge of the operation, concluded his discussion of the princely library with an anecdote:

> As it was something in illustration of character, I cannot forbear mentioning that one day, while Maj. Ogg and myself were turning over the leaves of these multifarious M.SS. one of the young princes who had been permitted to look in upon us, was overheard, in rather audible whisper, to observe to his attendants—"Only see how these hogs are allowed to contaminate my father's books."²⁶

That the indiscriminate handling of the royal library was considered a desecration was evident to Captain Price. He placed this anecdote just before his description of the looting of the *zenana* (women's quarter) located diagonally across from the library.²⁷

When this library was transferred to the Oriental Repository at the East India House in London, it was displayed on shelves in a well-appointed room dressed in "gold and azure" (**Plate 27**).²⁸ This room consisted of three compartments with two symmetrically arranged spaces flanking a domed square central space. Each room was furnished with bookshelves set within the walls. Generous windows in the side compartments admitted light. In the central space visitors were given a glimpse of Tipu's library.²⁹ They could also see alongside bound volumes "specimens of various ores and fossils which Major Ogg collected from the Mysore country."[30]

At first glance, the distinction between the library as a state vault in Seringapatam and the library as the trophy of a mercantile corporation in London appears stark. While they both served the goals of claiming sovereignty, the Oriental Repository was meant as a visual display that extended the existing iconography of the decorative program at the East India House, most clearly demonstrated by the ceiling painting that greeted visitors to the building: Spiridione Roma's *East Offering its Riches to Britannia* (1778) (**Plate 28**).[31] Painted decades before the consolidation of empire, Roma's painting presented colonial trade and plunder as "gifting": figures personifying India, Persia, China willingly offer their riches—tea, porcelain, bales of cotton, pearls—to Britannia as if they have recognized and accepted her innate superiority. Expropriation and gifting became unified in the figure of the library as a commodity on display.

This grand display of books alongside minerals and miscellaneous plundered treasures drew sharp criticism from one observer, Peter Gordon. A staunch critic of the EIC, Gordon disapproved of the Repository on two counts. The collection as trophy transplanted to the "metropolis of the conqueror" stood as an insult to the Indian who "cannot visit the depot in which the spoil of his country is exhibited." Note that Gordon describes the repository as a "depot" exactly in the manner that Tipu's library was described by the English soldiers. Gordon also recorded the "affecting sight" he had witnessed when Tipu's son, Jamal-ud-Din, visited the library and stood "in the midst of the plunder of Seringapatam"—on one side of the prince "lay Tipu's dream register, to another lay one of Tipu's illuminated Qurans."[32] For the visitor the original scene of plunder could be relived and reimagined.

The idea of the Repository as alienated patrimony was reinforced by its ineffective insertion in Britain's public life. Gordon noted that the collection amounted to a national treasure: "The most valuable collection of Oriental manuscripts in existence in Europe or in Asia." Yet the Directors possessed no recognition of such a valuable collection. The Repository severely limited public access.[33] The short hours of the library, the paucity of qualified personnel, its lack of suitable reference books, even its location in the city far away from "every other oriental establishment," made it ill-suited as a public library.

The functioning of the Oriental Repository, Gordon argued, mirrored the EIC's mercenary motives and its history of corruption.[34] The mere placement of books on shelves was not sufficient evidence of their availability for public enlightenment. The superficial emphasis on the library as a trophy detracted from the acquisition of knowledge that such a collection promised. Gordon was not troubled by the seizure of Tipu's library per se, but with the library's inadequate interface with the public (both in England and in India) and its utter neglect of public interest—that is, the failure of the library as an institution. The Court of Directors had reduced the collection to a hidden space once more—"except the venerable librarian, no person knows what treasures it contains."[35] Gordon saw in the library's lack of public access a mirror of that oriental excess and despotism that so colored the history of Tipu Sultan. If bibliomigrancy depended on circulation of books, travel between languages, of the exchange of ideas—the bases of an emergent nineteenth-century public sphere—the Oriental Repository thwarted this possibility. The commodification of the library in the imperial metropolis that drew Gordon's critique was a constant refrain in descriptions of libraries in colonial India. Its spatial articulation, however, carried different meanings.

The Material Culture of Reading

The diffusion of printed books in India in the late eighteenth century, beyond the confines of royal courts and European factories and missions, changed the spaces of reading, publishing, literary exchange, and archiving.[36] For a while, as in the Western world, books, loose folios, and manuscript scrolls jostled for space in trunks, chests, and wall niches, before the bookshelf became a standard piece of household furniture.[37] The newness of the form of the bookshelf in the first decades of the nineteenth century was clearly articulated in Bhavanicharan Bandopadhyay's *Kalikata Kamalalaya* (Calcutta the Abode of Lakshmi, the Goddess of Prosperity), a didactic tract published in 1823.[38] Set as a conversation between a city dweller and a country dweller (newcomer to the city) about new modes of socialization that the upper-caste Hindus appeared to be undertaking in early-nineteenth-century Calcutta, the text takes the form of two archetypal characters discussing the emergence of a new Bengali society in which religious rituals appear to have taken a back seat. The main point of contention is contamination: the pollution of the sacred Hindu household caught in the socioeconomic nexus of the colonial city where men spent long hours performing salaried work in the office, neglecting the religious duties of the householder. Their speech, clothing, modes of socialization, and the material culture of their residences betray foreign influence: hence the fear of ritual contamination. The outside world of the foreign colonizers is seen as invading the inner world of ritual observance, thereby posing a threat to the household's caste status.

One piece of furniture that serves as a point of discussion is the bookshelf. The visitor to the city asks in puzzlement about the fashion of buying books in Persian, English, and Arabic to fill one- and two-leaf glass-door "almirahs." The orderly display of the expensive collection appears in inverse relation to its use—seemingly the books are only handled by the manager and binder. Is this the educational equivalent of the practice of building temples?—some do it for cultivating virtue and others to display wealth—asks the country dweller.[39] At this the city dweller irritably responds: there is no reason for a person of means to use a collection all the time; he does it when he needs to—his livelihood does not depend on daily use of books. And, of course, there are those whose livelihoods depend on daily perusal of books.

Three points are noticeable in this staged conversation. The English word "bookshelf" is not used; but the Portuguese/Old English word "almirah" or "almery" (which by that time had become indigenized in Bengali as *almari*) is used to refer to the bookcase, suggestive of a process of cultural incorporation: of course, all kinds of valuable goods could be stored in an *almari*. A book *almari* conveys the transformation of an older article of household furniture to meet the specific purpose of storing books.[40] Second, a distinction is made between the symbolic role of personal libraries comprising elegant bookshelves as markers of wealth and desire for knowledge acquisition, and the utilitarian use of collections for the sake of livelihood. Neither case, we are given to understand, presents a risk of contamination: books concern dealings with the outside world where economic and social norms of the rulers have to be followed. Not all wealthy people have libraries, we learn later. While the colonial marketplace has created opportunities for economic advancement for all castes and professions, not every man of means is invested in literary pursuits. The presence of a library in a house and its use differentiate upper-caste/classes from the merely wealthy. Third, there is no mention of Bengali books in this new library. Publication of Bengali books was a new enterprise, in which Bhavanicharan as writer, editor, publisher was one of the pioneers.

The library in nineteenth-century mansions of the Indian elite in Calcutta and provincial towns in Bengal would usually be located in the outer, public compartments of the house linked to the sphere of male sociality.[41] By the late nineteenth century bookshelves had also become common in middle-class households and residences of the burgeoning professional class of lawyers, educators, doctors.[42] While the library might still be located near the space of male sociality—the *baithakkhana* (salon)—it was just as likely to be a connecting piece between public (outer/male) and private (inner/female) compartments, as an increasing number of women were educated and fostered ambitions of partaking in the public sphere of letters.[43]

Vidyasagar's Library

Vidyasagar's library did not fully accord with this spatial distinction between inner and outer compartments. Nor did Vidyasagar's understanding of public and private worlds comply with the distinction articulated by Bhavanicharan. Vidyasagar's book collection was not confined to a room designated as a library, but consisted of several rooms on the upper floor of his two-story house. The scale, scope, and organization of his library were noted by contemporaries. In addition to collecting books and manuscripts in Indian languages, he sourced English books directly from London, where booksellers were instructed to send him the books uniformly bound. The books were organized by subject—history, literature, philosophy—and represented this "Sanskrit pundit's deep affection for Western history, science and philosophy."[44]

The singular feature of Vidyasagar's life as an educator, author, publisher, social reformer was his nonconformism: his refusal to obey caste, religious, and political norms simply because it would have been convenient to acquiesce for economic or social succor. Secular biographies and reminiscence of Vidyasagar read the spatial organization of his orderly library and its furniture arrangement as an index of his bibliomigrancy, rational outlook, and upright disposition in matters both public and personal. Take this description, for example. In 1883, a young writer Muhammad Reazuddin Ahmad (1861–1933) came to meet Vidyasagar and was led into a large room in which ten to twelve glass-case almirahs were filled with books, all bound beautifully and with golden lettering. A servant was taking the books out one at a time and wiping each with a clean cloth. A massive table with twelve or thirteen chairs completed the room's furnishing. After a few minutes, he was "led into another room also lined with almirahs filled with books" where Vidyasagar was sitting erect on a chair next to a large table.[45] In another reminiscence these two rooms are described as his library and study. Though set up for both private reading and meeting with friends and guests, the rooms did not represent the *baithakkhana* of the Bengali household, where men sat on a large carpet (*jajim*) on the floor. The *baithakkhana* had a connotation of gentlemanly indolence with which Vidyasagar, though known for his conversational aptitude, did not identify.[46]

The spatial articulation of the public self, and the distinction between private and public spheres, took on a peculiar configuration in nineteenth-century Bengal. Partha Chatterjee argues that the distinction between an inner "spiritual" domain and an outer "material" domain was the leitmotif of nineteenth-century Bengali nationalism.[47] The spiritual domain that Bhavanicharan described as the domain of the household and caste community by the second half of the nineteenth century was redefined as a domain of the "cultural." This cultural domain had to be protected from colonial intrusion, whereas the material domain was the outer sphere of politics and statecraft in which European superiority had to be recognized, replicated, and ultimately superseded. Long before the Bengali nationalist elite launched a political struggle in the outer domain, it began its self-definition in the domain of the cultural. Education and the purpose and value of education were some of the most debated aspects of this self-definition. Vidyasagar's library entered the history of Bengali thought as a site of such debate. The event was his legendary meeting with Sri Ramakrishna narrated by Mahendranath Gupta (1854–1932) in *Sri Sri Ramakrishna Kathamrita* (translated into English as The Gospel of Shri Ramakrishna; hereafter *RK*).

An Encounter

The meeting was initiated at Ramakrishna's request. Perpetually curious about spirituality and religious experience, he wanted to meet the man so famed for his erudition and kindness (Vidyasagar literally means "ocean of learning" and his other sobriquet was *karunasagar*: "ocean of kindness"). The narrative of this meeting was posed as an encounter between two divergent modes of being in the colonial world and two different paths to salvation. Although both were Brahmins, unlike Vidyasagar, Ramakrishna had little education. He was a poor priest who had become, by the time this meeting took place, the most sought-after spiritual guide among the educated Hindu Bengali middle class. Increasingly disillusioned with the prospect of material advancement under colonial rule, they found refuge in Ramakrishna's teachings that emphasized freedom from salaried labor. Though usually dressed in a rustic manner, Ramakrishna had a fondness for fineries, particularly Western leather shoes, an accessory that Vidyasagar famously never wore. The story of Vidyasagar's experience at the Asiatic Society Library where he was a member but was refused admission because he wore wooden sandals was already the stuff of lore.[48] Both of them were living legends and "worshipped" for two diametrically opposite reasons: one for his peculiar mix of kindheartedness and erudition, nonconformity and civic engagement, and the other for his godliness and sayings that combined the simplicity of rural speech with a dense body of theological scholarship.

RK is narrated in four registers. It contains the specifics of date, time, and location and description of the physical settings. These documentary details written in formal urban Bengali attend to the historicity of the narrative and are interspersed with contextual and biographical information about the persons Ramakrishna met. When Mahendranath records Ramakrishna's speech he moves to rustic Bengali and "surrenders himself completely in his journey with Ramakrishna through the fluid space of mythic time," making myriad connections across time and space.[49] It is also an explicitly bilingual text that repeatedly employs English terms to translate Ramakrishna's theological oeuvre for a Western-educated audience well-versed in the traditions of European philosophy.[50] This narrative structure is deployed to a specific effect in the description of the meeting of Vidyasagar and Ramakrishna in August 1882.

When Ramakrishna arrived with Mahendranath and a few disciples at Vidyasagar's house, they encountered a two-story building "built in an English manner" (**Plate 29**). Unlike the Bengali urban courtyard house, Vidyasagar's residence was a freestanding three-bay structure with a central hall. Situated in the middle of the property enclosed by a boundary wall, the house was surrounded by a garden planted with flowering trees. Their carriage stopped at the porch on the south. Ramakrishna was so "impressed with this representation of bourgeois respectability," that he asked Mahendranath if it would be okay to appear at this meeting with his shirt unbuttoned.⁵¹ Ramakrishna was assured that this would not pose a problem. Mahendranath then provides a description of the upstairs rooms—the hall, study, and Vidyasagar's bedroom—all of which were filled with a "valuable collection of books." This scholarly setting would have been daunting for Ramakrishna:

> Vidyasagar is sitting on the north end of the hall facing south. A polished long rectangular table in front. On the east of the table is a bench with backrest. A few chairs on the south and west side of the table. Vidyasagar is conversing with a few friends. He stands up to greet Ramakrishna ... Thakur (Ramakrishna) stands on the east end (of the table), with his left hand on the table. He is intently looking at Vidyasagar as if he is an old acquaintance, smiling, in a trance-like state ... Soon the room is full of people.⁵²

Here the narrative pivots and we witness the emergence of a new figure of space centered around Ramakrishna. Rather than the bookshelves, the people in the room now serve as the frame. The next section of the narrative is titled "Vidyasagar's worshipful offering (*puja*) and address to Sri Ramakrishna." Ramakrishna emerges from his trance and speaks: "Until now I have seen canals, ponds, puddles, rivers, today I see the ocean," referring to his host's title, "ocean of learning." Vidyasagar responds with a smile: "[T]hen take away some salt water if you please." In the long conversation that follows, Ramakrishna attempts to gauge Vidyasagar's position on spiritual matters, with Vidyasagar responding briefly, obliquely, and with humor. The narrative is rigged in favor of Ramakrishna, but we sense the awkwardness of the meeting in which the two men with such divergent conceptions about the aim of life—public good and spiritual salvation—undertake a delicate "public" performance of reason, knowledge, respect, and reputation. What concerns us here is the technique of reframing the secular space of the library as a sacred space of spiritual encounter in *RK*.

A New Figure of Space

Vidyasagar's library was his work space in which the bookshelves were a protective frame of sorts. In the first instance the library was his refuge from the entanglements of family and society. The bookshelves also served as a key piece in his articulation of the self in relation to the colonial public sphere. The plan of his residence and his library, and the social life that he constructed around it, helped secrete a set of spatial layers between him and the literary public sphere that he helped construct and that which remained in a heterogeneous relation to the colonial public sphere. In the narrative of his encounter with Ramakrishna, the bookshelves representing the expanding cosmopolitan network of knowledge is reframed to interrogate the ultimate object of knowledge acquisition. What begins as a detailed but factual description of the house is turned around as the two men meet face to face. Mahendranath's meticulous attention to the orientation of the house, the room, and the positions of the protagonists serves to transform the library into a sacred topography in which orientation and cardinal directions are suffused with cosmic significance. The focus is turned away from the bookshelves to the library as a space of Ramakrishna's divine utterance.

It is possible to configure two different spatial moves in the relation between books, bookshelves, and buildings in the two sets of stories I have assembled above. The removal of Tipu's library from the "dark" warehouse-like space to the "gold and azure" display room of the Oriental Repository in London constitutes an architectural correspondence of the move from a secret collection of a barbaric monarch to a corporate library with an enlightenment promise that is ultimately thwarted by its logic of commodification. As the book collection moves from one space to another, the bookshelf mediates the construction of meaning between the object, building, institution, and the universal claims of empire. The bookshelf here functions as the synecdoche of empire and helps create the colonial library as a figure of space around which questions of governance and the empire as public good could be launched.

In contrast, Vidyasagar's library, remembered for its orderly display, refutes that impress of empire and trajectory of knowledge acquisition. As a private library took on a different agency and urgency in a colonial city where access to the nominally public libraries could not to be taken for granted, Vidyasagar imagined his bookshelves would define a new kind of residential space and help articulate a different set of relations between public, private, and domestic space, determined neither by the racialized logic of colonial rule nor by the strictures of Bengali caste society. The bookshelves mediate these uneven relations to give the collection a unity and to affirm its collector's unique identity. But that articulation we have seen was not immune to contestation: the library as an object and space in the secular world was wrenched from its profane context and rendered susceptible to a different kind of universalism, away from public engagement and into the immaterial space of self-reflection and spiritual quest.

Seen through the lens of an emergent anticolonial nationalism, these two invocations of the library were not entirely antithetical. Vidyasagar's bookshelves and book collection would find their way into Bangiya Sahitya Parishat Library, a public library instituted in 1893 as a nationalist response to colonial dominance. Those bookshelves, as objects of veneration, accommodate, somewhat uneasily perhaps, the secular meaning that Vidyasagar conferred upon them and the spiritual aura that Ramakrishna sought to induce within its architectural framing.

17

A Box of Medicine

I am standing next to my bookcase, leafing through a frail early-twentieth-century book, contemplating a strategy to bring this work to a conclusion. In the patch of light falling on the shelf, I notice a thin layer of dust that has settled on the books through months of neglect. It reminds me of the description of a visitor to Vidyasagar's house who on arrival on the upper floor notices a servant taking books out of the book cases one at a time and wiping them.[1]

Those who come to meet Vidyasagar without ever having seen him often mistake him for a servant. His unpretentious clothes and willingness to do work that in upper-class households would be consigned to a servant upsets expectations of a learned upper-caste man: Vidyasagar is found working in his garden and mistaken for a *mali*; he shows in the visitors and asks them to wait; a few minutes later he discloses his identity to the embarrassment of his guests.[2] His close acquaintances recall his skilled handling of domestic chores—"women's work"—as he prepares a plate of fruits for his guest.[3] By the same token, he can just as well show up the pretensions of mastery of his British counterparts: Vidyasagar enters the office of J. Carr, principal of Hindu College, on business; the principal doesn't offer him a seat and deems it unnecessary to take off his outstretched legs from the table while speaking; a few days later Vidyasagar reciprocates in like manner, except he is wearing sandals instead of shoes; when Carr lodges a complaint about Vidyasagar's rude behavior, Vidyasagar responds that he is merely emulating British manners.[4]

There are many ways to interpret these stories, not least of which is Vidyasagar's canny recognition of the social significance of how clothing, furniture, and gestures order the relations of masters and servants in a colonial world. Vidyasagar in his negotiation with colonial authorities and his assumption of reciprocity in these interactions challenged the symbolic construction of colonial dominance.

Regardless of whether visitors mistook Vidyasagar for the master or the servant of the household, an unlettered servant dusting books would relate to the bookshelf very differently than Vidyasagar or his lettered guests. Did the servant know how to read? Did he sometimes put the books back on the bookshelf upside down because it made no difference to him? Or did he "read" the texts on the books' spine as a pattern and so had no problem putting them right side up? Did he know how to arrange the many volumes of a work in their right sequence? Did he ever unfurl a manuscript that transported him to the world of his childhood village?

The bookshelf as small space provides openings from which other actors could imagine lifeworlds beyond the ken of Vidyasagar, notwithstanding the capaciousness of his reach. His bookshelf does not just serve as a space for congregating books from across the world in an effort to locate oneself and negotiate the tracks of colonial power, it is also both literally and metaphorically a space of dispersal—of books, ideas, and affects. As a framing device, the bookshelf declares the collector's terms of containment as a mode of dwelling in a changing world. But collections, as I have noted earlier, are also always a scattering. They reorganize terms of engagement among objects, bodies, space, and knowledge systems.

I have suggested that we reposition our point of view and the vantage from which we experience spaces and social relations. My invocation of the bottlekhana, backstairs, passages, verandah, daowa, terrace as small spaces is intended to demonstrate that these often-undistinguished spaces proliferate modes of engaging with the world. Such repositioning allows us to understand relations across space that we fail to notice otherwise—the various ways in which the very infrastructure of empire that projects connections among certain constituencies, localizes, and disconnects others. And yet sometimes these localizations open up modes of imagining land and community that endure other rhythms and patterns of space and time.

If the bookshelf as a figure of space configures social relations and serves as an embarkation point for conversation and debate, how else might it have slipped through the "grey zone" between object and space to extend the range of social imaginations, of ways of dwelling in a colonial milieu?[5] What else besides the master's tool could be brought to unlock the possibilities of the grey zone? The story with which I wish to conclude this work suggests a mode of access to knowledge systems that depends on a process of vernacularization and describes a form of spatial unfolding that is dispersive. Its route is through a box of homeopathic medicine.

Vernacularization

Among Vidyasagar's book collection were sixty-five works on homeopathy.[6] He taught himself homeopathy and is recognized as one of the handful of key figures who were responsible for popularizing homeopathy among the Bengali middle class. He kept detailed notes of the application of his knowledge, recording symptoms of disease, doses of medicine, and cure. He is remembered as busy dispensing homeopathic medicine among the Santals at his residence in Karmatar.[7]

Homeopathy rapidly rose to popularity in the second half of the nineteenth century in India, and particularly in Bengal, where medical practitioners trained in Western allopathic medicine turned to homeopathy as a more suitable therapeutic. Scores of men and women began to teach themselves homeopathic methods of cure and collect books on homeopathy. Pharmacies became booksellers as well. A robust print culture extended the reach of homeopathy in the form of debates among professional practitioners and amateurs, and as household medical advice and housekeeping guides in both English and Bengali.

Scholars working on the history of homeopathy's origination in Germany and its subsequent successful indigenization in India have debated the process by which homeopathy was "naturalized." Surinder Bhardwaj notes that homeopathy was seen as Western and modern but not colonial (because of its origination in Germany rather than in Britain) and in resonating with Indian *unani*, *ayurvedic*, and *hakimi* systems of medicine, it became more culturally acceptable than allopathy—that is, the system of Western medicine which the colonial state backed.[8] This narrative can be conveniently folded into a narrative of Indian nationalism. David Arnold and Sumit Sarkar have cautioned against such a smooth transition narrative. In their essay on Dr. Mahendralal Sirkar, who received a medical degree from the Calcutta Medical College but after four years of practicing allopathy "converted" to homeopathy, they point out the important role of European practitioners of homeopathy in India. Indian proponents of homeopathy, such as Sirkar, valued homeopathy because they deemed it superior to existing Indian systems of medicine as well as allopathy. Homeopathic medicine crossed cultural, racial, and religious divides to gain popularity across the subcontinent. No doubt, its cheapness compared with allopathy and its early popularization among Bengali intellectual elites helped this propagation. Its DIY appeal had much to do with its popularity and "the easy entrance through Hahnemann's *Organon* and *Materia Medica Pura*, in sharp contrast to the increasingly formidable and esoteric corpus of official modern medicine." They continue:

> In this respect, as in the actual language of its dissemination, homoeopathy was particularly open to processes of vernacularisation. It became indigenised largely through a world of autodidacts, practitioners who had little or no formal training . . .
> The barrier between fully trained doctor and "quack", specialised practitioner and lay patient, becoming increasingly formidable with the development of allopathic medical science, were made more permeable through homoeopathy.[9]

Homeopathy, Arnold and Sarkar argue, was considered a new "rational and humane" system of Western medicine as opposed to the old and barbaric one practiced by the official medical establishment that included bloodletting, caustic bandages, cauterization, and surgery.[10] Arnold and Sarkar make the important point that early practitioners of homeopathy, such as

Sirkar or Rajendralal Dutta who established the first commercial firm for homeopathic medicine in Calcutta and was Sirkar's senior, were unabashedly in favor of modern, rationalist, scientific arguments. What was rational and deserving of universal scientific approbation was not easily settled, however.

Homeopathy's superiority, Shinjini Das argues in her analysis of Bengali print publications since the 1860s, was anchored in the field's claim of being founded on a "absolute and universal law" that could be experimentally tested through therapeutics.[11] The universal law of homeopathy was an axiom: *similia similibus curentur* ("like cures like"). Fixed, definite laws were seen as the "hallmark of respectable science," and for the promoters of homeopathy, the other Western medical system of allopathy could show no such law. Allopathic medical practitioners on their part argued that such a law was a complete fabrication. Importantly, homeopathy was based on "infinitesimal" doses of drugs, a method considered superior to the large doses of drugs prescribed by allopathic practitioners. Small amounts of "poison" made homeopathy a "gentle" remedy, to which allopaths responded by saying it was no remedy at all.[12] The discussion in print media exceeded these disagreements among medical professionals, and extended well into the realm of housekeeping guides addressed specifically to educated women. Homeopathy administered by women in their capacity as mothers and guardians of household health, it was argued, would stabilize the declining health of the family unit and therefore the larger national community.[13]

The popularization of homeopathy was thus based on its claims of being founded on a universal and fixed law, its experimental method, and successful vernacularization not just in language but in methods as well. As Das writes, homeopathy "traversed the domains of the western and the indigenous, the elite and the popular, the subaltern and the state. To that extent, the vernacular was more of a product of the colonial encounter rather than an already existing category or domain ... the 'vernacular' itself was put together in the colonial period."[14] I want to consider this proposition by focusing on the relation between the homeopathic box of medicine that became a common household artifact in middle-class homes and the spaces in which the vernacularization of homeopathy interceded.[15]

Therapeutic Kit

Housekeeping guides, whether in English or Indian vernacular languages, routinely provided home recipes for common ailments and accidents: colds, stomach aches, indigestion, fever, bruises, burns, and insect bites. Dozens of remedies for dyspepsia and fevers, such as Edward Tonic "anti-malarial specific," and antiseptics intended to treat ailments from sore throat to pneumonia, were peddled by pharmacies in small and large towns.[16] These same pharmacies would also sell allopathic medicine as well as homeopathic kits and books.

Homeopathic medicine came in boxes of different sizes and elaboration, and could be purchased from stores or ordered over mail. In 1875, the Homeopathic Laboratory of B. Dutta and Co., located on Chitpore Road, Calcutta, advertised various sizes of "clean," varnished boxes, containing 2-dram phials. A small box for the treatment of cholera contained 9 phials of medicines, a phial of camphor, and a guide to the application of the medicines, while a larger box with 26 phials could be purchased as well. The advertisement recommended boxes of 12, 16, 24, and 30 phials for household use. Medical practitioners could choose from larger boxes with multiple shelves and trays containing 40, 60, or 80 phials. The company assured its customers that a fresh supply of medicines was received monthly from Britain and America.[17]

The homeopathic medicine box was essentially an expandable grid (**Plate 30**). The phials were placed in the box within a gridded wood frame with each small square containing a circular aperture for one phial. The grid kept the bottles in place and emblematized a vision of precision and universal order. The portable kits came with explanatory literature and families could choose from a range of options, depending on the extent of self-medication they desired. It dispensed with the need to fetch a doctor for ordinary ailments, and in locations where doctors were not easily available, it substituted expertise. The portable homeopathy box became a locus of trust and comfort in middle-class households, but more importantly it became an antidote to the severe paucity of transportation and health infrastructure in colonial India. Listen to this story.

Death and Survival

Kulachandra Dey, father of Rani Chanda whose memoir I discuss in Chapter 12, wrote a Bengali book on homeopathy in verse and dedicated it to his wife, Purnashashi Debi.[18] Kulachandra was employed in the colonial government's Department of Agriculture and his job necessitated postings in *sadar* stations (headquarters) far from the rural home where his wife lived with their children. Published in 1907, the book began with an ode to Samuel Hahnemann, the founder of homeopathy, and the dedicatory note that followed recounted a painful, intimate family story of "despair, angst, maddening pain and sorrow."[19] Their eldest son and eldest daughter contracted cholera and died on the same night. On hearing the news, he took leave from work and came home: "You were beset with grief. A vast void stood between us. Hopelessness got the better of us."[20] The fact that the children died without any medical treatment, that she could not give them "a single drop of medicine," hurt the most.[21]

Recognizing the paucity of medical practitioners, Purnashashi wanted to learn homeopathy. Kulachandra eagerly complied and brought home everything he could think of: a 16-phial box, books, and periodicals. They both started studying. But she got "caught in the tangle of medicinal details and the maze of texts." Her enthusiasm waned and she stopped soon after. This was inevitable, Kulachandra noted, because the differentiation among symptoms and complications about doses and dilutions were all difficult to fathom, and the strange combination of Latinized nomenclature and the awkward translation of Western scientific terms into Bengali in a heavily Sanskritized idiom were bewildering: "The new language looked like the personification of the learned Maxmuller! You paid respect from a distance and retreated in fear. And I heaved a sigh of relief and quit!"[22]

Later when the couple again had to move to two separate locations, Purnashashi felt the need to be better-versed in homeopathy. So Kulachandra went to Calcutta to study homeopathy in a systematic manner and distilled the therapeutic advice in a verse form and called it *Homeogatha* (*gatha* = saga in verse).[23] He concluded the dedicatory statement with:

With great hesitation I came to place this garland around your neck; you were ecstatic with joy and presented me with a bouquet of smiles. And within a few hours pretty much memorized these preparatory verses. It is on the strength of that certificate I have today mustered the courage to submit this small work in the hands of educated Bengali women.[24]

As Kulachandra and Purnashashi's story tells us, entrée into homeopathy was not easy and its popularization cannot be attributed to its rather simple axiomatic system; becoming a homeopathic autodidact was limited to a small minority. Its arcane diagnostics and therapeutics were beyond the ken of most people, despite many works offering simplified instructions as evidenced in the very titles of the popular books, such as *Saral Chikitsa* (1926, Simplified Treatment) and *Homeopathic Sachitra Pustakabali* (1876, Illustrated Homeopathic Book Series). Popularization needed consideration of the mode of communication rather than the content of communication.

When Rani Chanda related her family story in her memoir, she remarked that her father saw in her mother's predicament the larger picture of rural Bengal where a doctor could be five or six villages away and the patient could die before any medical aid could arrive. These rural women were mostly unlettered, but they had remarkable capacity for memorizing: "how many hundreds of stories and songs have been handed down by them by word of mouth in the form of rhythmic verses."[25] The verse form operationalized homeopathy's universality in a regional mode of communication. It crossed milieus—urban to rural, elite to subaltern—by effectively mediating in verse the larger corpus of knowledge and the box of medicine. The method must have been found effective as such verse-form books on homeopathy were published into the 1920s.[26]

The tragedy of losing children to cholera was shared by many families, and there is no evidence that homeopathy had any cure for cholera or malaria, two of the scourges of the region. Both of these diseases are related to infrastructural inadequacy. Cholera as a waterborne disease has a direct relation to the inadequate access to clean potable water, and even the large cities such as Dhaka had minimal water and sewage infrastructure into the early twentieth century. In the case of malaria, the construction of railways obstructed the natural flow of water across the land, and resulted in marked proliferation of the disease. And yet, this box of medicine, by assuring women that they have therapeutics at hand, relieved them from a sense of "helplessness."[27] The portable box of medicine became from their point of view an infrastructural element that took the place of a reliable medical and transportation infrastructure. In recalling her mother's authority as the head of the extended family in a remote village, Rani Chanda noted that neighbors in that rural community looked to her for medical aid: "My mother always carries a large box of homeopathic medicine. She never goes anywhere without it." The box of medicine represented her resourcefulness and enabled her to extend her hospitality to a larger community. Sitting at the intersection of scattered lives, gatherings of texts and dissemination of a knowledge system, the box of medicine accrued value through vernacularization, serving as a small intervention and a fragile protection against precarity.

18

Epilogue

Throughout this book, I have made an argument for thinking through small things and small spaces. Not all these spaces are dimensionally small. Some of them come in clusters. Others function in isolation. And some of these are conjunctural spaces created at the momentary intersections of space and time. Let me return to that point in conclusion to chart out some possibilities of smallness and scalar alterity.

I have invoked smallness in a multitude of senses: in terms of scale, size, power, location, distance, status, visibility, duration, race, portability, aberrance, and affect. A range of meanings attaches to them.

scale: minor, micro, local

size: big, small

power: disenfranchised, subjugated, unauthorized, silenced

location: peripheral, marginal, confined, scattered

distance: separation, distancing, movement, isolation

status: subaltern, colonized, untouchable, outcaste

visibility: obscure, hidden, submerged, subterranean

duration: ephemeral, transitory, impermanent, contingent

race: Black, native, half-caste, low-caste, contaminant, dark, dirty

portability: mobile, moveable, connective, accretive

aberrance: exceptional, singular, nonconforming

affect: embodied, emotive, memorable, emergent, abhorrent.

These constellations of meaning help delineate certain modalities through which small spaces operate: restriction and diminution that work through the imperial right to command, and the techniques of negation that operate through scalar alterity, reassembly, antinomy, and opacity.

Restriction: Smallness is produced through the micro dynamics of power in everyday life and through coercive tools to break down the body into a set of constituent parts that can be apprehended to capture labor.[1] Power works to confine and regulate movement, access to food and shelter whether it is in the plantation, servants' quarters, or the famine camp. Smallness is a function of distancing the subalterns from elites. Subalternity, as Ranajit Guha explains, is "expressed in differentials of wealth, status and culture."[2] The subaltern learns to "recognize himself not by the properties and attributes of his own social being but by the diminution, if not negation, of his superiors."[3] It is through spatial methods that inequity is structured, the disenfranchised are made to appear insignificant or of less relevance.

Diminution: Smallness as a hierarchical scalar relation is a modality by which imperial power constitutes the conquered, the enslaved, and the subordinate as less-than. Here inequality is assumed as is the authority's right to command. The architectural correlates of this modality are so ubiquitous that we only venture to *notice* them when the master's spaces cannot be described without recourse to those service spaces—the kitchen, smoke house, slave quarters, corn cribs, stables, and hog pens—in which the enslaved and servants labor. These spaces add value by being subordinate, like the throngs of Indian servants that surrounded European figures as visible signs of European authority to command. There is no contradiction between lending value or increasing the master's property and being made to appear undeserving and insignificant. When in a conceptual twist, the enslaved Sixo informs the master that killing a "shoat" and eating it is not stealing but improving property—"Sixo take and feed Sixo give you more work"—Sixo is reminded by a beating that "definitions belonged to the definers—not the defined."[4] It is by depleting, exhausting their own value, that the small spaces and the subordinates register themselves in the matrix of power.

Scalar Alterity: At the same time, as spaces infiltrated with myriad sinews of power, small spaces surprise when they are revealed as porous entities where relations of dominance may be turned around by acts of resistance and recalcitrance, small and significant. Their subordinate location notwithstanding, small spaces becoming sites of alternate world-building. Being distanced from the center of power, people residing in the peripheral spaces view the land differently. The enslaved's view of opportunities in the land—of sources of sustenance and escape—is fundamentally different from that of the master's.[5] By shifting coordinates, each coercive move can be turned around and read otherwise: significant instead of insignificant, the peripheral as the threatening squatter, the unauthorized as resilient, and a range of in-betweens.

Micro here doesn't mean a diminished version of a bigger entity, but a scalar identity that is ordered by different rules. These rules might help defy the master's tools and language and support a repertoire of options that the master doesn't possess. Here distance becomes closeness, lack of visibility becomes the opportunity for the illicit, contingency becomes the emergent, contamination turns out to be a potent weapon to confront power. Striking *mehtar*s (nightsoil cleaners) hurled the harvest of their labor—excreta—at the police when they attempted to break the municipal sweepers' strike.[6]

Scalar alterity is their binding cord. It is also here that smallness becomes a tool to reconstitute, reframe, reposition. Small spaces are chameleon-like. They morph into other entities without too much trouble, and it is here that they become potent sites of imagination and engagement.

Reassembly: The head servant Turab Ali turns a remnant of consumption, the empty Heinz can, into a gift through an act of rehabilitation, by conferring a value that does not properly belong to the colonizer's economy. A dimensionally small portable artifact, the product of global trade and foodways, precisely because of its size becomes manipulable, reinscribable. No change of scale takes place in such a transformation; the tin can made into a jewelry case is placed in a circuit of gift exchange to generate a new scalar connection. It is by leaving the bottlekhana-cook room-dining room circuit as exhausted material that it becomes primed to attain new inscriptions of identity and belonging. In the pile of tin cans in Turab Ali's one-room dwelling lingers the shadow of lives lived differently. This heap of empty containers mirrors the stacks of provisions in the bottlekhana and the amassed grain sacks in the Madras beach that are kept just beyond the reach of a population starving in a famine. As if seen through a stereoscope, that quintessential technology of colonial optics, Turab Ali's artifice assembles these separate fields of view into one composite image to the bewilderment of his white mistress.

Antinomy: If small space is constituted in relation to that which is large by way of a self-congratulatory power, imagine the diminutive *dhoti*-clad figure of Mohandas Gandhi walking up the grand entry stairs of the newly finished Viceroy's Palace in 1931. Winston Churchill found the sight/spectacle both "alarming" and "nauseating." The scalar antinomy created by the small fragile figure against the wide marble stairs appeared as an indictment of the grand claims and legitimacy of the empire. Gandhi, who had a political knack for recognizing the value of small gestures and actions as aberrant acts (a pinch of salt, a hand *charkha*, a small meal) and their multiplying effects, made smallness the anchor of his defiance of empire. Smallness here questions the moral order of the dominant and emerges as an antinomian stance. Gandhi had both hoped to enlist the expanding potential of small things in aggregate and was troubled by its scalar effect, when defiance turned violent. Small gatherings, becoming large, overwhelmed its compass of restraint to reveal the anger that fuel mass mobilizations.

Opacity: The imperial insistence of forcing small enterprises of distilling liquor and famine-struck households into larger contained spaces speak of the sheer threat of large numbers of small-scaled entities dispersed across a large territory. These small footholds have to be uprooted to make imperial governance possible—visible. Richard Temple's complaint that, unlike Bengal with its enumerable villages, the Deccan with its scattered rural hamlets amid rugged terrain forestalled surveillance, is important. The imperial state needs a form of spatial legibility that emphasizes geometrically defined enclosures, transparent and easily surveilled. This is the basis of what William Glover describes as the "colonial spatial imagination."[7] Social and material environments had to be made intelligible within a grid of knowledge and caught within a set of signifying forms by "disaggregating, larger-scale phenomena into their component parts and then reassembling them into a variety of synthetic (and programmatic) constructions."[8] And yet, the topography of trade, commerce, civil and military administration was far from smooth, orderly, and transparent. The opacity of the small spaces of empire continued to pose problems from the point of governance. It contributed to the lumpy geography of empire in which opportunities for escape and withdrawal could not be completely eradicated.

These acts of negation seen in spatial terms might be thought of as openings. Small spaces offer differentiated openings to imagine possibilities other than those normed into the dominant logic of material relations. These openings that I am calling "another place" emerges out of a discordance between space and affect. Joseph Pugliese speaks of the imprisoned Ahmed Errachidi in the detention camp of Guantanamo where he is kept in penal isolation for four years. Errachidi in his devastating solitude befriends a trail of ants who keep him company:

> These beautiful creatures would visit me in my metal prison carrying with them hope and life. I'd save food for them. I'd put in a corner away from the prying eyes of the soldiers, if they saw my visitors they'd either spray them with insecticide or squash them with their boots. If I was caught feeding the ants I knew I'd be punished with smaller rations or extra days of punishment, but despite this, I continued to encourage them . . . These ants were a rare sign of life, and when they appeared animation would creep into the deadness of my solitary cell, and for that moment, I'd feel optimism rather than despair.[9]

Errachidi extends to the ants one thing he is denied, compassion. The ants in turn offer Errachidi entomological lessons in community. The company of ants, flies, birds, feral cats, and iguanas in forming interspecies relationships "transform Guantanamo, momentarily, into an entirely different order of space."[10] Even if it is momentary, the ability to form meaningful connections in the world across and beyond the walls of caged life, "however fragile," is an opening. Reframing Martin Heidegger's understanding of unconcealment (disclosure of being) as the Open through an interspecies lens, Pugliese describes the healing power of feeling "complete" after years of brutal fragmentation. "Transitory and wholly contingent on the fragile moment" made possible by the experience of fellowship at the intersection of deprivation/delight, isolation/connection, distancing/proximity, that we sense the emergence of another place.[11] Another place from which to imagine, interact, and intercede.

The promise of another place that we glimpse in Harriet Jacobs's story resonates in myriad different guises in the small spaces that describe Turab

Ali's artifice, servants and famished victims demanding fair wages (the latter at the risk of dying of starvation), Minnie Wood planning an escape, Rani Chanda's rememoring, Kulachandra and Purnashashi Dey's grief, Iris Macfarlane's despair, Vidyasagar's bookish trust, Rabindranath Tagore's faith in transcendence. Another place is that designation of the world in which the masters, too, would become servants, as Minnie Wood was reminded during the Sepoy Rebellion. These stories do not carry the same valence and they do not convey a shared space. The stories, however, help us shift our way of thinking about empire as a geographical fact or defined by clear entry and exit points. The multistranded repository of sources and sites when unarchived becomes a form of disarticulation. No interpretation of Government House as a singular edifice, no discussion of cities as urban ensembles of imperial institutions, no insistence on reading buildings as architectural frames for containing bodies will suffice. In unarchiving we create openings that are otherwise imperceptible.

The departures that demonstrate the connections between nineteenth-century practices of saving the labor time of the enslaved and coolies, and the prevailing practices of service spaces and mechanical articulation of space, might help us to rethink how the grey zones between buildings and objects operate and place these operations within our current concerns with the environment. The insinuation of small spaces, from the closet to the detention camp, might broker the promise of finding submarine anchors and links and the buried traces that the empire-as-geographical-fact denies. If that means rethinking the structures of spatial disciplines and strategies of knowledge acquisition, that would be a good outcome. In a geography of small spaces forgotten, that promise flickers.

APPENDIX

Tulloh and Company's Catalogue, 1819

Europe, China & Country
GOODS
To be Sold by Public Auction
By Tulloh and Company
At their Auction Room
This-day, Friday the 24th Dec 1819
A choice assortment of
Prime Europe Goods
By the recent arrivals;
Including a selection of superfine
British Piece Goods
With some Fresh
Confectionary & Grocery
Likewise
A Variety of Fresh
China and Country Goods . . .

Queen's-Ware
Dinner Service of the finest Queen's-Ware with very handsome brown flouered (*sic*) border and brown edges consisting
2 soup tureens with covers
1 gravy dish
2 fish drainers
4 curry dishes with two covers
4 baking dishes
2 salad bowls
Plates:
    55 flat
    20 dessert
    12 muffin
    17 hotwater
4 pickle tureens with covers and stands
4 sauce bowls

Breakfast Sets
A Breakfast Set of the finest Queen's Ware, with very large beautiful brown flowered border and brown edges consisting of
1 coffee pot
1 slop bason
12 Coffee Cups and Saucers, and
12 Breakfast Plates

Spare Queen's-Ware
Viz
Soup Tureens

Beefsteak and Vegetable Dishes
Two of the finest queen's ware brown verge line bordered Beefsteak dishes, with covers and liners for hot water
Two ditto vegetable dishes

Curry Dishes
Three of the finest queen's ware brown verge line border curry dishes with covers
Three ditto

Salad Bowls and Gravy Dishes
Three queens ware salad bowls with brown verge line border
Four ditto
Four ditto gravy dishes
Four ditto smaller dishes

Fish drainers ad Pickle Tureens
Eight of the best queen's ware fish drainers, with brown verge line border
Nine ditto pickle tureens with covers, stands & ladles
Ten ditto
Eighteen sauce boats with stands
Eleven ditto preserve pots with covers.

Jugs
A set of very fine handsome drab-colored Wedgewood-ware Jugs with handles
A set ditto
A set ditto
A set ditto

Conditions as usual.

Source: British Library IOR 9056ggl

NOTES

Preface and Acknowledgments

1. Swati Chattopadhyay, "Colonial Port Cities and the Infrastructure of Empire: Tracing the Geography of Alcohol in British Colonial India," in Harald Fischer-Tiné and Maria Framke, eds., *Routledge Handbook of the History of Colonialism in South Asia* (London: Routledge, 2021), 294–308.
2. Swati Chattopadhyay, "Architectural History or a Geography of Small Spaces?," *Journal of the Society of Architectural Historians* 81, no. 1 (March 2022), 5–20.
3. Swati Chattopadhyay, "Roofscapes: A Speculative History of Terraces in Calcutta," in Anuradha Roy and Melitta Waligora, eds., *Kolkata in Space, Time and Imagination: Rethinking Heritage* (Delhi: Primus, 2019), 56–93.

Chapter 1

1. For two recent works that address this building type, see Jonathan A. Farris, *Enclave to Urbanity: Canton, Foreigners, and Architecture from the Late Eighteenth to the Early Twentieth Centuries* (Hong Kong: Hong Kong University Press, 2016); and Cole Roskam's discussion of godowns in nineteenth-century Canton and Shanghai in *Architecture and Governance in Shanghai, 1843–1937* (Seattle: University of Washington Press, 2019).
2. For a description of hiding spaces, see Harriet Jacobs's narrative, *Incidents in the Life of a Slave Girl: Written by Herself*, ed. L. Maria Child (Boston: Published for the Author, 1861); for slaving spaces, including the cellar and block, see Louis P. Nelson, *Architecture and Empire in Jamaica* (New Haven: Yale University Press, 2016); for cellar in which runaway enslaved people hid, see James A. Delle and Jason Shellenhamer, "Archaeology at the Parvin Homestead: Searching for the Material Legacy of the Underground Railroad," *Historical Archaeology* 42, no. 2 (2008), 38–62.
3. Of these, the most often invoked are verandahs. See Garth Myers, *Verandahs of Power: Colonialism and Space in Urban Africa* (New York: Syracuse University Press, 2003).
4. See, for example, the discussion of dumbwaiters and access patterns that ensured privacy to Jefferson in Monticello in Dell Upton, *Architecture in the United States* (Oxford: Oxford University Press), Chapter 1, and the role of

verandahs in colonial houses in Swati Chattopadhyay, *Representing Calcutta: Modernity, Nationalism, and the Colonial Uncanny* (London: Routledge, 2005), Chapter 2.

5   John Michael Vlach, "'Appropriated for the Use of Colored People': Urban Slave Housing in the North Slavery in the City," in Clifton Ellis and Rebecca Ginsberg, eds., *Slavery in the City* (Charlottesville: University of Virginia Press, 2017), 64–5.

6   See, for example, Ariella Aiisha Azoulay, *The Civil Contract of Photography* (New York: Zone Books, 2012); Saidiya Hartman, "A Minor Figure," *Wayward Lives, Beautiful Experiments: Intimate Histories of Riotous Black Girls and Troublesome Women, and Queer Radicals* (New York: W.W. Norton & Co., 2019).

7   Probate inventory is a list of a person's property after their death. It typically includes a list of objects in the household and/or farm and business.

8   Frederick Douglass, *Narrative of the Life of Frederick Douglass, an American Slave, Written by Himself* (Boston: Anti-Slavery Office, 1845), 6–8. On the effort to look elsewhere—where terror can hardly be seen—for the "routinized violence of slavery," see Saidiya V. Hartman, *Scenes of Subjection: Terror, Slavery and Self-Making in Nineteenth-century America* (New York: Oxford University Press, 1997).

9   Jacobs, *Incidents*, 173.

10 Jacobs, *Incidents*, 174–5.

11 For more on the phrase "loophole of retreat," see Valerie Smith, "'Loopholes of Retreat': Architecture and Ideology in Harriet Jacobs's 'Incidents in the Life of a Slave Girl'," in Henry Louis Gates, Jr., ed., *Reading Black, Reading Feminist* (New York: Penguin Books/Meridian, 1990), 212–26; Daneen Wardrop, "I stuck a Gimlet in and Waited for Evening: Writings and Incidents in the Life of a Slave Girl," *Texas Studies in Literature and Language* 49, no. 3 *Dialectics and Discursive Communities* (Fall 2007), 209–29; Miranda A. Green-Barteet, "'The Loophole of Retreat': Interstitial Spaces in Harriet Jacobs's 'Incidents in the Life of a Slave Girl'," *South-Central Review* 30, no. 2 (Summer 2013), 53–72.

12 It is telling that the nineteenth-century panorama had to be constructed out of fragments. I thank Zirwat Chowdhury for alerting me to this point.

13 Antonio Gramsci, *Selections from Prison Notebooks*, ed. and trans. Quintin Hoare and Geoffrey Nowell Smith (New York: International Publishers), 54–5.

14 Gyanendra Pandey's discussion of writing the history of the fragment—minority groups—in the context of the nation-state and the historiographical procedure of taking "a prescribed center (of a state formation, a nation state) as one's vantage point and the 'official' archive as one's primary source for the construction of an adequate general 'history'" (50) is as relevant today as it was thirty years ago. See Gyanendra Pandey, "In Defense of the Fragment: Writing About Hindu-Muslim Riots in India Today," *Representations* 37, Special Issue: Imperial Fantasies and Postcolonial Histories (Winter 1992), 27–55.

15 Chattopadhyay, *Representing Calcutta*, 176–7.

16 Robin Evans, *Translations from Drawings to Buildings and Other Essays* (Cambridge, MA: MIT Press, 1997), 56.

17 Evans, *Translations*, 77.

18 Edward Said, *Culture and Imperialism* (New York: Vintage Books, 1994), 12.

19 An exception is Itohan Osayimwese, *Colonialism and Modern Architecture in Germany* (Pittsburgh, PA: University of Pittsburgh Press, 2017).

20 Said, *Culture and Imperialism*, 14.

21 For an approach to architectural analysis that assumes "construction only on the way to construing," see Dell Upton, "Architectural History or Landscape History," *Journal of Architectural Education* 44, no. 4 (August 1991), 195–9.

22 See Sujit Sivasundaram, "Towards a Critical History of Connections: The Port of Colombo, the Geographical 'Circuit', and the Visual Politics of New Imperialism ca. 1880–1914," *Comparative Studies in Society and History* 59, no. 2 (2017), 346–84.

Chapter 2

1 Christine Furedy, "British Tradesmen of Calcutta 1830–1900: A Preliminary Study of Their Economic and Political Roles," in C. B. Sealy, ed., *Women Politics and Literature in Bengal* (East Lansing: Asian Studies Center, Michigan State University, 1981), 43–62.

2 Rajat Ray, "Asian Capital in the Age of European Domination: The Rise of the Bazaar, 1800–1914," *Modern Asian Studies* 29, no. 3 (1995), 449–554. Also see C. A. Bayly, *Rulers, Townsmen and Bazaars: North Indian Society in the Age of British Expansion* (Cambridge: Cambridge University Press, 1988); Kumkum Chatterjee, *Merchants, Politics and Society in Early Modern India, Bihar: 1733–1820* (Leiden: Brill, 1996); Sudipta Sen, *Empire of Free Trade: The East India Company and the Colonial Marketplace* (Philadelphia: University of Pennsylvania Press, 1998).

3 Ray, "Asian Capital," 453.

4 Ray, "Asian Capital," 455.

5 Tirthankar Roy, *The East India Company: The World's Most Powerful Corporation* (London: Penguin, 2016), 208.

6 For general merchandise, see B. R. Tomlinson, "From Campsie to Kedgeree: Scottish Enterprise, Asian Trade and the Company Raj," *Modern Asian Studies* 36, no. 4 (October 2002), 779.

7 Tomlinson, "From Campsie to Kedgeree," 769–91; Huw Bowen, "Sinews of Trade and Empire: The Supply of Commodity Exports to the East India Company During the Late Eighteenth Century," *The Economic History Review* 55, no. 3 (August 2002), 466–86.

8 Huw Bowen, "The Consumption of British Manufactured Goods in India, 1765–1813: A Prologue," in Douglas Haynes, Abigail McGowan, Tirthankar

Roy, and Haruka Yanagisawa, eds., *Towards a History of Consumption in South Asia* (New Delhi: Oxford University Press, 2010), 27.

9   For the substantial literature on the subject, see Amales Tripathi, *Trade and Finance in the Bengal Presidency, 1793–1893* (Calcutta: Oxford University Press, 1979); Stephanie Jones, *Merchants of the Raj: British Managing Agency Houses in Calcutta Yesterday and Today* (Basingstoke: Macmillan, 1992); P. J. Marshall, *East India Fortunes: The British in Bengal in the Eighteenth Century* (Oxford: Clarendon Press, 1976); Huw Bowen, *The Business of Empire: The East India Company and Imperial Britain, 1756–1833* (Cambridge: Cambridge University Press, 2006); Claude Markovits, *Global World of Indian Merchants, 1750–1947: Traders from Sind and Bukhara to Panama* (Cambridge: Cambridge University Press, 2008); J. Forbes Munro, *Maritime Enterprise and Empire: Sir William Mackinnon and his business network, 1823–93* (Woodbridge: Boydell Press, 2003); Tirthankar Roy, "Trading Firms in Colonial India," *Business History Review* 88 (Spring 2014), 9–42; Tony Webster, "An Early Global Business in a Colonial Context: the Strategies, Management, and Failure of John Palmer and Company, Calcuttta, 1780–1830," *Enterprise and Society* 6, no. 1 (March 2005), 98–133; Anthony Webster, "The Strategies and Limits of Gentlemanly Capitalism: the London East India Agency Houses, Provincial Commercial Interests, and the Evolution of British Economic Policy in South and South East Asia, 1800–50," *The Economic History Review, New Series*, 59, no. 4 (November 2006), 743–64; Ray, "Asian Capital"; Alex Bremner, "Tides that Bind: Waterborne Trade and the Infrastructure Networks of Jardine, Matheson & Co.," *Perspecta* 52 (2019), 31–47.

10 For example, for the export trade to Britain, see Maxine Berg, "In Pursuit of Luxury: Global History and British Consumer Goods in the Eighteenth Century," *Past and Present* 182 (February 2004),:85–142; Erika Rappaport, *Thirst for Empire: How Tea Shaped the Modern World* (Princeton: Princeton University Press, 2017).

11 David Arnold, "Global Goods and Local Usages: The Small World of the Indian Sewing Machine, 1875–1952," *Journal of Global History* 6 (2011), 407–29; David Arnold, *Everyday Technologies: Machines and the Making of India's Modernity* (Chicago: University of Chicago Press, 2013). For a history of consumption in South Asia from the late nineteenth century onwards, see Haynes et al., *Towards a History of Consumption*.

12 Elizabeth Collingham, *The Taste of Empire: How Britain's Quest for Food Shaped the Modern World* (New York: Basic Books, 2017).

13 East India Company, "Accounts Presented to the House of Commons, 1808: Report on the External Commerce of Bengal as carried by Individuals in the Year 1811–12 or from 1st June 1811 to 30th April 1812;" East India Company, "An Account of all Goods exported from Great Britain to the East indies and China for two years, Ending 5th Jan 1820, specifying the Value of the principal Articles, and also distinguishing India from China; so far as they may be ascertained," British Library, IOL 1947 B 629.

14 An Account of all Goods, 1820.

15 Tripathi, *Trade and Finance*, 78.

16. The market size for imported consumables was an estimated 1 million people in the first decades of the twentieth century, cited in Ray, "Introduction," *Entrepreneurship and Industry*, 17–18.
17. Sanjay Subrahmanyam, "Connected Histories: Notes towards a Reconfiguration of Early Modern Eurasia," *Modern Asian Studies* 31, no. 3 (July 1997), 735–62.
18. Dipesh Chakrabarty, "The Climate of History: Four Thesis," *Critical Inquiry* 35, no. 2 (Winter 2009), 197–222.
19. Zachary Horton, *The Cosmic Zoom: Scale, Knowledge, and Mediation* (Chicago: University of Chicago Press, 2021), 6.
20. George R. Parkin, *Imperial Federation: The Problem of National Unity* (London: Macmillan & Co., 1892).
21. For an example of expertise swapping on water infrastructure, see Karen Piper, "The Architecture of Water," in Swati Chattopadhyay and Jeremy White, eds., *The Routledge Companion to Critical Approaches to Contemporary Architecture* (London: Routledge, 2019), 287–99.
22. Subrahmanyam, "Connected Histories," 762.
23. Jonathan Saha, "No, You're Peripheral" (July 18, 2013) https://colonizinganimals.blog/2013/07/18/no-youre-peripheral/.
24. Antoinette Burton, "Not Even Remotely Global? Method and Scale in World History," *History Workshop Journal*, no. 64 (Autumn 2007), 323–8.
25. Burton, "Not Even Remotely Global?," 327.
26. Lara Putnam, "To Study the Fragments/Whole: Microhistory and the Atlantic World," *Journal of Social History* 39, no. 3 (Spring 2006), 615.
27. Tonio Andrade, "A Chinese Farmer, Two African Boys, and a Warlord: Toward a Global Microhistory," *Journal of World History* 21, no. 4 (December 2010), 573–91.
28. Ariella Aïsha Azoulay, *Potential History: Unlearning Imperialism* (London: Verso, 2019).
29. Putnam, "To Study the Fragments/Whole," 615.
30. Edward Kamau Brathwaite, "Caribbean Man in Space and Time," *small axe* 66 (1975; November 2021), 90.
31. Brathwaite, "Caribbean Man," 96.
32. Brathwaite, "Caribbean Man," 93.
33. Brathwaite, "Caribbean Man," 100.
34. Charles Correa, *The New Landscape* (Bombay: Book Society of India, 1985).
35. Joya Chatterjee, "The Fashioning of a Frontier: The Radcliffe Line and Bengal's Border Landscape, 1947–52," *Modern Asian Studies* 33, no. 1 (February 1999), 185–242.
36. Horton, *The Cosmic Zoom*.
37. Horton, *The Cosmic Zoom*.
38. Horton, *The Cosmic Zoom*, 14, 17.

39 Horton, *The Cosmic Zoom*, 15.
40 Zachary Horton, "Viral Zoom: Covid-19 as Multiscalar Immune Failure," *International Journal of Performance Art and* Media 16, no. 3 (2020), 320.
41 Horton, *The Cosmic Zoom*, 18.
42 Horton, *The Cosmic Zoom*, 18.
43 Andrew James Hamilton, *Scale and the Incas* (Princeton: Princeton University Press, 2019), 5.
44 Hamilton, *Scale and the Incas*, 48.
45 Adam Moore, "Rethinking Scale as a Geographical Category: From Analysis to Practice," *Progress in Human Geography* 32, no. 2 (2008), 204.
46 These debates are usefully summarized in Sallie Marston, John Paul Jones, and Kevin Woodward, "Human Geography without Scale," *Transactions of the Institute of British Geographers, New Series* 30, no. 2 (April 2005), 416–32; Adam Moore, "Rethinking Scale as a Geographical Category: From Analysis to Practice," *Progress in Human Geography* 32, no. 2 (2008); Stephen Legg, "Of Scales, Networks and Assemblages: The League of Nations Apparatus and the Scalar Sovereignty of the Government of India," *Transactions of the Institute of British Geographers, New Series* 34, no. 2 (April 2009), 234–53;
47 Legg, "Of Scales, Networks and Assemblages," 243–5.
48 In a review of Elizabeth Collins Cromley, *Food Axis: Cooking, Eating, and the Architecture of American Houses* (Charlottesville: University of Virginia Press, 2010), Kenneth L. Ames's remarks that spaces concerned with food production and storage, such as "bake ovens, smokehouses, root cellars, kitchen ranges, pantries, ice boxes, microwave ovens" were "important" but not "pivotal" as Cromely argued. *Journal of the Society of Architectural Historians* 71, no. 1 (March 2012), 121–2.
49 For a critique and a method, see Arijit Sen, "Walking the Field in Milwaukee," PLATFORM July 13, 2020, https://www.platformspace.net/home/walking-the-field-in-milwaukee; and "Stories from the Flatlands," PLATFORM, September 28, 2020, https://www.platformspace.net/home/stories-from-the-flatlands
50 Upton, "Architectural History or Landscape History."
51 Dell Upton, "The VAF at 25: What Now?," *Perspectives in Vernacular Architecture* 13, no. 2 (2006/2007), 7–13.
52 Saidiya Hartman, *Wayward Lives, Beautiful Experiments: Intimate Histories of Riotous Black Girls, Troublesome Women and Queer Radicals* (New York: W.W. Norton & Co., 2019), 34.
53 Kathleen Stewart, *Ordinary Affects* (Durham, NC: Duke University Press, 2007).
54 Samir Amin, *Delinking: Towards a Polycentric World* (London: Zed Books, 1990); Walter Mignolo, "Delinking," *Cultural Studies* 21, no. 2 (2007), 449–514.

Chapter 3

1. The suffix was added to the function of a space, such as *diwankhana* (living room), *abdarkhana* (the room for storing beverages), *saraikhana* (tavern).

2. The word "gymkhana" was also used to refer to a sports meet. See, for example, Marchioness of Dufferin & Ava, *Our Viceregal Life in India: Selections from My Journals, 1884–1888*, vol. II (London: John Murray). Throughout this book I will be using the term "Anglo-Indian" to refer to the British community in colonial India.

3. Robin Evans, "The Rights of Retreat and the Rights of Exclusion: Notes Towards the Definition of Wall," *Translations from Drawing to Building and Other Essays* (Cambridge, MA: MIT Press, 1997), 45.

4. Evans, "The Rights of Retreat," 46–7.

5. Thomas Hubka, *Big House, Back House, Little House, Barn: The Connected Farm Buildings of New England* (Hanover, NH: University Press of New England, 1984), Chapter 7.

6. Fraser D. Neiman, "Domestic architecture of the Clifts Plantation Site: The Social Context of Early Virginia building," *Northern Neck Historical Magazine* 28 (1978), 3096–128. Also see Barbara J. Heath, "Dynamic Landscapes: The Emergence of Formal Spaces in Colonial Virginia," *Historical Archaeology* 50, no. 1 (2016), 27–44.

7. John Michael Vlach, *Back of the Big House: Architecture of Plantation Slavery* (Chapel Hill: University of North Carolina Press, 1993).

8. John P. Corry, "The Houses of Colonial Georgia," *The Georgia Historical Quarterly* 14, no. 3 (September 1930), 195.

9. Ellen Beasley, *The Alleys and Back Buildings of Galveston: An Architectural and Social History* (Houston: Rice University Press, 1996), Chapter 1.

10. Richard C. Wade, *Slavery in the Cities: The South 1820–1860* (London: Oxford University Press, 1964), 59–60.

11. For South Africa, see Rebecca Ginsburg, *At Home with Apartheid: The Hidden Landscapes of Domestic Service in Johannesburg* (Charlottesville: University of Virginia Press, 2011); for the Caribbean, see Louis P. Nelson, *Architecture and Empire in Jamaica* (New Haven: Yale University Press, 2016); Elizabeth C. Clay, "Landscape and Labor on the Periphery: Built Environments of Slavery in Nineteenth-century French Guiana," in James A. Delle and Elizabeth C. Clay, eds., *The Archaeology of Domestic Landscapes of the Enslaved in the Caribbean* (Gainesville: University of Florida Press, 2019), 166–87.

12. Vlach, *Back of the Big House*; Nelson, *Architecture and Empire*; Rebecca Ginsburg and Clifton Ellis, eds., *Cabin, Quarter, Plantation: Architecture and Landscape of North America Slavery* (New Haven: Yale University Press, 2010).

13. I am grateful to Sudipta Sen for this point.

Chapter 4

1. Eliot James, *A Guide to Indian Household Management* (London: Ward, Lock and Company, 1901), 61.
2. Hobson-Jobson, *A Glossary of Anglo-Indian Words and Phrases* (London: John Murray, 1903). It has an entry for godown.
3. *Calcutta Gazette*, February 7, 1790.
4. *Calcutta Gazette*, June 10, 1790.
5. Elizabeth Garrett, *Morning Hours in India: Practical Hints on Household Management* (London: Trubner & Co., 1887), 6, 14, 28.
6. Jonathan A. Farris, *Enclave to Urbanity: Canton, Foreigners, and Architecture from the Late Eighteenth to the Early Twentieth Centuries* (Hong Kong: Hong Kong University Press 2016); and Cole Roskam, *Architecture and Governance in Shanghai, 1843–1937* (Seattle: University of Washington Press, 2019).
7. Robert Kerr, *The Gentleman's House or How to Plan English Residences* (London: John Murray, 1865), 221.
8. Marchioness of Dufferin & Ava, *Our Viceregal Life in India: Selections from My Journals, 1884–1888*, vol. II (London: John Murray), 295.
9. Dufferin, *Our Viceregal Life*, vol. II, 296.
10. Dufferin, *Our Viceregal Life*, vol. II, 296.
11. Kipling, "The Mother Lodge", *Sussex Edition*, 152.
12. Emma Roberts, *Scenes and Characteristics of Hindustan* (London: W. H. Allen & Co, 1835), 7.
13. Auction notice in the *Calcutta Gazette*, April 1, 1784. Seton-Karr, *Selections*, vol. 1, 34.
14. *Calcutta Gazette*, April 15, 1784. Seton-Karr, *Selections*, vol. I, 40.
15. *Calcutta Gazette*, June 29, 1797.
16. *Calcutta Gazette*, April 22, 1784. Seton-Karr, *Selections*, vol. I, 41.
17. *Calcutta Gazette*, June 28, 1809, Sandeman, *Selections*, vol. IV, 436.
18. Richard Temple, ed., *The Diaries of Streynsham Master, 1675–1680, and Other Contemporary Papers Relating Thereto*, vols. I and II (London: John Murray, 1911), 48, 213.
19. *Calcutta Gazette*, May 7, 1814. Sandeman, *Selections*, vol. IV, 454.
20. Plan of the Cachar Cutcherry, Report on the Administration of the District of Cachar, From J. W. Allen to A. R. Young, dated December 16, 1858, Home Public Proceedings 1859. For a discussion of record rooms in provincial towns in colonial India, see Tania Sengupta, "Papered Spaces: Clerical Practices, Materialities and Spatial Cultures of Provincial Governance in Bengal, Colonial India, 1820s–60s," *Journal of Architecture* 25, no. 2 (May 2020), 111–37.
21. Chattopadhyay, *Representing Calcutta*, 97.
22. Plans of Jails, Cutcheries, Circuit Houses, &c., in the Lower Provinces, 1823; British Library IOR X1004.
23. James, *A Guide*, 62.

24 Maud Diver, *The Englishwoman in India* (Edinburgh: William Blackwood & Sons, 1909), 68.
25 James, *A Guide*, 78.
26 Mrs. Deane, *Tour Through*, 98.
27 Plan of Lieutenant Colonel W. R. Gilbert's bungalow at Hazaribagh, *c.* 1825.
28 Jane Vansittart, ed., *From Minnie, with Love: The Letters of a Victorian Lady (Maria Lydia Blane Wood) 1849–1861* (London: Peter Davies, 1974), 118.
29 For more on this aspect, see Chattopadhyay, *Representing Calcutta*, Chapter 2.
30 In 1894, decrying the absence of servants' accommodation in hotels, Major General Hallam Parr observed that the Bombay Hotel's narrow corridors were crowded with the "encampment of ayah or khidmatgar or bearer, etc." Hobbs, *John Barleycorn*, p. 72.
31 For more on Belvedere House, see Swati Chattopadhyay, "The Other Face of Primitive Accumulation: The Garden House in British Colonial Bengal," in Peter Scriver and Vikram Prakash, eds., *Colonial Modernities: Building, Dwelling and Architecture in British India and Ceylon* (Routledge, 2007), 169–97.
32 *Viceregal Establishments in India* (New Delhi: The Governor-General's Press, 1949), 3.
33 *Viceregal Establishments*, 1.
34 Robert Grant Irving, *Indian Summer: Lutyens, Baker and Imperial Delhi* (New Haven: Yale University Press, 1981).
35 Notes for the Viceroy Elect, December 31, 1930. British Library L/PJ/7/107.
36 Irving, *Indian Summer*, 231.
37 Dufferin, *Our Viceregal Life*, vol. II, 296.
38 Kerr, *The Gentleman's House*, 255.
39 Kerr, *The Gentleman's House*, 36.
40 Kerr, *The Gentleman's House*, 45, 54.
41 Kerr, *The Gentleman's House*, 256.
42 Leslie Harris, *In the Shadow of Slavery: African Americans in New York City, 1626–1863* (Chicago: University of Chicago Press, 2003), 76.
43 Harris, *In the Shadow of Slavery*, 77, 90, 103–4.
44 Harris, *In the Shadow of Slavery*, 209.
45 Irving, *Indian Summer*, 227–9.
46 Irving, *Indian Summer*, 231.
47 See Dell Upton's discussion of the basement in *Architecture in the United States*.
48 F.A. Steel and G. Gardiner, *The Complete Indian Housekeeper and Cook*, 7th ed. (London: William Heinemann, 1909), 4.
49 For analysis of the economic structure of the bazaar, see Rajat Ray, "Asian Capital in the Age of European Domination: The Rise of the Bazaar 1800–1914," *Modern Asian Studies* 29, no. 3 (July 1995), 449–554; and Sudipta Sen,

Empire of Free Trade: The East India Company and the Making of the Colonial Marketplace (Philadelphia: University of Pennsylvania Press, 1998).

50 James, *A Guide*, 50.

51 For a discussion of collecting native artifacts, see Mrs. M. Rivett-Carnac, "An Afternoon's Ramble in an Indian Bazaar," *Journal of Indian Art* 1, no. 3 (1886), 6–8.

Chapter 5

1 Henry Hobbs, *John Barleycorn Bahadur: Old Time Taverns in India* (Calcutta: Thacker and Spink, 1944), 174–5.

2 I am using the term "subaltern" in the original sense of low-ranked soldier in the army.

3 Hobbs, *John Barleycorn*, 174–5.

4 Hobbs, *John Barleycorn*, 124–5.

5 Douglas Peers, "Imperial Vice: Sex, Drink and the Health of British Troops in North Indian Cantonments, 1800–1858," in David Killingray and David Omissi, eds., *Guardians of Empire* (Manchester: Manchester University Press, 2004), 25–52; N. Cherian, "Spaces for Races: Ordering of Camp Followers in the Military Cantonments, Madras Presidency, c. 1800–1864," *Social Scientist* 32, no. 5/6 (2004), 32–50; Harald Fischer-Tiné, "'The Drinking Habits of Our Countrymen': European Alcohol Consumption and Colonial Power in British India," *The Journal of Commonwealth and Imperial History* 40, no. 3 (2014), 338–408; Erica Wald, "Governing the Bottle: Alcohol, Race and Class in Nineteenth-Century India," *The Journal of Commonwealth and Imperial History* 46, no. 3 (2018), 397–417.

6 Frederick Cooper, "Back to Work: Categories, Boundaries and Connections in the Study of Labour," in Peter Alexander and Rick Halpern, eds., *Racializing Class, Classifying Race: Labour and Difference in Britain, the USA and Africa* (Basingstoke: Palgrave MacMillan, 2000), 213–35.

7 K. T. Achaya, *Food Industries of British India* (Delhi: Oxford University Press, 1995), ?

8 See my discussion of this point in Chapter 2 in this volume.

9 William Milburn, *Oriental Commerce: Containing a Geographical Description of the Principal Places in India, China, and Japan with Their Produce, Manufacture, and Trade, Including the Coasting or Country Trade from Port to Port*, vol. 1 (London: Black, Perry and Co., 1813), 182; and vol. 2, 48, 112.

10 John Biddulph, *The Pirates of Malabar and An Englishwoman in India Two Hundred Years Ago* (London: Smith, Elder, & Co, 1907), 268.

11 Richard Temple, ed., *The Diaries of Streynsham Master, 1675–1680, and Other Contemporary Papers Relating Thereto*, vols. I and II (London: John Murray, 1911), 58.

12 Accounts of Lord Clive, 1752, British Library, Mss Eur G37/75/2; Accounts of Lord Clive, 1765: British Library, Mss Eur G37/80/2.

13 *The Calcutta Gazette*, June 25, 1812.
14 Milburn, *Oriental Commerce*, vol. 1, 182; vol. 2, 12 and 112.
15 Kate Platt, *The Home and Health in India and the Tropical Colonies* (London: Ballière, Tindall and Co., 1923), 27.
16 For price and reference to debt, see Jane Vansittart, *From Minnie, with Love, the Letter of a Victorian Lady (Maria Lydia Blane Wood) 1849–1861* (London: Peter Davies, 1974), 112, 136, 178; for "Parsee rapacity," see E. E. P. Tisdall, ed., *Mrs Duberly's Campaign: An Englishwoman's Experiences in the Crimean War and Indian Mutiny* (London: Jarrolds, 1963), 184.
17 H. D. Darukhanawala, *Parsi Lustre on Indian Soil*, vol. II (Bombay: G. Claridge, 1963).
18 Darukhanawala, *Parsi Lustre*.
19 Miles Ogborn, *Indian Ink: Script and Print in the Making of the East India Company* (Chicago: University of Chicago Press, 2007), 88–9.
20 Cited in Ogborn, *Indian Ink*, 89.
21 Hobbs, *John Barleycorn*, 82–3.
22 Ogborn, *Indian Ink*, 72.
23 Hobbs, *John Barleycorn*, 78–9.
24 Hobbs, *John Barleycorn*, 86.
25 Hobbs, *John Barleycorn*, 93.
26 Hobbs, *John Barleycorn*, 92.
27 Ravi Ahuja, "The Origins of Colonial Labour Policy in Late Eighteenth-Century Madras," *International Review of Social History* 44 (1999), 159–95.
28 Hobbs, *John Barleycorn*, 144.
29 Hobbs, *John Barleycorn*, 101–2, 139–44.
30 Hobbs, *John Barleycorn*, 160.
31 Hobbs, *John Barleycorn*, 144.
32 Despatch to Bengal, "Reply to Military Letter dated 15th June 1858, No 87. Correspondence bringing to notice the demoralization of the European soldiery by means of the liquor shops in Calcutta," Bengal Despatches, British Library, IOR E/4/855.
33 Milburn, *Oriental Commerce*, vol. 2, 171.
34 Estate of Robert Dunlop, January 31, 1859. British Library, L/AG/34/27/182.
35 Hobbs, *John Barleycorn*, 178.
36 Motilal Seal constructed a *ghat* on the Hooghly that bears his name, funded a college—Motilal Seal's Free College—and donated the land for the founding of the Calcutta Medical College Hospital. For more on Indian ownership of property in the colonial city, see Swati Chattopadhyay, *Representing Calcutta: Modernity, Nationalism and the Colonial Uncanny* (London: Routledge, 2005).
37 The reorganization of the city center and the platting of suburbs for the middle classes were concomitant phenomena. See Susan Lewandowski, "Urban Planning in the Asia Port City: Madras, an overview, 1920–1970," *South Asia:*

The Journal of South Asian Studies 21, no. 2 (1975), 30–45; Swati Chattopadhyay, "The Other Face of Primitive Accumulation: The Garden House in Colonial Bengal," in Peter Scriver and Vikramaditya Prakash, eds., *Colonial Modernities: Building, Dwelling and Architecture in British India and Ceylon* (London: Routledge, 2007), 169–98; Nikhil Rao, *House but No Garden* (Minneapolis: University of Minnesota Press); Preeti Chopra, "Free to Move, Forced to Flee: the Formation and Dissolution of Suburbs in Colonial Bombay, 1750–1918," *Urban History* 39, no. 1 (2012), 83–107.

38   See, for example, the plans of Colonel Mackenzie's garden house in Madras in the collection of the British Library: http://www.bl.uk/onlinegallery/onlineex/apac/other/largeimage66575.html, accessed March 16, 2017.
39   Hobbs, *John Barleycorn*, 105.
40   Hobbs, *John Barleycorn*, 68–9.
41   For a critical reading of the trope of Venus, see Saidiya Hartman, "Venus in Two Acts." *Small Axe* 12, no. 2 (June 2008), 1–14.
42   Seton-Karr, *Selections from Calcutta Gazettes*, 1864, 38–9.
43   Mrs. Latimer, "Journal, Rajkot," January 1912, and "Stores for Malakand," May 1927, Sir Courtenay Latimer papers. British Library, Mss Eur D1143.
44   Colonel Harvey to D. T. Monteath, Notes for the Viceroy Elect, 31 December 1930, British Library L/PJ/7/107.
45   Notes for the Viceroy Elect.
46   Chota Mem, *The English Bride in India, Being Hints on Housekeeping* (London, 1909), 45.
47   Estate of Elizabeth Tilyard, Inventories of Deceased Estates, Oriental and India Office Collection, British Library, L/AG/34/27/163.
48   A Lady Resident, *The Englishwoman in India* (London: Smith, Elder and Co., 1865), 26–7.
49   Servants Account Book Presented by the Representative of the Marquess Wellesley, General List of Servants in the Establishment at Government House, June 1805. British Library, Add Ms 13893.
50   *Viceregal Establishments in India* (New Delhi: Governor-General's Press, 1949), 5–6.
51   F. A. Steel and G. Gardiner, *The Complete Indian Housekeeper and Cook*, 7th ed. (London: William Heinemann, 1909), 60.
52   For a visual depiction of uncoordinated and raucous service, see George F. Atkinson, "Our Burra Khana," *Curry and Rice on Forty Plates* (London: Day & Son, 1859).
53   Data collected from the English-language *Thacker's Indian Directory, 1915* (Calcutta: Thacker, Spink & Co., 1915), and the Bengali-language *Kalikata Street Directory* (Calcutta: P. M. Bagchi, 1915; repr. Kolkata: P. M. Bagchi, 2016).
54   See, for example, David Fahey and Padma Manian, "Poverty and purification: the politics of Gandhi's campaign for prohibition," *The Historian* 67, no. 3 (2005), 489–506.

55 Ahuja, "Origins of Colonial Labour Policy," 168.
56 James Ranald Martin, *The Sanitary History of the British Army in India: Past and Present* (London: Savill, Edwards and Company, 1868), 41, 45.
57 Monier Monier-Williams, *A Few Remarks on n the Use of Spirituous Liquors Among the European Soldiers, and on the Punishment of Flogging in the Native Army of the Honourable the East India Company* (London: D. S. Maurice, 1833), 11–12.
58 Wald, "Governing the Bottle," 405.
59 Peers, "Imperial Vice"; Cherian, "Spaces for Races"; Wald, "Governing the Bottle."
60 K. T. Achaya, *Food Industries of British India* (Delhi: Oxford University Press, 1995), 43.
61 C. E. Buckland, *A Report on the Systems of Abkari Administration with Respect to the Taxation of Country Liquor in the Presidencies of Bombay and Madras* (Calcutta: Bengal Secretariat Press, 1888), 25–7.
62 Achaya, *Food Industries*, 43; Buckland, *A Report*, 27. One lakh is 100,000.
63 Buckland, *A Report*, 4.
64 Buckland, *A Report*, 4.
65 Buckland, *A Report*, 10–11.
66 Buckland, *A Report*, 5.
67 Buckland, *A Report*, 6.
68 Buckland, *A Report*, 21.
69 Buckland, *A Report*, 21.

Chapter 6

1 Advertisement of provisions, *Calcutta Gazette*, May 18, 1797.
2 S. B. Singh, *European Agency Houses in Bengal, 1783–1833* (Calcutta: Firma KLM, 1966); Tomlinson, "From Campsie to Kedgeree: Scottish Enterprise, Asian Trade and the Company Raj," *Modern Asian Studies* 36, no. 4 (October 2002), 769–91.
3 William Milburn, *Oriental Commerce, Containing a Geographical Description of the Principal Places in India, China, and Japan with Their Produce, Manufacture, and Trade, Including the Coasting or Country Trade from Port to Port*, vol. II (London: Black, Perry and Co. 1813), 123.
4 Christine Furedy, "British Tradesmen of Calcutta 1830–1900: A Preliminary Study of Their Economic and Political Roles," in Clinton B. Seely, ed., *Women Politics and Literature in Bengal* (East Lansing: Asian Studies Center, Michigan State University, 1981), 43–62.
5 The examples are numerous. In 1812, Lady Nugent noted that the breakfast service at the Lucknow Nawab's palace was Colebrookdale china (Cohen, *Lady Nugent's East India Journal*, 136). Afterwards Lady Nugent sent him "a present of a dessert service, of Colebrooke Dale china, each piece painted differently,

and all highly gilt, with three dozen tea cups—they are very showy, and I dare say will please him very much, particularly as I did not see anything of the sort among his English china at Lucnow" (153). For discussion of interiors with European furnishing, see Swati Chattopadhyay, "Goods, Chattels and Sundry Items: Constructing Nineteenth-century Anglo-Indian Domestic Life," *Journal of Material Culture* 7, no. 3 (November 2002), 243–71, and "The Other Face of Primitive Accumulation: : the Garden House in British Colonial Bengal," in Peter Scriver and Vikram Prakash, eds., *Colonial Modernities* (London: Routledge, 2007), 169–97; Jaffer, "Indo-Deco," in Charlotte Benton, T. Benton and G. Wood, eds., *Art Deco 1910–1939* (London: V&A Publications, 2003); Deepika Ahlawat, "Empire of Glass: F. C. Osler in India, 1840–1930," *Journal of Design History* 21, no. 2 (Summer 2008), 155–70.

6   There are frequent mentions of tinned biscuits, butter, jams, and preserves in Bengali memoirs of elite households such as the Tagores from the 1870s onwards. We know from a description of a boat trip from Calcutta to Benaras taken by Rwitendranath Tagore that canned provisions—fish, vegetables, milk, cocoa—were taken along with grains, lentils, tea, butter, etc. to prepare meals. For special events in which Europeans were invited, the meals were catered by European tavern owners and food suppliers. Rwitendranath Tagore, *Jalpathe Kashi Jatra, Punya* 1 (*Ashwin-Bhadra*, Bengali 1304 [1897]), 214.

7   Milburn, *Oriental Commerce*, vol. II, 123.

8   Some commission agents, such as Morgan, Williamson, Davidson, and Co., sent their own boats up-country once each month from Calcutta to Futtyghur to supply residents and retailers who did not have their own agents in Calcutta, at the same rate as they would do in the Commission Warehouse in Calcutta, with the additional information about how such shipment could be insured. *Calcutta Gazette*, October 18, 1787.

9   Milburn, *Oriental Commerce*, vol. II, 123.

10 Milburn, *Oriental Commerce*, vol. II, 123.

11 Vicente Raphael, *The Promise of the Foreign* (Durham, NC: Duke University Press, 2005).

12 Preserving fish by smoking and salting had been practiced by Indians in coastal areas of the subcontinent for centuries. In Hugli, the Dutch used timber brought from Batavia to manufacture wooden casks for storing the salted pork they produced downstream at Baranagar. Richard C. Temple, ed., *The Diaries of Streynsham Master, 1675–1680, and Other Contemporary Papers Relating Thereto*, vols. I and II (London, John Murray, 1911), 41.

13 *John Barleycorn Bahadur: Old Time Taverns in India* (Calcutta: Thacker and Spink, 1944), 103–4.

14 *Calcutta Gazette*, November 18, 1806. Sandeman, *Selection from the Calcutta Gazettes*, vol. IV, 422.

15 *Calcutta Gazette*, August 9, 1814. Sandeman, *Selections*, vol. IV, 454–5.

16 *Calcutta Gazette*, August 9, 1814. Sandeman, *Selections*, vol. IV, 455.

17 Havell advertised in the *Calcutta Gazette*.

18 Mrs. Latimer, "Journal, Rajkot," January 12, 1936, Sir Courtenay Latimer papers. British Library, Mss Eur D1143.

19 Table Expenses for the month of June 1798. Presented by the Representatives of the Marquess of Wellesley Table Expenses June 1798 to July 1799. British Library Add Ms 13887.

20 Eliot James remarked that all English vegetables flourished well "with proper care and attention," that included peas, beans, radishes, "melons, green-fleshed, pink-fleshed, and yellow-fleshed," "vegetable-marrows, cucumbers—trained to hang down from sticks—tomatoes, capsicums, chillies, egg-plants and cabbages, spinach and lettuces, and plenty of native products, yams, bringals (*sic*), and Indian corn" *A Guide to Indian Household Management* (London: Ward, Lock and Co., *c.* 1880), 64–5. Wyvern included asparagus, artichokes, watercress, some of which required "growing in the hills" *Culinary Jottings: A Treatise in Thirty Chapters of Reformed Cooking*, 5th ed. (Madras: Higginbotham & Co., 1885), 127–8.

21 Elizabeth Garrett, *Morning Hours in India: Practical Hints on Household Management* (London: Trubner & Co., 1887), 46–7. Annual reports of horticulture and botanic gardens in India carried lists of people and institutions to whom seeds were distributed. See, for example, Nathaniel Wallich's report on the Calcutta Botanic Gardens, British Library, IOR/P/13/36 7 April 1841 Nos 26–32, 1840–1. For private correspondence regarding distribution of seeds, see, for example, Letter from William Carey, 1824, British Library, Mss Eur C583.

22 Garrett, *Morning Hours*, 14.

23 Some of the most popular ones that went through multiple editions were W. Gollan, *The Indian Vegetable Garden* (Allahabad: Indian Press, 1892); Landolicus, *The Indian Amateur Gardener* (Calcutta: W. Newman & Co, 1881); E. W. Grindal, *Everyday Gardening in India* (Bombay: Taraporevala Sons and Co., 1942).

24 Major C. Dutton, writing in 1882, remarked that it is "essential to keep up a garden for the sake of the vegetables" *Life in India* (London: W. H. Allen, 1882), 68, and his sentiments were repeated in various details in advice to Englishmen and women; see F. A. Steel and G. Gardiner, *The Complete Indian Housekeeper and Cook*, 7th ed. (London: William Heinemann, 1909), 130; Garrett, *Morning Hours*, 11.

25 Steel and Gardiner, *Complete Indian Housekeeper*, 131.

26 George W. Clutterbuck, *In India, Bombay the Beautiful* (London: Ideal Publishers, 1897), 241.

27 James, *A Guide*, 64; Cuthell, *My Garden in the City of Gardens*, 12, 23, 120–1, 219.

28 *Calcutta Gazette*, May 31, 1787.

29 *Calcutta Gazette*, January 1814. For long river voyages, the pinnace would be exclusively used for food storage and preparation, while other larger boats were used for dining, sleeping, and resting. See Mrs. Deane, *Tour Through the Upper Provinces*, for example.

30 A Lady Resident, *The Englishwoman in India*, 89–93.

31 Steel and Gardiner, *Complete Indian Housekeeper*, 148, 156.

32 Steel and Gardiner suggested preserved haricot beans and the French product, Chollet's compressed vegetables, to be taken on the march (151).

33 Steel and Gardiner, *Complete Indian Housekeeper*, 150–1.

34 Examples are numerous. For a particularly interesting notes, see E. E. P. Tisdall, ed., *Mrs Duberly's Campaign: An Englishwoman's Experiences in the Crimean War and Indian Mutiny* (London: Jarrolds, 1963), 178, 184.

35 Steel and Gardiner, *Complete Indian Housekeeper*, 151.

36 Mrs. Latimer, "To Nathia Gate," April 14, 1918. Sir Courtenay Latimer papers. British Library, Mss Eur D1143.

37 Steel and Gardiner, *Complete Indian Housekeeper*, 152.

38 See, for example, Steel and Gardiner, *Complete Indian Housekeeper*, 152; Jane Vansittart, ed., *From Minnie, with Love: The Letters of a Victorian Lady (Maria Lydia Blane Wood) 1849–1861* (London: Peter Davies, 1974) 57; Mrs. Deane, *Tour Through the Upper Provinces*, 2.

39 Garrett, *Morning Hours*, 35.

40 Vansittart, *From Minnie*, 136. Eliot James's estimation of wine, beer, and incidentals for her household in Multan in the 1880s is comparable (37), but this she thought was without undue economy or hardship.

41 James, *A Guide*, 73.

42 Steel and Gardiner, *Complete Indian Housekeeper*, 14; Garrett, *Morning Hours*, 14.

43 Wyvern, *Culinary Jottings*, 28.

44 Wyvern, *Culinary Jottings*, 28–9. Other bottled items he recommended included "a little bottle of American 'Tabasco', 'Messers Brand & Co.'s preparations for invalids, potted meats, soups, and strong essences of beef, chicken, &c., Harvey's sauce, Moir's sauces, Reading sauce, Sutton's 'Empress of India' sauce, and mushroom and walnut ketchup, tomato preserve, caviar, olive farcies, and anchovies in oil" (28, 35).

45 Major Dutton, writing in 1882, remarked: "One cannot avoid having a great many tinned things, owing to the difficulty of making a really good dinner without them ... At dinner-parties the fish would be tinned, the bacon, the pâté de foie gras, asparagus and cheese, if all these things were used, and maybe others as well" (100–1). On social implications of curried soups, see Modhumita Roy, "Class, Gender and Empire in the Making of Mulligatawny Soup," *Economic and Political Weekly* 45, no. 32 (August 2010), 68–70.

46 Hobbs, *John Barleycorn Bahadur*, 158.

47 Chattopadhyay, "Goods, Chattles," 257; Lizzy Collingham, *Taste of Empire: How Britain's Quest for Food Shaped the Modern World* (New York: Basic Books, 2017), 183–4. See Wyvern, *Culinary Jottings*, 25–6.

48 Wyvern, *Culinary Jottings*, 500.

49 Sidney L. Blanchard, *Yesterday and Today in India* (London: W. H. Allen, 1867), 45.

50 Wyvern, *Culinary Jottings*, 286.

51 Mildreth W. Pinkham, *A Bungalow in India, Intimate Glimpses of Indian Life and People* (New York: Fleming H. Revell Company, 1928), 44.

52 Wyvern, *Culinary Jottings*, 16, 28, 273. The same advice was given about "spices" that were supposed to be doled out to the cook in "atoms" (16).

53 Accounts of Lord Wellesley's Table Expenses June 1798 to July 1799; Presented by the Representatives of the Marquess of Wellesley, British Library Add Ms 13887.

54 George F. Atkinson, *Curry and Rice on Forty Plates* (London: Day & Son, 1859), np.

55 Estate of Robert Dunlop, January 21, 1859, Inventories of Deceased Estates, British Library, L/AG/34/27/182.

56 Garrett, *Morning Hours*, 10.

57 John Coatman, *Portrait of an Englishwoman* (London: Peter Skelton, 1964), 39.

58 Jon Godden and Rumer Godden, *Two Under the Indian Sun* (New York: Alfred A. Knopf; Viking Press, 1966), 58. I thank Arun Nag for directing my attention to this text.

59 Godden and Godden, *Two Under the Indian Sun*, 58.

60 *The Englishwoman in India*, 71.

61 Estate of John Graham, February 5, 1859, Inventories of Deceased Estates British Library, L/AG/34/27/182, pp.141-143; Estate of Robert Dunlop.

62 Chattopadhyay, "Goods, Chattels," 260–4.

63 Steel and Gardiner, *Complete Indian Housekeeper*, 13.

64 Vansittart, *From Minnie*, 68.

65 Vansittart, *From Minnie*, 68.

66 Steel and Gardiner, *Complete Indian Housekeeper*, 5–6.

67 Coatman, *Portrait*, 40.

68 Wyvern, *Culinary Jottings*, 24.

69 Wyvern, *Culinary Jottings*, 26.

70 Pinkham, *A Bungalow in India*, 48.

71 Wyvern, *Culinary Jottings*, 291.

72 Steel and Gardiner, *Complete Indian Housekeeper*, 13.

73 Steel and Gardiner, *Complete Indian Housekeeper*, 67.

74 Some of them such as Henry Pattullo tied the prospect to improved proprietary rights in land to acceptance of "British furniture and way of living" (Ranajit Guha, *A Rule of Property in Bengal: An Essay on the Idea of Permanent Settlement* [Durham, NC: Duke University Press, 1981], 44), while others hoped English education and Christianity might help the process of dissemination of English tastes.

75 Omkar Goswami estimates that "by World War II the purchasing power of the urban populace had almost doubled in real terms compared to the 1900–1 level." Goswami, "Sahibs, Babus and Banias: Changes in Industrial Control in

Eastern India", in Rajat Ray, ed., *Entrepreneurship and Industry in India, 1800–1947* (New Delhi: Oxford University Press, 1992), 255–6.

76 Amritalal Basu, "*Patit Daktar,*" *Koutuk Joutuk* (Calcutta, 1929), 4.

77 For a snapshot of this, see Utsa Ray, *Culinary Culture in Colonial India: A Cosmopolitan Platter and the Middle-Class* (New Delhi: Cambridge University Press, 2015), Chapter 1.

Chapter 7

1 Mildreth Worth Pinkham, *A Bungalow in India: Intimate Glimpses of Indian Life and People* (New York: Fleming H. Revell Company, 1928), 26.

2 William Digby, *The Famine Campaign in Southern India, 1876–1878*, vol. 1 (London: Longmans, Green and Co, 1878), 55.

3 George F. Atkinson, "Our Cook Room," *Curry and Rice on Forty Plates* (London: Day & Son Ltd., 1859), np.

4 Pinkham, *A Bungalow*, 24.

5 Pinkham, *A Bungalow*, 24.

6 Achille Mbembe, *On the Postcolony* (Berkeley: University of California Press, 2001), 32.

7 Mbembe, *On the Postcolony*, 35.

8 Mbembe, *On the Postcolony*, 28.

9 David Arnold, "The Discovery of 'Malnutrition' and Diet in Colonial India," *The Indian Economic and Social History Review* 31, no. 1(1994), 3–12.

10 Elizabeth Collins Cromley, *The Food Axis: Cooking, Eating, and the Architecture of American Houses* (Charlottesville: University of Virginia Press, 2010), 3.

11 Cromley, *The Food Axis*, 2.

12 Cromley, *The Food Axis*, 3.

13 Cromley, *The Food Axis*, 6–7.

14 Cromley, *The Food Axis*, 7, 48–53.

15 See Ruth Goodman's discussion of this point in *The Domestic Revolution: How the Introduction of Coal into Victorian Homes Changed Everything* (New York: Liveright Publishing, 2020), 218–19.

16 For an architectural analysis of kitchens in Indian homes in British India, see William J. Glover, "Changing Houses: Rethinking and Rebuilding Townhouses and Neighborhoods," *Making Lahore Modern: Constructing and Imagining a Modern City* (Minneapolis: University of Minnesota Press, 2008), 132–40.

17 Angela Gill Cooley, *To Live and Dine in Dixie: The Evolution of Urban Food Culture in Jim Crow South* (Athens: University of Georgia Press, 2015), 9–11.

18 Alan Macfarlane, ed., *Twenty Years in Tea: The Letters of Iris Macfarlane from Assam Tea Gardens, 1946–65* (2019), 104. https://doi.org/10.17863/CAM.57018.

19 Lady Anne Wilson, *Letters from India* (Edinburgh: William Blackwood, 1911),

20 See the exception in the Viceroy's Palaces discussed in Chapter 4 in this volume.

21 Elizabeth Garrett, *Morning Hours in India: Practical Hints on Household Management, the Care and Training of Children, &C.* (London: Trubner & Co., 1887), 19.

22 Wyvern, *Culinary Jottings: A Treatise in Thirty Chapters of Reformed Cooking*, 5th ed. (Madras: Higginbotham & Co., 1885), 1.

23 Wyvern, *Culinary Jottings*, 3.

24 Wyvern, *Culinary Jottings*, 333.

25 Wyvern, *Culinary Jottings*, 15.

26 Wyvern, *Culinary Jottings*, 16.

27 Wyvern, *Culinary Jottings*, 15.

28 Wyvern, *Culinary Jottings*, 14.

29 Wyvern, *Culinary Jottings*, 14.

30 Wyvern, *Culinary Jottings*, 23.

31 Wyvern, *Culinary Jottings*, 500.

32 Mary Douglas, *Purity and Danger: An Analysis of the Concepts of Pollution and Taboo* (1966; London: Routledge, 2002).

33 Stephanie Newell, *Histories of Dirt: Media and Urban Life in Colonial and Postcolonial Nigeria* (Durham, NC: Duke University Press, 2020), 3, 117.

34 Wyvern, *Culinary Jottings*, 500–2.

35 Wyvern, *Culinary Jottings*, 503.

36 Kate Platt, *The Home and Health in India and the Tropical Colonies* (London: Baillière, Tindall and Cox, 1923), 44.

37 Wyvern, *Culinary Jottings*, 18.

38 Wyvern, *Culinary Jottings*, 18.

39 Wyvern, *Culinary Jottings*, 19.

40 Wyvern, *Culinary Jottings*, 508–9.

41 Wyvern, *Culinary Jottings*, 42.

42 Pinkham, *A Bungalow*, 25.

43 Radhika Mohanram, "Gastronomia Anglo-India: Culinary Jottings in the Age of Famine," *Journal of Continuum: Media and Cultural Studies* 25, no. 5 (October 2011), 770–1.

44 Wyvern, *Culinary Jottings*, 103.

45 The famine resulted in severe loss of cattle, and because the famished people could not afford grain, they ate the meat of the cattle as the last resort.

46 This is rephrasing Ramachandra Guha's question in his *How Much Should a Person Consume? Environmentalism in India and the United States* (Berkeley: University of California Press, 2006).

47 Nick Cullather, "The Foreign Policy of the Calorie," *American Historical Review* (April 2007), 337. Also see Nick Cullather, *The Hungry World: America's Cold War Battle Against Poverty in Asia* (Boston, MA: Harvard University Press, 2013).

48 Cullather, "The Foreign Policy," 338; Arnold, "The Discovery of 'Malnutrition'"; Tom Scott-Smith, *On an Empty Stomach: Two Hundred Years of Hunger Relief* (Ithaca: Cornell University Press, 2020).

49 Cullather, "The Foreign Policy," 338.

50 Cullather, "The Foreign Policy," 340.

51 For more on the effect of Atwater's ideas on good physique and governmental intervention, see Rachel Louis Moran, "Body Politic: Government and Physique in Twentieth-century America," Ph.D. dissertation, The Pennsylvania State University, August 2013.

52 For a discussion of the rise of unit as an architectural measure, see Andrew M. Shanken, "Unit: A Semantic and Architectural History," *Representations* 143 (Summer 2018), 91–117.

53 A summary of this is provided in the US Department of Agriculture's bulletin: W. O. Atwater and Chas. D. Woods, *The Chemical Composition of American Food Materials* (Washington, DC: Government Printing Press, 1896), 5–6.

54 W. O. Atwater and Chas. D. Woods, *Dietary Studies with Reference to the Food of the Negro in Alabama in 1895 and 1896*, US Department of Agriculture's Bulletin No 38 (Washington, DC: Government Printing Press, 1897), 16.

55 Atwater and Woods, *Dietary Studies*, 7.

56 Atwater and Woods, *Dietary Studies*, 17.

57 Atwater and Woods, *Dietary Studies*, 19.

58 On this point, see Prathama Banerjee's discussion of colonial construction of primitives in relation to a money economy in *Politics of Time: "Primitives" and History-Writing in a Colonial Society* (Delhi: Oxford University Press, 2006).

59 Atwater and Woods, *Dietary Studies*, 7

60 Atwater and Woods, *Dietary Studies*, 23.

61 Atwater and Woods, *Dietary Studies*, 24.

62 Arnold, "The Discovery of 'Malnutrition'"; Scott-Smith, *On an Empty Stomach*, 46–7.

63 Scott-Smith, *On an Empty Stomach*, 46–7.

64 Cullather, "The Foreign Policy," 341–2.

65 Scott-Smith, *On an Empty Stomach*, 53.

66 Cullather, "The Foreign Policy," 348–50.

67 Cited in Moran, "Body Politic," 43.

68 For a connection between colonialist and nationalist policies in India, see Sunil S. Amrith, "Food and Welfare in India, c. 1900–1950," *Comparative Studies in Society and History* 50, no. 1 (October 2008), 1010–35.

69 Amartya Sen, "Ingredients of Famine Analysis: Availability and Entitlement," *The Quarterly Journal of Economics* 96, no. 3 (August 1981), 433–64. Also see Amartya Sen, *Poverty and Famines: An Essay on Entitlement and Deprivation* (Oxford: Oxford University Press, 1981).

70 Indian nationalists such as Dadabhai Naoroji and Romesh Chunder Dutt made this argument by relating famine to the "drain of wealth": David Arnold, *Famine: Social and Historical Change* (Chichester: Wiley-Blackwell, 1991); and Amrith, "Food and Welfare." Also see, Madhusree Mukherjee, *Churchill's Secret War: The British Empire and the Ravaging of India during World War II* (London: Basic Books, 2011).

71 William Digby, *The Famine Campaign in Sothern India*, vol. 1 (London: Longmans, Green and Co., 1878), 1–7; Mike Davis, *Late Victorian Holocausts: El Niño Famines and the Making of the Third World* (New York: Verso, 2000), 25–50.

72 Ranjini Ray, Atreyee Bhattacharya, Gaurav Arora, et al., "Extreme Rainfall Deficits Were Not the Cause of Recurring Colonial-era Famines of Southern Indian Semi-arid Regions," *Science Report* 11, 17568 (2021).

73 Davis, *Late Victorian Holocausts*, 27.

74 Davis, *Late Victorian Holocausts*, 39.

75 Scott-Smith, *On an Empty Stomach*, 13.

76 Digby, *The Famine Campaign*, 48.

77 Digby, *The Famine Campaign*, 55

78 Report of the Famine Commission 1898 (Simla: Government Central Printing Press, 1898), 6.

79 Digby, *The Famine Campaign*, 54, 76, 336; For later extension of this principle, see Report of the Indian Famine.

80 Digby, *The Famine Campaign*, 26.

81 Digby, *The Famine Campaign*, 214. Also see Report of the Indian Famine.

82 Digby, *The Famine Campaign*, 483.

83 Aidan Forth, *Barbed Wire Imperialism: Britain's Empire of Camps, 1876–1903* (Berkeley: University of California Press, 2017), 105.

84 Digby, *The Famine Campaign*, 37–8.

85 Digby, *The Famine Campaign*, 82, 89.

86 Digby, *The Famine Campaign*, 483.

87 Digby, *The Famine Campaign*, 55, 61.

88 Digby, *The Famine Campaign*, 372–3.

89 Forth, *Barbed Wire Imperialism*, 103.

90 Report of the Famine, 18.

91 Digby, *The Famine Campaign*, 376. Also see Aidan Forth's discussion in *Barbed Wire Imperialism*, 59–60.

92 Forth, *Barbed Wire Imperialism*, 60.
93 Digby, *The Famine Campaign*, 112.
94 For a longer treatment on this subject, see Forth, *Barbed Wire Imperialism*.
95 Forth, *Barbed Wire Imperialism*, 60.
96 Forth, *Barbed Wire Imperialism*, 58–63.
97 Digby, *The Famine Campaign*, 340.
98 Cited in Davis, *Late Victorian Holocausts*, 59.

Chapter 8

1 Mrs. (Elizabeth Augusta) Robert Moss King, *The Diary of a Civilian's Wife in India 1877–1882*, vol. 1 (London: Richard Bentley & Son, 1884), 128–9. In the 1950s in the age of electricity and automobiles, Iris Macfarlane's bungalow in the Cherideo Parbat tea plantation in Assam had 13 servants (3 bearers, 1 cook, 2 paniwallahs (water carriers), 4 malis (gardeners), 1 sweeper, 2 horse folk, 1 driver, and 2 cow men), while the manager at the apex of the Assam Tea Company had 24 servants (3 bearers, 2 paniwallahs (water carriers), 8 malis (gardeners), 2 sweepers, 2 horse folk, 2 drivers, and 2 cow men). Source: Alan Macfarlane, ed., *Twenty Years in Tea: The Letters of Iris Macfarlane from Assam Tea Gardens, 1946–65* (2019), 146. https://doi.org/10.17863/CAM.57018.
2 Swati Chattopadhyay, *Representing Calcutta: Modernity, Nationalism, and the Colonial Uncanny* (London: Routledge, 2005), Chapter 1.
3 This is the classic understanding of subalternity. The subaltern appears in the archive through acts of negation. See Ranajit Guha, *Elementary Aspects of Peasant Insurgency in Colonial India* (Delhi: Oxford University Press, 1983).
4 Saidiya V. Hartman, *Scenes of Subjection: Terror, Slavery, and Self-Making in Nineteenth-Century America* (New York, 1997); Krista A. Thompson, "The Evidence of Things not Photographed: Slavery and Historical Memory in the British West Indies," *Representations* 113 (Winter 2011), 39–71.
5 Krista Thompson, *An Eye for the Tropics: Tourism, Photography, and Framing the Caribbean Picturesque* (Durham, NC: Duke University Press, 2006).
6 Mark Girouard, *Life in the English Country House: A Social and Architectural History* (New Haven: Yale University Press), 285.
7 Tanika Sarkar, "Making and Remaking Caste and Labour," in Anuradha Roy and Melitta Waligora, eds., *Kolkata in Space, Time and Imagination*, vol. 1 (Delhi: Primus Books), 188.
8 Vijay Prashad, *Untouchable Freedom: A Social History of a Dalit Community* (New Delhi: Oxford University Press, 2000), 4.
9 Dean T. Ferguson, "Nightsoil and the 'Great Divergence': Human Waste, the Urban Economy, and Economic Productivity," *Journal of Global History* 9 (2014), 382.

10 Prashad, *Untouchable Freedom*, Chapter 1; Tanika Sarkar, "Making and Remaking Caste."
11 Kate Platt, *The Home and Health in India and the Tropical Colonies* (London: Baillière, Tindall and Cox, 1923), 20.
12 Prashad, *Untouchable Freedom*, 8–9.
13 Prashad, *Untouchable Freedom*, 10.
14 Prashad, *Untouchable Freedom*, 52.
15 Tanika Sarkar has noted that "tribals" dominated Calcutta's sweeper class in the nineteenth century: "Making and Remaking Caste," 186–7; Prashad, *Untouchable Freedom*, 22.
16 Nikhil Rao, *House, But No Garden: Apartment Living in Bombay's Suburbs, 1898–1964* (Minneapolis: University of Minnesota Press, 2013), 123–9.
17 Rao, *House, But No Garden*, 131.
18 In the 1960s and 1970s, I lived in this house. My father's state government accommodation, it was demolished in 2010.
19 Remarkably, among the commands cited in *Dialogues*, instructing English speakers how to communicate with Indians is "let the servants sleep on the floor": "nuokuron ko zumeen pur sone do." John Borthwick Gilchrist, *Dialogues, English and Hindoostanee* (London: Kingsbury, Parberry, Allen, 1826), 83.
20 Mrs. Deane, *Tour Through the Upper Provinces*, 2; Jane Vansittart, ed., *From Minnie with Love, the Letters of a Victorian Lady (Maria Lydia Blane Wood) 1849–1861* (London: Peter Davies, 1974), 57; F.A. Steel and G. Gardiner, *The Complete Indian Housekeeper*, 7th ed. (London: William Heineman, 1907), 152; King, 62–3, 70.
21 See Dell Upton's analysis of Monticello in *Architecture in the United States* (Oxford: Oxford University Press, 1998), Chapter 1.
22 For punkah design and use in the American South, see Dana Byrd, "Motive Power: Fans, Punkahs, and Fly Brushes in the Antebellum South," *Buildings & Landscapes* 23, no. 1 (Spring 2016), 29–51.
23 Thomas Jefferson, "To fix a fan over the Dining room table," Notebook of Improvements, Monticello (Virginia, 1804–7), K 162–7. The Coolidge Collection of Thomas Jefferson Manuscripts, Massachusetts Historical Society.
24 Jefferson, "To fix a fan."
25 Stephen B. Hodin, "The Mechanisms of Monticello: Saving Labor in Jefferson's America," *Journal of the Early Republic* 26, no. 3 (Fall 2006), 377.
26 Nitin Sinha, "Who is (Not) a Servant Anyway? Domestic Servants and Service in Early Colonial India," *Modern Asian Studies* 55, no. 1 (Spring 2021), 154. For a discussion of the "service sector" in the Madras Presidency, see Dharma Kumar, "The Forgotten Sector: Services in the Madras Presidency in the First Half of the Nineteenth Century," *The Indian Economic and Social History Review* 24, no. 4 (1987), 367–93.
27 See, for example, Ravi Ahuja, "Labor Relations in an Early Colonial Context: Madras, c. 1750–1800," *Modern Asian Studies* 36, no. 4 (October 2002), 793–826.

28 Sinha, "Who is (Not) a Servant," 153.
29 Sinha, "Who is (Not) a Servant," 161–2.
30 Gilchrist, *Dialogues*, 31.
31 Transportation of labor from India was not new to the nineteenth century, but mass transportation to plantations started in 1834, first to Mauritius, and then to British Guiana in 1838. See Ashutosh Kumar, "Naukari, Networks of Knowledge: Views of Indenture in Nineteenth-century North India," *South Asian Studies* 33, no. 1 (2017), 52–67.
32 Ahuja, 801.
33 Ahuja, 802.
34 King, *The Home*, 130.
35 King, *The Home*, 130.
36 Michael H. Fisher, "Bound for Britain: Changing Conditions of Servitude, 1600–1857," in Indrani Chatterjee and Richard Eaton, eds., *Slavery and South Asian History* (Bloomington: Indiana University Press, 2006), 187–209.
37 For a discussion of this painting, see Chattopadhyay, *Representing Calcutta*, 123–5.
38 Chattopadhyay, *Representing Calcutta*, 132–5.
39 Vansittart, *From Minnie*, 95.
40 Vansittart, *From Minnie*, 136.
41 Vansittart, *From Minnie*, 140.
42 Vansittart, *From Minnie*, 179.
43 Maud Divers, *The Englishwoman in India* (Edinburgh: W. Blackwood, 1909), 55.
44 Vansittart, *From Minnie*, 137.
45 Vansittart, *From Minnie*, 90.
46 King, *The Home*, 70.
47 King, *The Home*, 107.
48 King *The Home*, 104–5.
49 King, *The Home*, 103–4.
50 George F. Atkinson, "Our Bed Room," *Curry and Rice on Forty Plates* (London: Day & Son, 1859), n.p.
51 "House of Commons question on the sentence passed to Pte John Rigby who kicked a punkah coolie to death," British Library, IOR/L/P/J/6/360, File 2170, 9 November 1893. Sudipta Sen, "Confessions of the Unfriendly Spleen," in Rohan Deb Roy and Guy N. A. Attewell, eds., *Locating the Medical: Explorations in South Asian History* (London: Oxford University Press, 2018), 71–102.
52 Atkinson, "Our Colonel," *Curry and Rice*, n.p.
53 *Allen's Indian Mail*, September 6, 1878.
54 Major E. Stokes-Roberts, *Some Practical Points in the Design and Construction of Military Buildings in India* (Calcutta, Superintendent Government Printing, India, 1910), 49.

55 Stokes-Roberts, *Some Practical Points*, 50.
56 This is exemplified in the mid-twentieth-century work of Louis Kahn. See Swati Chattopadhyay, "Architectural History or a Geography of Small Spaces?," *Journal of the Society of Architectural Historians* 81, no. 1 (March 2022), 5–20.
57 See Ranajit Guha's discussion on this point about the connections the subalterns made between the triad of the government–moneylender–landlord in the figures *sarkari*, *sahukari*, and *zamindari* property as the target of peasant insurgency. Ranajit Guha, *Elementary Aspects of Peasant Insurgency* (New Delhi: Oxford, 1983), 25.
58 Vansittart, *From Minnie*, 150.
59 It is useful to note here that it is unlikely that the servants used the term "king" to refer to Bahadur Shah II. Rather it is the British who insisted on referring to the Mughal emperor as a king and not an emperor.
60 Vansittart, *From Minnie*, 118.
61 Vansittart, *From Minnie*, 182–3.

Chapter 9

1 Rani Chanda, *Amar Ma'r Baper Bari* (My Mother's Father's House) (Calcutta: Visvabharati, 1977), 39.
2 I borrow this phrase from Antoinette Burton, "Not Even Remotely Global? Method and Scale in World History," *History Workshop Journal*, no. 64 (2007), 323–8.
3 Paul Carter, *The Road to Botany Bay: An Exploration of Landscape and History* (1988; Minneapolis: University of Minnesota Press, 2010), xvi.
4 Carter, *The Road to Botany Bay*, xvi.
5 Carter, *The Road to Botany Bay*, "Introduction: A Cake of Portable Soup," xxv. For a visual counterpart to this presenting history as a classical stage, see Thomas Cole, *The Architect's Dream*, 1840.
6 David Arnold, *Tropics and the Traveling Gaze* (Seattle: University of Washington Press, 2007), 28.
7 John Lewis Gaddis, *The Landscape of History: How Historians Map the Past* (Oxford: Oxford University Press, 2002), 4–5.
8 Fernando Luiz Lara, "Abstraction is a Privilege," PLATFORM, June 7, 2021.
9 Philip Arnold, *Eating Landscape: Aztec and European Occupation of Tlalocan* (Boulder: University Press of Colorado, 1999), 54.
10 For histories of these traditions, see Paul Groth and Chris Wilson, "The Polyphony of Cultural Landscape Study: An Introduction," in Paul Groth and Chris Wilson, eds., *Everyday America: Cultural Landscape Studies after J. B. Jackson* (Berkeley: University of California Press, 2003), 1–22; Dianne Harris and D. Fairchild Ruggles, eds., *Sites Unseen: Landscape and Vision* (Pittsburg: University of Pittsburg Press, 2007).

11 For a recent volume that addresses the idea of seeing in the Arab-Persianate world, see Samer Akkach, *Nazar: Vision, Belief and Perception in Islamic Cultures* (Leiden: Brill, 2022). I thank Samira Fathi and Nuha Khoury for sources and conversation on this subject.

12 It belongs to the domain of "judicative reasoning which elaborates and discerns the logical validity of statements and seeks understanding through mental processes" (Latiri, 3). See Lamia Latiri, "The Meaning of Landscape in Classical Arabo-Muslim Culture," *Cybergeo: European Journal of Geography*, no. 196 (October 16, 2001), 1–17.

13 Here see D. Fairchild Ruggles's argument about representation and Islamic landscape art in "Making Vision Manifest: Frame, Screen and View in Islamic Culture," in Harris and Ruggles, eds., *Sites Unseen*, 131–56.

14 Arnold, *Eating Landscape*, 237.

15 Arnold, *Eating Landscape*, 237.

16 Lara, "Abstraction is a Privilege."

17 Kathleen Stewart, *Ordinary Affects* (Durham, NC: Duke University Press, 2007), 4.

18 Tim Ingold, "Bringing Things to Life: Creative Entanglements in a World of Materials," ESRC National Center for Research Methods, NCRM Working Paper Series (July 2010).

19 Arjun Appadurai, *Modernity at Large* (Durham, NC: Duke University Press, 1996), 13.

20 Michel de Certeau, *The Practice of Everyday Life* (Berkeley: University of California Press, 1984), 116–18.

21 de Certeau, *The Practice of Everyday Life*, 128.

22 Dell Upton, "Architectural History or Landscape History," *Journal of Architectural Education* 44, no. 4 (August 1991), 195–9.

Chapter 10

1 Robin Evans, "Figures, Doors and Passages," *Translation from Drawing to Building and Other Essays* (Cambridge, MA: MIT Press, 1997), 56.

2 Andrew Jackson Downing, *The Architecture of Country Houses, Including Designs for Cottages, Farmhouses and Villas* (New York: D. Appleton, 1851); Bernard Herman, "The Embedded Landscapes of the Charleston Single House, 1780–1880," *Perspectives in Vernacular Architecture*, vol. 7, *Exploring Everyday Landscapes* (1997): 41–57; Therese O'Malley, with contributions from Elizabeth Kryder-Reid and Anne L. Helmreich, *Keywords in American Landscape Design* (New Haven: Yale University Press, 2010).

3 Jiat-Hwee Chang and Anthony D. King, "Towards a Genealogy of Tropical Architecture: Historical Fragments of Power-knowledge, Built Environment and Climate in the British Colonial Territories," *Singapore Journal of Tropical Geography* 32 (2011): 283–300; Jiat-Hwee Chang, *A Genealogy of Tropical Architecture: Colonial Networks, Nature and Technoscience* (London:

Routledge 2016); Cole Roskam, *Improvised City: Architecture and Governance in Shanghai, 1843–1937* (Seattle: University of Washington Press, 2019).

4 James Pope Hennessey, *Verandah: Some Episodes in the Crown Colonies* (New York: Alfred Knopf, 1964).

5 Garth Myers, *Verandahs of Power: Colonialism and Space in Urban Africa* (New York: University of Syracuse, 2003).

6 See Anthony D. King, *Bungalow: The Production of a Global Culture* (London: 1976). For a contemporary description, see Divers, *The Englishwoman in India*, 61–2.

7 Edith E. Cuthell, *My Garden in the City of Gardens: A Memory with Illustrations* (London: John Lane, 1905), 206.

8 Edith E. Cuthell, *Tent and Bungalow* (London: Metheun and Co. 1892), 152.

9 Tania Sengupta, "Papered Spaces: Clerical Practices, Materialities and Spatial Cultures of Provincial Governance in Bengal, Colonial India, 1820s-60s," *Journal of Architecture* 25, Issue 2 (May 2020): 111–137.

10 In a large estate, the garden house at Pultah on the Hooghly near Calcutta, a real estate advertisement referred to circular verandahs on both upper and lower stories, and the lower story had an "extra verandah." *Calcutta Gazette*, June 21, 1820.

11 See To W. Dorrin Esq, Register of Nizamat Adawlut from D. Morrieson, 3rd Judge, 16 Oct 1820, Bhagaulpore, Judicial Proceedings (Criminal), 1820. British Library IOR/P/128/62; and To the Suptd. of Public Buildings, Lower Provinces from H. T. Prinsep, Actg. Secy to Government, 13 Dec 1822, Judicial Proceedings (Criminal), 1822, British Library IOR/P/135/30.

12 PW (Revenue) 18 Nov 1857. The "substitution of a permanent for a thatched verandah at the Collector's Cutchhery at Mymensingh" cost Rs. 522. Despatches to Indian and Bengal, British Library, IOR/E/4/848.

13 From Captain I. H. Warner, Executive Engineer, Lower Provinces to Colonel R. Tiekell, Bauleah, 8 May 1835, Judicial Proceedings (Criminal), July 4 1835, British Library IOR/P/140/69.

14 Warner to Colonel R. Tiekell. See also, To the Secy to the Governor from I. R. Elphinstone 2nd Judge, Arrah, 4 May 1819, Judicial Proceedings (Criminal), 6 Aug 1819. British Library IOR/P/133/67.

15 In an advertisement of a residence on 17 Chrowringhee in the *Calcutta Gazette*. May 24, 1810, specifies that the "verandah lately built to the west," as an improvement to the property.

16 Advertisement by Dring Cleland & Co, *Calcutta Gazette*, Thursday May 15, 1794.

17 Sunshades were added to the eastern verandah of the sub-division bungalow at Govindpore at a cost of Rs, 246.9.11. India PW (Judicial) 24th June 1857.

18 The advertisement for a large garden house with three halls and six bedrooms contained an "inclosed verandah to the northward," presumably as a protection from the wind. *Calcutta Gazette*, Thu Nov 25, 1790. Other references appear in the *Calcutta Gazette*, March 29, 1810.

19 *Calcutta Gazette*, April12, 1810.
20 Public Works Consultations, 5th April 1855. No 80. British Library IOR/P/15/93.
21 For a more detailed treatment of this see Swati Chattopadhyay, "Spaces of Conversation: : The Avant-garde in 1920s Calcutta," in Regina Bittner and Kathrin Rhomberg, eds., *Transcultural Avant-Garde Laboratory: The Bauhaus in Calcutta, 1922* (Berlin: 2013), 161–72.
22 Ruggles, "Making Vision Manifest," 153.
23 Abanindranath Tagore, *Apan Katha, Abanindra Rachanabali*, vol 1. (Kolkata: Prakash Bhavan 1973), 15.
24 For a discussion of the importance of the *otla* in the imagination of princely architecture in the state of Jaipur see Sugata Ray, "Colonial Frames: 'Native' Claims: The Jaipur Economic and Industrial Museum," *The Art Bulletin* XCVI, no 2 (June 2014): 196–212.
25 Chanda, *Amar Ma'r Baper Bari*, 21–22.
26 Chanda, *Amar Ma'r Baper Bari*, 30.
27 Polier's letter to Nawab Shuja-ud-Daula, 26 Rajab, 1187, in Muzaffar Alam and Seema Alavi, *A European Experience of the Mughal Orient the I'jāz-i Arsalānī (Persian letters 1773–1779) of Antoine-Louis Henri Polier* (Delhi: Oxford University Press, 2001), 101; and Polier to Oshra Mistri Gora, 7 Shawwal, in Alam and Alavi, *A European Experience of the Mughal Orient*, 113–114.
28 For more on this see Swati Chattopadhyay, "Anomalous Spaces: Representations of Dance Performance in Colonial India," in Prarthana Purakayastha and Anurima Banerjee, eds., *The Oxford Handbook of Indian Dance* (Delhi: Oxford University Press, 2023 forthcoming).
29 Malini Roy, "Origins of the Late Mughal Painting Tradition in Awadh," in Stephen Markel, and Tushara Bindu Gude, eds., *India's Fabled City: The Art of Courtly Lucknow*, 165–186 (Los Angeles: Los Angeles County Museum of Art and Del Monico Books, Prestel, 2011), 171.
30 Peter Alford Andrews, "The Generous Heart or the Mass of Clouds: the Court Tents of Shahjahan," *Muqarnas* vol. 4 (1987): 148–165.
31 See Chattopadhyay, *Representing Calcutta*.
32 Lady Maria Nugent, *Lady Nugent's East India Journal*, ed. Ashley L. Cohen (1839; London: Oxford University Press, 2014), 55.
33 Nugent, *Lady Nugent's East India Journal*, 59, 63 and passim.
34 Colesworthy Grant, *Anglo-Indian Domestic Sketch* (Calcutta: Thacker and Spink, 1862), 11.
35 W. S. Seton-Kerr, *Selections from Calcutta Gazettes*, vol 3 (Calcutta: Military Orphan Press, 1864), 567.
36 Chattopadhyay, *Representing Calcutta*, Chapter 2.
37 William Clerihew, "View of the Cenotaph and Governor's House seen from across the river, Barrackpore," 1843. Royal Institute of British Architects Collections, RIBA 37341.
38 The only other images of Calcutta drawn by British artists where terraces are clearly indicated are those drawn from the terraces and glacis of Fort William,

which no doubt was meant to be a power vantage. For example, William Hodges, "A view of Calcutta taken from Fort William," 1781. Line Engraving with etching by W. Byrne from Hodges' *Travels in India*, London, 1793; Samuel Davis, "View of Calcutta from Fort William," c 1805, Colored aquatint engraved by C. Duburh, 1807. See Jeremy Losty, *Calcutta City of Palaces* (London: British Library, 1990).

39 Kalyani Dutta notes that in her childhood, in the first half of the twentieth century, the *nyara chhad* was the place, among other found spaces, for school-going girls to hang out. Kalyani Dutta, *Thor Bori Khara* (Kolkata: Thema, 1998), 90.

40 For a good discussion and images of these terraces at #6 Dwarakanath Tagore Lane, see Suranjana Bhattacharya, *Kabi'r Abas*, vol. 1 (Kolkata: Ananda Publishers, 2015).

Chapter 11

1 Edith E. Cuthell, *My Garden in the City of Gardens: A Memory with Illustrations* (London: John Lane, 1905), 37–8.
2 Cuthell, *My Garden*, 3.
3 Cuthell, *My Garden*, 3.
4 Cuthell, *My Garden*, 163.
5 See Part Two of this volume. For earlier works, see Nupur Chaudhuri's discussion of the treatment of servants in "Memsahibs and their Servants in Nineteenth-centiry India," *Women's History Review* 3 (1994).
6 F.A. Steel and G. Gardiner, *The Complete Indian Housekeeper and Cook*, 7th ed. (London: William Heineman, 1909), 7. For a discussion of the empire of home, see Rosemary Marangoly George, "Homes in the empire, empires in the home," *Cultural Critique* (Winter 1993–4), 95–127; Mary Procida, *Married to the Empire: Gender, Politics and Imperialism in India, 1883–1947* (Manchester: Manchester University Press, 2002), Chapter 2; Alison Blunt, "Imperial Geographies of Home: British Domesticity in India, 1886–1925," *Transactions of the Institute of British Geographers*, New Series 24, no. 4 (1999), 421–40.
7 Swati Chattopadhyay, "Goods, Chattels and Sundry Items: Constructing Nineteenth-century Anglo-Indian Domestic Life," *Journal of Material Culture* 7, no. 3 (November 2002), 245–6.
8 Maud Divers, *The Englishwoman in India* (Edinburgh: W. Blackwood, 1909), 62.
9 I am indebted to Sudipta Sen for suggesting the phrase "everyday fussiness that comes with the plenitude of power."
10 Divers, *The Englishwoman in India*, 132–3. Most housekeeping guides for British women in India had something to say about it, and a good many memoirs by Englishwomen in India dwell on that topic. See Divers, *The Englishwoman in India*, 67. Even in the post-World War I years, Theodora

Coatman's "passing-out parade" in household management in Peshawar took the form of passing out dozens of dusters to a large household of servants. John Coatman, *Portrait of an Englishwoman* (London: Peter Skelton), 40.

11 See, for example, Ann Campbell Wilson's letters of her experience in northern India in the 1880s and 1890s: *Letters from India* (London: William Blackwood and Sons, 1911), 46.

12 An Anglo-Indian, *Indian Outfits and Establishment: A Practical Guide to Persons About to Reside in India* (London: L. Upcott Gill, 1882), 63.

13 Cuthell, *My Garden*, 12.

14 Cuthell, *My Garden*, 69–70.

15 Cuthell, *My Garden*, 121.

16 Cuthell, *My Garden*, 10.

17 For mutiny narratives constructed from site visits, see Manu Goswami, "'Englishness' on the Imperial Circuit: Victorian Englishness, Mutiny Tours in Colonial South Asia," *Journal of Historical Sociology* 9, no. 1 (1996), 54–84, and Ian Baucom, "The Path from War to Friendship: E. M. Forster's Mutiny Pilgrimage," *Out of Place: Englishness, Empire and the Locations of Identity* (Princeton: Princeton University Press, 1999), 101–34.

18 Edith married Captain Cuthell in the early 1870s at his first posting in Lucknow. Captain Cuthell began his military career with the 38th (1st Staffordshire) Regiment of Foot in 1865, and joined the 13th Hussars, Lucknow, in 1870 at the rank of Captain. He subsequently rose to the rank of Lieutenant Colonel.

19 Margaret Macmillan, *Women of the Raj* (London: Thames & Hudon, 1988), 154.

20 Cuthell, *My Garden*, 164.

21 Among her books based in India are a children's storybook, *Little Nellie's Days in India* (1883) and *In the Mutiny Days* (1892); the short story collections *Indian Idylls, by an Idle Exile* (1890) and *In Camp and Cantonment: Stories of Foreign Service* (1897); and two novels, *A Baireuth Pilgrimage* (1894) and *Sweet Irish Eyes* (1897).

22 Martin Heidegger, "The Thing," *Poetry, Language, Thought*, trans. and intro. Albert Hofstadter (New York: HarperCollins, 1971), 163–80.

23 Cuthell, *My Garden*, 74. *Chabutra* refers to a pavilion, in this case set in the garden.

24 Cuthell, *My Garden*, 74.

25 Cuthell, *My Garden*, 89.

26 Cuthell, *My Garden*, 89.

27 Swati Chattopadhyay, "Blurring Boundaries: the Limits of 'White' Town," *Representing Calcutta: Modernity, Nationalism and the Colonial Uncanny* (London: Routledge, 2005).

28 For a representative case of getting a "hold" on household matters, see Steel and Gardiner, *Complete Indian Housekeeper*, 3, 4–5, and A Lady Resident, *The Englishwoman in India*, 2nd ed. (London: Smith Elder and Co., 1865), 5.

29 Cuthell, *My Garden*, 196–7.
30 Cuthell, *My Garden*, 4.
31 Cuthell, *My Garden*, 5.
32 George F. Atkinson, *Curry and Rice on Forty Plates* (London: Day & Sons, 1859), n.p.
33 Cuthell, *My Garden*, 5.
34 Cuthell, *My Garden*, 70.
35 Cuthell, *My Garden*, 14.
36 Cuthell, *My Garden*, 195–6.
37 Cuthell, *My Garden*, 206–7.
38 Cuthell, *My Garden*, 209.
39 Cuthell, *My Garden*, 219.
40 Cuthell, *My Garden*, 277.
41 Cuthell, *My Garden*, 273.
42 Cuthell, *My Garden*, 119.
43 Cuthell, *My Garden*, 25.
44 Atkinson, *Curry and Rice*.
45 For a more detailed account, see Veena Talwar Oldenburg, *The Making of Colonial Lucknow, 1856–1877* (Princeton: Princeton University Press, 1984), Chapter 2.
46 Atkinson, *Curry and Rice on Forty Plates*, n.p.
47 Kenneth L. Ames, *Death in the Dining Room and Other Tales of Victorian Culture* (Philadelphia: Temple University Press, 1992), 196–9.
48 Ames, *Death in the Dining Room*, 202.
49 Ames, *Death in the Dining Room*, 203.
50 Atkinson, *Curry and Rice*, n.p.
51 See Chapter 7 in this volume.
52 I have extended this line of argument in a reading of "nautch" paintings in Chattopadhyay, "Anomalous Spaces: Representations of Dance Performance in Colonial India," in Prarthana Purakayastha and Anurima Banerjee, eds., *The Oxford Handbook of Indian Dance* (Delhi: Oxford University Press, 2023 forthcoming). See reference to one such painting in Chapter 10 in this volume.
53 Thomas Babington Macaulay, "Government of India," Speech Delivered in the House of Commons on the 10th of July 1833.
54 Indeed extraction of even more revenue would be foreseeable in exchange of good governance. The precise language is as follows: "If we have made a good pecuniary bargain for India, but a bad political bargain, if we have saved three or four millions to the finances of that country, and given to it, at the same time, pernicious institutions, we shall indeed have been practising a most ruinous parsimony. If, on the other hand, it shall be found that we have added fifty or a hundred thousand pounds a-year to the expenditure of an empire

which yields a revenue of twenty millions, but that we have at the same time secured to that empire, as far as in us lies, the blessings of good government, we shall have no reason to be ashamed of our profusion. I hope and believe that India will have to pay nothing. But on the most unfavourable supposition that can be made, she will not have to pay so much to the Company as she now pays annually to a single state pageant, to the titular Nabob of Bengal, for example, or the titular King of Delhi. What she pays to these nominal princes, who, while they did anything, did mischief, and who now do nothing, she may well consent to pay to her real rulers, if she receives from them, in return, efficient protection and good legislation."

55 Removal of crippling anomalies that create uncertainties would lead him to suggest a uniform code of laws.
56 Lieutenant Colonel Cuthell, Late 13th Hussars, "Practical Hints on Taxidermy," *The Boy's Own Book of Indoor Book and Recreations*, ed. G. A. Hutchison (Philadelphia: J. B. Lippincott Company, 1890), 298–307.
57 Cuthell, "Practical Hints," 302.
58 Cuthell, "Practical Hints," 304.
59 Cuthell, *My Garden*, 39.
60 Karen R. Jones, "Fantastic Beasts in the Great Indoors: Taxidermy, Animal Capital and the Domestic Interior, 1851–1921," *Home Cultures: The Journal of Architecture, Design and Domestic Space*, October 13, 2021.
61 Jones, "Fantastic Beasts," 7.
62 Donna Haraway, "Teddy Bear Patriarchy: Taxidermy in the Garden of Eden, New York City, 1908–1936," *Social Text*, no. 11 (Winter 1984–5), 23.
63 Haraway, "Teddy Bear Patriarchy," 25.
64 Cuthell, *My Garden*, 40.
65 William T. Hornaday with W. J. Holland, *Taxidermy and Zoological Collecting: A Complete Handbook for the Amateur Taxidermist, Collector, Osteologist, Museum-Builder, Sportsman, and Traveller* (New York: Charles Scribner's Sons, 1891), 99.

Chapter 12

1 Two of her mother's brothers lived at "home." Others had salaried jobs in Asansol and Dhaka. Rani Chanda, *Amar Ma'r Baper Bari* (My Mother's Father's House) (Calcutta: Visvabharati, 1977), 61.
2 Chanda, *Amar Ma'r Baper Bari*, 1.
3 Chanda, *Amar Ma'r Baper Bari*, Preface.
4 Rani Chanda's other works include *Purnakumbha* (1952), *Patheghate* (1978), *Jenana Phatak* (1983), *Sab Hotey Apan* (1984), and three biographies, *Alapchari Rabindranath* (1942), *Gurudev* (1962), and *Shilpaguru Abanindranath* (1972). *Jenana Phatak* was based on her experience of imprisonment in 1942 for her involvement in the nationalist movement.

5 Chanda, *Amar Ma'r Baper Bari*, 136.
6 Kathleen Stewart, *Ordinary Affects* (Durham, NC: Duke University Press, 2007), 3–4.
6 Chanda, *Amar Ma'r Baper Bari*, 12.
7 I am grateful to Arijit Sen for discussion on this point.
8 Pargana is an administrative unit, a subdivision.
9 Chanda, *Amar Ma'r Baper Bari*, 1.
10 See Chapter 8 in this volume for a discussion of the daowa as architectural form.
11 Chanda, *Amar Ma'r Baper Bari*, 7. Angyina in Bengali or *angna* in Hindi refers to a forecourt or courtyard.
12 Chanda, *Amar Ma'r Baper Bari*, 9.
13 Chanda, *Amar Ma'r Baper Bari*, 66.
14 Chanda, *Amar Ma'r Baper Bari*, 66–8.
15 Chanda, *Amar Ma'r Baper Bari*, 7–8.
16 Chanda, *Amar Ma'r Baper Bari*, 6–7. Other sources such as Mukul Dey's reminiscences note the name of the village as Sridharpur.
17 In a discussion of the politics of women's domestic labor and its aestheticization in colonial Bengal, see Utsa Ray, *Culinary Culture in Colonial India: A Cosmopolitan Platter and the Middle Class* (Cambridge: Cambridge University Press, 2015), 130–3. Reading Rani Chanda's description as simply ideology misses something important about the mode of narration and why small spaces such as kitchens needed an aesthetic code.
18 Chanda, *Amar Ma'r Baper Bari*, 104.
19 Chanda, *Amar Ma'r Baper Bari*, 66.
20 Chanda, *Amar Ma'r Baper Bari*, 39.
21 Mukul Dey, "My Reminiscences," *The Statesman*, Calcutta, 1938.
22 Chanda, *Amar Ma'r Baper Bari*, 72–3.
23 Chanda, *Amar Ma'r Baper Bari*, 127–9.
24 This is the term used by Sanjoy Chakraborty, "Alpona and Chittagong Ailbana," 1st Karnaphuli Folk Triennial Publication, Chittagong Bangladesh & *Kolal, A Research Journal*, 2015.
25 See Gurusaday Dutta, *Banglar Lokshilpa o Loknritya* (Kolkata: Chatim Books, 2000), 183–9. Chakraborty cites Rabindranath's letter to Surendranath Dasgupta of Chittagong requesting "vintage" examples of alpona: "Alpona and Chittagong Ailbana."
26 Nandalal Bose, *Shilpakatha* (Kolkata: Viswabharati Granthan Bibhag, 1944); Sudhangshu Kumar Roy, "Banglar Alpona," in *Meyeli Brata Bishoye* (Kolkata: Loksanskriti Gabeshana Parishad, 1995); Swati Ghosh, *Rabindrabhavanay Santiniketan'e Alpona* (Kolkata: Ananda Publishers, 2011) and *Design Movement in Tagore's Santiniketan—Alpana, An Experiment in Aestheticism* (Delhi: Niyogi Books, 2018).

27 Chanda, *Amar Ma'r Baper Bari*, 48–50.
28 Chanda, *Amar Ma'r Baper Bari*, 48.
29 Chanda, *Amar Ma'r Baper Bari*, 1.
30 Chanda, *Amar Ma'r Baper Bari*, 5.
31 *Boyndi* refers to elder sister in the local dialect, and *bhai* is brother.
32 Chanda, *Amar Ma'r Baper Bari*, 5.
33 Chanda, *Amar Ma'r Baper Bari*, 9–10.
34 Chanda, *Amar Ma'r Baper Bari*, 14–18.
35 Chanda, *Amar Ma'r Baper Bari*, 39–41.
36 Chanda, *Amar Ma'r Baper Bari*, 39–41.
37 Chanda, *Amar Ma'r Baper Bari*, 106–7.
38 Chanda, *Amar Ma'r Baper Bari*, 115–16.
39 Chanda, *Amar Ma'r Baper Bari*, 9.
40 Chanda, *Amar Ma'r Baper Bari*, 136.
41 The dreaded diseases were malaria and cholera. The incidence of malaria had increased rapidly with the construction of the railways in eastern Bengal that impeded natural draining and led to water stagnation.
42 A growing body of works has attempted to understand the complexity of floods in colonial Bengal and how one might effectively understand floods as process. See, for example, Christopher V. Hill, "Water and power: Riparian legislation and agrarian control in colonial Bengal," *Environmental History Review* 14, no. 4 (1990), 1–20, and *River of Sorrow: Environment and Social Control in Riparian North India, 1770–1994* (Ann Arbor: Association for Asian Studies, 1997); Rohan D'Souza, *Drowned and Dammed: Colonial Capitalism and Flood Control in Eastern India* (New Delhi: Oxford University Press, 2006); and "Event, Process and Pulse: Resituating Floods in Environmental Histories of India," *Environment and History* 26 (2020), 31–49; Iftekhar Iqbal, *The Bengal Delta: Ecology, State and Social Change, 1840–1943* (New York: Palgrave Macmillan, 2010); K. Kuntala Lahiri-Dutt and Gopa Samanta, *Dancing with the River: People and Life on the Chars of South Asia* (New Haven: Yale University Press, 2013); Nitin Sinha, "Fluvial Landscapes and the State: Property and the Gangetic Diaras in Colonial India, 1790s–1890s," *Environment and History* 20 (2014), 209–37.
43 Chanda, *Amar Ma'r Baper Bari*, 61.
44 Chanda, *Amar Ma'r Baper Bari*, 140.
45 Susan Stewart, *On Longing: Narratives of the Miniature, the Gigantic, the Souvenir, the Collection* (Durham, NC: Duke University Press, 1993), 23.
46 Joya Chatterjee, "The Fashioning of a Frontier: The Radcliffe Line and Bengal's Border Landscape, 1947–52," *Modern Asian Studies* 33, no. 1 (February 1999), 223.
47 Chatterjee, "The Fashioning of a Frontier," 225.

Chapter 13

1. Rabindranath Tagore, *Boyhood Days* (*Chelebela*), trans. Radha Chakravarty (New Delhi: Puffin Classics, 2007), 48. In the references that follow, I have indicated where I have used Radha Chakravarty's translation. When I have resorted to my own translation I have indicated the original source in *Rabindra Rachanabali*.
2. Rabindranath Tagore, *Char Adhyay* (Four Episodes), Rabindra Rachanabali, vol. 9 (Calcutta: Visvabharati, 1994).
3. Rabindranath was at least 7 years old at that time and it is likely that the parapet walls of the *andarmahal* terrace at that time were higher than the extant one.
4. Garden of the Singha family.
5. Rabindranath Tagore, "Jibansmriti," *Rabindra Rachanabali*, vol. 9 (Calcutta: Visvabharati, 1994), 416.
6. Rabindranath, "Jibansmriti," 411.
7. Rabindranath, "Jibansmriti," 411.
8. Uma Dasgupta, *Rabindranath Tagore: My Life and Words* (New Delhi: Penguin, 2006), xii.
9. Rabindranath, "Jibansmriti," 411.
10. Rabindranath, "Jibansmriti," 412.
11. For Rabindranath's views on history, see Dipesh Chakrabarty, *The Calling of History: Jadunath Sarkar and his Empire of Truth* (Chicago: University of Chicago Press, 2015).
12. In this connection, see Dipesh Chakrabarty's explanation of the idea of imagination in Rabindranath's poetry: "Nation and Imagination," *Provincializing Europe* (Princeton: Princeton University Press, 2000).
13. The ostensible reason for their strained relationship was Digambari's objecting to Dwarakanath's relaxing the strictures of Hinduism, including serving forbidden meat and liquor to his European guests.
14. Dwarakanath's youngest son Nagendranath died at the age of 29, without children, and his wife Tripurasundari Debi was given property elsewhere in Calcutta.
15. These are the house numbers found in plans from the late nineteenth century. These numbers have since been changed.
16. Extended family here refers to both multigenerational living and the siblings with their spouses and children living in the same house with other relatives.
17. Rabindranath Tagore, *Boyhood Days*, 48–50.
18. Sumintendranath Tagore's recollection of these rituals in the 1930s and early 1940s contains wonderful details. Sumintendranath Tagore, *Thakurbarir Jana Ajana* (Kolkata: Mitra & Ghosh, 2001), 58–9.
19. Purnima Debi, *Thakurbariri Gaganthakur* (Calcutta: Punascha, 1999), 68.
20. Purnima Debi, *Thakurbariri Gaganthakur*, 47.

NOTES

21 Rabindranath Tagore, *Boyhood Days*, 48.
22 Rabindranath, "Jibansmriti," 448.
23 Rabindranath, "Jibansmriti," 458.
24 Rabindranath, "Jibansmriti," 488.
25 In this context, see my discussion of Rabindranath's *Strir Patra* for an elaboration of *abasar* as expressed through the protagonist Mrinal, who needed to step out of marital bonds to claim such a space. Chattopadhyay, *Representing Calcutta*, 250.
26 Purnima Debi, *Thakurbariri Gaganthakur*, 10–11.
27 Purnima Debi, *Thakurbariri Gaganthakur*, 64.
28 Abadindranath Tagore, "Apankatha," *Abanindra Rachanabali*, vol. 1 (Kolkata: Prakash Bhavan 1973), 45–7.
29 Rabindranath Tagore, "Chelebela," *Rabindra Rachanabali*, vol. 9, 725.
30 Rabindranath, "Chelebela," 466.
31 Rabindranath, "Chelebela," 466.
32 For a charming description of this, see Abanindranath Tagore, "Gharoa," *Abanindra Rachanabali*, vol. 1 (Calcutta: Prakash Bhavan, 1973), 93–5.
33 Purnima Debi, *Thakurbariri Gaganthakur*, 59–60. These prayer meetings could be seen and heard from the next-door terrace at No. 5.
34 Rabindranath, "Chelebela," 726.
35 Sarala Debi, *Jibaner Jharapata* (Kolkata: Subarnarekha, 2007), 16.
36 Rabindranath, *Boyhood Days*, 63.
37 Rabindranath, "Chelebela," 732.
38 Rabindranath., *Boyhood Days*, 62–3.
39 Rabindranath., *Boyhood Days*, 38.
40 Rabindranath, "Jibansmriti," 508–10.
41 Rabindranath, "Jibansmriti," 509.
42 Rabindranath, "Jibansmriti," 491.
43 Saudamini Debi, Debendranath's eldest daughter, recalled that their neighbors complained that the young women could be *seen* on the rooftop terrace. Saudamini Debi, *Pitrismriti*, cited in Chitra Deb, *Antahpurer Antahkatha* (Kolkata: Ananda Publishers, 1992), 32.
44 Abanindranath Tagore, "Apankatha," *Abanindra Rachanabali*, vol. 1 (Calcutta: Prakash Bhavan, 1973), 12.
45 Niradchandra Chaudhuri, *Aji Hote Satabarsha Aage* (Kolkata: Mitra and Ghosh, 2000), 26. Nirad Chaudhuri's various recollections of Calcutta life contain snippets of information on terraces and views from terraces. For a description of pigeon flying, see p. 32. For the story of his infatuation with a young woman whom he saw drying clothes on the rooftop terrace next door, see Niradchandra Chaudhuri, *Amar Debottor Sampatti* (Kolkata: Ananda Publishers, 2013), 211–12.
46 Sumitendranath Tagore, *Thakurbarir Jana Ajana*, 75–6.

47 For descriptions of pigeon and kite flying in Dhaka in the early twentieth century, see Paritosh Sen, *Jindabahar O Ananya Rachana* (Kolkata: Punascha, 2003).
48 Sumitendranath Tagore, *Thakurbarir Jana Ajana*, 75–6.
49 Sisir Kumar Basu, *Basubari* (Kolkata: Ananda Publishers, 1995), 26.
50 Basu, *Basubari*, 74.
51 See Partha Chatterjee, "Two Poets and Death: Civil Society in a non-Christian World," in Timothy Mitchell and Lila Abu-Lughod, eds., *Questions of Modernity* (Minneapolis: University of Minnesota Press, 2000), for one of the controversies on the form and format of public meetings, in this case the memorial meeting held after novelist Bankim Chandra Chattopadhyay passed away in 1894.
52 Swati Chattopadhyay, "Politics, Planning, and Subjection: Anticolonial Nationalism and Public Space in Calcutta," in *City Halls and Civic Materialism: Towards a Global History of Urban Public Space* (London: Routledge, 2014), 199–216.

Chapter 14

1 Nii Kwate Owoo, *You Hide Me* (1970), 16 mins, b/w.
2 Owoo in interview with Agustina Andreoletti, Cinema RESIST!, *Nii Kwate Owoo on his film You Hide Me*, posted May 11, 2021, https://www.youtube.com/watch?v=W2EHjYjtdeg.
3 Interview with Agustina Andreoletti.
4 Robert Young, "The Violent State," *Naked Punch Supplement*, Issue 2 (October 2009), http://www.nakedpunch.com/articles/38.
5 Bénédicte Savoy, *Africa's Struggle for its Arts: History of a Postcolonial Defeat* (Princeton: Princeton University Press, 2022), 13.
6 Savoy, *Africa's Struggle*, 83–6.
7 Savoy, *Africa's Struggle*, 38.
8 Savoy points out that these kinds of arguments were made even whether museum officials knew that their museum buildings and storage facilities were failing by their own standards.
9 Savoy, *Africa's Struggle*, 7.
10 Quoted in Savoy, *Africa's Struggle*, 124.
11 I am thinking of the way that Fred Moten considers fugitive practices. Fred Moten, "The Case of Blackness," *Criticism* 50, no. 2 (Spring 2008), 177–218.
12 Frantz Fanon used the term "occult instability" to refer to the native's estrangement from their own culture with the onslaught of colonialism. Frantz Fanon, *Wretched of the Earth* (London: Penguin, 1967 [1961]), 183.
13 Danielle Bobker, *The Closet: the Eighteenth-century Architecture of Intimacy* (Princeton: Princeton University Press, 2020).

14 Niradchandra Chaudhuri, *Aji Hotey Sata Barsha Aage* (Kolkata: Mitra and Ghosh, 1999), 9.
15 Chaudhuri, *Aji Hotey*, 9.
16 Niradchandra Chaudhuri, *Amar Debottor Sampatti*, 6th ed. (Kolkata: Ananda Publishers, 2013), 149.
17 In Iris Macfarlane's bungalow in a tea plantation in Assam a tin roof replaced thatch only in the mid-1950s—with the result that instead of the muffled sound of rain on the roof, rain sounded loud and rattling. Alan Macfarlane, ed., *Twenty Years in Tea: The Letters of Iris Macfarlane from Assam Tea Gardens, 1946–65* (2019), 37–8, https://doi.org/10.17863/CAM.57018.
18 Charlotte Ashby and Mark Crinson, eds., "Grey Zones," in *Building/Object: Shared and Contested Territories of Design and Architecture* (London: Bloomsbury, 2022), 20.
19 Romita Ray, "Ornamental Exotica: Transplanting the Aesthetics of Tea Consumption and the Birth of a British Exotic," in Yota Batsaki, Sarah Burke Cahalan, and Anatole Tchikine, eds., *The Botany of Empire in the Long Eighteenth Century* (Washington, DC: Dumbarton Oaks, 2016); Luke Keogh, *The Wardian Case: How a Simple Box Moved Plants and Changed the World* (Chicago: University of Chicago Press, 2020).
20 Advertisement in the Calcutta Directory, 1920.
21 Eliot James, *A Guide to Indian Household Management* (London: Ward, Lock and Co., *c.* 1880), 22–3.
22 James, *A Guide*, 26.
23 F. A. Steel and G. Gardiner, *The Complete Indian Housekeeper and Cook*, 7th ed. (London: William Heineman, 1909), 202.
24 Steel and Gardiner, *The Complete Indian Housekeeper*, 200–1.
25 Steel and Gardiner, *The Complete Indian Housekeeper*, 202.
26 Steel and Gardiner, *The Complete Indian Housekeeper*, 201.
27 Bobker, *The Closet*, 20.
28 Mud and thatch carry social and cultural significance that are not perfectly aligned with their material properties. Thatch and mud as symbols of poverty are patently modern constructs. For more on this, see Sheetal Chhabria, *Making a Modern Slum: The Power of Capital in Colonial Bombay* (Seattle: Washington University Press, 2019).
29 Tim Ingold, "Bringing Things to Life: Creative Entanglements in a World of Materials," ESRC National Center for Research Methods, NCRM Working Paper Series (July 2010).

Chapter 15

1 John Coatman (1889–1963) served in the British colonial government in various capacities. He joined the Indian Police Service in 1910 and served with Frontier Constabulary between 1914 and 1919. He studied at Pembroke

College, Oxford, and returned to India in 1926 where he was a member of the Indian Legislative Assembly and the Director of Public Information. He was Professor of Indian Economic Relations, University of London, funded by the Imperial Marketing Board, between 1930 and 1934, https://www.nottingham.ac.uk/research/groups/conferencing-the-international/delegates/people.aspx?id=e31b0f1c-40f2-416d-a5ea-8c543c59f150.

2 John Coatman, *Portrait of an Englishwoman* (London: n.p., 1960), 163.
3 Coatman, *Portrait*, 84.
4 Coatman, *Portrait*, 47.
5 Coatman, *Portrait*, 125.
6 Coatman, *Portrait*, 65.
7 Coatman, *Portrait*, 48.
8 Coatman, *Portrait*, 44.
9 Coatman, *Portrait*, 42–3.
10 Coatman, *Portrait*, 48–9.
11 Homi Bhabha, *The Location of Culture* (London: Routledge, 1994).
12 The conceptual link between gardening and political acumen and ambition is old. Monarchs frequently styled themselves as cultivators par excellence. This tradition of thought had been well established in modern politics since the eighteenth century—Horace Walpole, Lord Shaftesbury, George Washington, Thomas Jefferson, James Madison, to name just a handful, were known for their views on gardening.
13 Sara Jeanette Duncan, *On the Other Side of the Latch* (London: Metheun & Co., 1901), 230.
14 Duncan, *On the Other Side*, 199–200.
15 Duncan, *On the Other Side*, 231.
16 Landolicus, *The Indian Amateur Gardener*, 4th ed. R. Ledlie (Calcutta: W. Newman & Co., 1936), 294.
17 Thomas F. Gieryn, "Boundary-Work and the Demarcation of Science from Non-Science: Strains and Interests in Professional Ideologies of Scientists," *American Sociological Review* 48, no. 6 (1983), 781–95.
18 Gieryn, "Boundary-Work," 782.
19 Stephen Frenkel, "Jungle Stories: North American Representations of Tropical Panama," *Geographical Review* 86, no. 3 (July 1996), 330–1.
20 Frenkel, "Jungle Stories," 328.
21 Margaret Willes, *The Gardens of the English Working Class* (New Haven: Yale University Press, 2014).
22 Alan Macfarlane, ed., *Twenty Years in Tea: The Letters of Iris Macfarlane from Assam Tea Gardens, 1946–65*, 146, https://www.repository.cam.ac.uk/handle/1810/309918.
23 *Viceregal Establishments in India* (New Delhi: The Governor-General's Press, 1949), 3.

24 G. Marshall Woodrow, *Gardening in India*, 3rd ed. (Bombay: Bombay Education Society Press, 1903), 1.
25 Agnes W. Harler, *The Garden in the Plains*, 4th ed. (London: Oxford University Press, 1962), 3.
26 Harler, *The Garden*, 11.
27 Harler, *The Garden*, 14–15.
28 Harler, *The Garden*, 16–17.
29 David Arnold, "Agriculture and 'Improvement' in Early Colonial India: a Pre-History of Development," *Journal of Agrarian Change* 5, no. 4 (2005), 505–25; Laura Tavolacci, "Vegetable Gardens versus Cash Crops: Science and Political Economy in the Agricultural and Horticultural Society of India, 1820–40," *History Workshop Journal* 88 (Autumn 2019), 24–46.
30 For discussion of dismissal of indigenous knowledge of plants, see Kavita Philip, "Global Botanical Networks, Political Economy, and Environmentalist Discourses in Cinchona Transplantation to British India," *Revue francaise d'histoire d'outre-mer* (1999), 119–42.
31 Woodrow, *Gardening*, 123–5.
32 Woodrow, *Gardening*, 123.
33 Woodrow, *Gardening*, 125.
34 Margaret Willes, *The Making of the English Gardener* (New Haven: Yale University Press, 2011); Mark Laird, *A Natural History of English Gardening 1650–1800* (New Haven: Yale University Pres, 2015).
35 Woodrow, *Gardening*, 134.
36 Woodrow, *Gardening*, 134.
37 For elaborate instructions on filling out beds with flowering plants, see, for example, Landilocus, *The Indian Amateur Gardener*, 306.
38 Willes, *The Making of the English Gardener*, 60; Mark Laird, *A Natural History*, 46–9.
39 Only in horticulture and botanical gardens, government houses, and similar buildings that had a very large number of gardeners do we see the toolshed as a defined entity.
40 Elizabeth Kent, *Flora Domestica or the Portable Flower-Garden* (London: Taylor and Hessey, 1823).
41 See Chapter 11 in this volume.
42 Iris Macfarlane, *Daughters of the Empire: A Memoir of Life and Times in the British Raj* (Oxford: Oxford University Press, 1996), 163.
43 Macfarlane, *Daughters of the Empire*, 164.
44 Macfarlane, ed., *Twenty Years in Tea*, 37–8.
45 Macfarlane, ed., *Twenty Years in Tea*, 85.
46 Macfarlane, ed., *Twenty Years in Tea*, 164.
47 Macfarlane, *Daughters of the Empire*, 163.
48 Macfarlane, *Daughters of the Empire*, 146.

49 Macfarlane, *Daughters of the Empire*, 146–7.
50 Macfarlane, *Daughters of the Empire*, 146.
51 Dell Upton, "The Seen, Unseen and Scene," in Paul Groth and Todd W. Bressi, eds., *Understanding Ordinary Landscapes* (New Haven: Yale University Press, 1997), 176.
52 Macfarlane, *Daughters of the Empire*, 160.
53 Macfarlane, *Daughters of the Empire*, 162.
54 Macfarlane, *Daughters of the Empire*, 160–1.
55 Homi Bhabha, *The Location of Culture*.
56 Michael R. Dove, "Forest Discourses in South and Southeast Asia: A Comparison with Global Discourses," in Paul Greenough and Anna Tsing, eds., *Nature in the Global South: Environmental Projects in South and Southeast Asia* (Durham, NC: Duke University Press, 2003), 107–9.
57 For a genealogy of the English idea of waste, see Vittoria Di Palma, *Wasteland: A History* (New Haven: Yale University Press, 2014).
58 The discourse on wastelands did not die off by the late nineteenth century as Vittoria Di Palma suggests; its trailing off in England was accompanied by an expansion of the idea in the colonies. The Forestry Acts in late-nineteenth-century India are critical to understand the displacement of this discourse and the contribution of the idea of waste to imperial expansion.
59 Major Browne, *India Tracts Containing A Description of the Jungle Terry Districts* (London: n.p., 1788), 11, 25, 54, 66.
60 Evelien de Hoop and Saurabh Aurora, "Material Meanings: 'Waste' as a Performative Category of Land in Colonial India," *Journal of Historical Geography* 55 (2017), 87.
61 Vinay K. Gidwani, "'Waste' and the Permanent Settlement in Bengal," *Economic and Political Weekly* 27, no. 4 (January 25, 1992): PE 39–PE 46.
62 For example, the Sunderbans is referred to as "woods infested by tygers" as well as "thick jungles" by James Rennell in the 1760s, as "jungle" by W. E. Morrieson *c.* 1814, and "forest" with intertwined and immense trees and low brushwood. For a discussion of these, see Swati Chattopadhyay, "Traverse, Territory and the Ecological Uncanny: James Rennell and the Mapping of the Gangetic Plains," in Karen Bishop, ed., *The Cartographic Necessity of Exile* (London: Routledge, 2016), 89–109.
63 K. Sivaramakrishnan, personal communication with author, March 31, 2022.
64 For various perspectives on the specificity of the use of the term "jungle" to refer to tropical forests, see Frenkel, "Jungle Stories"; Meg Fumiss Weisberg, "Jungle and Desert in Postcolonial Texts: Intertextual Ecosystems," *Cambridge Journal of Postcolonial Literary Inquiry* 2, no. 2 (2015), 173.
65 Weisberg, "Jungle and Desert," 173.
66 For clearing a "sanitated zone" in the "jungles," see Frenkel's discussion of the Canal Zone at the head of the Panama Canal in "Jungle Stories."

67 For an excellent study of such reclamation, removal, and afforestation of land that was seen as waste, see Dotan Halevy, "Sand and the City: On Colonial Development and its Evasive Enemies in Twentieth-century Palestine," *Environment and History* (February 2022), doi: 10.3197/096734022X16384451127302.

68 Macfarlane, *Twenty Years in Tea*, 319–20.

69 Macfarlane, *Daughters of the Empire*, 146.

Chapter 16

1 The number of bookshelves is specified in his will, dated 1875. Santosh Kumar Adhikary, *Vidyasagarer Jibaner Shesh Dinguli* (Kolkata: Ananya Prakashan, 1986), 115.

2 Vidyasagar's son had carelessly sold off some of his books, ignoring the instructions in the will. Subsequently the Raja of Lalgola purchased the book collection and donated the bulk of it to the Bangiya Sahitya Parishat Library in 1913. This collection of books from Vidyasagar's library at present contains 324 Sanskrit and Bengali *puthi* (manuscripts), 322 Sanskrit and Hindi books, 191 Bengali books, and 2,910 books in English. Ramenkumar Sar, "Bangiya Sahitya Parishade Vidyasagar Samgraha," Vidyasagar Special Issue, *Bangiya Sahitya Parishat Patrika* 126, no. 4. (2020), 206–8.

3 Sambhuchandra Vidyaratna, *Vidyasagar Jibancharit o Brhamanirash* (Kolkata: Chirayata Prakashan, 1992), 122.

4 B. Venkat Mani, *Recoding World Literature* (New York: Fordham University Press, 2017), 52.

5 For the spatial significance of the library in early modern England, see Susie West, "An architectural typology of the early modern country house library, 1660–1720," *Library* 14, no. 4 (2013), 441–64.

6 Walter Benjamin, "Unpacking my Library," *Illuminations*, trans. Harry Zohn (New York: Schocken Books, 1969).

7 Benjamin, "Unpacking," 59.

8 In this context, see Amitav Ghosh, "The March of the Novel Through History: The Testimony of My Grandfather's Bookcase," *The Kenyon Review* 20, no. 2 (Spring 1998), 13–24.

9 Bernard S. Cohn, "The Command of Languages and the Languages of Command," *Colonialism and its Forms of Knowledge: The British in India* (Princeton: Princeton University Press, 1995), 16–56.

10 Thomas Babington Macaulay, "Minute on Education," 1835.

11 See, for example, Angel Rama, *The Lettered City*, trans. John Charle Chasteen (Durham, NC: Duke University Press, 1996); Elizabeth Hill Boone and Walter D. Mignolo, eds., *Writing without Words: Alternative Literacies in Mesoamerica and the Andes* (Durham, NC: Duke University Press, 1994); José Rabasa, *Tell Me the Story of How I Conquered You: Elsewheres and*

Ethnosuicide in the Colonial Mesoamerican World (Austin: University of Texas Press, 2011).

12 Modhumita Roy, "The Englishing of India," *Social Scientist* 21 (May–June 1993), 36–62.

13 Instruction in Indian languages was also instituted at the East India College at Haileybury in 1807.

14 David Price, *Memoirs of the Early Life and Service of a Field Officer on the Retired List of the Indian Army* (London: W. H. Allen, 1839), 446. About the number of books in the library, see the discussion of Joshua Ehrlich, "Plunder and Prestige: Tipu Sultan's Library and the Making of British India," *South Asia: Journal of South Asia Studies* 43, no. 3 (2020), 478–92.

15 Ehrlich, "Plunder and Prestige."

16 Ehrlich, "Plunder and Prestige," 482–3.

17 Ehrlich, "Plunder and Prestige," 483.

18 Incidentally the location of the library next to the private compartments away from state rooms was a practice also followed in early modern English country houses. See Susie West, "Studies and status: spaces for books in seventeenth-century Penhurst Place, Kent," *Transactions of the Cambridge Bibliographic Society* 12, no. 3 (2002), 266–92.

19 Alexander Beatson, *A View of the Origin and Conduct with the War with Tipoo Sultaun* (London: W. Bulmer and Co., 1800), 179; Price, *Memoirs*, 446.

20 Ehrlich, "Plunder and Prestige," 483.

21 Price, *Memoirs*, 445.

22 Price, *Memoirs*, 445.

23 Price, *Memoirs*, 446. Captain Price, one of the officers in charge of selecting manuscripts from Tipu's library, conveyed his desire to possess a book on magic which he considered to be "an article of extraordinary rarity and value" because of its beautifully executed "diagrams, and pictorial illustrations."

24 Beatson, *A View of the Origin*, 179, 195–7.

25 Henry Petroski, *The Book on the Bookshelf* (New York: Alfred Knopf, 1999), 57–8.

26 Petroski, *The Book*, 57–8.

27 Price, *Memoirs*, 447.

28 Ehrlich, "Plunder and Prestige," 488.

29 Ehrlich, "Plunder and Prestige," 488–9.

30 Peter Gordon, "The Oriental Repository at the India House," typescript notes, British Library Mss Eur D 656, p. 3.

31 For a discussion of this image see Swati Chattopadhyay, *Representing Calcutta*, 37–8.

32 Ehrlich, "Plunder and Prestige', 491.

33 Gordon, "The Oriental Repository," 13.

34 Gordon, "The Oriental Repository," 15.

35 Gordon, "The Oriental Repository," 14.
36 Abulfazal M. Fazle Kabir, "English Libraries in Eighteenth-century Bengal," *The Journal of Library History* 14, no. 4 (Fall 1979), 436–56.
37 Purnima Thakur, *Thakurbarir Gaganthakur* (Kolkata: Punascha, 1999); Gautam Bhadra, *Nyara Battlalay Jay K'bar* (Kolkata: Chhaatim: 2011); Anindita Ghosh, "Coming of the Book, Early Print Cultures in Colonial India," *Book History* 6 (2003), 23–55.
38 Bhavanicharan Bandopadhyay, *Kalikata Kamalalaya*, ed. Bishnu Basu (1823; Kolkata: Pratibhas, 1986).
39 Bandopadhyay, *Kalikata Kamalalaya*, 140–1.
40 Originating in the Latin *armarium* for "closed cabinet" in which all kinds of valuable objects would be stored, it had come down as *armoire, almery, almirah*. Petroski, *The Book on the Bookshelf*, 63.
41 The large library of the Sobhabazar Rajbari occupied the long hall next to the outer courtyard, a connecting piece between the public spaces organized around the courtyard and the Natmandir—meeting hall—built as a separate structure to facilitate political and social gatherings. See Swati Chattopadhyay, *Representing Calcutta*, Chapter 3.
42 See Chapter 14 in this volume.
43 For a cinematic recreation of this mode of spatial connection, see Satyajit Ray's *Charulata* (1964), where a verandah links Charulata's private apartments and the library.
44 Sashibhusan Basu, "Vidyasagar Smriti," *Prabashi*, Sravana, Bengali 1343 (July–August 1936), 584, cited in Indramitra, *Karunasagar Vidyasagar* (1969; Kolkata: Ananda Publishers, 1997), 29.
45 Indramitra, *Karunasagar Vidyasagar* (1969; Kolkata: Ananda Publishers, 1997), 12. For another description of this space, see Dinesh Chandra Sen, *Gharer Katha o Jugasahitya* (1922; Kalikata: Jignasa, 1960), 130.
46 Vidyasagar, when he visited friends in their *baithakhana*, always sat on a chair.
47 Partha Chatterjee, *The Nation and Its Fragments* (Princeton: Princeton University Press, 1993).
48 He returned insulted, but penned a letter of complaint where he discussed the superstitious practices of the British regarding footwear (and implicitly hypocritical practice, as they refused to take off their shoes where Indians did).
49 Chatterjee, *The Nation and Its Fragments*, 54.
50 Chatterjee, *The Nation and Its Fragments*, 52–3. These English terms appear in chapter headings, in parentheses and footnotes, and form part of a citational apparatus that is remarkable for its bibliomigrancy.
51 Brian A. Hatcher, *Vidyasagar: The Life and After-Life of an Eminent Indian* (London: Routledge, 2014), 44.
52 Mahendranath Gupta, *Sri Sri Ramakrishna Kathamrita* (Kolkata: Kamini Prakashaloy, 2001), 453–4.

Chapter 17

1. Indramitra, *Karunasagar Vidyasagar* (1969; Kolkata: Ananda Publishers, 1997), 12.
2. Indramitra, *Karunasagar*, 62.
3. Indramitra, *Karunasagar*, 49, 601–2.
4. Indramitra, *Karunasagar*, 126.
5. See Chapter 14 in this volume.
6. These books are now housed in the Bangiya Sahitya Parishad Library, Kolkata.
7. Indramitra, *Karunasagar*.
8. Surinder M. Bhardwaj, "Homoeopathy in India," in Giri Raj Gupta, ed., *The Social and Cultural Context of Medicine in India* (Delhi: Vikas Publications, 1981).
9. David Arnold and Sumit Sarkar, "In Search of Rational Remedies: Homeopathy in Nineteenth-century Bengal," in W. Ernst, ed., *Plural Medicine, Tradition and Modernity, 1800–2000* (London: Routledge, 2002), 43.
10. Cited in Arnold and Sarkar, "In Search of Rational Remedies," 46.
11. Shinjini Das, "Debating Scientific Medicine: Homoeopathy and Allopathy in Late Nineteenth-century Medical Print in Bengal," *Medical History* 56, no. 4 (2012), 463–80.
12. Das, "Debating Scientific Medicine," 473.
13. Shinjini Das, "Healing the Home: Indigeneity, Self-Help and the Hindu Joint Family," *Vernacular Medicine in Colonial India* (Cambridge: Cambridge University Press, 2019), 155–99. There is a much larger literature that addresses the role of medicine in colonial India, including David Arnold, *Colonising the Body: State Medicine and Epidemic Disease in Nineteenth Century India* (Berkeley: University of California Press, 1993) and *Science, Technology and Medicine in Colonial India*, New Cambridge History of India III: 5 (Cambridge: Cambridge University Press, 2000); Mark Harrison, *Public Health in British India: Anglo India Preventive Medicine 1859–1914* (Cambridge: Cambridge University Press, 1994); Mark Harrison and Biswamoy Pati, eds., *Health, Medicine and Empire: Perspectives on Colonial India* (New Delhi: Orient Longman, 2001); Kavita Sivaramakrishnan, *Old Potions, New Bottles: Recasting Indigenous Medicine in Colonial Punjab, 1850–1945* (Hyderabad: Orient Longman, 2006); Projit Bihari Mukharji, *Nationalising the Body: The Medical Market, Print and Daktari Medicine* (London: Anthem Press, 2009); Ishita Pande, *Medicine, Race and Liberalism in British Bengal: Symptoms of Empire* (London: Routledge, 2009); Rachel Berger, *Ayurveda Made Modern: Political Histories of Indigenous Medicine,1900–1955* (Basingstoke: Palgrave Macmillan, 2013).
14. Das, "Epilogue: A Familiar Science," *Vernacular Medicine in Colonial India*, 246.

15 For more on vernacularization, see Brian A. Hatcher, *Idioms of Improvement: Vidyasagar and Cultural Encounter in Bengal* (Oxford: Oxford University Press, 1996).
16 Advertisement by Savory and Moore, London; Dinneford & Co., London; C. K.Sen & Co. Calcutta, in Bengal Directory (Calcutta: Thacker & Spink, 1875); and Butto Kristo Paul, Bengal Directory (Calcutta: Thacker & Spink, 1918).
17 Advertisement in homeopathy book published by Berini & Co., 12 Lalbazar, Calcutta, 1875. This emphasis on pure and imported merchandise continued well into the twentieth century. For a representative advertisement of "Pure American Homeopathic Medicine" from 1928, see Das, "Healing the Home," 170.
18 Kulachandra Dey, *Homeogatha* (Kalikata: Kuntalin Press, 1907).
19 Dey, *Homeogatha*, i.
20 Dey, *Homeogatha*, i.
21 Rani Chanda, *Amar Ma'r Baper Bari* (My Mother's Father's House) (Calcutta: Viswabharati, 1977), 122.
22 Dey, *Homeogatha*, i.
23 Chanda, *Amar Ma'r Baper Bari*, 122.
24 Dey, *Homeogatha*, ii.
25 Chanda, *Amar Ma'r Baper Bari*, 122.
26 See Das, "Healing the Home," 180.
27 Chanda, *Amar Ma'r Baper Bari*, 122.

Chapter 18

1 See Ariella Aïsha Azoulay's discussion of the tools of torture in *Potential History: Unlearning Imperialism* (London: Verso, 2019).
2 Ranajit Guha, *Elementary Aspects of Peasant Insurgency* (New Delhi: Oxford, 1983), 18.
3 Guha, *Elementary Aspects*, 18.
4 Toni Morrison, *Beloved* (London: Chatto & Windus, 1987), 190.
5 John Michael Vlach, *Back of the Big House: The Architecture of Plantation Slavery* (Chapel Hill: University of North Carolina Press, 1993); Mechal Sobel, *The World They Made Together: Black and White Values in Eighteenth-century Virginia* (Princeton: Princeton University Press, 1987); Rebecca Ginsburg, "Freedom and the slave landscape," *Landscape Journal* 26, no. 1 (2007), 37–44.
6 Tanika Sarkar, "Making and Remaking Caste and Labour," in Anuradha Roy and Melitta Waligora, eds., *Kolkata in Space, Time and Imagination*, vol. 1 (Delhi: Primus Books), 209.

7   William J. Glover, *Making Lahore Modern: Constructing and Imagining a Colonial City* (Minneapolis: University of Minnesota Press, 2008), Chapter 2.
8   Glover, *Making Lahore Modern*, 29.
9   Joseph Pugliese, *Biopolitics of the More-Than-Human: Forensic Ecologies of Violence* (Durham, NC: Duke University Press, 2020), 141.
10 Pugliese, *Biopolitics*, 148.
11 Pugliese, *Biopolitics*, 147.

INDEX

aberrance 26, 275
abkari
   administration/department 67, 78–9
   revenue 65, 77
   system pl.10
abstraction 145, 150–2, 252
access 5, 20, 126, 187, 223, 269
   pattern of 65, 161
   to food, water, relief 119, 274–5
   to labor 103, 117, 120
   to public space 216, 219, 261–2, 267
   to space 41, 53, 107, 128, 130, 138, 162, 166–7, 196, 204, 232–3
adjunct space 4, 45, 132, 141, 156
advertisement 16
   Gammidge and Saunders 82
   homeopathic medicine 272
   John Lewis 82
   provisions 82, 294 n.1
   real estate 39, 42–3, 159, 166, 308 n.10, n.15, n.17, n.18
   Tulloh and Company 280–1
aesthetic 107, 171–2, 176, 185, 200, 214–15, 232–3
   episode 186–9, 216
   landscape 168
   theory/idea 9, 11
aestheticization 102–3, 183, 314 n.17
aesthetics 4, 17, 32, 187–8, 194
   of comfort 132, 145
affect 6, 19–20, 26, 185, 206, 210, 215, 269, 275, 278
   ordinary 26, 187–8
   see also landscape
affective 94, 202, 251
   ecology 93–5
   modalities 214–15

spark 154, 187, 205
   value 117, 172
African American 58, 103, 115
African art 223–4
agency 4, 16, 96, 188, 267
   house 15, 64–7, 70–2, 80–1
Alabama 115–16
Ali, Turab 25, 91–4, 99, 277–8
allopathy 270–1
alpona 192–5, 199, 314 n.25
alterity 20, 22–3, 172
   see also scalar alterity
andarmahal 149, 207–10, 212–14
Andrews, Charles 192
anomaly/anomalous 79, 164, 168, 180–2, 313 n.55
another place 12, 278–9
antinomy 275, 277
army 171, 223, 246, 291 n.2
   colonial/EIC's 15, 65, 84, 86, 135, 137, 143, 243
   officer 86, 110, 117
Assam 104, 244–7
   Cherideo Parbat 244–5, 248, 249, 251, pl. 23
   Deopani 248, 251, pl.24
   Nazira tea plantation 245, 251
   Tea Company 251–2
Atkinson, George F. 88–9, 97–8, 104, 140–3, 173–4, 178–80
atmosphere 17, 139, 152, 175, 190
Atwater, Wilbur O. 113, 115–18, 122
Auriol, Charles, James Auriol and John 135–6, pl.11
Auriol, Charlotte and Sophia 136, pl.11
Awadh 139, 163–4, 174

bahirmahal 207, 212–13
baithakkhana 216, 263–4
   baithakkhana bari 206–7
Balasore 69
balustrade 165–6
Bandopadhyay, Bhavanicharan 262–4
baradari 163–4
barrack 62, 77, 112, 116, 121, 143–4
basement 43, 48–9, 52, 54, 57–60, 131, 223–4, 290 n.47
Basu, Amritalal 95–6
bawarchi 106, 133
bawarchikhana 39
bazaar 14, 37, 59–61, 62–3, 86, 290 n.49, 291 n.51
Beatson, Alexander 260, 324
beel, 197, 199
   see also marsh
beer 15–16, 53, 58, 64–5, 69, 71, 73–7, 86, 171, 174
Bell, Richard Clarke 74
belonging 200, 202, 210, 228, 277
Belvedere House, Calcutta, 43, 49–50
Bengal 121, 149, 164, 187, 194, 204, 211, 263–4, 273, 277, 315 n.42, 313 n.54
   eastern 162, 188, 226, 315 n.41
   Lieutenant Governor of 43
   Partition 21, 202
   Permanent Settlement of 250, 298 n.74
   Presidency/province 10–11, 38, 43, 65, 81, 118, 143, 158–9
   School of Art 159
   see also famine
Bengali 10, 82, 96, 262, 265, 267, 269
   books/publication/writing 95–6, 200, 206, 263, 227, 271–3, 295 n.6, 323 n.2
   home/household 207, 227, 264–5
   language 13, 186, 192, 202, 250, 253, 257, 263, 265, 270, 273
   nationalism 20, 264
   terms 156, 159, 166, 314 n.11
Benjamin, Walter 255–6
Bhanja, Gouri 194
bhisti 128, 175
   see also watercarrier

bibliomigrancy 255–7, 262, 264
bigness 6, 17–19, 151
biopolitics 107
Black ontology 225
Blake, William 20
Bombay 65, 67, 72, 77–8, 83, 85, 122, 128–9, 192, 241–2, 290 n.30
   Presidency 77–9, 101, pl.10
bookshelf 11, 227, 253–69, 322 n.1, 325 n.40
Bose, Bhowany 25, 74–5
Bose, Nandalal 194
Bose, Sarat Chandra 218
Bose, Sisir Kumar 218–19
botanical garden 84, 177, 237, 242, 321 n.39
bottle 3, 71, 73–4, 88, 90, 93–4, 96, 174–5, 228, 272
   bottled provisions/foodstuff 17, 39, 57, 81–5, 87–8, 95, 106, 187, 297 n.44
bottlekhana 3, 13, 18, 31, 36, 38–49, 61, 64–7, 73–6, 81, 88–91, 93, 95–6, 104, 159, 269, 277
   sircar 25, 74–5
   tent 85
boundary 21, 79, 202, 235, 247, 249
   boundary-work 132, 234–5, 243
   wall 43, 45, 165, 235, 265
box 85, 90, 94, 187, 199, 223, 225–6, 228–9, 246
   boxwallah 158
   icebox 108
   of medicine 11, 230, 268–9, 271–4, pl.30
Brathwaite, Edward Kamau 20
Britain 9, 36, 40, 57–8, 64, 80, 117–18, 184, 224, 261, 270, 272
   see also England
British 4, 15, 25, 40, 122, 137, 141, 169, 170, 178, 185, 232–6, 243, 257–60, 268, 281, 288 n.2, 306 n.59, 309 n.38, 325 n.48
   colonial 38, 63, 69, 101–2, 113, 118, 127, 133, 157, 176, 178, 234, 244–5, 319 n.1
   empire 3, 13–14, 17, 26, 36, 38, 40, 157, 180, 302 n.70

government 122, 232
Guiana 305 n.31
India 10, 47–8, 97, 321 n.30
Museum 223
Parliament 180
social life 140–1, 178, 180
brothel 61, 63, 67, 70
Browne, James W. pl. 9
Buckland, C.E. 78–9
building type 10, 185
bungalow 39, 72, 94, 99, 109, 124, 141, 178, 180–5, 231–5, 242–9, 308 n.17, 319 n.17
   Assam pl.23, pl.24
   compound 43, 55, 99, 104, 122, 158, 169–70, 175, 232, 237, 239–40, 249
   Gageepore pl.5
   garden 84, 168–9, 171–2, 175, 233, 235, 247, 249
   Hazaribagh pl.6, pl.7
   Jhelum 44, 137
   plan 137, 146
   verandah 158, 170, 172, 176, 244
   see also circuit house
Buriganga River 196

Calcutta 3, 53, 62, 65, 67–72, 76, 144, 186–7, 191, 200, 204–5, 210, 214, 217–18, 228, 244, 252–3, 257–8, 262–3, 270–3, 292 n.36, 295 n.6, and n.8, 310 n.38, 316 n.14
   buildings/residence 42–3, 45–9, 72, 128–30, 135–6, 159–60, 163–6, 207, 308 n.10, 317 n.25
   China Bazar 42, 69–70
   Chowringhee 42, 71, 165
   Garden Reach 165–6
   Government House 40, 47–8, 53, 72–4, 83, 134, 166, 279
   Lalbazar 70, 327 n.17
   suburb 43, 70, 72, 129, 166
   Tagore mansion 129, 159, 164, 210
   Town Hall 42, 70
   see also terrace, *and* public sphere
Calcutta Gazette, 39–40, 66, 82, 308 n.15 and n.18

calorie 113–14, 118, 123
   calorie transfer 117–18, 122
calorimeter 113–15, 117
camp 40, 65, 85–6, 89, 108, 110, 121–2, 124, 131, 169, 171
   concentration 118
   detention 121, 278–9
   followers 77, 86, 125
   famine relief 119, 121–2, 276
   site/ground 101, 120, 131
canal 18, 73, 119, 149–50, 194, 196–9, 235, 266
canned food/provisions 31, 81, 83, 86–8, 91, 93, 95, 246, 295 n.6
Canton 3
cantonment 37, 60, 63, 67, 73, 77, 83, 101, 137, 143, 146, 148, 169–72, 177–8, 184, 244
capital 6, 14, 20, 64, 71, 79, 224
capital city 48, 55, 187
capitalism 14, 17, 20, 115, 126, 191, 228, 255
caste 6–7, 24, 76, 133, 135, 140, 145, 196, 201, 255, 267, 268, 275
   "half-caste"/"mixed-caste" 68, 73, 275
   practice/prejudice 121, 125–9
   upper-caste 128, 162, 198, 227, 262–4
centering 27, 36
chair 88, 140, 159, 213, 245–6, 264, 266
   armchair 173–4, 179
Chand, Mihr 163–4, pl.17
Chanda, Rani 149, 162, 186–92, 194, 196–202, 272–4, 279, 313 n.1, 314 n.17
Chandannagar 214, 220
Chaudhuri, Nirad C./Niradchandra 217, 226–7, 317 n.45
chhad 166–7, 310 n.39
   see also terrace
childhood 140, 186, 194, 202, 204, 208, 210, 226, 269, 310 n.39
china 40, 57, 169, 229, 261, 294 n.5
China 42, 67, 82, 84, 152, 261, 280
Chinsurah 42
Chittagong 82
Churchill, Winston 277

circuit house, 43, 158, 178, pl.5
  see also bungalow
circumscription 7, 211, 215, 220
civil station/lines 74, 128, 170, 172, 178, 184
class 36, 43, 68, 72, 78, 81, 133–4, 145, 161–2, 184, 216–18, 229, 263, 268
  middle 95–6, 101–2, 128, 216–18, 226, 228, 263, 265, 269, 271–2, 292 n.37
  and race 24–5, 53, 59, 63, 70, 76, 87, 126, 170, 243, 255
  sorting 6, 62, 70
  working 17, 62, 66, 70, 76, 113, 115, 125, 236, 304 n.15
classical 58–9, 159
cleanliness 102, 107–9, 145
  see also dirt
Clerihew, William 166
Clifts Plantation, VA 33
Clive, Robert 65
closet 42, 226–7, 230
club 31, 41, 62–3, 67, 70, 73, 109, 244–6, 248
Coatman, John 233, 319 n.1
Coatman, Theodora 90, 231
collecting 11, 183, 194, 226–7, 230, 232, 255–6, 263
collection 10, 223–7, 230–3, 253, 256–63, 266–7, 269, 323 n.2
colonial 69, 75, 89–90, 103–4, 113, 128–9, 131, 137–8, 141, 150, 169, 179–81, 183, 191, 210, 223, 251, 263–71, 277, 301 n.58
  Africa 10, 157
  America 4–5, 32, 36, 131
  archive 13, 67, 83, 125–7
  army 15, 65, 84, 86, 144
  Asia 3, 10, 35
  authority 63, 70, 76–9, 95, 99, 174, 268
  building/house/residence 9, 31, 43–8, 53–62, 74, 97, 100–1, 126, 165, 241
  economy 36–7, 107
  milieu 9, 41, 202, 230, 243, 248, 254–5, 269

  rule 18–19, 38, 69, 73, 96, 99, 101, 133–4, 157, 178, 265, 267
  spatial imagination 79, 278
  state 47, 66, 79, 118–22, 219, 257, 270
  see also garden/gardening, collecting, India, sovereignty *and* trade
colonial city 15, 80, 127, 164, 187, 200, 205, 210, 262, 267, 291 n.36
colonialism 9, 14, 27, 31, 101–2, 117–18, 123, 156–7, 172, 178, 187, 202, 224–5, 228, 255, 318 n.12
coloniality 184, 224
comfort/discomfort 4, 25–6, 36, 41, 75, 81, 86, 88, 90, 101, 103, 116, 120, 130, 132–40, 143, 145, 175, 177, 179, 186, 212, 214, 236, 244–5, 247, 252, 255, 272
command 14, 31, 99–104, 117–18, 122, 256–7, 276, 304 n.19
commandement 99–100
commodity 16, 23, 67, 71, 81, 152, 261
community 4, 59, 70, 75, 80, 127–8, 187, 191, 196–8, 201–2, 217, 264, 269, 271, 274, 278
compound 31, 35, 37, 39, 59–61, 69, 88, 93, 126, 196
  see also under bungalow
connector 6, 156, 218
construction 4, 9–10, 31–3, 54, 57, 97, 110, 120–1, 144, 189, 206, 235, 284 n.21
  of canal 18, 40, 119
  materials 158, 230
  of railways 18, 274, 315 n.41
  of Viceroy's Palace 40
  see also infrastructure *and* materials
consumption 5, 10–11, 15–16, 26–7, 36–7, 83, 87, 95–6, 113–14, 133, 145, 183, 226–8, 234, 277
  of food 74, 101–3, 116
  see also liquor *and* Europe Goods
container 11, 95–6, 225–30, 254, 256, 277

containment 58, 63, 184–5, 220, 223–4, 226–7, 237, 269
cook 39, 82, 86, 88, 93–5, 97–100, 105–12, 133–4, 137, 298 n.52, 303 n.1
cook room 3, 31, 38–40, 42–5, 49, 54, 61, 81, 89, 97–9, 104–8, 112, 121, 159, 277
cooking range 111–12, 115
coolie 54, 73, 133–4, 228, 252, 279
  see also punkah coolie
Correa, Charles 21
corridor 8, 48, 53, 57–8, 126, 156, 290 n.30
country house 40, 43, 53, 55, 57–8, 126
country still 64–5, 67
courtyard 11, 149–50, 153–4, 161–3, 188, 190–2, 196–9, 202, 209, 259, 265, 314 n.11, 325 n.41, pl.16, pl.19
  see also yard
craft/crafting/craftsmanship 4, 9, 154, 170, 173, 183–5, 189, 204, 239
culinary racism 99, 103, 113, 117, 123
  see also race/racial
culture 22, 19–20, 22, 24, 62, 80, 95–6, 107, 114, 164, 183, 223–4, 227, 238, 256–7, 268, 276
  see also material culture
cutcherry/kachhari 43, 146, 158
Cuthell, Edith E. 168–85, 243, 311 n.18
Cuthell, Thomas, 168, 171, 173, 175, 183

Dacca/Dhaka 65, 186, 196, 200, 274, 313 n.1, 318 n.47
dalan 162, 196
daowa 149, 153–4, 156, 162, 167, 188–92, 194, 198–9, 201, 269, pl.16
Dashwood, Thomas 135–6, pl.11
death 143, 169, 182–5, 186, 191, 205, 207, 214–15, 224, 253, 272, 283 n.7
Debi, Digambari 207, 316 n.13

Debi, Kadambari 212–16
Debi, Purnashashi 197, 272–4, 279
Debi, Purnima (Thakur) 209–11
Debi, Sarada 210–11, 213
Debi, Saudamini 211, 317 n.43
Debi, Sukumari 194
Deccan 65, 118, 277
de Certeau, Michel 154
Deetz, James 5, 15, 25
degradation test 119, 121
delinking 26–7
  strategic 27
Dey, Kulachandra 191, 272–3, 279
dhai 135
Dhaleswari River 196
Digby, William 119, 121, 199
diminution 275–6
dirt 120–1, 127, 145
  see also cleanliness
disciplinary tool, practice, thinking 9, 21, 24, 120, 149, 151
discipline 24, 28, 112, 120–1, 125
  of history/art history 17, 34
  test 119
disease 109, 120–1, 145, 202, 251, 269, 274
distance 9, 44, 47, 58, 97, 102, 104, 109, 118–19, 151–2, 168, 175, 179, 187, 197, 199–200, 206, 215, 251, 273, 275–6
  test 119
  see also long-distance trade
distress test 119–20
domestic 64–5, 76–7, 84, 88, 90–1, 112, 170–1, 177, 179, 182–4, 191, 207, 209, 211, 216, 234, 255
  labor/service/task 40–1, 46, 59–61, 93–100, 161–2, 174, 189, 191, 198, 207, 210, 232, 280, 314 n.17
  space/confines 8–9, 37, 41, 119, 145, 156, 158, 183–4, 216, 236, 242, 267
  worker/servant 41, 59, 125, 133, 135, 137, 172–3, 176
domesticity 94, 102, 173, 206, 215, 255
D'Oyly, Charles 257, pl.13, pl.25
Dufferin, Lady Hariot 40, 57

dumbwaiter 4, 131, 145, 282 n.4
Duncan, Sara 234
Dunlop, Robert 73, 89
duration 163, 189–90, 194, 196, 210, 245, 275
durational
  aesthetic 185
  imagination 149
Dutta, Rajendralal 271
dwelling 6, 11, 41, 153, 167, 204, 239, 255, 269, 277

East India Company (EIC) 14–16, 47, 65–9, 73, 134–5, 137, 180–1, 258, 260–1
efficiency 21, 77, 100–1, 111–13, 117–18, 131, 144, 169
empire 5–6, 9–19, 21–3, 117, 150, 155, 157–8, 169, 171, 179, 187, 230, 242–3, 247, 251, 253–6, 261, 267, 269, 277, 312 n.54
  architectural history of 25–7
  biopolitics of 107
  geography of 10–13, 22–6, 71, 79, 278–9
  historiography of 3, 17–19, 62–4
  imagination of 181–2, 232–5
  see also British empire, foodways and imperialism
England 16, 91, 102, 108–9, 116, 126, 136, 146, 164, 169–71, 175–6, 184, 227, 229, 231, 233, 236, 238, 242–8, 250, 252, 261, 322 n.58
  see also Britain
Englishness 93, 169–70, 176, 231, 235
enslaved/enslaved labor 3–4, 6–8, 10, 31–6, 58–9, 103, 116, 125–6, 130–7, 145, 228, 276, 279
entrepreneurship 71, 83
environment 178, 215, 228, 245, 279
environmental 32, 99, 114
  determinism 107, 127
  history 315
  racism 107
  violence 17
ephemeral 5, 194, 202, 275
escape 7, 122, 145, 212, 225, 245, 276–9

Europe 9, 14, 25–6, 37–8, 40, 63, 65, 68–9, 80–4, 89, 93, 107, 113, 128, 149, 255, 257, 261, 280
Europe Goods 15–16, 80–3, 280
European
  community/society 16, 70, 81–2
  domination 10, 14
  imperialism/colonialism 9–10, 31
  settlement 43, 101
  soldiers 63, 73, 76–7, 84, 134, 238
  staff 53–5
  women 40, 61, 76
  see also liquor, Europe Goods, and provisions
Evans, Robin 8, 32, 156
exposure 141, 178, 185

factory 65, 68, 74, 79, 104
famine 101, 113, 117–27, 277, 300 n.45, 302 n.70
  camp 119, 121, 276
  feeding shed 120
  kitchen 101, 121
  wage 101, 118–20
fan 22, 110, 131–2, 138, 140, 176
  see also punkah
fetish 81, 93, 226
flood 26, 149–50, 188–9, 198–200, 202
food 3, 37, 39–40, 45–6, 49, 53, 57, 59–60, 74–6, 88, 90, 95–125, 135, 159, 161, 209–10, 214, 223, 246–7, 275, 278, 295 n.6, 296 n.29
  axis 101–2, 113, 117, 122, 287 n.48
foodstuff 11, 16, 61, 64, 81–5, 90, 189
foodways 16, 83, 86–7, 91, 95, 101–3, 112, 277
Fort St. George 70, 134
Fort William 62, 309 n.38
Fort William College 257–8
Fourth Anglo-Mysore War 258
fungible 3, 115–16, 154
Futteygurh 82, 295 n.8

Galveston, Texas 35
Gandhi, Mohandas (Mahatma) 218, 277

INDEX

Gangetic delta 164, 250, 315, 155, 158–9, 161–4
Gangadharpur, Bikrampur 186, 188, 196
garden 35, 48, 55, 72, 84–6, 104, 139, 145, 168–78, 204–5, 213, 215, 231, 233–43, 245–9, 251, 265, 268, 270, 308 n.18
   design 234–41, p.22
   house 72, 166, 214, 220, 269
   portable 242
   vegetable/kitchen 173–4, 177, 249
   see also botanical garden *and* horticulture garden
gardener 49, 81, 84, 169, 175, 232–8, 241, 303 n.1, 321 n.37
   see also mali
gardening 17, 169, 171, 176, 233, 235–8, 240–2, 251, 320 n.12
   guide 84, 234, 238, 240–2, 251
garret 7
Garrett, Elizabeth 86, 89, 104
gender 6, 19, 25, 36, 67, 104, 162, 184, 213, 216
   feminine 174, 194, 232, 243
   gendered 115, 169, 173, 208, 217
   manhood 184
   masculine/masculinist 25, 171, 174, 179
geography 5, 7, 11, 13, 22, 26, 62, 71, 79, 118–19, 121, 149, 152, 191, 197, 202, 230–3, 243, 250, 254, 278
   of foodways 86, 91
   of liquor 62, 65
   lumpy 81
   of overseas trade 64, 69
   portable 232
   of small spaces 7, 12, 279, 306 n.56
Gibbs, James 165
Gilchrist, John Borthwick 134, 257
glassware 15–16, 74–5, 81
Godden, Jon and Rumer 90–1
godown 3, 4, 11, 25, 31, 38–40, 42–3, 47, 49, 58, 64–5, 68, 71–5, 79–80, 90, 93, 95, 106–8, 159, 246, pl.3, pl.4
   see also wine godown
Gordon, Peter 261–2

governance 100, 146, 78, 180–1, 257, 267, 277–8, 312 n.54
Gramsci, Antonio 7
Grant, Colesworthy 166
Green Hill, VA 33–5
grey zone 225–8, 269, 279
grid 3, 72, 91, 150, 210, 239, 272, 278
Guantanamo 278
Gupta, Mahendranath 264–7

habitation 6, 172, 192, 204, 235, 249, 251–2
   see also inhabitation
Halhed, Nathaniel Brassey 250
Hancock, Madeline 105, 139
Harler, Agnes H. 236–7
Hazara 232–3
Hazaribagh 44, pl.6, pl.7
Heidegger, Martin 171
Hickey, William 136
hill station 159, 169, 176, 234
   see also Simla, *and* station
history 4–6, 17–19, 64, 100–1, 113, 127, 130, 179, 181, 184, 206, 224, 256, 260–2, 264, 270, 283 n.14
   architectural 8–13, 24–5, 36, 284 n.21
   art 149, 153
   connected 18, 26
   global 17–19
   imperial 149–51
   microhistory 19
home 22, 25, 40, 48, 76, 86, 115–17, 119–20, 123, 127, 135–7, 140, 146, 149, 168–72, 176, 182–8, 191, 196–7, 208, 212, 218, 226–7, 243, 251–3, 313 n.1
   economics 103, 117
   in India 103, 170, 231, 248
   like 108, 169, 235
   made 90, 187
   maker 10, 84
   medicine 17, 271
   village/rural 149, 187, 197, 201, 272
   see also comfort

homeopathy/homeopathic medicine 191, 269–74, 327 n.17
    Homeopathic Laboratory, B. Dutta & Co. 272
    see also box of medicine
hookahburdar 135
horticulture garden 84, 237–8, 296 n.21
housekeeping 17, 88, 91–3, 102
    guide 25, 31, 38–9, 42, 59, 75, 83–4, 87–91, 102–6, 109, 124, 172, 234, 270–1, 310 n.10
hunt 170–2, 181, 183–4, 248
Hunter, William W. 250–1
hurkarah 135

Ichhamati River 196–7
imperialism 9, 17, 20, 102, 104
    see also empire
Impey, Lady Mary 136
India 38, 47, 62–3, 66, 98, 101, 125–6, 131, 133, 135, 138, 156, 234, 262, 272, n.2
infrastructure 10, 14, 23–4, 40, 63, 75, 86, 196, 269, 272
    social 21, 252
    transportation 3, 17–18, 187, 200, 228, 274
inhabitation 154, 230
interspecies 278
    see also non-human/other than human
invisible/invisibility 4, 6–7, 9, 24, 31, 36, 58–9, 75, 102, 104, 123–7, 131, 140, 145
Irwin, Lord (Edward Wood) 53, 74

Jacobs, Harriet 7, 278
jali/jaffri 161, 173–4
James, C.L.R. 20
James, Eliot J. 43–4, 61, 84, 86, 228, 296 n.20, 297 n.40
jangal/jungle 110, 224, 234–6, 246–51, 322 n.62
Jefferson, Thomas 131–2, 320 n.12
Jhelum, Punjab, 44, 137

Kaghan Valley 231
Kent, Elizabeth 242

Kerr, Robert 8, 57–8, 145
khal 149, 196–8
    see also canal
khansamah 36, 41–2, 88, 91, 106, 133
khidmutger 41–2, 45, 91, 133
King, Elizabeth A. 124, 134–5
Kipling, Rudyard 42
Kishoreganj 226
kitchen 4, 7, 11, 31, 33, 35–6, 39–40, 47, 49, 57, 59, 88, 90, 107–12, 119, 129, 167, 188, 190, 193, 197, 199, 213, 276
    entry 53–5
    equipment 39, 43, 97–104, 106
    range 97, 108, 112, 287 n.48.
    see also under garden
Koodrutwoollah 74–5
Krishnanagar 164
Kwa, Chow pl.4

labor 3–6, 11, 23, 25, 38, 46–7, 63, 86, 88, 105, 118–20, 122–3, 126–8, 143–6, 169, 171, 176, 179, 183–5, 204, 209, 211, 236, 241, 250–1, 265, 275–6, 305 n.31
    efficiency 100, 114, 131–3, 144
    menial 36, 134, 138, 140
    migrant 140, 228
    relation 32–6
    time 112, 131, 279
    unfree/slave 13, 131–3, 144
    see also coolie and domestic labor
laboratory 114, 184, 272, 279
laboring
    body 32, 75, 102, 115, 135, 137, 145
    population 67, 125, 180
Lakshmi Puja 191–3
land
    art 193
    imagination 11, 149, 151–2, 182, 193, 200–1, 269
    and water 20, 23, 188, 196, 198, 203, 233
    see also waste
landscape 6, 11, 14, 24, 64, 67, 72–3, 77, 121, 133, 135, 145, 157,

163, 184–5, 189–90, 194, 197, 212, 217, 235, 239, 243, 246
aesthetic 168
affect 170
of empire/colonial/imperial 63, 133, 149–51, 184–5
vernacular 4
see also property *and under* liquor
Latimer, Mrs. (Lady Primrose) 83
lawn 158, 176, 235, 237, 239, 242, 244–5
laziness 119–20, 143, 250
leisure 61, 138, 141, 158–9, 163–4, 169, 172–3, 177, 185, 204, 209, 211, 236, 248
library 253–67, 323–5
    Asiatic Society 258, 265
    Bangiya Sahitya Parishat 253–4, 267
    see also under Tipu Sultan *and* Iswarchandra Vidyasagar
liquor 31, 37, 39–40, 81, 83, 89–90, 277
    cabinet 67
    landscape 68–73, 77–9
    shop 61, 64–7, 71, 77–9
    trade 62–79
literary magazines 213, 227
    Bamabodhini Patrika 227
    Basumati 191
    Bharati 192, 216, 268
    Modern Review 192
    Prabasi 191–2, 227
    Pradip 227
    see also print culture
London 64, 67, 74, 165, 191–92, 223, 242, 258, 263
    East India House 260–1, pl.28
    Oriental Repository 258, 260–2, 76, pl.27
loophole of retreat 7
Lucknow 163, 168, 170, 172, 177, 184, 294 n.5, 311 n.18
lumpy geography 79, 278
Lutyens, Edwin 49, 52–4

Macaulay, Thomas Babington 256–7
Macfarlane, Alan 248–52
Macfarlane, Iris 104, 236, 243–52, 279, 303 n.1, 319 n.17

Madras 47, 65, 69–70, 76, 87, 93, 106
    Famine 101, 113, 118–23, 277
    Presidency 77, 121, 134
    suburb 72, 292 n.37
maidan 165–6
mali 169, 236, 241, 268
    see also gardener
map 10, 13, 17, 21, 48, 69, 71, 79, 150–1, 202, 237, 251–2
    collection 230–3
march 77, 85–6, 169, 297 n.32
market 4, 14–16, 72, 75, 81, 85, 95, 113, 225, 263, 286 n.16
marsh 170, 184, 197
    see also beel
Martin, Ranald 76
material culture 15–16, 64, 95–6, 104
    of reading 253, 262–3
materiality 53, 230
    of place 187
    of sound 196
    of space 23, 190
materials
    bamboo 93, 173, 189–90, 198–9, 211, 227
    mud 43, 97, 104, 162, 190, 227, 246
    pucca/pucka 43, 62, 159, 162
    tin 189–90, 227, 319 n.17
    see also construction
mehtar/mehtarni 126–8, 133, 276
memoir 13, 25, 31, 39, 65, 149, 153, 160, 170, 200, 204, 220, 243, 245–51
military 10, 62–5, 81, 85, 99–100, 178, 231, 243, 250
    administration 144, 146, 179, 278
    force 121, 134
    infrastructure 40, 86
    see also cantonment
modern 55, 117, 150, 154, 188, 190, 213, 270, 319 n.28
    living/house 129, 145, 164, 213, 218, 222
    method 32, 111
    metrics 100
    technology 98–9, 103, 112, 127–8
    world 9–10, 14, 17, 99, 151

modernity 7, 17–19, 27, 152
Monier-Williams Monier 76–7
Monticello, VA 35, 59–60, 125, 131–2
Moore, Robert 74
Mount Vernon, VA 35, 125
mufassil 43, 82
munshi 133, 173, 232, 257, pl.25
Murshidabad 164
Mysore 85, 258–61

Nabob 136
Nakra, Edulji Bhikaji 65
naming 31–2, 38–9
narrative 7, 13, 25–7, 32, 88, 97–9, 104, 137, 143, 149, 153–5, 265–70
  of everyday life 40
  frame 73, 99, 150, 152
  historical 3, 5–6, 17, 150, 154, 223–4
  vantage 153
  see also empire, nationalist, Edith E. Cuthell, Rani Chanda, Theodora Coatman, *and* Iris Macfarlane
nation/national 17–18, 22, 115, 117, 135, 191, 194, 261, 271, 263 n.14
nationalism 102, 185, 187, 205, 216, 264, 267, 270
nationalist 103, 155, 187, 194
  imagination 200
  movement 218–19, 313 n.4
  narrative 155, 202
  procession 218
negation 235, 275–6, 278, 303 n.3
neighborhood 127–8, 162, 165, 189, 191, 197, 217
network 23, 26–7, 72, 76, 121, 178, 267
  of small spaces 73
  transportation 228
  see also trade
New Delhi 127
  Viceroy's Palace 40, 48–59, 74–5, 236, 277
New York City 58, 192
Nizam of Hyderabad 65
noise 32, 58, 162, 179
  see also sound

nomenclature 4, 16, 36, 95, 112, 167, 273
  of rooms 38, 40, 57, 73, 102
nonhuman/other than human 154, 170, 183, 191, 194
  ants 278
  deer 170, 173, 227, 245–7
  gibbon 246
  pigeons 211–12
  zootic 184
Nugent, Lady Maria 165

oilman's store 67, 823, 86, 90–1
otla 156, 162
outhouse 31, 43, 45, 72
Owoo, Nii Kwate 223–6

Padma River 214, 220
Parkin, George 17, pl.2
Pearson, William 192
pickle 80, 82–5, 87, 167, 187–8, 209, 280–1
Pinkham, Mildreth 87–8, 93–4, 98–100, 104, 112
placemaking 32, 194, 202
placement 4, 31–3, 35, 57–8, 119, 163, 185, 200
  of books 259–61
plantation 4, 7, 10, 33–5, 134–5
  coconut 116
  house 125
  tea 244–53, 276
platedware 15–16, 67
Platt, Dr. Kate 109, 127
Polier, Antoine-Louis Henri 163–4, pl.17
poorhouse 119
port city 3, 15, 37, 39, 63–4, 67, 80–3, 157, 264, 292 n.37
portability 26, 275
portable
  artifact/object 11, 220, 230, 272
  European home 243
  garden 237, 242–3
  geographies 231–2, 252
  see also box
potted plant 233, 242–3
power 4, 14, 17, 26–7, 31, 93, 99, 118, 131–2, 151, 156, 183–4, 233, 255–8, 269, 275, 277

colonial/imperial 180, 255, 269, 276
divine 20
explanatory 19
leisure-as- 169
microdynamics of 95, 100, 145
site of 153
see also under labor *and* verandah
Price, Captain David 260
Prinsep, John 135–6
print culture 191, 202, 270
see also literary magazines
privacy 90, 132, 141, 163, 173, 207, 282 n.4
private
  space 159
  sphere 178, 255
probate inventory 5, 25, 71, 73–4, 89, 125, 283 n.7
property 4, 31, 35, 42, 71, 235, 237, 265, 276, 283 n.7, 292 n.36, 306 n.57, 308 n.15, 316 n.14
prosthetic trace 130–2, 145
provisions 67, 71, 74, 80, 81–94, 228, 277
  canned 31, 86–7, 91, 93, 295 n.6
  room 38
  store 64
  see also under liquor *and* Europe Goods
public 84, 127, 158, 177, 234, 261, 263
  building 43, 72, 138, 165
  gathering 70
  house 68
  life/role 100, 164, 169, 231–3, 261, 263
  project/work 119, 158
  space 3–4, 27, 63, 103, 163, 216–20, 255, 325 n.41
  sphere 178, 216, 251–3, 262–6
Punjab 44, 137
punkah/fan 22, 88, 110, 130–2, 136, 138–44
  coolie 138, 140, 143, 145, pl.13
  Mortimer frame 143–4
puthi 253, 232 n.2

race/racial 6, 19, 24–5, 36, 42, 55, 67, 68, 76, 113, 115–16, 145, 232, 243–4, 255, 275
  anxiety 135
  difference/distinction/hierarchy 59, 70, 87, 103, 114, 126, 143
  lines/boundaries 43, 143, 180, 270
  premise of empire 63
  privilege 59, 170
  relations 53
  sorting 62
  see also culinary racism *and* empire
railway 18, 68, 86, 118–19, 146, 251, 274, 315 n.41
Ram, Sita pl.3, pl.8
Ramakrishna, Sri Paramhamsa 264–7
rebellion/insurgency 137, 146, 146, 306 n.57
  see also Sepoy Rebellion
recalcitrance 24, 36, 101, 110–11
Redheffer, Charles 131–3
refuge 157, 172–8, 243, 265–6
regimental canteen 67, 76
  see also cantonment
remembrance/reminiscence 170, 186, 205–6, 217, 227, 256, 264, 276
  sites of 202
  see also memoir
Rennell, James 250
repatriation/restitution 223–4
Rhodes, Cecil 17–18
rice 35, 85, 87, 90, 97, 188, 191, 198–9, 201, 246
  beer 77
  field 26, 72, 199
  paste 5, 192–3
riverine 190–1, 197, 250
Roberts, Emma 41
roof 7, 33, 154, 162, 173, 175, 189–90, 197, 230, 234
  roofline 163–7
  roofscape 204–20
  thatch 93, 158, 227
  tile 99, 212–13, 227
  tin 190, 246, 319 n.17

sadar 79, 91, 272
sanitation 119, 127–9
Santiniketan 191, 194–5, 220
sarkar/sircar 25, 74–5, 133, 135
Savannah, GA 35

scalar
  alterity 20–3, 275–7
  imagination 6, 21, 23
scale 4–6, 17–20, 26–7, 37
  large 6, 13–14, 48, 59, 77, 102, 278
  proximate 39
  small 14, 17, 22–3, 96
scattering 35, 225, 230, 269
Scotland 231
screen 59, 159–61, 172, 175
scullery 36, 39–40, 47, 53, 57, 90–1, 104, 107–8
Seal, Motilal 71, 292 n.36
seam 58, 62–4, 155, 157, 178, 182–5
Second Anglo-Afghan War 122
separation 4, 32–6, 43–4, 58–9, 63, 104, 119, 137, 161, 207, 231, 244, 275
Sepoy Rebellion 137, 140, 143, 146, 170–1, 178, 184, 234, 279
Serampore pl.1
servant 6, 8, 10, 32, 36–7, 39–43, 53–5, 57, 67, 71–5, 86–93, 99, 100–1, 104–10, 125–6, 135–8, 140, 143–6, 168–9, 172, 176–80, 184, 204, 207–13, 229, 236, 244–6, 264, 268, 276–7, 279, 290 n.30, 303 n.1, 304 n.19, 306 n.59, 311 n.10
  hierarchy 36, 38, 75, 125–6, 133–5
  list 25, 124
  of the East India Company 65
  population 36, 53, 60, 125, 209
  servants' quarters 4, 31, 32–6, 43–5, 48–60, 95, 106, 109, 239, 248, 276
  servants' spaces 42–5, 49, 58–9, 130, 145
  wages 86–7, 135
sewage 127–8, 274
shankhari 199
sight 4, 36, 97, 115, 125, 202, 212, 216, 277
  of the city 161
  lines 19
  privileging 151–2
Simla 49, 74, 234
  Viceregal Lodge 40, 55–8

Sirkar, Mahendralal 270–1
size 4–6, 19, 27, 31, 25, 42–3, 47–8, 64, 73, 88, 94, 121, 173, 176, 182, 204, 208, 216, 228, 243, 272, 275, 277
  domain 22
  of lot 57
  of market 16, 286 n.16
  mid- 81
  of space/room 3, 137–8, 158
slave auction block 4, 34–5
slow looking 26, 150, 153
small spaces 3–12, 14, 17, 23, 25–7, 37, 73, 70, 82, 94–5, 102, 145, 155–6, 203, 220
smallness 3, 5–6, 12, 14, 19, 23, 26–7, 35, 64, 275–7
smell 5, 23, 32, 41–2, 44, 58, 104, 161
smoke 43, 44, 74, 97, 107–8, 169, 171, 175, 224, 244, 276
  house 287 n.48
sociopoetics 211–15, 220
sound/noise 32, 42, 44, 161, 175, 186, 190–1, 194, 196, 199, 319 n.17
sovereignty 146, 250, 258–9, 261
  colonial 23, 79, 181
space
  everyday 194, 204, 212
  figure of 255, 266–7, 269
  mechanical 146
  see also small spaces
spatial
  architectonic 172
  ensemble 169, 213, 217
  event 150, 154
  knot 196
  relations 9–12, 23, 25, 32, 102, 182, 228, 235
  stories 154
spatializing food 119, 126
stair 8, 53, 59, 128–9, 131–2, 116, 166–7, 205, 253, 277
  back 126–30, 269
  service 4, 53–4, 57–61, 166, pl.1
state 10, 100, 113, 117, 119–21, 123, 134, 226, 257–8, 271
  centric- 251
  craft 117, 264
  revenue 79

rooms 53–4
see also anomaly/anomalous, nation/national, sovereignty *and under* colonial
station 62, 67, 79–82, 85, 93, 125, 176–8, 236, 243
police 71
see also civil station/lines, hill station, cantonment *and sadar*
Steel, Flora Annie and Grace Gardiner 59, 84–7, 91–2, 94, 109
storeroom 7, 43–4, 87–91, 104, 137–8
see also bottlekhana *and* godown
subaltern 7, 62, 271, 273, 275–6, 291 n.2
histories 17
practice 24
subalternity 276, 303 n.3
suburb 59, 72, 128, 178, 196
see also under Calcutta, Bombay *and* Madras
Sunderbans 250, 322 n.62
sweeper *see mehtar/mehtarni*
Syfollah 25, 74–5

Tagore mansion *see under* Calcutta
Tagore, Abanindranath 159, 161, 192
Tagore, Debendranath 207, 211–12
Tagore, Dwarakanath 206
Tagore, Gaganendranath 159, 192
Tagore, Jyotinindranath 213
Tagore, Rabindranath 186, 204–20
Tagore, Rwitendranath 295 n.6
Tagore, Samarendranath 159
Tagore, Sumitendranath 217, 316 n.18
tailor 141, 158, 173, 180
taste 40, 82–6, 95, 97, 100, 103, 105, 107, 114, 117, 189, 205, 212, 236, 253, 256, 298 n.74
tavern 37, 62–3, 68–73, 82, 288 n.1, 295 n.6, pl.8
taxidermy 168, 170–1, 175, 182–5
see also under seam
technology, *see under* modern
Temple, Richard 118–22, 277
Temple wage 119
tent 72, 110, 125, 164, 229, 232, 244
godown 40
see under bottlekhana

terrace 153–4, 269
garden 213–15
rooftop 163–7, 204–20, 316 n.3, 317 n.33 and n.45, pl.17, pl.18, pl.21
salon 215–16, 255
terrain 23, 121, 150, 185, 277
territorial
ambition 172
control 22, 122
entity 170
fact 10
imagination 22
occupation 13, 181–4, 234, 236
possession 180, 185
prerogative 171, 181, 233
scale 22, 37
sublime 14
territory 26, 153, 155, 171–2, 203, 233, 243, 277
Afghan 231–2
colonial 79, 184–5
English 232
thakurghar 209
Thana 78
therapeutic 270–4
threshold 22, 155, 157, 162–3, 178, 180
time 5, 7, 11, 93, 170, 182, 190–6, 209–11, 248
-gap 214
and money 236
and space 19–20, 150–3, 172, 185, 187, 265, 269, 275
-space 202, 211–12, 215, 256
see also labor time
Tipu Sultan 258–62, 267, pl.26
tool house/shed 239–41
trade 10–11, 40, 43, 61, 122, 135, 181, 228, 261, 277–8
colonial 14–15, 102, 261
long-distance 13–17, 25, 64, 82, 95, 102
network 11, 13–14, 64
slave 126
see also liquor *and* Europe Goods
travel 149–52, 178, 199, 233, 244, 247, 256, 262
traveling gaze 150

trunk 11, 192, 198, 226–9, 262
Tuckahoe Plantation, VA 33

unarchive 25, 279
United States 4, 9, 64, 101–2, 131, 184, 187
Uran 77–8

vantage 149–55, 157, 166, 168, 178, 204, 220, 269, 310 n.38, pl.14
venetian blind 159, 161
verandah/*baranda* 4, 11, 26, 40, 42, 44, 47, 53–4, 57–9, 61, 85, 156, 159–60, 107, 109, 128–9, 141, 145, 152–4, 156–62, 165, 167, 169–85, 206, 212, 217–19, 243–7, 255, 308 n.18, 325 n.43, pl.15, pl.19, pl.20
  front verandah 158, 173, 237
  back verandah 107–8, 119, 168, 170, 174, 181
vernacular 117, 238
  architectural history 24–5
  buildings 158, 162
  landscape 4
vernacularization 269–74
Vidyasagar, Iswarchandra 253–4
  library 263–9
  residence 265–6, pl.29
village 77, 86, 121, 134, 149, 151, 162, 170, 186–204, 209, 246, 269, 273–4, 277, 314 n.16
  headmen 119
  modernity 19
  see also under home
visibility 4, 26, 223, 250, 275–6

Wardian case 228
warehouse 43, 64–5, 67, 71–2, 259, 295 n.8
  see also godown

waste 103, 112–14, 145, 248, 132, 248–51
  land 239, 250–1, 322 n.58
  removal 4, 126–8
water 40, 94, 104, 107, 109, 112, 136, 138, 152, 184, 188, 214, 236, 239, 280–1
  body 72, 191, 194, 197–9; *see also* marsh
  carrier 128, 303 n.1; *see also bhisti*
  cooler 133
  country 191
  infrastructure 23–4, 129, 163–4, 212, 217, 246, 248, 251, 274
  movement of 20, 196, 200, 203; *see also* flood
Wellesley, Richard Colley, 1st Marquess of Wellesley 257–8
wilderness 234
Williams, Eric 20
Wilson, Lady Anne 104, 108
wine 15–16, 31, 64–70, 74–6, 86–7, 91, 105
  cask/bottle 175, 228
  cellar/cellaret 53, 58–9, 73
  godown 25
  merchant 76
Wolseley's field kitchen 110–11
Wood, Captain Arthur (Archie) 137–8, 146
Wood, Minnie 90–1, 146, 279
Woodrow, George 238–42
Wyvern, Colonel Kenny Herbert 84, 87–8, 93–4, 104–13

yard 35, 60, 129, 188, 194, 237
  see also courtyard

Zain al-din, Shaikh 136
zamindar 176, 227
Zoffany, Johann 135–6, pl.11